DYNAMIC HTML

Master the Essentials

DYNAMIC HTML

Master the Essentials™

Joseph Schmuller

SYBEX®

San Francisco • Paris • Düsseldorf • Soest

Associate Publisher: Amy Romanoff
Contracts and Licensing Manager: Kristine Plachy
Acquisitions & Developmental Editor: Suzanne Rotondo
Editor: Kristen Vanberg-Wolff
Project Editors: Kim Wimpsett and Kim Crowder
Technical Editor: David Shank
Book Designers: Patrick Dintino and Catalin Dulfu
Graphic Illustrator: Andrew Benzie
Electronic Publishing Specialists: Cyndy Johnsen, Bob Bihlmayer,
    and Robin Kibby
Production Coordinator: Duncan Watson
Production Assistant: Beth Moynihan
Indexer: Ted Laux
Cover Designer: Design Site
Cover Illustrator: Design Site

Screen reproductions produced with Collage Complete.

Collage Complete is a trademark of Inner Media Inc.

SYBEX and Master the Essentials are registered trademarks
of SYBEX Inc.

TRADEMARKS: SYBEX has attempted throughout this book to
distinguish proprietary trademarks from descriptive terms by
following the capitalization style used by the manufacturer.

Netscape Communications, the Netscape Communications logo,
Netscape, and Netscape Navigator are trademarks of Netscape
Communications Corporation.

Netscape Communications Corporation has not authorized,
sponsored, endorsed, or approved this publication and is not
responsible for its content. Netscape and the Netscape
Communications Corporate Logos are trademarks and trade
names of Netscape Communications Corporation. All other prod-
uct names and/or logos are trademarks of their respective owners.

The author and publisher have made their best efforts to prepare
this book, and the content is based upon final release software
whenever possible. Portions of the manuscript may be based
upon pre-release versions supplied by software manufacturer(s).
The author and the publisher make no representation or war-
ranties of any kind with regard to the completeness or accuracy of
the contents herein and accept no liability of any kind including
but not limited to performance, merchantability, fitness for any
particular purpose, or any losses or damages of any kind caused
or alleged to be caused directly or indirectly from this book.

Library of Congress Card Number: 97-61955
ISBN: 0-7821-2277-9

Manufactured in the United States of America

10 9 8 7 6 5 4 3 2 1

For Kathryn Marie,
Love of my life,
Girl of my dreams,
And as dynamic a soulmate
as a man could have.

Acknowledgments

Throughout the creation of this book, the members of the Sybex team have been wonderful to work with, and it's my pleasure to acknowledge all they've done. Editor Kris Vanberg-Wolff played a major role in making my words readable. I greatly appreciate her cooperation, her patience, and her many editorial insights. Kim Crowder started as Project Editor, and then moved on to a larger role within Sybex. Kim Wimpsett then became the Project Editor. I've been fortunate to work with this abundance of Kims, both of whom adeptly managed the whole process, kept it on an even keel, and kept me on schedule.

Acquisitions & Developmental Editor Suzanne Rotondo was responsible for setting the whole thing in motion. I'm extremely grateful for her confidence in me and for helping me through the early stages of the book.

This brings me to Technical Editor David Shank of Microsoft. More a partner than a technical editor, David carefully read the manuscript and painstakingly worked through all the exercises. He provided numerous constructive comments and questions that made this a stronger book. I greatly appreciated the opportunity to interact with him. I, as the author, and you, as the reader, both benefit from his extensive knowledge and technical insights. I've worked with Dave and with Kim Wimpsett on two books now, and I fear they've both gotten to know me better than anyone should have to.

Kris, Kim, Kim, Suzanne, and Dave did a marvelous job. Any errors or inconsistencies that remain are under the direct ownership of the author.

My thanks also to the Sybex production team, particularly to Electronic Publishing Specialist Cyndy Johnsen and Production Coordinator Duncan Watson. Their tireless work on every page turned my manuscript into the book you're holding.

In addition to the Sybex team, others made important contributions. David Fugate of Waterside Productions catalyzed the process that resulted in this book. My friends and colleagues at Barnett Technologies and at Adcomtek provided support and information. I'm also indebted to my friends at *PC AI* magazine (a publication I edited from 1991 through 1997) for their cooperation and understanding.

As always, my deepest thanks to my mother and my brother David for their love, support, and patience throughout the project … and my love and gratitude to Kathy (LOML and GOMD) for absolutely everything.

Contents at a Glance

Table of Contents

Introduction

As the World Wide Web grows in popularity, users demand increased sophistication from the Web pages that appear in their browsers. Dynamic HTML (DHTML) offers a way to provide that sophistication. Combining HTML with Cascading Style Sheets and scripting languages, DHTML is a rich toolset for creating eye-catching effects and new dimensions in functionality. Animation, dragging and dropping, changing the content of downloaded pages—all these and more become easy to implement with DHTML.

I wrote this book to give you the skills you'll need to harness the DHTML toolset. I assume that you're somewhat familiar with HTML, and that you're using Windows 95 on your machine. At present, Microsoft and Netscape have separate versions of DHTML. Each vendor's version is, not surprisingly, compatible with its own browser. Accordingly, the book includes exercises designed for Microsoft's Internet Explorer 4.*x* (IE) and Netscape Navigator 4.*x* (Navigator), so I also assume that you have a working, fully licensed copy of each browser installed on your computer.

The Organization of the Book

I've found that the best way to present a technical subject is often to start by leading students step-by-step through hands-on exercises. The knowledge they've gained then becomes a framework for understanding the subject's foundational concepts in a more formal way. Too many books reverse the order: They present the formal concepts first, and then the experience. While the flow seems logical and natural to the author, it's typically not as natural for the reader.

I've laid out the book in three parts. Part I, "Forming the Foundations," immediately immerses you in both versions of the technology. You'll develop DHTML applications for IE and for Navigator, review the fundamentals of HTML, learn about Cascading Style Sheets, and write programs in Visual Basic, Scripting Edition (VBScript) and in JavaScript. IE interprets programs in VBScript and in JScript (the Microsoft version of JavaScript). Navigator interprets programs in JavaScript. For the most part, the IE exercises you'll work through in this book are in VBScript. Occasionally, you'll see a JScript program in an IE exercise. Navigator exercises, of course, are all in JavaScript. I felt this was the most efficient way of covering the scripting languages.

After Part I builds your experience base and your skill set, Part II, "Getting Dynamic," enables you to apply your newly acquired skills and experience. You'll create Web pages that incorporate animation, multimedia, dragging and dropping, data manipulation, and more.

Part III, "Storming the Foundations," examines the models and the scripting languages that form the basis of DHTML. The knowledge and experience you gained in the first two parts provide the backdrop for understanding.

Each part consists of a set of Skills designed to make you a seasoned DHTML developer. Let's take a look at the Skills in each Part of *Dynamic HTML: Master the Essentials*.

Part I: Forming the Foundations

Part I consists of Skills 1 through 6. Skill 1, "Exploring and Navigating Dynamic HTML," introduces the technology, shows you how to organize your files for the book's exercises, shows you how to prepare your development tools, and leads you through the development of a DHTML page for IE and another for Navigator. Skill 2, "Learning the Basics of HTML: Text, Hypertext, and Frames," and Skill 3, "Learning the Basics of HTML: Graphics and Tables," provide a refresher in some of the most frequently used aspects of Hypertext Markup Language.

Skill 4, "Cascading Style Sheets," introduces the style sheet, a construct that enables efficient and imaginative styling of Web page elements. Because the scripting languages you'll use are object-based, Skill 5, "Orienting Toward Objects," gives you a firm grounding in object orientation—today's dominant software development technique. Skill 6, "Getting into Scripting," takes you through the nuts and bolts of writing scripts in VBScript and JavaScript. Skill 6 also shows you how IE and Navigator process events like mouse-clicks, keystrokes, and mouse movement.

Part II: Getting Dynamic

In Part II, which consists of Skills 7 through 11, you apply the tools and techniques you learned in Part I. Skill 7, "Adding Animation," shows you how to write scripts that perform timed repositioning of Web page elements, thus creating the illusion of movement on the page. In Skill 8, "Multiplying the Media," you'll learn how to add audio and video to your Web pages. Skill 9, "Adding Interactivity: Dragging and Dropping," provides the essentials for incorporating a useful technique that increases user interactivity. This Skill also takes you through the development of an application that's based on this technique.

Skill 10, "Working with Data and Dialog Boxes," introduces Microsoft's Tabular Data Control, a software component that enables users to manipulate data on downloaded pages. In this Skill, you'll also learn how to build modal dialog boxes that communicate with a Web page. Skill 11, "Working with Text: Dynamically Changing Content," shows you how to empower users to manipulate a downloaded Web page's text. An important aspect of Skills 10 and 11 is that the techniques they provide enable changes to pages without tedious round-trips between a client and a server.

Part III: Storming the Foundations

Part III consists of Skills 12 through 15. Skill 12, "Understanding Browser Object Models," dissects the object models at the foundation of IE and Navigator. Skill 13, "Working with VBScript," examines the details of Visual Basic, Scripting Edition. Skill 14, "Working with JavaScript," does the same for JavaScript. Skill 15, "Summing Up, Dynamically," discusses possible applications of DHTML and presents an exercise that acquaints you with the Active Desktop.

Code Examples

The code for the hands-on exercises in the pages that follow appears on the Sybex Web site. Instead of having to type in each code listing, you can save time and energy by downloading certain listings. Each code file that's on the site is noted in the book with its name along with this icon:

Downloading the Code

You can download the code examples from http://www.sybex.com. Click on the Catalog link, and then either search for this book or click on the Master the Essentials logo to get to the series page. Once you're at this book's page, click on the Download button to access the code files.

Listings

One more word about the code. When you're learning a new language and a new technology, it's often helpful to see the whole listing for a programming exercise. You might not always download the code from the Web, but you'll still want to see the code so that you can check your own work. In most cases, the book presents the entire listing for a particular exercise.

Notation Conventions

Throughout the book, our discussion will take various forms. Sometimes, I'll ask you to type something. Sometimes, I'll direct your attention to features of your display or your keyboard. At other times, I'll bring new terminology into the fray.

To help keep things comprehensible, here are some conventions for our notation:

- When I ask you to type a word or a phrase, I'll put the word or phrase in **bold** font.

- I'll use `monospaced` font to indicate a word or phrase that is in a code listing.

- When I refer to on-screen items—like titles of windows, folders, buttons, elements in lists, items in dialog boxes, menus, or menu choices—I'll put those items in Initial Capital Letters, regardless of how they appear on-screen.

- When I refer to named keys on your keyboard, I'll put those in Initial Capital Letters, too (for example, Alt, Tab, Esc, Ctrl).

- To indicate keystroke combinations, I'll put a plus sign (+) between a pair of keys. For example, Alt+Tab means "hold down the Alt key while you press the Tab key."

- To indicate a menu choice, I'll use this symbol: ➢. Thus, "File ➢ Save" refers to the Save choice under the File menu.

- New terminology can sometimes be confusing—particularly when you don't know that it's new. For this reason, I'll use *italics* to signal the first appearance of an important word or phrase, which I'll then define for you.

- Sometimes a line of code is too long to fit on a line of text, and I'll have to continue it on the following line. When that happens, I'll start the continued line with ➡.

Here are some other items you'll see along the way:

NOTE This is a Note. It provides a piece of additional information about a topic.

This Is a Sidebar

Occasionally, I'll discuss an area that requires more space than a Note. If putting the discussion into the main body of the text would disrupt the flow, I'll present it to you in a sidebar that looks like this.

TIP This is a Tip—a shortcut or a trick that helps you become more productive.

WARNING This is a Warning. It indicates a condition or an action that could be potentially harmful to your work or your computer.

Let's Get Going

The information in the pages to come is intended to excite your imagination and stimulate your creativity. As you go through each exercise, try to envision how you can apply each technique to your specific needs.

Fire up your computer, open your mind, turn to Skill 1, and get ready to master the essentials of Dynamic HTML.

PART I

Forming the Foundations

Dynamic HTML provides a new direction for Hypertext Markup Language. You can use its capabilities to produce striking effects on a downloaded Web page without return trips to a Web server. In Part I, you'll see how DHTML works, and you'll acquire the skills necessary to apply it. You'll refresh your knowledge of HTML, harness the power of Cascading Style Sheets, and learn about object orientation and scripts.

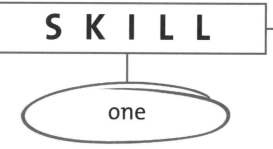

Exploring and Navigating Dynamic HTML

❑ Setting up your tools

❑ Building a dynamic Web page for Internet Explorer 4.0

❑ Building a dynamic Web page for Netscape Navigator 4.0

❑ Analyzing your DHTML code

With the explosion of interest in the World Wide Web, *Hypertext Markup Language (HTML)* has assumed a prominent place in the computer world. HTML has evolved to meet the increasing demand for eye-catching—and mind-catching—Web sites. Until recently, however, the evolutionary process mostly involved new and improved tags and attributes. The end-products, static Web pages that often required repeated time-consuming round-trips between client and server machines, clearly showed that a new direction was in order.

Dynamic HTML (DHTML) is that new direction. It combines HTML with Cascading Style Sheets (CSSs) and scripting languages. What role does each member of this combination play?

- As you're undoubtedly aware, HTML specifies a Web page's elements, like a table, a heading, a paragraph, or a bulleted list.

- CSSs enable you to decide how a Web browser renders those elements: You can use a CSS to determine (i.e., to *style*) an element's size, color, position, and a number of other features.

- Scripting languages enable you to manipulate the Web page's elements, so that the styles you assigned to them can change in response to an end-user's input.

That last point is extremely important. Before DHTML, you often had to jump through complicated hoops to give end-users the ability to change a Web page's features after it downloaded. One of those hoops, as I mentioned before, involved repeated communication with the server machine. This takes a lot of time, and detracts from the Web-surfing experience. How many times have you clicked your browser's Stop button because everything was just taking too long? DHTML makes Web page events instantaneous: They occur within the browser after the page has downloaded. With DHTML, Web pages become very much like other software applications.

Microsoft and Netscape, the companies behind the two most popular Web browsers, each have a version of DHTML. Both are called "DHTML," and each vendor's version is compatible only with its own browser. Microsoft and Netscape have proposed separate versions of DHTML to the World Wide Web Consortium. Each, of course, hopes the Consortium adopts its proposal and stamps it the official version, but it's probably the case that a sort of hybrid will emerge. This book will give you a firm grounding in both, so that you'll be ready for any decisions the Consortium makes.

NOTE   If you're at all serious about Web development, I highly recommend that you check out the World Wide Web Consortium's Web site (http://www.w3.org). You'll find a wealth of information about HTML, Cascading Style Sheets, and a variety of other topics related to the care and feeding of the World Wide Web.

Setting Up

We'll jump into DHTML shortly, but first we have to set up the tools we're going to work with. I'm assuming you have a computer that operates under Windows 95 or later. Windows NT 4.0, or later, is compatible with what we'll do, but you may find a quirk here or there along the way. I'm also assuming that you've installed either Microsoft's Internet Explorer 4 (IE), Netscape's Navigator 4 (Navigator), or both. You can learn a lot from our discussion if you have only one of these browsers, but the Skills in this book mostly center around hands-on exercises geared toward both. As you surf the Web, you'll have numerous opportunities to click on-screen buttons that take you to either the Microsoft site or the Netscape site so that you can obtain these browsers. IE is free, but Navigator is not.

 NOTE   If you're developing a Web site that will go on the Internet, it's a good idea to have both browsers on your system. For a corporate intranet, of course, an organization can specify a particular browser. Each browser can render graphics, colors, sound, and even text in very different ways, as you'll see in our first exercise. As you add elements to your page, be sure to review the page in each browser to make sure you're not catering to one browser audience over another. If you favor one over the other, you'll be sure to pay the price in diminished visits—it's an all too common oversight, but easy to avoid.

A Directory Structure

You'll be doing a lot of developing, so you'll need a place to put your work.

1. On your hard drive, create a new folder called DHTML MTE, and open this folder.

2. Within this folder, create a separate folder for the work you'll do in each Skill.

3. When you read a Skill, open that Skill's folder and store your work in it as you go along.

I keep this file structure on my E: drive. Obviously, if you keep yours on some other drive, your path names won't look the same as mine. This is also the way we'll organize the files of source code from the book, so that you can download them from the Web.

NOTE   You can download this book's source code from the Sybex Web site at http://www.sybex.com/. Click the Downloads link and find this book's page by title, ISBN number or software topic. You'll find many other utilities and tools to download and check out as well, along with links to other useful sites.

Preparing a Development Tool

An HTML file is just a text file that a browser can process and display. If you have a favorite text editor, feel free to use it throughout the exercises. If not, Windows 95 has provided one for you: Notepad.

You can set up Notepad to act as a convenient HTML editor.

1. Find Notepad in your system, open it, and select File ➢ New.

2. Next, select File ➢ Save As. Name the file Template and save it in your DHTML MTE folder.

3. In this file, type these lines:

```
<HTML>
<HEAD>
<TITLE>New Page</TITLE>
</HEAD>
<BODY>

</BODY>
</HTML>
```

4. Select File ➢ Save.

Whenever you have to create an HTML file, you can open Template and then save it under a new name with the extension .htm.

Your Template file should look like Figure 1.1.

FIGURE 1.1: Your Template file in Notepad

You now have a starting point for creating any HTML document. Save the Template file, close Notepad, and we'll move on.

NOTE If you want to step up several notches from Notepad, try a terrific text editor called EditPad. To get EditPad, visit http://www.tornado.be/~johnfg/. EditPad is neither freeware nor shareware—it's "postcardware." If you use it and like it, all you have to do is thank its creator, Jan Goyvaerts, by sending him a postcard! As Jan says, "If everyone would say 'thank you' when someone else said or did something nice, this world would be a much better place."

Connecting Your Text Editor

You'll find that your development efforts will proceed a lot more efficiently if you don't have to find your text editor, open it, and then select File ➤ Open each time you want to edit an HTML file. Instead, it will be helpful if you just locate the icon for your HTML document, right-click it, and then select your text editor from the menu that pops up. Your file will open in your text editor, and you can start working.

Here's how to make that happen:

1. Double-click your My Computer icon.

2. In the window that opens, select View ➤ Options. This opens the Options dialog box, which presents a set of tabbed pages.

3. Select the File Types tab.

4. Scroll down the list of Registered File Types and highlight Internet Document (HTML). Figure 1.2 shows the appearance of the File Types tab after you do this.

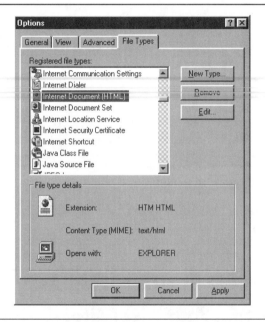

FIGURE 1.2: The Options dialog box, with the File Types tab selected and Internet Document (HTML) highlighted

5. Click the Edit button to open the Edit File Type dialog box.

6. In the Edit File Type dialog box, click New to open the New Action dialog box.

7. In the Action: box, type **Edit with Notepad** (or substitute your favorite text editor).

8. Click Browse, and then keep clicking until you find the icon for Notepad or whatever text editor you're going to use.

9. Click Open in the Open With dialog box. The path to your text editor now appears in quotes in the Application Used To Perform Action: box. Figure 1.3 shows what the New Action dialog box should look like. (Your file path to Notepad might be somewhat different.)

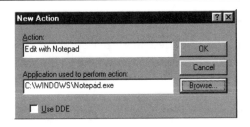

FIGURE 1.3: The New Action dialog box after you've selected Notepad as the program that performs the new action you created

10. Click OK to close the New Action dialog box.

11. In the Edit File Type dialog box, scroll through the Actions: list to find the action you just created.

12. Click Close in the Edit File Type dialog box, and then click Close in the Options dialog box.

WARNING As you've surely noticed, IE comes with a development tool called FrontPage Express, and Navigator comes with a development tool called Composer. Why bother with a text editor? It turns out that both tools might have some problems with DHTML. Earlier editions of FrontPage Express, then known as FrontPad, didn't save DHTML-related code, and early editions of Composer had some similar quirks. You can connect a text editor to Composer, but if you're not careful, you might lose some information when you add DHTML-related code to your document.

Connecting Your Browsers

In a similar fashion, you'll increase your efficiency if you can right-click on an HTML file and use the pop-up menu to open it in either IE or Navigator. With IE installed on Windows 95, it's probably the case that the Open action on an HTML file's pop-up menu activates IE. If not, go through the steps in the preceding section to create an action called Open with IE for the Internet Document (HTML) file type. (In Step 8, of course, you'll look for the icon for IE.) Repeat these steps to create an action called Open with Navigator for the HTML file type, with the appropriate adjustment to Step 8.

Switching between Your Editor and IE

When you've added all the selections to the pop-up menu, you'll find that you can switch back and forth between your text editor and IE. After you create and save an HTML file (i.e., a text file whose extension is .htm), don't close the file. Minimize it, find its newly created icon in the appropriate folder, and right-click on the icon. Use the pop-up menu to open the file in IE and see your creation. If you want to make some changes, leave IE open, click Alt+Tab, and then hold down the Alt key. In the little display that opens, press the Tab key until you land on the icon for your text editor. Release the Tab key, and you're back in the text editor.

If you then make and save changes in your text editor and want to see them in IE, press Alt+Tab once again to return to IE. Press F5 to refresh the page and put those changes into effect.

Switching between Your Editor and Navigator

To switch back and forth between your text editor and Navigator, follow almost the same steps. After you create and save an HTML file, minimize the file, right-click on the file's newly created icon, and select Open with Navigator from the pop-up menu. Your document will appear in Navigator.

If you want to make some changes, press Alt+Tab to switch back to your text editor. After you make your changes, press Alt+Tab to switch back to Navigator. To see those changes take effect, select View ➤ Reload from Navigator's menu bar or press Ctrl+R on your keyboard. Either operation has the same effect as pressing F5 in IE. (Selecting View ➤ Refresh in Navigator won't reload the page.)

Using DHTML in IE

In traditional "Master the Essentials" fashion, you're going to dive right into DHTML. You'll work with HTML, CSS, and scripting. You'll start with a page in IE and you'll endow it with a number of *dynamic effects*—effects that depend on user actions. Here are the dynamic effects you'll build into your first page:

- Moving your mouse through a heading on the top of the page will cause a hidden text display to appear and will change the color of the heading.

- Moving your mouse through the heading will also change the color and the content of a small box on the page.

- Clicking on the heading will cause a box in the center of the page to split into four boxes that move outward toward the corners of the page, revealing a short message in the center of the page.

- The centered message will appear to be layered above the text display.

- Moving the mouse out of the heading will return the page to its original appearance.

Figure 1.4 shows what the page will look like when you first open it in IE, and Figure 1.5 shows its appearance after a few mouse-clicks on the heading.

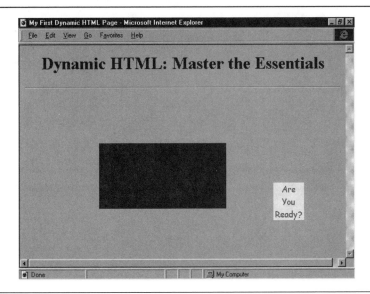

FIGURE 1.4: Your first DHTML Web page, opened in IE

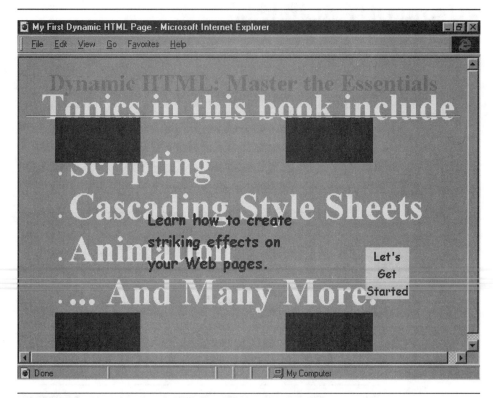

FIGURE 1.5: The Web page after several mouse-clicks on the heading

The Heading and the Horizontal Line

Let's get started. Open your Template file, select File ➢ Save As, and save the file as First Dynamic IE.htm in Skill 1. Change the title of the page by typing **My First Dynamic Web Page** between <TITLE> and </TITLE> in place of New Page. Inside the <BODY> tag, type **Style = "background-color : 'Silver'"** to give your page that macho silver-gray color you see in many applications. This expression is called a *style sheet*. Because it's inside a tag, it's an *inline* style sheet. As you can see, in this context, Style is an attribute and its value is a string. The string contains a style property, a colon, and the value of the property. A style sheet can hold more than one property-value pair, and when it does, a semicolon separates adjacent pairs. (You'll see an example of this in the next section, "The Hidden Message.") We'll have more to say about style sheets later in this skill, and much more in Skill 4.

If you've worked with HTML 3.*x*, you've probably used the attribute bgcolor to specify a Web page's background color. In HTML 4.0, this attribute is *deprecated*, meaning that (1) newer features of the language provide Web developers with greater capabilities, and (2) it may become obsolete in future versions of HTML.

Next, center an H1 heading by typing

```
<H1 Style = "text-align:center">Dynamic HTML: Master the Essentials</H1>
```

after the <BODY> tag. To follow the heading with a horizontal line, type **<HR>**.

At this point, we're going to add an extremely important attribute to the <H1> tag. This attribute, ID, will give us a way of referring to the header when we have to work with it in a scripting language. Inside the <H1> tag, type **ID = h1Header**.

What's in a Name?

When I assign an ID to an HTML element, I'll begin the ID with a lower-case prefix. That prefix will be the element tag (like h1, div, or p). The rest of the ID will be a descriptive term that tells you something about the element. It will begin with an uppercase letter, and all the rest will be lower-case (h1Header, for example).

This is similar to a naming convention that software developers use in other contexts. The prefix usually is an abbreviation, but every HTML element has a short name, so I'll use that name as the prefix.

If you're familiar with object-oriented programming, you've already seen this kind of notation. Is this naming convention subtly trying to tell you that DHTML turns HTML elements into objects? Exactly!

Your document should look like this:

```
<HTML>
<HEAD>
<TITLE>My First Dynamic HTML Page</TITLE>
</HEAD>
<BODY Style = "background-color:'silver'">
<H1 ID = h1Header Style = "text-align:center">Dynamic HTML: Master the
Essentials</H1>
<HR>
</BODY>
</HTML>
```

The page in IE looks like Figure 1.4, but without anything below the line under the heading.

NOTE   Throughout this book, I'll write HTML tags in UPPERCASE letters.

The Hidden Message

To create the remaining elements of the page, we'll divide the page into segments called DIVs. Each segment starts with <DIV> and ends with </DIV>. After we've created our segments, we'll script them to exhibit the desired effects.

Let's create a segment to hold the hidden message that you see in large, bold, white font in Figure 1.5. Just after the <HR> tag, type

```
<DIV ID = divMessage>
</DIV>
```

Next, type the message between these two DIV tags. Put the message in a paragraph (that is, enclose it with a <P> and a </P>), and make it a bulleted list. Here's the HTML to type between the DIV tags:

```
<P> Topics in this book include
<UL>
<LI> Scripting
<LI> Cascading Style Sheets
<LI> Animation
<LI> ... And Many More!
</UL>
</P>
```

We've typed the message, but so far its appearance in IE would be pretty non-descript. We haven't colored the text white, enlarged it, or made it bold. We also haven't positioned the message on the page.

To take care of the message's size, appearance, and position, we'll add information to the <DIV> tag. We add the information as a group of styling specifications in an inline style sheet. Within the <DIV> tag, type

```
Style = "Position:Absolute;Left:5%;Top:10%;
Visibility:Hidden;z-index:-1;font-style:normal;font-weight:bold;
font-family:Normal;font-size:50;color:'White'"
```

The first property-value pair, `Position:Absolute`, tells the browser to position the DIV with respect to the top edge and left edge of the browser window.

NOTE   Another possible value for `Position` is `Relative`. In contrast with `Absolute`, `Relative` situates an element in relation to other elements on the page.

The next two property-value pairs show one way that style sheets let you specify position—via percentages of distance from the left edge and the top edge of the browser window. The first of the two pairs positions the DIV's left side 5% of the distance from the left edge to the right, and the second positions its top edge 10% of the distance from the top of the browser to the bottom. The fourth pair, `Visibility:Hidden`, keeps the message invisible when the page opens.

The next pair positions the DIV in the "third dimension." If you look closely at Figure 1.5, you'll see that the large white-lettered message appears to be underneath the message in the center of the screen and underneath the page's heading. The `z-index` styling property determines this kind of layering: the lower the `z-index`, the deeper the apparent layer of its element.

NOTE   The word "layer" is important in Netscape's version of DHTML. For this reason, I'll try to avoid this word during our discussion of IE.

The remaining property-value pairs determine the message font's size, weight, appearance, and color. The `font-size` attribute's value, 50, specifies a font whose size is 50 pixels.

NOTE   In HTML 3.*x*, developers used the <FONT> tag to specify a font's aspects. In HTML 4.0, the <FONT> tag is *deprecated*. As I said in a previous note, this means (1) newer features of the language provide Web developers with greater capabilities, and (2) this element may become obsolete in future versions of HTML. Font-size is a good example of "greater capabilities." Through its Size attribute, the <FONT> tag supports only seven possible font sizes. The newer font-size style property, on the other hand, can give you pixel-level precision when you specify the size of a font.

The Message at the Center of the Page

Now we'll create the message at the center of the page. Create a <DIV> called divLearn, and we'll position it by pixels, rather than percentages. We'll position it 180 pixels from the left edge of the page, and 200 pixels from the top edge:

```
<DIV ID = divLearn Style ="POSITION:ABSOLUTE;LEFT:180;TOP:200;">
```

It will be helpful to confine the message to a specific width—say, 210 pixels—so that we can make its text cover three lines. To overlay the message on top of the large white-font text display, we'll give it a z-index of 0. (Remember that the text display's z-index is –1.) Adding these specifications to the style sheet gives us

```
<DIV ID = divLearn Style
="Position:Absolute;Left:180;Top:200;Width:210;
z-index:0;">
```

The message will reside in a paragraph:

```
<P>
Learn how to create striking effects on your Web pages.
</P>
```

and we'll add some styling information to the <P> tag. In this tag, we can specify an appearance, size, and weight for the font. The entire <P> tag should look like this:

```
<P ID = pLearn Style = "font-family:cursive;font-size:15pt;font-weight:bold">
```

Here's the HTML for the DIV:

```
<DIV ID = divLearn Style ="POSITION:ABSOLUTE;LEFT:180;TOP:200;Width:210;
z-index:0;">
<P ID = pLearn Style = "font-family:cursive;font-size:15pt;font-weight:bold">
```

```
Learn how to create striking effects on your Web pages.
</P>
</DIV>
```

The Moving Boxes

To create the effect of a box that splits into four boxes, we position four boxes in the center of the page and give them all the same background color. Each box will be a separate DIV. I used blue as the background-color, but you can pick any color you like. I also specified a color property and a text-align property, because we'll use them in an exercise.

Here is one way to write the DIVs for the boxes:

```
<DIV ID = divBox1 Style="background-color:blue;color:blue;
text-align:center;Position:Absolute;Left:150;Top:180;Width:120;
Height:60;z-index:1 ">
</DIV>

<DIV ID = divBox2 Style="background-color:blue;color:blue;
text-align:center;Position:Absolute;Left:270;TOP:180;Width:120;
Height:60;z-index:1">
</DIV>

<DIV ID = divBox3 Style="background-color:blue;color:blue;
text-align:center;Position:Absolute;Left:150;Top:240;Width:120;
Height:60;z-index:1">
</DIV>

<DIV ID = divBox4 Style="background-color:blue;color:blue;
text-align:center;Position:Absolute;Left:270;Top:240;Width:120;
Height:60;z-index:1">
</DIV>
```

If you write the DIVs this way, you'll create the boxes in Figures 1.4 and 1.5, but the CSS syntax presents another possibility. Instead of writing the colors, text alignment, width, and height four times, we can put the style specifications for these properties at the beginning of the document between <HEAD> and </HEAD>, give those specifications a name, and then use that name within each box's <DIV> tag.

Here's how to do it. After the <HEAD> tag in your document, type

```
<STYLE Type = "text/css">
</STYLE>
```

We'll put the style information between these two tags. To give a name ("bluebox") to the style specifications and specify the background-color, color, text-alignment, width, and height, for the boxes, type

```
.bluebox {background-color:blue;
          color:blue;
          text-align:center;
          width:120;
          height:60}
```

after your newly created <STYLE> tag. When you prefix the name of a style with a dot, you create a style *class*. Note the consistent syntax for the style sheet. We still use a colon to separate a property from its value and a semicolon to separate adjacent property-value pairs.

 TIP   In the Microsoft version of DHTML, you can omit Type = "text/css", as CSS is the only type of style sheet that Microsoft supports. In the Netscape version, you can't omit this expression, because Netscape supports another type of style sheet in addition to CSS.

With the style specified as a class in the head of your document, you insert the name of the class in each box's DIV. Here's the HTML for the movable boxes:

```
<DIV ID = divBox1 Class = "bluebox"
Style="Position:Absolute;Left:150;Top:180;z-index:1">
</DIV>

<DIV ID = divBox2 Class = "bluebox"
Style="Position:Absolute;Left:270;Top:180;z-index:1">
</DIV>

<DIV ID = divBox3 Class = "bluebox"
Style="Position:Absolute;Left:150;Top:240;z-index:1">
</DIV>

<DIV ID = divBox4 Class = "bluebox"
STYLE="Position:Absolute;Left:270;Top:240;z-index:1">
</DIV>
```

Save your work, open the page in IE, and you'll see a display that looks like Figure 1.4, but without the little box in the lower-right corner.

Here's the exercise that uses the `color` and `text-align` properties you just set. It will show you how style sheets can combine to produce an HTML element's appearance. Follow these steps:

1. For the first movable box, between <DIV> and </DIV>, insert a paragraph that identifies the box:

   ```
   <P>Box<BR>1</P>
   ```

2. Do the same for the fourth movable box:

   ```
   <P>Box<BR>4</P>
   ```

3. In the first movable box's inline style sheet, add

   ```
   color:white
   ```

4. In the fourth movable box's inline style sheet, add

   ```
   background-color:white
   ```

In your document, the HTML for the movable boxes should now look like this:

```
<DIV ID = divBox1 Class = "bluebox"
Style="Position:Absolute;Left:150;Top:180;z-index:1;color:white">
<P>Box<BR>1</P>
</DIV>

<DIV ID = divBox2 Class = "bluebox"
Style="Position:Absolute;Left:270;Top:180;z-index:1">
</DIV>

<DIV ID = divBox3 Class = "bluebox"
Style="Position:Absolute;Left:150;Top:240;z-index:1">
</DIV>

<DIV ID = divBox4 Class = "bluebox"
STYLE="Position:Absolute;Left:270;Top:240;z-index:1;
background-color:white">
<P>Box<BR>4</P>
</DIV>
```

With these changes in place, Figure 1.6 shows the appearance of your page in IE.

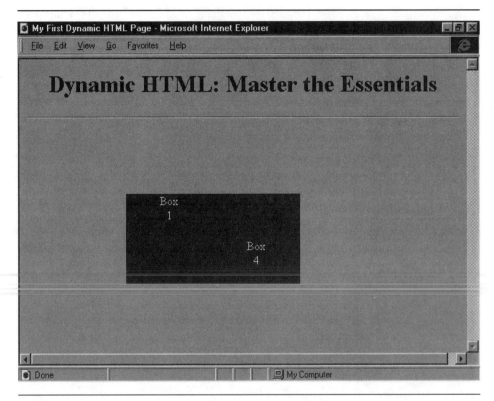

FIGURE 1.6: Your page in IE, with modified styling specifications for two of the movable boxes

The effects of these changes tell you that you can combine styles from the specification at the beginning of the document (between the <STYLE> and </STYLE> tags) and style from inline specifications. This combination is referred to as *cascading*—the "C" in CSS. Cascading is just one of the benefits that style sheets provide. You'll see others as you progress through the book, and you'll learn more about style sheets in Skill 4.

Remove those changes from divBox1 and divBox4, and we'll move on to the next element.

The Changeable Box

We finish off the page design by creating the box in the lower-right corner. The box changes color and content when you pass the mouse through the heading at the top of the page. You can see this by comparing Figure 1.4 to Figure 1.5. By now, you've probably guessed that we'll implement the effect by writing two DIVs, assigning them different z-indices, and making one visible and one invisible. We'll write a script that switches the visibility of the DIVs when the mouse passes into the heading and returns to the original values when the mouse passes out of the heading.

Here's the HTML that sets up the two DIVs:

```
<DIV ID = divReady Style =
"Position:Absolute;Top:70%;Left:80%;Width:10%;
z-index:1;Visibility:Visible">
<P Align = Center Style = "font-family:cursive;
Background-Color:'Beige';Color:Chocolate">
Are<BR>You<BR>Ready?</P>
</DIV>

<DIV ID = divStarted Style =
"Position:Absolute;Top:70%;Left:80%;Width:10%;
z-index:0;Visibility:Hidden">
<P Align = Center Style = "font-family:cursive;
Background-Color:'BlanchedAlmond';Color:Blue">
Let's<BR>Get<BR>Started</P>
</DIV>
```

A Word about Color

We've used numerous color-names in the HTML for our first page. What other color-names can you use in your code? Table 1.1 presents some of the colors that IE and Navigator can render. For completeness, I've included their hexadecimal codes. It's important to test a color in both browsers. As our work with Netscape will show later in this Skill, the browsers react differently to different color-names.

TABLE 1.1: Color-Names and Their Hexadecimal Codes

Color Name	Code	Color Name	Code
ALICEBLUE	#F0F8FF	ANTIQUEWHITE	#FAEBD7
AQUA	#00FFFF	AQUAMARINE	#7FFFD4
AZURE	#F0FFFF	BEIGE	#F5F5DC
BISQUE	#FFE4C4	BLACK	#000000
BLANCHEDALMOND	#FFEBCD	BLUE	#0000FF
BLUEVIOLET	#8A2BE2	BROWN	#A52A2A
BURLYWOOD	#DEB887	CADETBLUE	#5F9EA0
CHARTREUSE	#7FFF00	CHOCOLATE	#D2691E
CORAL	#FF7F50	CORNFLOWER	#6495ED
CORNSILK	#FFF8DC	CRIMSON	#DC143C
CYAN	#00FFFF	DARKBLUE	#00008B
DARKCYAN	#008B8B	DARKGOLDENROD	#B8860B
DARKGRAY	#A9A9A9	DARKGREEN	#006400
DARKKHAKI	#BDB76B	DARKMAGENTA	#8B008B
DARKOLIVEGREEN	#556B2F	DARKORANGE	#FF8C00
DARKORCHID	#9932CC	DARKRED	#8B0000
DARKSALMON	#E9967A	DARKSEAGREEN	#8FBC8B
DARKSLATEBLUE	#483D8B	DARKSLATEGREY	#2F4F4F
DARKTURQUOISE	#00CED1	DARKVIOLET	#9400D3
DEEPPINK	#FF1493	DEEPSKYBLUE	#00BFFF
DIMGRAY	#696969	DODGERBLUE	#1E90FF
FIREBRICK	#B22222	FLORALWHITE	#FFFAF0
FORESTGREEN	#228B22	FUCHIA	#FF00FF
GAINSBORO	#DCDCDC	GHOSTWHITE	#F8F8FF
GOLD	#FFD700	GOLDENROD	#DAA520
GRAY	#808080	GREEN	#008000
GREENYELLOW	#ADFF2F	HONEYDEW	#F0FFF0
HOTPINK	#FF69B4	INDIANRED	#CD5C5C
INDIGO	#4B0082	IVORY	#FFFFF0
KHAKI	#F0E68C	LAVENDER	#E6E6FA
LAVENDERBLUSH	#FFF0F5	LAWNGREEN	#7CFC00
LEMONCHIFFON	#FFFACD	LIGHTBLUE	#ADD8E6
LIGHTCORAL	#F08080	LIGHTCYAN	#E0FFFF
LIGHTGOLDENRODYELLOW	#FAFAD2	LIGHTGREEN	#90EE90
LIGHTGREY	#D3D3D3	LIGHTPINK	#FFB6C1
LIGHTSALMON	#FFA07A	LIGHTSEAGREEN	#20B2AA

TABLE 1.1 CONTINUED: Color-Names and Their Hexadecimal Codes

Color Name	Code	Color Name	Code
LIGHTSKYBLUE	#87CEFA	LIGHTSLATEGRAY	#778899
LIGHTSTEELBLUE	#B0C4DE	LIGHTYELLOW	#FFFFE0
LIME	#00FF00	LIMEGREEN	#32CD32
LINEN	#FAF0E6	MAGENTA	#FF00FF
MAROON	#800000	MEDIUMAQUAMARINE	#66CDAA
MEDIUMBLUE	#0000CD	MEDIUMORCHID	#BA55D3
MEDIUMPURPLE	#9370DB	MEDIUMSEAGREEN	#3CB371
MEDIUMSLATEBLUE	#7B68EE	MEDIUMSPRINGGREEN	#00FA9A
MEDIUMTURQUOISE	#48D1CC	MEDIUMVIOLETRED	#C71585
MIDNIGHTBLUE	#191970	MINTCREAM	#F5FFFA
MISTYROSE	#FFE4E1	MOCCASIN	#FFE4B5
NAVAJOWHITE	#FFDEAD	NAVY	#000080
OLDLACE	#FDF5E6	OLIVE	#808000
OLIVEDRAB	#6B8E23	ORANGE	#FFA500
ORANGERED	#FF4500	ORCHID	#DA70D6
PALEGOLDENROD	#EEE8AA	PALEGREEN	#98FB98
PALETURQUOISE	#AFEEEE	PALEVIOLETRED	#DB7093
PAPAYAWHIP	#FFEFD5	PEACHPUFF	#FFDAB9
PERU	#CD853F	PINK	#FFC0CB
PLUM	#DDA0DD	POWDERBLUE	#B0E0E6
PURPLE	#800080	RED	#FF0000
ROSYBROWN	#BC8F8F	ROYALBLUE	#4169E1
SADDLEBROWN	#8B4513	SALMON	#FA8072
SANDYBROWN	#F4A460	SEAGREEN	#2E8B57
SEASHELL	#FFF5EE	SIENNA	#A0522D
SILVER	#C0C0C0	SKYBLUE	#87CEEB
SLATEBLUE	#6A5ACD	SLATEGRAY	#708090
SNOW	#FFFAFA	SPRINGGREEN	#00FF7F
STEELBLUE	#4682B4	TAN	#D2B48C
TEAL	#008080	THISTLE	#D8BFD8
TOMATO	#FF6347	TURQUOISE	#40E0D0
VIOLET	#EE82EE	WHEAT	#F5DEB3
WHITE	#FFFFFF	WHITESMOKE	#F5F5F5
YELLOW	#FFFF00	YELLOWGREEN	#9ACD32

Scripting the Dynamic Effects

We've set up a number of segments in our Web page, and if you open it in IE at this point, you'll see a display that looks like Figure 1.4. In its present form, however, a user can't interact with this page to make it look like Figure 1.5. To enable interactivity, we have to add scripts.

Scripts make a Web page come alive. If we think of the elements on a page as actors on a stage, then a script tells them how to behave and interact with one another.

You write a script in a *scripting language*, a computer language designed to work inside a specific environment like an HTML document. Two scripting languages are prominent. One, VBScript or VBS, is a subset of Microsoft's popular Visual Basic. The other, JavaScript, has some of the syntax of Java, but is very different from Java. Both VBS and JavaScript work with software structures called *objects*, which we'll discuss in detail in Skill 5.

Unlike programming languages that can create applications that run by themselves, a scripting language requires a piece of software called an *interpreter* to run its programs. IE has built-in interpreters for VBScript and JavaScript, and Navigator has a built-in interpreter for JavaScript. In this first IE-based exercise, we'll work with VBScript.

In an HTML document, one way to write scripts is to put them inside this set of tags:

```
<SCRIPT Language = "VBScript">
<!--
-->
</SCRIPT>
```

You place this code in your document somewhere between <HEAD> and </HEAD>.

You put the body of your script between <!-- and -->. These two structures represent the beginning and end of a comment. Since a browser ignores comments, it won't process your script if it doesn't have the interpreter specified by the Language attribute in the <SCRIPT> tag.

Our script will set up the behaviors for the Web page elements for these situations:

- The mouse passes into the heading

- Mouse-clicks occur with the cursor in the heading

- The mouse passes out of the heading

The Mouse Passes into the Heading

As I said earlier, when the mouse passes into the heading, we want the color of the heading to change, the large-font message to become visible, and the box in the lower-right corner to change its colors and its content.

Passing the cursor into the heading is an *onMouseOver* event. (Think of an *event* as a signal to the Web page from the outside world.) Remember that we've given the heading an ID, so we can refer to it in our script. We'll write a *subroutine* for the heading's onMouseOver event.

We start the subroutine with this line:

```
Sub h1Header_onMouseOver
```

Sub lets the browser know that a subroutine definition follows, h1Header is the ID we gave the heading, and onMouseOver is the specific event that causes the subroutine to respond.

One of the behaviors that we want to happen as a result of this event is the change in the heading's color. We represent the heading's color as

```
h1Header.Style.Color
```

You can read this expression as "h1Header's Style's Color." In this context, a dot is like an apostrophe followed by "s."

NOTE   A more detailed explanation is that h1Header is an object, Style is a property of the object, and Color is a property of Style. We'll elaborate on the details in Skill 5.

To change the heading's color from the default black to something a bit livelier, like goldenrod, type

```
h1Header.Style.Color = "Goldenrod"
```

Next, we'll make the message with the large font visible. The ID for that message is divMessage, so the code to make it visible is

```
divMessage.Style.Visibility = "Visible"
```

Similarly, we switch the Visibility property for the two boxes in the lower-right corner of the page:

```
divReady.Style.Visibility = "Hidden"
divStarted.Style.Visibility = "Visible"
```

We must end every subroutine with

```
End Sub
```

The entire subroutine for the heading's onMouseOver event is:

```
Sub h1Header_onMouseOver
    h1Header.Style.Color = "Goldenrod"
    divMessage.Style.Visibility = "Visible"
    divReady.Style.Visibility = "Hidden"
    divStarted.Style.Visibility = "Visible"
End Sub
```

The script in this subroutine illustrates a fundamental principle of DHTML—it changes CSS information in response to a user event.

Mouse-Clicks Occur with the Cursor in the Heading

When the mouse passes into the heading and the user clicks the mouse, the message in the middle of the page becomes visible, and the box in the middle of the page splits into four boxes that move toward the corners of the page with each click. The effect is something like animation, as the boxes appear to move across the page. We'll get into animation in Skill 7, when we script movement that proceeds without mouse-clicks.

You already know how to make an element visible:

```
pLearn.Style.Visibility = "Visible"
```

Now for the tricky part—moving the boxes. Let's say we want the first box, divBox1, to move 20 pixels to the left and 20 pixels toward the top each time we click the mouse. This composite movement will take divBox1 toward the upper-left corner. The box to its immediate right, divBox2, should go 20 pixels to the right and 20 toward the top (i.e., toward the upper-right corner). divBox3 should move 20 to the left and 20 toward the bottom, and divBox4 should move 20 to the right and 20 toward the bottom. (You can use other numbers of pixels if you like.) In the coordinate system of browsers, the upper-left corner is at (0,0) so that movement toward the right is positive, movement toward the left is negative, movement toward the bottom is positive, and movement toward the top is negative.

With all these considerations in mind, we can set up the desired movement with:

```
Call MoveElementBy(divBox1,-20,-20)
Call MoveElementBy(divBox2,20,-20)
Call MoveElementBy(divBox3,-20,20)
Call MoveElementBy(divBox4,20,20)
```

Each line calls the subroutine MoveElementBy, which takes three *arguments* (items a subroutine needs in order to do its job)—the ID of the element to move, the number of pixels to move it in the horizontal direction, and the number of pixels to move it in the vertical direction.

This is all very straightforward, except for one problem: VBScript has no built-in subroutine called MoveElementBy. Where will this subroutine come from? We have to build it ourselves. The first line of the subroutine's definition should look like this:

```
Subroutine MoveElementBy(ElementID, LeftMovementAmount, TopMovementAmount)
```

Setting this up is a little more challenging than it looks, because MoveElementBy has to move an element a specified number of pixels. The positional information of an element, however, is not in numerical form—it's in a string.

For example, if divBox1 is 200 pixels from the left edge of the window, the value of divBox1.Style.Left isn't the number 200, it's the string "200px". We somehow have to turn "200px" into the number 200.

 NOTE   There's a way around this, but I want to take the opportunity to show you some of the aspects of VBScript.

Fortunately, VBScript provides some help. We'll use two built-in *functions* to turn the string "200px" into the string "200", and another built-in function to convert the string "200" into the integer 200. (In VBS, a function is like a subroutine except that it returns a value.)

The function InStr searches a string for the presence of a target string. If InStr finds the target, it returns the position in which the target begins. For example,

```
InStr("200px", "px")
```

returns 4. Our strategy, then, will be to set a variable equal to

```
InStr(ElementID.Style.Left,"px")
```

and another variable equal to InStr(ElementID.Style.Top,"px"), where ElementID is the ID of the element we're moving:

```
intPxPositionLeft = InStr(ElementID.Style.Left,"px")
intPxPositionTop = InStr(ElementID.Style.Top,"px")
```

The int prefix indicates that the variables hold integer information. We then use these variables in another built-in function, called Left. This function starts from the leftmost character in a string and returns a specified number of characters. The expression

```
Left("200px",3)
```

returns the string "200". We'll take the value that Left returns and use it as the argument for the VBS function CInt, which converts a string into an integer. The expression

```
CInt(Left(ElementID.Style.Left, intPxPositionLeft-1))
```

turns an element's Left edge location into an integer, and

```
CInt(Left(ElementID.Style.Top, intPxPositionTop-1))
```

turns the element's Top edge location into an integer.

Here's the VBScript for moving the boxes in response to a mouse-click:

```
Sub h1Header_onClick
    pLearn.Style.Visibility = "Visible"
    Call MoveElementBy(divBox1,-20,-20)
    Call MoveElementBy(divBox2,20,-20)
    Call MoveElementBy(divBox3,-20,20)
    Call MoveElementBy(divBox4,20,20)
End Sub


Sub MoveElementBy(ElementID,LeftMovementAmount,TopMovementAmount)
    dim intPxPositionLeft
      dim intPxPositionTop
    intPxPositionLeft = InStr(ElementID.Style.Left,"px")
    intPxPositionTop = InStr(ElementID.Style.Top,"px")
    ElementID.Style.Left = _
      CInt(Left(ElementID.Style.Left,intPxPositionLeft-1)) + _
        LeftMovementAmount
    ElementID.Style.Top = _
      CInt(Left(ElementID.Style.Top,intPxPositionTop-1)) +
        TopMovementAmount
End Sub
```

NOTE   The underscore is VBScript's line continuation character.

In the second subroutine, the dim statement defines the variables we use to store the returned values of the InStr function. VBScript allows you to create variables on the fly, but it's a good idea to define them explicitly as we've done here. (You'll learn more about this in Skill 13.)

The Mouse Passes Out of the Heading

After the scripting you've just created, the script for moving the mouse out of the heading is pretty tame:

```
Sub h1Header_onMouseOut
    h1Header.Style.Color = "Black"
    divBox1.Style.Top = 200
    divBox1.Style.Left = 150
    divBox2.Style.Top = 200
    divBox2.Style.Left = 270
    divBox3.Style.Top = 235
    divBox3.Style.Left = 150
    divBox4.Style.Top = 235
    divBox4.Style.Left = 270
    divMessage.Style.Visibility = "Hidden"
    divReady.Style.Visibility = "Visible"
    divStarted.Style.Visibility = "Hidden"
    pLearn.Style.Visibility = "Hidden"
End Sub
```

This Sub just returns all the elements to their original settings.

An Important Tip

If you save your work and open the page in IE, it will look like Figure 1.4 and your scripts will enable you to perform mouse actions that activate the dynamic effects. You'll encounter one problem, however. Moving the mouse into and out of the heading will result in flicker: Because it's text, the heading sets off an irregularly shaped area—sometimes the cursor is in that area, sometimes it's not, and it's not always obvious which is which. The irregularity of the heading area's shape causes another problem—mouse-clicks on the heading might not work as you'd like them to.

You can easily solve these problems by wrapping the heading in a DIV, and positioning the DIV at the top of the page. Here's what the HTML for the heading should look like:

```
<DIV Style = "Position:Absolute;Left:10;Top:0;Width:100%">
<H1 ID = h1Header Style = "text-align:center">Dynamic HTML:
Master the Essentials</H1>
<HR>
</DIV>
```

Including the <HR> tag in the DIV preserves the positional relationship between the heading and the horizontal line.

The Whole File

Here's the entire First Dynamic IE.htm file

 First Dynamic IE.htm

```
<HTML>
<HEAD>
<STYLE Type = "text/css">
.bluebox {background-color:blue;
        color:blue;
        text-align:center;
        width:120;
        height:60}
</STYLE>

<SCRIPT LANGUAGE = "VBSCRIPT">

Sub h1Header_onMouseOver
        h1Header.Style.Color = "Goldenrod"
        divMessage.Style.Visibility = "Visible"
        divReady.Style.Visibility = "Hidden"
        divStarted.Style.Visibility = "Visible"
End Sub

Sub h1Header_onMouseOut
        h1Header.Style.Color = "Black"
        divBox1.Style.Top = 180
        divBox1.Style.Left = 150
        divBox2.Style.Top = 180
        divBox2.Style.Left = 270
        divBox3.Style.Top = 240
        divBox3.Style.Left = 150
        divBox4.Style.Top = 240
        divBox4.Style.Left = 270
        divMessage.Style.Visibility = "Hidden"
        divReady.Style.Visibility = "Visible"
        divStarted.Style.Visibility = "Hidden"
End Sub

Sub h1Header_onClick
        pLearn.Style.Visibility = "Visible"
        Call MoveElementBy(divBox1,-20,-20)
        Call MoveElementBy(divBox2,20,-20)
        Call MoveElementBy(divBox3,-20,20)
        Call MoveElementBy(divBox4,20,20)
End Sub
```

```
Sub MoveElementBy(ElementID,LeftMovementAmount,TopMovementAmount)
    pPositionTop = InStr(ElementID.Style.Top,"px")
    pPositionLeft = InStr(ElementID.Style.Left,"px")
    ElementID.Style.Top = _
      CInt(Left(ElementID.Style.Top,pPositionTop-1)) + _
        TopMovementAmount
    ElementID.Style.Left = _
      CInt(Left(ElementID.Style.Left,pPositionLeft-1)) + _
        LeftMovementAmount
End Sub

</SCRIPT>
<TITLE>My First Dynamic HTML Page</TITLE>
</HEAD>
<BODY Style = "background-color:'Silver'">
<DIV Style = "Position:Absolute;Left:10;Top:0:Width:100%">
<H1 ID = h1Header Style = "text-align:center">Dynamic HTML:
Master the Essentials</H1>
<HR>
</DIV>
<DIV ID = divMessage Style = "Position:Absolute;Left:5%;Top:10%;
Visibility:Hidden;z-index:-1;font-style:normal;font-weight:bold;
font-family:Normal;font-size:50;color:'White'">
<P> Topics in this book include
<UL>
<LI> Scripting
<LI> Cascading Style Sheets
<LI> Animation
<LI> ... And Many More!
</UL>
</P>
</DIV>

<DIV ID = divLearn Style="Position:Absolute;Left:180;Top:200;Width:210;
z-index:0;">
<P ID = pLearn Style = "font-family:cursive;font-size:15pt;
font-weight:bold">
Learn how to create striking effects on your Web pages.
</P>
</DIV>

<DIV ID = divBox1 Class = "bluebox"
Style="Position:Absolute;Left:150;Top:180;z-index:1">
</DIV>

<DIV ID = divBox2 Class = "bluebox"
Style="Position:Absolute;Left:270;Top:180;z-index:1">
</DIV>
```

```
<DIV ID = divBox3 Class = "bluebox"
Style="Position:Absolute;Left:150;Top:240;z-index:1">
</DIV>

<DIV ID = divBox4 Class = "bluebox"
STYLE="Position:Absolute;Left:270;Top:240;z-index:1">
</DIV>

<DIV ID = divReady Style =
"Position:Absolute;Top:70%;Left:80%;Width:10%;
z-index:1;Visibility:Visible">
<P Style = "text-align:center;font-family:cursive;Background-Color:
'Beige';Color:Chocolate">
Are<BR>You<BR>Ready?</P>
</DIV>

<DIV ID = divStarted Style =
"Position:Absolute;Top:70%;Left:80%;Width:10%;
z-index:0;Visibility:Hidden">
<P Style = "text-align:center;font-family:cursive;Background-Color:
'BlanchedAlmond';Color:Blue">
Let's<BR>Get<BR>Started</P>
</DIV>

</BODY>
</HTML>
```

Open this file in IE to see all the effects that turn Figure 1.4 into Figure 1.5.

Using DHTML in Navigator

To round out your introduction to Dynamic HTML, let's put a similar page together for Netscape Navigator. We'll have to make a few changes, but most of the effects will remain:

- Moving the mouse into the heading will change the color of the heading and make a large-font message appear.

- Mouse-clicks will make boxes in the middle of the page move out toward the corners. In this version, the mouse-click will occur on an on-screen button, rather than on the heading.

- A mouse-click on another button will return all the elements to their original settings.

I've eliminated the small changeable box from this page, but you can put it in as an exercise. Figure 1.7 shows what this page looks like, rendered in Netscape, with the dynamic effects visible.

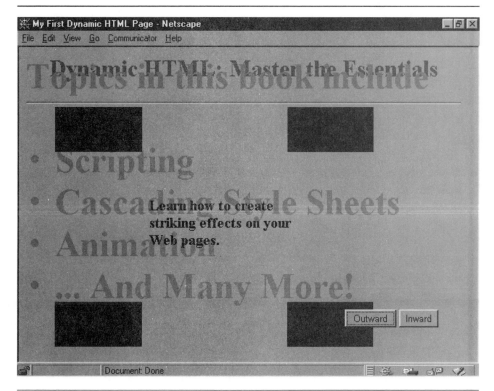

FIGURE 1.7: Your DHTML page in Netscape, with dynamic effects visible

To start things off, open your `Template`, save it as `First Dynamic Nav.htm` in Skill 1, and change the title to **My First Dynamic Web Page**. Next, change the background color to silver. In the IE version, you did this by putting the style sheet

```
Style = "background-color:'silver'"
```

into the <BODY> tag. If you do that in the Navigator version, you'll run into trouble. As you'll see again and again, Navigator is quirky when it comes to rendering colors specified in style sheets. (Future versions of Navigator will no doubt solve this problem.) To work around this, insert the deprecated attribute `Bgcolor` into the <BODY> tag:

```
Bgcolor = "Silver"
```

The Heading and the Horizontal Line

We start out as before, by creating the heading and the horizontal line beneath it. The HTML is the same as before, so your file should look like this:

```
<HTML>
<HEAD>
</HEAD>
<TITLE>My First Dynamic HTML Page</TITLE>
<BODY Bgcolor = "Silver">
<Center>
<H1>Dynamic HTML: Master the Essentials</H1></Center>
<HR>
</BODY>
</HTML>
```

The *<LAYER>* Tag

In our IE version, we used <DIV> tags to divide our page into segments. We then used VBScript to apply dynamic effects to those divisions.

To segment a Web page, Navigator provides the <LAYER> tag. You begin a segment with <LAYER> and end it with </LAYER>. Although <LAYER> and <DIV> both segment a page, and both support the z-index, they differ in important ways.

Netscape designed the <LAYER> to behave like a piece of transparent paper laid on top of a Web page. Between <LAYER> and </LAYER>, you insert HTML elements. You provide the <LAYER> with an ID (via either ID or Name) and with attributes and values that specify its appearance and position. You use JavaScript to change those values in response to user events. Dynamic effects result from these scripted changes.

NOTE   As I write this, <LAYER> is a cornerstone of Netscape's Dynamic HTML. This may change, however, as the World Wide Web Consortium has rejected the <LAYER> tag.

One of the important differences between <DIV> and <LAYER> is that the <LAYER> tag doesn't work with inline style sheets. You can use inline style sheets to set styles for HTML elements that reside inside a layer, but you can't assign IDs to these elements and then script them. You can only script behaviors for the <LAYER> tag, and programmatically change only the attributes that the <LAYER> tag supports. This limits the type of scripting you can do, compared with the Microsoft version. To create similar effects from one browser to the other, you often have to exercise some ingenuity, as you'll see later in this Skill.

Default positioning presents another important difference. If you don't include values for TOP and LEFT, a <DIV> defaults to a position based on where it appears in the flow of the HTML document. A <LAYER>, on the other hand, defaults to a position seven pixels from the left edge of the browser window and seven pixels from the top. With multiple layers this can get messy, as they will all default to the same position.

Back to the Heading and the Horizontal Line

Now that you know about the Netscape <LAYER> tag, let's put the heading and the horizontal line into a layer. Remember, we start with <LAYER> and end with </LAYER>, and we have to provide positional information:

```
<LAYER Name = layerHeader Left = 10 Top = 10 z-index = 0
<Center>
<H1>Dynamic HTML: Master the Essentials</H1></Center>
<HR>
</LAYER>
```

Notice the Name attribute, and note also that we've provided a z-index value. This value, 0, puts the layer at the same level as the document. Higher numbers make the layer appear on top of the document, negative numbers make the layer appear below the document.

We added the z-index because we can't reference the heading and change its color with a script. Instead, we have to exercise the ingenuity I mentioned in the last section. To make the heading appear to change color, we'll create another heading which resides in a layer just below this one, give the new heading a different color, make the layer invisible, and script a visibility swap. Here's the other heading and its enclosing layer:

```
<LAYER Name = layerUnderHeader Left = 10 Top = 10 z-index = -1
Visibility = "hide">
<Center>
<H1 Style = "color:'khaki'">Dynamic HTML: Master the
Essentials</H1></Center>
<HR>
</LAYER>
```

The z-index, -1, and the Visibility value, "hide", hint at the script that will appear to change the color of the page's heading.

NAVIGATOR, COLORS, AND CSS

I didn't use goldenrod for the new heading-color this time, because Navigator renders it as a darkish green when you specify this color in a CSS. Of course, Navigator also renders khaki as a darkish green in this context, too. As I pointed out before, Navigator—at least my release—is iffy with respect to colors when you specify them in CSSs. If you use the code values instead of the names, you'll get the same result.

You can prove to yourself that Navigator understands the colors in Table 1.1, however. Within any of the <LAYER> tags that we create in this exercise, set the Bgcolor attribute equal to any of the color-names in Table 1.1. You'll find them rendered very nicely as background colors when you open the file in Navigator. In fact, we'll use one of those colors when we set up our movable boxes. (Remember that we used Bgcolor as a substitute for Style = "background-color: 'Silver'" when we set the background color for the body of the page.)

The Hidden Message

As in the IE version, we'll implement the large-font hidden message by putting it inside a paragraph, and we'll provide the styling specifications in an inline style sheet:

```
<P Style = "color:'green';  font-size:50px; font-weight:bold">Topics in
this book include
<UL Style = "color:'green';  font-size:50px; font-weight:bold">
<LI> Scripting
<LI> Cascading Style Sheets
<LI> Animation
<LI> ... And Many More!
</UL>
</P>
```

You'll immediately see three differences between the IE version and this one:

- In the IE version, we didn't put a style sheet in the <UL> tag. In IE, the <UL> tag inherited the <P> tag's style. In Navigator, it doesn't, although the <LI> elements do inherit the <UL>'s style.

- In IE, we didn't put px after the font size value. With no unit after the value, IE defaults to px. Navigator does not. If you omit the unit name after the value, Navigator defaults to normal-size font.

- Although Figure 1.7 isn't in color, you probably noticed that the color of the large-font message isn't white. As you can see from the style sheets, we've set it to green. Why? In the context of a style sheet, Navigator doesn't render white as a text color—it defaults to black. (This is consistent with the situation I described in the sidebar "Navigator, Colors, and CSS.") Later releases of Navigator 4.*x* will probably clear this up. If you like, you can use the <FONT> tag to set the text color to white, but I'd rather you became accustomed to working with style sheets than with deprecated elements.

Now let's put this message in a layer, give the layer a name, a position, a visibility, and a z-index. Precede the <P> tag with

```
<LAYER ID = layerMessage Left=10 Top=10 Visibility = "hide" z-index = -2 >
```

and follow the </P> tag with

```
</LAYER>
```

The Message at the Center of the Page

The paragraph that holds the centered message is the same as the one in the IE version, except that it has no ID. The <LAYER> tag that precedes it holds the position, width, and z-index specifications:

```
<LAYER NAME = layerLearn LEFT = 180 TOP = 200 Width = 210 z-index = 0>
<P  Style="font-family:Cursive;font-weight:bold;font-size:15pt">
Learn how to create striking effects on your Web pages.
</P>
</LAYER>
```

The Movable Boxes

The easiest way to implement the movable boxes is to create each one as a separate layer, and position them appropriately. To make them appear as blue boxes, we set the (somewhat infamous) Bgcolor attribute to blue:

```
<LAYER NAME = layerBox1 Bgcolor = "blue" LEFT = 150 TOP = 180 Width = 120
Height = 60 z-index = 1>
</LAYER>

<LAYER NAME = layerBox2 Bgcolor = "blue" LEFT = 270 TOP = 180 Width = 120
Height = 60 z-index = 1>
</LAYER>

<LAYER NAME = layerBox3 Bgcolor = "blue" LEFT = 150 TOP = 240 Width = 120
Height = 60 z-index = 1>
</LAYER>

<LAYER NAME = layerBox4 Bgcolor = "blue" LEFT = 270 TOP = 240 Width = 120
Height = 60 z-index = 1>
</LAYER>
```

The Clickable Buttons

This version of our Web page has two buttons in the lower-right corner of the page. One is labeled Outward, and the other Inward. Clicking on the Outward button will move the boxes toward the corners, and clicking on the Inward button will return them to their original positions.

I put these buttons on the page because they support the onClick event. The <LAYER> tag does not support this event, so clicking on the heading would have no effect. Since I wanted a mouse-click to move the boxes, I added these buttons.

The buttons are examples of *form controls*, so named because they reside between <FORM> and </FORM> tags. You specify a button inside an <INPUT> tag by assigning the value button to the attribute Type. You label the button by assigning a string to the attribute Value:

```
<FORM>
<INPUT Type = button Value = "Outward"
<INPUT Type = button Value = "Inward">
</FORM>
```

We wrap the form in a layer, so that we can position it within the page. Precede the <FORM> tag with

```
<LAYER Left = 450 Top = 350>
```

and follow the </FORM> tag with </LAYER>.

Scripting the Dynamic Effects

Once again, we'll write scripts to make our Web page come alive. This time we'll write our scripts in JavaScript, the only scripting language Navigator supports.

In our IE version, we put VBScript between <SCRIPT> and </SCRIPT> tags. In this version, we'll write our JavaScript inline (i.e., inside HTML tags). It's not necessary to do it this way—I'm just illustrating another way to add script. Both ways, tagged and inline, work in both browsers.

The Mouse Passes Into and Out of the Heading

We begin our inline scripting with the events associated with the heading. The heading, you'll remember, resides in a LAYER called `layerHeader`. Since we're concerned with the mouse moving into and out of the heading, we'll write script for the `onMouseOver` and `onMouseOut` events inside the <LAYER> tag for `layerHeader`.

When the mouse moves into the heading, we want to make the large-font message appear and have the heading's color change. We're making the heading seem to change colors by making `layerHeader` invisible and `layerUnderHeader` visible. This means that we'll want these settings:

```
layerMessage.visibility = "show"
layerHeader.visibility = "hide"
layerUnderHeader.visibility = "show"
```

To put these settings into inline JavaScript code, you write them inside a quoted string and separate them with semicolons. (Make sure you change the double quotes around the attribute values to single quotes.) Then you set this string as the value of `onMouseOver` and put the whole thing inside the <LAYER> tag:

```
<LAYER Name = layerHeader Left = 10 Top = 10 z-index = 0
onMouseOver = "layerMessage.visibility = 'show';
               layerHeader.visibility = 'hide';
               layerUnderHeader.visibility = 'show'"
```

Don't add the closing angle-bracket yet, because you still have to add the code for onMouseOut, which returns the settings to their starting values:

```
onMouseOut = "layerMessage.visibility = 'hide';
              layerUnderHeader.visibility = 'hide'
              layerHeader.visibility = 'show'" >
```

Note the closing angle-bracket, indicating that we've finished scripting the behaviors for this layer.

 **WARNING**   JavaScript is case-sensitive, so don't even think about beginning visibility with an uppercase "V."

Mouse-Clicks Occur on the Response Buttons

We finish by scripting behaviors for the onClick event in the tags that define the on-screen response buttons. When we click the button labeled Outward, we want the boxes to move outward, and when we click the button labeled Inward, we want the boxes to move back into their starting positions.

Fortunately, JavaScript layers have built-in *methods* that will handle these effects for us. (Think of a method as a procedure that the layer knows how to follow.) The first method, offset, is something like the MoveElementBy subroutine we wrote. It takes two arguments—the distance to move the layer in the horizontal direction and the distance to move it in the vertical direction. Here's the code to write inside the first response button's <INPUT> tag:

```
<INPUT Type = button Value = "Outward"
    onClick = "layerBox1.offset(-20,-20);
               layerBox2.offset(20,-20);
               layerBox3.offset(-20,20);
               layerBox4.offset(20,20);">
```

The second built-in method is called moveTo. As its name suggests, moveTo moves a layer to a location specified by the method's two arguments:

```
<INPUT Type = button Value = "Inward"
    onClick = "layerBox1.moveTo(150,180);
               layerBox2.moveTo(270,180);
               layerBox3.moveTo(150,240);
               layerBox4.moveTo(270,240);">
```

The Whole File

Here's the entire First Dynamic Nav.htm listing:

First Dynamic Nav.htm

```
<HTML>
<HEAD>
</HEAD>
<TITLE>My First Dynamic HTML Page</TITLE>
<BODY Bgcolor = "Silver">
<LAYER Name = layerHeader Left = 10 Top = 10 z-index = 0
onMouseOver = "layerMessage.visibility = 'show';
                layerHeader.visibility = 'hide';
                layerUnderHeader.visibility = 'show'"

onMouseOut = "layerMessage.visibility = 'hide';
                layerUnderHeader.visibility = 'hide'
                layerHeader.visibility = 'show'" >
<Center>
<H1>Dynamic HTML: Master the Essentials</H1></Center>
<HR>
</LAYER>

<LAYER Name = layerUnderHeader Left = 10 Top = 10 z-index = -1
Visibility = "hide">
<Center>
<H1 Style = "color:'khaki'">Dynamic HTML: Master the Essentials</H1></Center>
<HR>
</LAYER>
<Layer ID = layerMessage Left=10 Top=10
Visibility = "hide" z-index = -2 >

<P Style = "color:'green';  font-size:50px; font-weight:bold">Topics in this
book include
<UL Style = "color:'green';  font-size:50px; font-weight:bold">
<LI> Scripting
<LI> Cascading Style Sheets
<LI> Animation
<LI> ... And Many More!
</UL>
</P>
</LAYER>
```

```
<LAYER NAME = layerLearn LEFT = 180 TOP = 200 Width = 210 z-index = 0>
<P  Style="font-family:Cursive;font-weight:bold;font-size:15pt">
Learn how to create striking effects on your Web pages.
</P>
</LAYER>

<LAYER NAME = layerBox1 Bgcolor = "blue" LEFT = 150 TOP = 180 Width = 120
Height = 60 z-index = 1>
</LAYER>

<LAYER NAME = layerBox2 Bgcolor = "blue" LEFT = 270 TOP = 180 Width = 120
Height = 60 z-index = 1>
</LAYER>

<LAYER NAME = layerBox3 Bgcolor = "blue" LEFT = 150 TOP = 240 Width = 120
Height = 60 z-index = 1>
</LAYER>

<LAYER NAME = layerBox4 Bgcolor = "blue" LEFT = 270 TOP = 240 Width = 120
Height = 60 z-index = 1>
</LAYER>

<LAYER Left = 450 Top = 350>
<FORM>
<INPUT Type = button Value = "Outward"
    onClick = "layerBox1.offset(-20,-20);
                layerBox2.offset(20,-20);
                layerBox3.offset(-20,20);
                layerBox4.offset(20,20);">

<INPUT Type = button Value = "Inward"
    onClick = "layerBox1.moveTo(150,180);
                layerBox2.moveTo(270,180);
                layerBox3.moveTo(150,240);
                layerBox4.moveTo(270,240);">

</FORM>
</LAYER>
</BODY>
</HTML>
```

Open this file in Navigator to see the scripted effects. Mousing over the heading will make the heading's color appear to change, and will display the hidden message. Moving the mouse out of the header will return the heading color to its starting value. Clicking the Outward button will make the box in the middle split apart, and the resulting four boxes will move toward the four corners of the Web page. Clicking the Inward button will immediately move all the boxes back to the center.

Summary

DHTML combines CSS, HTML, and scripting, and you've already worked with all three in this Skill. You developed a couple of Web pages in HTML, complete with style sheets and scripts, and you even used two different scripting languages.

Chances are you now have a feel for the similarities and differences between the dueling DHTMLs. The Microsoft version supports the W3C standards on CSSs and makes CSS style elements available for scripting. Consequently, every attribute of every element on an IE-compatible Web page is programmatically changeable. By contrast, the Navigator version supports the W3C standards on CSSs, but not inside the <LAYER> tag, which is Netscape's vehicle for creating dynamic effects. Also, Navigator provides shaky support, at the time of this writing, for CSS color specifications.

We're just beginning, so get ready for a long ride.

Have You Mastered the Essentials?

Now you can...

☑ Set up a work environment for developing DHTML in both IE and Navigator

☑ Build a dynamic Web page that changes element visibility, moves objects, and changes an object's appearance, all in response to user events

☑ Modify a dynamic Web page built for IE to run in Navigator

☑ Create inline style sheets and understand the style sheet concept

☑ Write simple scripts in VBScript, including an original subroutine that converts string-based position information into integers

☑ Write simple inline scripts in JavaScript

☑ Use built-in functions and methods in VBScript and JavaScript

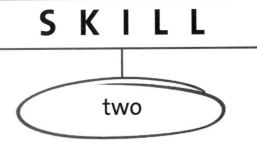

Learning the Basics of HTML: Text, Hypertext, and Frames

- ❏ HTML overview
- ❏ Creating a mini Web site
- ❏ Working with hypertext
- ❏ Frames and navigation buttons
- ❏ Frames and HTML-based navigation

Skill 1 immersed you in DHTML, but now is a good time to step back and take a look at HTML. If you already know HTML, this Skill and the next one will be a refresher for you. If not, read and follow the exercises, as you'll have to know HTML in order to understand DHTML.

Overview

Originally designed by scientists as a vehicle for exchanging research papers over the Internet, Hypertext Markup Language (HTML) has grown and developed in response to the demands of Web site builders. HTML tags and attributes define the structure of a Web page.

Growth in the language has typically been manifested in new tags and attributes that refine the *presentation* of a Web page (its fonts, color, and background, for example), rather than its structure. As we pointed out in Skill 1, many of these tags and attributes have been deprecated. Style sheets are replacing them and are, accordingly, becoming an important tool in the Web developer's arsenal. We'll examine style sheets in Skill 4. In this Skill, we'll discuss some of the aspects of the latest version of HTML.

Let's begin our discussion by taking a look at the template you designed in Notepad. You created this set of tags:

```
<HTML>
<HEAD>
<TITLE>New Page </TITLE>
<BODY>

</BODY>
</HTML>
```

You created these tags for a reason: They encompass all the important fundamental *elements* of an HTML document.

 NOTE   An element typically consists of a start-tag, content, and an end-tag, although some elements (like the line-break element BR) have no content, and some (again, like BR) have no end-tag. Thus, an element is not the same as a tag.

The *HTML* Element

The HTML element encloses the document. The <HTML> tag begins the document and the </HTML> tag ends it.

The *HEAD* Element

The HEAD element contains information about the Web page. It holds the title, indicated by the <TITLE> and </TITLE> tags, and it can hold keywords that search engines are able to access. In every HTML document, exactly one title in the HEAD element is required.

Within this element (i.e., between <HEAD> and </HEAD>), a developer can place a <META> tag that describes the document. The META element accepts a number of useful attributes. One of these attributes, Name, specifies the name of a property. You use it in conjunction with Content, which specifies the property's value. For example, if I wanted to specify myself as the author of a Web page, I'd do it like this:

```
<META Name = "Author" Content = "Joseph Schmuller">
```

Another application of META, Name, and Content is geared toward search engines:

```
<META Name = "Keywords" Content = "education, learning, design">
```

These <META> tags (and more) may appear within the HEAD element.

From Skill 1 you'll recall two more useful elements that can reside between <HEAD> and </HEAD>: STYLE and SCRIPT. STYLE contains the style sheets we'll use throughout the book (and discuss in Skill 4), and SCRIPT holds the scripts we write to make things happen on the page (we've also written inline scripts that reside inside other tags. We'll use scripts throughout the book, and discuss them in greater depth in Skill 6.

The *BODY* Element

The BODY element holds the content of the Web page. If you look at the source code for documents written in earlier versions of HTML, you'll find attributes for this element that specify the presentation aspects of a page. These attributes include:

- background—whose value is a URL for an image file that tiles the page's background
- bgcolor—a color for the page's background
- text—a color for the document's text
- link—a color of the text for hypertext links not yet visited
- vlink—a color of the text for visited links
- alink—a color of the text for links the user has selected

In HTML 4.0, these attributes have been deprecated in favor of style sheet properties.

NOTE As I mentioned in Skill 1, a "deprecated" element is one that may be obsolete in future versions of HTML because newer features provide greater capabilities.

NOTE How do you know which version of HTML an author used to develop a document? Most authors include a <!DOCTYPE> tag at the beginning of a document, just before the <HTML> tag. The tag looks something like this: <!DOCTYPE HTML PUBLIC "//W3C/DTD HTML 4.0 Final//EN>. This tag tells you the document is written in the final specification of HTML 4.0. EN indicates that the language is English.

Within the BODY element, you can place a wide range of elements that structure a Web page. One element we placed on both versions of our first Web page was H1, a heading. This is one of six possible headings—H1 produces the largest font, H6 the smallest.

The P element is one of the most pervasive. It's designed to hold text information in the form of a paragraph.

The A element allows you to isolate text so that you can style it differently from surrounding text, as you'll see in the first exercise in this Skill. In the second exercise, you'll see that it allows you to link your page to other pages.

From Skill 1, you'll recall that DIV is one of the most useful elements to put into the body of a document. With it, you can divide the page into segments or add a STYLE attribute to specify its position and appearance (or disappearance). You can also include other HTML elements within DIV.

FORM is another element that comes in handy. It allows you to create on-screen controls that enable interactivity, like the buttons we added to our Navigator-compliant Web page in Skill 1. Each control is represented by a value of the Type attribute inside an <INPUT> tag, and the <INPUT> tags reside in the FORM element. In addition to buttons, some other types of form controls are

- text—a single-line text box

- password—a single-line text box that shows a series of asterisks in response to user keystrokes

- checkbox—a toggle which allows the user to make selections from a set of alternatives; several checkboxes can work together so that a user can make more than one selection

- radio—an option button which allows the user to make a selection from a set of alternatives; when several radio controls work together, a user can make only one selection

Many Web pages use tables to present information. Tables are also often used to position elements on a page. With the advent of style sheets, however, element-positioning becomes exact and tables become unnecessary for presenting anything but traditional tabular information. In Skill 3, you'll go through an exercise on table construction.

Creating a Mini Web Site

Let's put our HTML knowledge to work. Imagine a fictional institution of higher learning called "The University of Cyberspace," a school whose colors are green and #FFFFCC (a pleasant light yellow). U of Cyb has a virtual campus, existing only on the Web. It specializes in learning-at-a-distance: U of Cyb professors present courses on the Web rather than in physical classrooms.

Let's use IE to develop a home page for the University. The finished page will look like Figure 2.1.

FIGURE 2.1: The Web page for the University of Cyberspace

Begin by saving your Template file as UofCyb.htm in Skill 2. (I'm assuming that you're using the Notepad template we defined in Skill 1.) After the <HEAD> tag, insert a style sheet that makes a class called UofCyb. We'll use it to style the phrase "University of Cyberspace" wherever it appears on the Web site:

```
<STYLE Type = "text/css">
.UofCyb{font-size:120%;color:'green';font-weight:bold;font-family:cursive}
</STYLE>
```

Notice the font-size value is 120%. This will make any font styled by the UofCyb class 20% larger than the font in the element in which it appears.

Change the title to The University of Cyberspace Home Page, and then give the page background a pleasant light yellow color. Use an inline style sheet to create the background color:

```
<BODY Style = "background-color:#FFFFCC">
```

The heading will be set as H1. Center it and make the University's name conform to the font-style and color in the UofCyb class. Don't forget the <HR> tag to create a line underneath the heading:

```
<H1 Style = "text-align:center">Welcome to the <A Class = "UofCyb">
University of Cyberspace</A> Home Page!</H1>
<HR>
```

Note that we've used the anchor tags, <A> and </A>, to set off "University of Cyberspace" so that we could apply our style.

Next, we'll create the paragraph that holds the text and the bulleted list of departments. We want to leave some room on the right for the three boxes, so we'll set a right margin of 40% (40% of the width of the page):

```
<P style = "margin-right:40%">At the
<A Class = "UofCyb">
University of Cyberspace</A>, we're proud of our faculty and
our students. Here are a few of our departments:

<UL>
    <LI>Web Page Design</LI>
    <LI>Web Access Statistics</LI>
    <LI>Cyberengineering</LI>
</UL>
</P>
```

You may recall that we used <UL> and <LI> in Skill 1. The UL element is an unordered list, and each LI element is a list item.

Next, create the paragraph that holds the text after the bulleted list:

```
<P style = "margin-right:40%">
<A Class = "UofCyb">University of Cyberspace</A> departments
are known virtually all over the world.
</P>
```

The boxes on the right of the screen are the final components to build. Each one is a DIV that contains a P element. As you can see in Figure 2.1, each box appears superimposed over the one that precedes it. We use increasing z-index, top, and left values to accomplish this (determined by experimentation):

```
<DIV style = "position:absolute;top:35%;left:65%;background-color:'blue';
color:'white';width:150;height:120;z-index:0">
<P style = "font-weight:bold;font-size:20;text-align:center">
Tops in Virtual Education</P>
</DIV>

<DIV style = "position:absolute;top:50%;left:70%;background-color:'green';
color:'white';width:150;height:120;z-index:1">
<P style = "font-weight:bold;font-size:20;text-align:center">
Number One Since 1994</P>
</DIV>

<DIV style = "position:absolute;top:65%;left:75%;background-color:'goldenrod';
color:'white';width:150;height:120;z-index:2">
<P style = "font-weight:bold;font-size:20;text-align:center">
The Premier Educational Organization on the World-Wide Web!</P>
</DIV>
```

Choose other colors if you like. Once you have input this HTML code, open the file in IE. You'll see a page that looks like Figure 2.1.

Here's the whole file:

```
<HTML>
<HEAD>
<STYLE Type = "text/css">
.UofCyb{font-size:120%;color:'green';font-weight:bold;font-family:cursive}
</STYLE>
<TITLE>The University of Cyberspace Home Page</TITLE>
</HEAD>
<BODY Style = "background-color:#FFFFCC">
<H1 Style = "text-align:center">Welcome to the <A Class = "UofCyb">University of
Cyberspace</A> Home Page!</H1>
<HR>

<P style = "margin-right:40%">At the
<A Class = "UofCyb">
University of Cyberspace</A>, we're proud of our faculty and
our students. Here are a few of our departments:

<UL>
    <LI>Web Page Design</LI>
    <LI>Web Access Statistics</LI>
    <LI>Cyberengineering</LI>
</UL>
```

```
</P>
<P style = "margin-right:40%">
<A Class = "UofCyb">University of Cyberspace</A> departments
are known virtually all over the world.
</P>

<DIV style = "position:absolute;top:35%;left:65%;background-color:'blue';
color:'white';width:150;height:120;z-index:0">
<P style = "font-weight:bold;font-size:20;text-align:center">Tops in Virtual
Education</P>
</DIV>

<DIV style = "position:absolute;top:50%;left:70%;background-color:'green';
color:'white';width:150;height:120;z-index:1">
<P style = "font-weight:bold;font-size:20;text-align:center">
Number One Since 1994</P>
</DIV>

<DIV style = "position:absolute;top:65%;left:75%;background-color:'goldenrod';
color:'white';width:150;height:120;z-index:2">
<P style = "font-weight:bold;font-size:20;text-align:center">
The Premier Educational Organization on the World-Wide Web!</P>
</DIV>
</BODY>
</HTML>
```

PLAYING THE PERCENTAGES

This is a good time to talk about positioning by percentage. In this document, and the others in this Skill, we position the DIVs by specifying percentage values, rather than pixel values, for Top and Left. The effect of this is that the page will look like Figure 2.1 if your browser window is maximized. If it's less than maximum size, the appearance changes to fit the percentages. You can see this for yourself by creating the document, opening it in your browser, and resizing the window.

Positioning this way can work to your advantage. For example, if you're creating a corporate Web page, you might always want the corporate logo to be visible regardless of how a user sizes a browser window. In the U of Cyb example, the overlapping boxes remain in view even when you shrink the window.

Hypertext: A Link to the World

One of the main attractions of the Web is hypertext, the linking of items in a nonlinear way. Hypertext frees users from having to view Web-resident items in a conventional page-after-page sequence defined by an author. Instead, users can jump around the Web in a user-defined path, choosing to examine topics that meet their own particular needs.

In this exercise, we add hypertext to our University of Cyberspace Web site. We'll start by creating pages for the U of Cyb home page to link to. We'll create a page for each department listed on the home page, and then we'll build a link from the home page to each department page. On each department page, we'll build a link back to the home page.

Use your text editor to create three new .HTM files—Cybereng.htm, WebAccessStats.htm, and WebPageDesign.htm. Each one will have the same style sheet as the U of Cyb page, and each one will just have a heading and a horizontal line. Here's Cybereng.htm:

```
<HTML>
<HEAD>
<STYLE Type = "text/css">
.UofCyb{font-size:120%;color:'green';font-weight:bold;font-family:cursive}
</STYLE>
<TITLE>Department of Cyberengineering</TITLE>
</HEAD>
<BODY Style = "Background-Color:#FFFFCC">
<H1 Style = "Text-Align:Center">
Cyberengineering at
the <A Class = "UofCyb">University of Cyberspace</A>
</H1>
<HR>
</BODY>
</HTML>
```

This is WebAccessStats.htm:

```
<HTML>
<HEAD>
<STYLE Type = "text/css">
.UofCyb{font-size:120%;color:'green';font-weight:bold;font-family:cursive}
</STYLE>
<TITLE>Department of Web Access Statistics</TITLE>
</HEAD>
<BODY Style = "Background-Color:#FFFFCC">
<H1 Style = "Text-Align:Center">
The <A Class = "UofCyb">University of Cyberspace</A>
Department of Web Access Statistics
```

```
</H1>
<HR>
</BODY>
</HTML>
```

And here's `WebPageDesign.htm`:

```
<HTML>
<HEAD>
<STYLE Type = "text/css">
.UofCyb{font-size:120%;color:'green';font-weight:bold;font-family:cursive}
</STYLE>
<TITLE>Department of Web Page Design</TITLE>
</HEAD>
<BODY Style = "Background-Color:#FFFFCC">
<H1 Style = "Text-Align:Center">
You've Found the Department of Web Page Design at the
<A Class = "UofCyb">University of Cyberspace</A>
</H1>
<HR>
</BODY>
</HTML>
```

NOTE   In Skill 4, you'll learn a technique that eliminates the need to enter the same style information in each page.

We won't bother with content for these pages just yet—we'll fill them in later Skills. For the moment, we're concerned about linking the home page to them. Reopen `UofCyb.htm` and turn your attention to the LI elements:

```
<LI>Web Page Design</LI>
<LI>Web Access Statistics</LI>
<LI>Cyberengineering</LI>
```

Let's set these items up as hyperlinks to the department pages. When we do, clicking on one of them should bring its department page into the browser. To make this happen, we use the A element. We used it before to apply a style, and now we use it to set up a link.

In the first LI element, just after the <LI> tag, type

```
<A Href = "E:\DHTML MTE\Skill 2\WebPageDesign.htm">
```

NOTE   Remember to substitute the appropriate drive, if you're not working from an E: drive.

The Href attribute of A has a string as its value, and the string holds the path to the linked page. Insert an </A> tag just before </LI>.

Make similar additions to the other LI elements. They should look like this when you're finished:

```
<LI><A Href = "E:\DHTML MTE\Skill 2\WebPageDesign.htm">Web Page
Design</A></LI>
<LI><A Href = "E:\DHTML MTE\Skill 2\WebAccessStats.htm">Web Access
Statistics</A></LI>
<LI><A Href = "E:\DHTML MTE\Skill 2\Cybereng.htm">
Cyberengineering</A></LI>
```

Now if you open UofCyb.htm in IE, you'll see that its appearance has changed. As Figure 2.2 shows, the items in the bulleted list are underlined and colored differently.

FIGURE 2.2: UofCyb.htm with hyperlinks established to department pages

Clicking on each of those links will cause the browser to display a department page.

Now, let's create a hyperlink back to the home page on each department page. In the lower-right corner of each page, we'll put a hyperlink that will send us home, as shown in Figure 2.3.

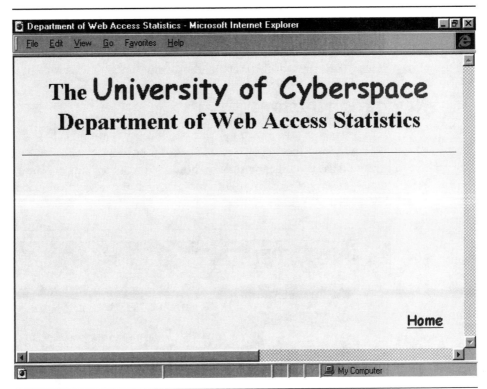

FIGURE 2.3: WebAccessStat.htm with a hyperlink to the UofCyb home page

Here's the HTML code to create the hyperlink back to the home page for each department page:

```
<DIV Style = "Position:Absolute;Top:90%;Left:90%">
<P Class = "UofCyb">
<A Href = "E:\DHTML MTE\Skill 2\UofCyb.htm">
Home
</A>
</P>
</DIV>
```

When you're done, open UofCyb.htm in IE and you'll find you can click back and forth between the home page and each department page. (Remember to adjust the file path if you're not using an E: drive.)

What's in a Frame?

HTML gives you the capability to split your browser into separate windows called *frames*. Each frame is an independent, fully functional window.

Navigation Buttons

Frames have numerous uses. One of the most common is to split the browser into two windows that aren't equal in size, and use the smaller one as a "navigation" frame. That is, you can put form buttons in the navigation frame and script their onClick events to display different pages in the larger frame. Figure 2.4 shows an example of this kind of setup.

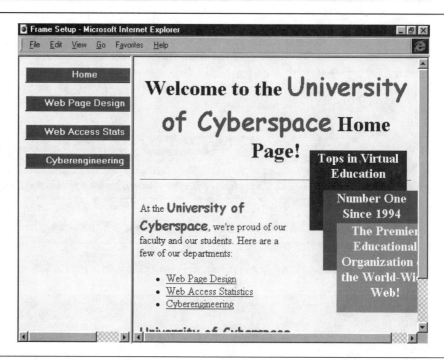

FIGURE 2.4: A page with two frames. In this setup, clicking the buttons in the smaller frame displays different pages in the larger frame.

Skill 2

The buttons in the left frame are standard form buttons. You usually see them colored gray, and the width usually varies with the number of letters on them. But here, we'll use a style sheet that specifies a color scheme to stay consistent with the school colors, and specifies their widths to stay consistent with each other.

Here's the HTML code that sets up the Frames.htm frame arrangement in Figure 2.4:

Frames.htm

```
<HTML>
<HEAD>
<TITLE>Frame Setup</TITLE>
</HEAD>
<FRAMESET Cols = 28%,72%>
<FRAME Name = "leftframe" Src = "E:\DHTML MTE\Skill 2\Navigation.htm">
<FRAME Name = "rightframe" Src = "E:\DHTML MTE\Skill 2\UofCyb.htm">
</FRAMESET>
</HTML>
```

NOTE   Notice the absence of <BODY> and </BODY> when you use a <FRAMESET> tag. This is a change from HTML 3.x.

The <FRAMESET> tag indicates that this file is setting up frames, and its Cols attribute divides the browser window into column-like windows with the indicated widths. I arrived at these widths via a little experimentation. When the display appears in your browser, you can adjust the on-screen widths by dragging the boundary between the frames.

The two <FRAME> tags use the Name attribute to provide names for the two frames. We'll use these names later. The Src attribute for each one provides a file path to the page that fills the frame when the display opens in the browser.

Here is the Navigation.htm file, displayed in the left frame:

```
<HTML>
<HEAD>
<STYLE Type = "text/css">
.UofCybButton {background-color:green;color:#FFFFCC;font-weight:bold;width:190}
</STYLE>
<TITLE>Navigation</TITLE>
</HEAD>
<BODY Style = "Background-Color:#FFFFCC">
<FORM>
<P>
<INPUT Type = button Value = "Home" Class = "UofCybButton">
<P>
```

```
<INPUT Type = button Value = "Web Page Design" Class = "UofCybButton">
<P>
<INPUT Type = button Value = "Web Access Stats" Class = "UofCybButton">
<P>
<INPUT Type = button Value = "Cyberengineering" Class = "UofCybButton">
</FORM>
</BODY>
</HTML>
```

The style sheet

```
<STYLE Type = "text/css">
.UofCybButton {background-color:green;color:#FFFFCC;font-weight:bold;width:190}
</STYLE>
```

creates a class that specifies the appearance of the buttons You link a button style to the style class by setting the button's `Class` attribute to `"UofCybButton"`.

Next, we must script the buttons so that clicking each one opens a different page in the larger frame. In order to do this, we have to

- Have a way to refer to the larger frame

- Change one of its properties (the one that specifies where its display comes from) as a result of the buttons' `onClick` event

Before we work out a way to refer to the larger frame, we have to understand how the browser is organized. Its window is an object, and it has properties, methods, and events, as you'll see in Skill 12. One of those properties, `top`, identifies what's top-most on the window's list of what to display. In our example, both our frames are on top when they appear in the browser. So, we can refer to `rightframe` as `window.top.rightframe`.

Now that we know the name, we have to specify that the frame's contents will come from a particular file when we click a particular button. How do we do this? A frame is like a window, and it has the same properties, methods, and events as a window. One of those properties is `Location`, which provides the location of the file displayed in the frame. `Location`, in turn, has a property called `Href`, which is the URL of the file in the frame.

 NOTE   We used `Href` in the previous exercise when we wanted to jump from one page to another. The principle is the same here: We use `Href` to jump to another page. This time the new page will show up in a frame, instead of the entire browser window.

Here's the bottom line: When we click one of the form buttons, we want to change the URL for the file in `rightframe`. That's how we direct the frame to display a different URL. When we click the Department of Web Page Design button, for instance, we want to set the URL to `WebPageDesign.htm`. This is the way to do it:

```
onClick = "window.top.rightframe.location.href = 'UofCyb.htm'
```

We vary this code (which is JavaScript, by the way) as necessary for the other three buttons.

> **WARNING** IE can't handle local file path names for the URLs in this context. If you try to use one, you'll get an error message. I'll elaborate on this in Skill 12.

Here is the `Navigation.htm` file with the scripting included:

 Navigation.htm

```
<HTML>
<HEAD>
<STYLE Type = "text/css">
.UofCybButton {background-color:green;color:#FFFFCC;font-weight:bold;width:190}
</STYLE>
<TITLE>Navigation</TITLE>
</HEAD>
<BODY Style = "Background-Color:#FFFFCC">
<FORM>
<P>
<INPUT Type = button Value = "Home" Class = "UofCybButton"
onClick = "window.top.rightframe.location.href = 'UofCyb.htm'">
<P>
<INPUT Type = button Value = "Web Page Design" Class = "UofCybButton"
onClick = "window.top.rightframe.location.href = 'WebPageDesign.htm'">
<P>
<INPUT Type = button Value = "Web Access Stats" Class = "UofCybButton"
onClick = "window.top.rightframe.location.href = 'WebAccessStats.htm'">
<P>
<INPUT Type = button Value = "Cyberengineering" Class = "UofCybButton"
onClick = "window.top.rightframe.location.href = 'Cybereng.htm'">
</FORM>
</BODY>
</HTML>
```

Open Frames.htm in IE, and you'll see a display like Figure 2.4. Clicking the buttons should get you around the mini Web site. Figure 2.5 shows the appearance of the frameset after you click on the Web Access Statistics button.

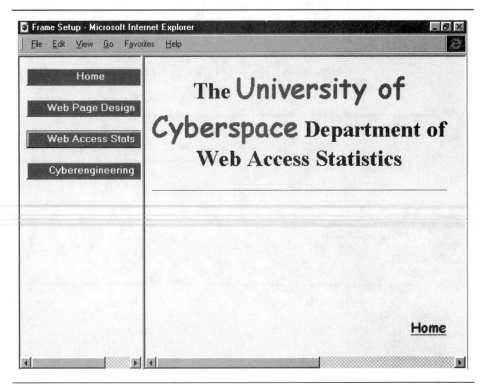

FIGURE 2.5: The appearance of frames.htm after you click on the Web Access Statistics button

The frameset and the code you created will work in Navigator. In order to accommodate Navigator's internal workings, however, you have to change the file path names in the Src attribute of Frame (within FRAMESET) to either just the name of the file (as I did in this exercise) or this format: file:///E:/DHTML MTE/ Skill 2/filename.htm. File paths written this way will also work in IE. Also, you'll find the appearance of the pages a bit different, due to Navigator's sporadic support for CSS: The navigation buttons on the left will be gray, and their widths will depend on the number of letters in the button caption. The three boxes on the right look nothing like they do in IE. In Navigator, they're smaller, their letters are in default font, and they don't overlap.

Another Way to Navigate

You can set up frame-based navigation another way. Instead of a frame with buttons next to a frame that shows pages, you can lay out two equally sized frames one above the other. The upper frame displays the home page, and clicking on its hyperlinks causes the other pages on the Web site to appear in the lower frame. This approach comes in handy if you always have to have the home page visible. It's also handy because it implements navigation entirely in HTML, with no need for any scripting. Figure 2.6 shows this arrangement.

FIGURE 2.6: Frames arranged as rows with the home page in the top frame. Clicking on the home page's bulleted list brings the departments' pages into the bottom frame.

I call the frameset for this display NewFrames.htm. Here it is:

NewFrames.htm

```
<HTML>
<HEAD>
<TITLE>New Frame Setup</TITLE>
</HEAD>
<FRAMESET Rows = 50%,50%>
<FRAME Name = "topframe" Src = "NewUofCyb.htm">
<FRAME Name = "bottomframe" Src = "WebPageDesign.htm">
</FRAMESET>
</HTML>
```

To make the frame-based navigation take place, we have to change UofCyb.htm a bit. As you can see from the frameset, I saved the changed file as NewUofCyb.htm. Specifically, we have to add the Target attribute to each <A> tag, and set Target to bottomframe:

```
<LI><A Href = "E:\DHTML MTE\Skill 2\WebPageDesign.htm" Target =
"bottomframe">Web Page Design</A></LI>
<LI><A Href = "E:\DHTML MTE\Skill 2\WebAccessStats.htm" Target =
"bottomframe">Web Access Statistics</A></LI>
<LI><A Href = "E:\DHTML MTE\Skill 2\Cybereng.htm" Target =
"bottomframe">Cyberengineering</A></LI>
```

Now, open NewFrames.htm in IE, and you'll see a display that looks like Figure 2.6. Click on the bulleted items in the home page in the top frame, and the appropriate pages will appear in the bottom frame.

Summary

Knowing HTML is the foundation for understanding some of the intricacies of DHTML. In this Skill, you saw how HTML elements construct a page and how hypertext links can deliver different pages to your browser. You worked with several useful tags, and you were introduced to the functionality of frames. Combining hypertext with frames resulted in some facilities that help users navigate through your Web site.

Although you accomplished a lot, you probably noticed that something was missing: graphics. Graphics brighten up a Web site, and are an important part of the Web experience. We'll cover graphics in Skill 3.

Have You Mastered the Essentials?

Now you can...

☑ **Work with HTML tags**

☑ **Set up hypertext links**

☑ **Build frames and implement frame navigation in JavaScript**

☑ **Add style to form buttons to control their color scheme and size in IE**

☑ **Implement frame navigation in HTML without scripting**

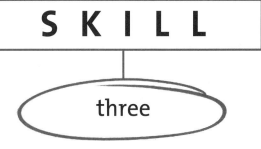

Learning the Basics of HTML: Graphics and Tables

☐ Introducing graphics

☐ Acquiring images

☐ Inserting an image into a Web page

☐ Adding a background to a Web page

☐ Using tables

True to its Internet roots as a medium for communication among scientific researchers, the Web features text wherever you surf. The explosion of interest in the Web, however, has brought a focus on graphics and on ways of presenting data in an organized way. Web developers everywhere now liven up their sites with snazzy drawings and photos, and present information in the form of carefully organized tables.

Introducing Graphics Formats

If you've worked with a package like Paint—the graphics-creation accessory in Windows 95—you already know something about graphics. The bitmap format that Paint works with, however, is large and cumbersome: Simple bitmap images, graphics files with a .BMP extension, can take up a lot of memory.

Draw something in Paint, and you'll see what I mean. A bitmap of just three simple overlapping shapes filled with color can approach 1MB. When the images get more complex, the file size can really explode. More importantly, a file this size on a Web page would translate into long, frustrating waits as the page unfolds in a browser.

People concerned with graphic transmission over the Internet have come up with a few solutions. The solutions compress images into much smaller packages that travel quickly over the Net.

CompuServe, a pioneer in online service for the masses, was one of the first organizations to tackle the challenges of graphic transmission. They called their solution *GIF* (Graphic Interchange Format). Each pixel in a GIF image can store up to eight bits. For our purposes, this means that a GIF image can have up to 256 colors. This format works well for line drawings.

The Joint Photographic Experts Group also tackled the problem. Their initials, JPEG, form the name of the format they derived for transmitting complex images like photographs. JPEG (pronounced "JAY-peg") stores 24 bits in each pixel. An image in this format can have over 16 million colors.

When you decompress a JPEG image, it isn't exactly the same as the pre-compressed original. Because JPEG compression loses information, JPEG is said to be *lossy*. The information that JPEG loses, however, is usually imperceptible to the human eye. Lossiness is adjustable: if you decrease the degree of compression, you increase the image quality and lower the lossiness. You're also likely to increase download time.

Acquiring Images

In order to work along with the exercises in this Skill, you'll need some image files in the proper format. The Web is the best place to get them. It's easy to copy any image from a Web page. Position your cursor anywhere on the image, right-click, and a menu will pop up. In IE, select Save Picture As from the pop-up menu. In Navigator, select Save Image As. In either browser, a dialog box opens. In that box, indicate the folder where you want to store a copy of the image file, and click OK.

Bear in mind that you shouldn't just copy an image and use it on a page that you'll put out on the Web, particularly for commercial purposes—the graphic artists who create those images don't like it, and copyright laws forbid it unless you have permission.

 NOTE This Skill shows you the fundamentals of working with ready-made graphics files, and doesn't cover graphics creation. This is a subject that typically takes up a whole book. If you strongly feel the need to create your own graphics, you'll find some surprisingly inexpensive yet powerful tools on the Web. Many of them are shareware packages. Three good places to start looking are: http://www.shareware.com, http://www.Windows95.com, and http://www.tucows.com.

For Web page graphics, it's helpful to have .GIF images of photographs, backgrounds, small images, and multicolored straight lines. California-based Lassen Technologies maintains a library of these kinds of images on its Web site, at http://www.snowcrest.net/lassen/images.html.

The images in Lassen Technologies' library are in five categories: solid/patterned backgrounds, photo backgrounds, bars, pictures, and little guys (small images you can use as buttons and bullets). Lassen Technologies grants permission to use these files on personal pages or on pages for nonprofit organizations. If you want to use them for commercial purposes, you have to pay a licensing fee (as I did). We'll use Lassen Technologies images in several Skills in this book.

When you download the Lassen images, save them in a folder called graphics within your DHTML MTE folder. Within graphics, set up a folder for each category to make it easy to find an image when you need it. (I use the names backgrounds, bars, pictures, photobks, and small for my folders.)

 NOTE Two more sources of GIF files are: http://www.3dcafe.com and http://www.mccannas.com.

Adding an Image

In this Skill, we'll work with pages you've already created, and we'll create an additional one. Copy the pages in your University of Cyberspace mini Web site from your Skill 2 folder to your Skill 3 folder. In the Href attributes of each page's HTML document, change the file paths to point to Skill 3 rather than to Skill 2.

Let's begin our foray into graphics by sprucing up the Web page for the Department of Web Page Design. When we're finished with our changes, it will look like Figure 3.1.

The centerpiece of the page is an image. We use an <IMG> tag to insert that image, and its Src attribute to provide the image's file path. Just below the <HR> tag in this page's HTML document, create this code:

```
<IMG Style = "Position:Absolute;Top:55%;Left:30%;"
Src = "E:\DHTML MTE\graphics\pictures\forest.gif">
```

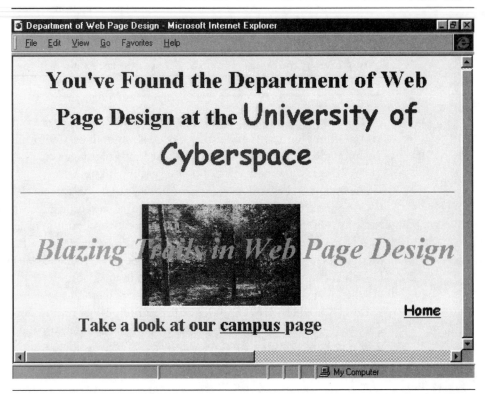

FIGURE 3.1: The finished Web page for the Department of Web Page Design

As you're aware by now, the `Style` attribute values position the image on the page. I'm assuming you downloaded the Lassentech images and put them in a file path like mine. If you're using some other image and a different file path, make the necessary adjustments.

Next, add the superimposed phrase

```
<DIV Style = "Position:Absolute;Top:65%;Left:5%;font-
size:40;color:gold;
font-style:italic;font-weight:bold;z-index:1">
<P> Blazing Trails in Web Page Design</P>
</DIV>
```

The `z-index`, 1, makes the phrase appear superimposed on the image.

Finally, add the phrase at the bottom of the page:

```
<DIV Style = "Position:Absolute;Top:95%;Left:15%;font-size:25;
font-weight:bold;color:green">
<P>Take a look at our <A Href = "E:\DHTML MTE\Skill 3\campus.htm">
campus </A>page
</P>
</DIV>
```

This is how the `WebPageDesign.htm` file should look:

```
<HTML>
<HEAD>
<STYLE Type = "text/css">
.UofCyb{font-size:120%;color:'green';font-weight:bold;font-family:cursive}
</STYLE>
<TITLE>Department of Web Page Design</TITLE>
</HEAD>
<BODY Style = "Background-Color:#FFFFCC">
<H1 Style = "Text-Align:Center">
You've Found the Department of Web Page Design at the
<A Class = "UofCyb">University of Cyberspace</A>
</H1>
<HR>
<IMG Style = "Position:Absolute;Top:55%;Left:30%;"
Src = "E:\DHTML MTE\graphics\pictures\forest.gif">
<DIV Style = "Position:Absolute;Top:65%;Left:5%;font-size:40;color:gold;
font-style:italic;font-weight:bold;z-index:1">
<P> Blazing Trails in Web Page Design</P>
</DIV>
<DIV Style = "Position:Absolute;Top:95%;Left:15%;font-size:25;
font-weight:bold;color:green">
<P>Take a look at our <A Href = "E:\DHTML MTE\Skill 3\campus.htm">
campus </A>page
</P>
```

```
</DIV>
<DIV Style = "Position:Absolute;Top:90%;Left:90%">
<P Class = "UofCyb">
<A Href = "E:\DHTML MTE\Skill 3\UofCyb.htm">
Home
</A>
</P>
</DIV>
</BODY>
</HTML>
```

The Href inside the <A> tag indicates a hyperlink to a "campus" page. Creating this page is our next order of business.

Adding a Background, and Then Some

Just for variety's sake, we'll make Campus.htm look a little different from the other U of Cyb pages we created so far. (A well-designed Web site, of course, would maintain consistency among its pages.) We'll create a tiled background, and put an image and some text inside a bordered box. Then we'll put a form button in the lower right corner. When we're finished, the page will look like Figure 3.2.

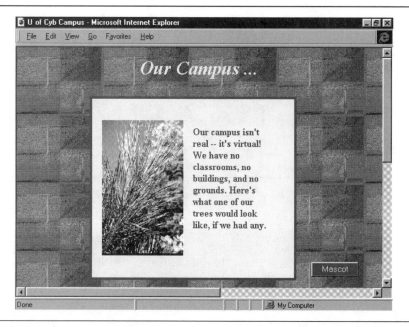

FIGURE 3.2: The campus Web page for the University of Cyberspace

Start by saving your TEMPLATE as `Campus.htm` in Skill 3, and changing the title to `U of Cyb Campus`.

The `<BODY>` tag will contain the file path to the background image that tiles the page. Here's how to use a style sheet to add that path:

```
<BODY Style = "background:url(E:\DHTML MTE\
graphics\photobks\ltp16a.gif)">
```

Notice that the value of `background` is written in a slightly different syntax from all the property values we've worked with so far. This syntax isn't scriptable, meaning that you can't change its specification programmatically. If you want to script changes to the background, use the `Background` attribute of the BODY element:

```
<BODY Background = "E:\DHTML MTE\graphics\photobks\ltp16a.gif">
```

TIP   You can use the style sheet syntax in the HTML element to set the background there instead of in the BODY element, and thus make setting backgrounds an out of <BODY> experience.

Next, we put a centered, italicized heading, written in one of the school colors, at the top of the page:

```
<H1 Style = "text-align:center;color:#FFFFCC;font-style:italic">Our
Campus ...</H1>
```

Now we'll add the image and the surrounding items. The easiest way to handle this is to put the image inside a DIV. We'll use a style sheet to position the DIV and style its appearance, and then we'll position the image within the DIV. In the HTML document, insert this code to style and position the DIV:

```
<DIV ID = divContainer1 Style = "position:absolute;
left:125;top:80;width:350;height:300;
background-color:#FFFFCC;color:green;font-weight:bold;
border:solid;border-color:green">
```

The ID is in preparation for the scripting I mentioned earlier, and it gives us a convenient way of referring to this DIV in the discussion that follows. I used `Container` in the name because it contains other elements, as all DIVs do, and the number 1 because we'll be creating another DIV like this one. The `background-color` and `color` properties put the school colors inside `divContainer1`, as colors for background and text. The border properties, `border` and `border-color`, define the green boundary that encloses `divContainer1`.

Next, add this code for the image:

```
<IMG Style = "position:absolute;top:12%;left:5%;"
Src = "E:\DHTML MTE\graphics\pictures\pine.gif"
Title = "Imaginary Tree">
```

The values for top and left may look a bit skimpy. That's because the image is within divContainer1, and the top and left are with respect to the top edge and the left edge of divContainer1—not the page. The Title attribute contains text that will appear in a small box whenever the mouse passes over the image. It's commonly called a *tool tip*.

In earlier versions of HTML, when you added an image to a Web page, you had to use the Align attribute to specify how text would flow around the image. With the advent of style sheets, however, you have more precise control. Accordingly, the W3C has deprecated Align in this context. To set the text next to the image, we'll

- Put a new DIV inside divContainer1

- Provide the new DIV with its own style sheet

- Embed the text in a paragraph in the new DIV

The styling information for the new DIV is

```
<DIV Style = "position:absolute;left:50%;top:15%;width:40%>
```

Notice that we don't have to specify a background color, a text color, or a font weight, as this DIV inherits those properties from divContainer1. Think of divContainer1 as the *parent* and the new DIV as the *child*.

Now we'll add a paragraph that contains the text:

```
<P>Our campus isn't real - it's virtual! We have no classrooms,
no buildings, and no grounds. Here's what one of our trees would look
like, if we had any.</P>
```

Finally, we have to make sure we close off both DIVs:

```
</DIV>
</DIV>
```

If you've been following along, your code should look like this:

```
<DIV ID = divContainer1 Style = "position:absolute;
left:125;top:80;width:350;height:300;
background-color:#FFFFCC;color:green;font-weight:bold;
border:solid;border-color:green">
```

```
<IMG Style = "position:absolute;top:12%;left:5%;"
Src = "E:\DHTML MTE\graphics\pictures\pine.gif"
Title = "Imaginary Tree">

<DIV Style = "position:absolute;left:50%;top:15%;width:40%">
<P>Our campus isn't real — it's virtual! We have no classrooms,
no buildings, and no grounds. Here's what one of our trees would look
like, if we had any.</P>
</DIV>
</DIV>
```

Open the page in IE, or link to it from `WebPageDesign.htm` to see a display that looks like Figure 3.2, but without the button in the lower-right corner.

Before we move on, let's leverage some of the knowledge you acquired in earlier skills. We'll script a dynamic effect that switches the school colors within `divContainer1` when you move your mouse through it. In other words, green elements will become #FFFFCC, and vice versa. When you move your mouse out of the DIV area, the colors will switch back.

We can make this happen easily in JavaScript (actually in JScript, the Microsoft version of JavaScript). In `divContainer1`, insert this code after the `Style` string:

```
onMouseOver = "this.style.backgroundColor = 'green';
               this.style.borderColor = '#FFFFCC';
               this.style.color = '#FFFFCC';"
```

The quoted string on the right of the equal sign takes advantage of the JavaScript expression `this`. It refers to the object, `divContainer1`, in which the code resides. Notice that a style property like `background-color` has to be in the intercap format, `backgroundColor`, when you script it, as JavaScript doesn't understand hyphens.

We'll complete our little script by creating the code for `onMouseOut`:

```
onMouseOut =  "this.style.backgroundColor = '#FFFFCC';
               this.style.borderColor = 'green';
               this.style.color = 'green'">
```

If you open the page in IE and position your mouse inside the central display (i.e., in `divContainer1`), it should look like Figure 3.3.

FIGURE 3.3: The appearance of Campus.htm when the mouse is positioned in the central display

The expressions in the quoted string reset the original values.

In your HTML document, divContainer1 now looks like this:

```
<DIV ID = divContainer1 Style = "position:absolute;
left:125;top:80;width:350;height:300;
background-color:#FFFFCC;color:green;font-weight:bold;
border:solid;border-color:green"

onMouseOver = "this.style.backgroundColor = 'green';
              this.style.borderColor = '#FFFFCC';
              this.style.color = '#FFFFCC';"

onMouseOut = "this.style.backgroundColor = '#FFFFCC';
             this.style.borderColor = 'green';
             this.style.color = 'green'">
```

```
<IMG Style = "position:absolute;top:12%;left:5%;"
Src = "E:\DHTML MTE\graphics\pictures\pine.gif"
Title = "Imaginary Tree">

<DIV ID Style = "position:absolute;left:50%;top:15%;width:40%">
<P>Our campus isn't real — it's virtual! We have no classrooms,
no buildings, and no grounds. Here's what one of our trees would look
like, if we had any.</P>
</DIV>
</DIV>
```

Now let's script that button in the lower-right corner. As Figure 3.2 shows, the word "Mascot" appears on the button. We'll write a script that causes a click on this button to replace the tree display in the center of the window with a display of the University of Cyberspace's mascot. Figure 3.4 shows the mascot display.

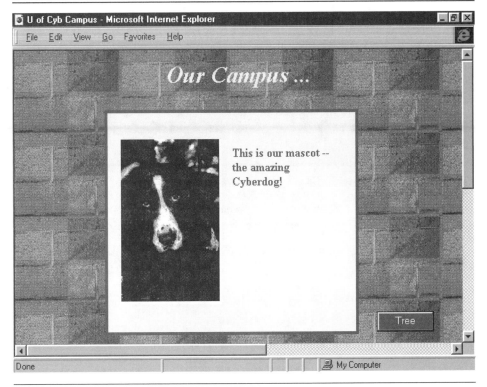

FIGURE 3.4: Clicking the button on the Campus page shows this display.

First, we have to create the DIV that contains an image of the mascot and one for its accompanying text—we'll call it divContainer2. The quickest way to create divContainer2 is to copy and paste divContainer1 and modify the copy appropriately:

```
<DIV ID = divContainer2 Style = "position:absolute;
left:125;top:80;width:350;height:300;
background-color:#FFFFCC;color:green;font-weight:bold;
border:solid;border-color:green"

onMouseOver = "this.style.backgroundColor = 'green';
               this.style.borderColor = '#FFFFCC';
               this.style.color = '#FFFFCC';"

onMouseOut = "this.style.backgroundColor = '#FFFFCC';
              this.style.borderColor = 'green';
              this.style.color = 'green'">

<IMG Style = "position:absolute;top:12%;left:5%"
Src = "E:\DHTML MTE\graphics\pictures\abi.gif"
Title = "Cyberdog">

<DIV ID Style = "position:absolute;left:50%;top:15%;width:40%">
<P>This is our mascot - the amazing Cyberdog!</P>
</DIV>
</DIV>
```

TIP   Some of the strings for our inline style sheets are becoming rather long. Make sure you put the close double-quote at the end. If you don't, you'll get errors in your display that may be hard to track down.

The modifications from divContainer1 to divContainer2 are

- The name

- The file path in the IMG element's Src attribute ("E:\DHTML MTE\ graphics\pictures\abi.gif")

- The IMG element's Title attribute (Cyberdog)

- The text in the P element (This is our mascot - the amazing Cyberdog!)

The beauty of the `this` expression is that we don't have to make any changes to the `onMouseOver` and `onMouseOut` scripts in `divContainer2`. Passing the mouse in and out of `divContainer2` will cause the same dynamic effects as passing the mouse in and out of `divContainer1`.

Now let's focus our attention on the button. To place the button in the HTML document

- Put the button in a paragraph inside a FORM element
- Put the FORM in a DIV
- Position the DIV with an inline style sheet

Here's the DIV followed by the <FORM> tag:

```
<DIV Style = "position:absolute; left:500;top:350;">
<FORM>
```

We use an inline style sheet to color the button green, give its text the light yellow color, and give it a width in pixels:

```
<P><INPUT Type = button ID = inputButton Value = "Mascot"
style = "background-color:green;color:#FFFFCC;width:80"
```

This is a substantial improvement over the pre-CSS days. HTML form buttons were always gray with black text, and their widths depended on the length of the `Value`—the text on the button face. With style sheets, you can control most of the aspects of a button's appearance.

Notice that I didn't include the right angle-bracket in the INPUT tag. That's because we still have to include the script for the button's `onClick` event. Let's script the button to be a toggle: If the tree display is visible, the button's `value` is `"Mascot"`, and clicking the button will reveal the mascot display, hide the tree display, and change the button's `value` to `"Tree"`. If the button's `value` is `"Tree"`, clicking the button will hide the mascot display, show the tree display, and change the button's `value` to `"Mascot"`. To script these behaviors, we use JavaScript's `if`...`else` structure:

```
if (test condition) {
… Steps to execute if the condition is true …
} else {
… Steps to execute if the condition is not true …
}
```

Skill 3

Applying this structure to our example gives us

```
onClick = "if (this.value == 'Tree') {
            this.value = 'Mascot';
            divContainer2.style.visibility = 'hidden';
            divContainer1.style.visibility = 'visible';
            } else {
            this.value = 'Tree';
            divContainer2.style.visibility = 'visible';
            divContainer1.style.visibility = 'hidden';
            }">
```

After this script, we close the paragraph, the FORM, and the DIV:

```
</P>
</FORM>
</DIV>
```

Here's the entire HTML document (Campus.htm):

 Campus.htm

```
<HTML>
<HEAD>
<TITLE>U of Cyb Campus</TITLE>
</HEAD>
<BODY Style = "background:url(E:\DHTML MTE\graphics\photobks\
ltp16a.gif)">
<H1 Style = "text-align:center;color:#FFFFCC;font-style:italic">
Our Campus ...</H1>

<DIV ID = divContainer1 Style = "position:absolute;
left:125;top:80;width:350;height:300;
background-color:#FFFFCC;color:green;font-weight:bold;
border:solid;border-color:green"

onMouseOver = "this.style.backgroundColor = 'green';
            this.style.borderColor = '#FFFFCC';
            this.style.color = '#FFFFCC';"

onMouseOut =  "this.style.backgroundColor = '#FFFFCC';
            this.style.borderColor = 'green';
            this.style.color = 'green'">
<IMG Style = "position:absolute;top:12%;left:5%;"
Src = "E:\DHTML MTE\graphics\pictures\pine.gif"
Title = "Imaginary Tree">
```

```
<DIV Style = "position:absolute;left:50%;top:15%;width:40%">
<P>Our campus isn't real - it's virtual! We have no classrooms,
no buildings, and no grounds. Here's what one of our trees would look
like, if we had any.</P>
</DIV>
</DIV>

<DIV ID = divContainer2 Style = "position:absolute;
left:125;top:80;width:350;height:300;
background-color:#FFFFCC;color:green;font-weight:bold;
border:solid;border-color:green;visibility:'hidden'"

onMouseOver = "this.style.backgroundColor = 'green';
            this.style.borderColor = '#FFFFCC';
            this.style.color = '#FFFFCC';"

onMouseOut =  "this.style.backgroundColor = '#FFFFCC';
            this.style.borderColor = 'green';
            this.style.color = 'green'">
<IMG Style = "position:absolute;top:12%;left:5%"
Src = "E:\DHTML MTE\graphics\pictures\abi.gif"
Title = "Cyberdog">

<DIV ID Style = "position:absolute;left:50%;top:15%;width:40%">
<P>This is our mascot - the amazing Cyberdog!</P>
</DIV>
</DIV>

<DIV Style = "position:absolute; left:500;top:350;">
<FORM>
<P><INPUT Type = button ID = inputButton Value = "Mascot"
style = "background-color:green;color:#FFFFCC;width:80"
onClick = "if (this.value == 'Tree') {
            this.value = 'Mascot';
            divContainer2.style.visibility = 'hidden';
            divContainer1.style.visibility = 'visible';
            } else {
            this.value = 'Tree';
            divContainer2.style.visibility = 'visible';
            divContainer1.style.visibility = 'hidden';
            }">
</P>
</FORM>
</DIV>
</BODY>
</HTML>
```

Jump to this page from `WebPageDesign.htm` to experience the behaviors you scripted. I'll leave it as an exercise for you to design and implement a hyperlink from this page back to `WebPageDesign.htm`.

Working with Tables

In addition to text and images, tables are a popular way to present information on the Web. Some might argue that tables have become *too* popular, as developers often use them to position images and text. Style sheet positioning will change that, so that you can expect to see tables fulfill their natural function—to organize data and present it in comprehensible ways.

To complete our look at the basics of HTML, we'll go through an exercise that produces a table. We'll add a table to our Cyberengineering page, and make the page look like Figure 3.5.

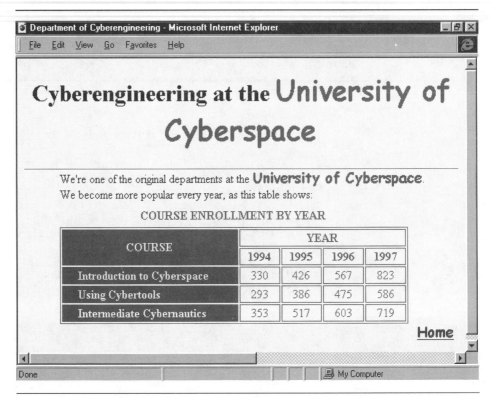

FIGURE 3.5: `Cybereng.htm` with a table

In the document, the table will reside between <TABLE> and </TABLE>. You start a table row with <TR> and end it with </TR>. Each cell in the table starts with <TD> and ends with </TD>. You put the cell's data between the two TD tags.

Before we begin constructing the table, reposition the Home text that links to UofCyb.htm, and use pixel positioning rather than percentage positioning. In its <DIV>, change Top to 360 and Left to 550. This will give you more room for the table.

We'll start with the text on the page, which is just a paragraph inside a DIV:

```
<DIV Style = "Position:Absolute;Top:145;Left:60;Width:576">
<P> We're one of the original departments at the
<A Class = "UofCyb">University of Cyberspace </A>.<BR>We become
more popular every year, as this table shows:
</P>
</DIV>
```

We begin defining the table with the <TABLE> tag, and include style information as well as specific table-related attributes:

```
<TABLE Style = "Position:Absolute;Top:200;Left:60;Width:480;
color:'green';font-weight:normal"
Cols = 5 Border Bordercolor = "green">
```

The color values in Style and Bordercolor keep the table consistent with the school colors, and Cols sets the number of columns in the table. Setting the font-weight to normal will keep the cell data in the normal font while we bold the font in the caption, the column headings, and the first column. We could have left this out and used the default normal font-weight, but I wanted you to see it explicitly: It's a good idea to distinguish the appearance of the column-headers and the row-identifiers from the appearance of the cell data.

Next, we'll create the caption that precedes the table:

```
<CAPTION Style = "font-weight:bold">COURSE ENROLLMENT BY YEAR</CAPTION>
```

We'll construct our table row by row. Let's move to the first row. Although it may be a little difficult to see, this row has only two cells: one holds the word "COURSE" and the other holds "YEAR." The "YEAR" cell covers four columns. The "COURSE" cell covers two rows. How do we specify this? We start the row with the <TR> tag and add Style values:

```
<TR Style = "text-align:center;font-weight:bold">
```

For the first cell, we use the Rowspan attribute to specify the number of rows this cell covers and Style to align the text, and we insert COURSE between <TD> and </TD>:

```
<TD Rowspan = 2 Style = "text-align:center">COURSE</TD>
```

We set up the next cell in a similar way, except that we use Colspan to specify the number of columns the cell covers, and we add </TR> to close the row.

```
<TD Colspan = 4 Style = "text-align:center">YEAR</TD>
</TR>
```

The next row holds the column headers that present the years:

```
<TR Style = "text-align:center;font-weight:bold">
<TD>1994</TD>
<TD>1995</TD>
<TD>1996</TD>
<TD>1997</TD>
</TR>
```

The Style property values in <TR> set the styles for the cells in this row. Notice that this row has four cells because the first cell in the first row also occupies space in the second row (as per the Rowspan attribute we set).

The remaining rows are straightforward, and each one has five cells:

```
</TR>
<TR Style = "text-align:center">
<TD>Introduction to Cyberspace</TD>
<TD>330</TD>
<TD>426</TD>
<TD>567</TD>
<TD>823</TD>
</TR>
<TR Style = "text-align:center">
<TD>Using Cybertools</TD>
<TD>293</TD>
<TD>386</TD>
<TD>475</TD>
<TD>586</TD>
</TR>
<TR Style = "text-align:center">
<TD>Intermediate Cybernautics</TD>
<TD>353</TD>
<TD>517</TD>
<TD>603</TD>
<TD>719</TD>
</TR>
```

Of course, we have to close off the table:

```
</TABLE>
```

If you open your work in IE at this point, you'll see the page shown in Figure 3.6.

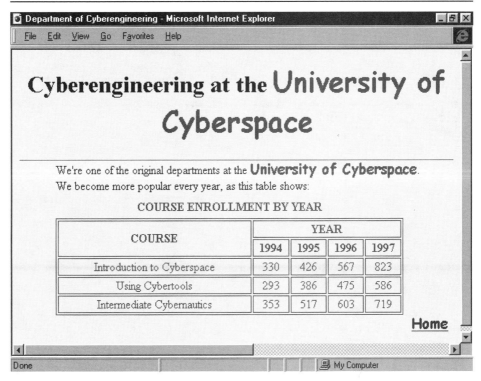

FIGURE 3.6 Cybereng.htm before you style the first column

The difference between this page and the one in Figure 3.5 is the styling in the first column. Two new elements in HTML 4.0 allow you to style all the cells in a column in the same way that you can style all the cells in a row. The new elements are COLGROUP and COL. COLGROUP sets up groups of columns and COL specifies styling for particular columns within the group. To produce the styling in our table's first column, we add this code just after the CAPTION element:

```
<COLGROUP>
<COL Style = "background-color:'green';color:#FFFFCC;
text-align:left;font-weight:bold;width:240">
```

We're not quite finished. This inline style sheet puts the course names flush against the left edge of the table. The first column will look prettier if we indent the course names by 20 pixels or so. But here's a quirk: if you add `margin-left:20` to COL's style sheet, it has no effect on the cells in the column. All the other style property values affect the appearances of the cells, but this one doesn't. (Go figure.) Instead, we have to include a style sheet that does the indentation in each cell. The cell that holds the course title "Introduction to Cyberspace," for example, has to look like this in the document:

```
<TD Style = "margin-left:20">Introduction to Cyberspace</TD>
```

Here's the listing for the `Cybereng.htm` page:

Cybereng.htm

```
<HTML>
<HEAD>
<STYLE Type = "text/css">
.UofCyb{font-size:120%;color:'green';font-weight:bold;font-family:cursive}
</STYLE>
<TITLE>Department of Cyberengineering</TITLE>
</HEAD>

<BODY Style = "Background-Color:#FFFFCC">
<H1 Style = "Text-Align:Center">
Cyberengineering at
the <A Class = "UofCyb">University of Cyberspace</A>
</H1>
<HR>

<DIV Style = "Position:Absolute;Top:145;Left:60;Width:576">
<P> We're one of the original departments at the
<A Class = "UofCyb">University of Cyberspace</A>.<BR>We become
more popular every year, as this table shows:
</P>
</DIV>
<TABLE Style = "Position:Absolute;Top:200;Left:60;Width:480;
color:'green'"
Cols = 5 Border Bordercolor = "green">
<CAPTION Style = "font-weight:bold">COURSE ENROLLMENT BY YEAR</CAPTION>
<COLGROUP>
<COL Style = "background-color:'green';color:#FFFFCC;
text-align:left;font-weight:bold">
<TR Style = "text-align:center;font-weight:bold">
<TD Rowspan = 2 Style = "text-align:center">COURSE</TD>
<TD Colspan = 4 Style = "text-align:center">YEAR</TD>
</TR>
```

```
<TR Style = "text-align:center;font-weight:bold">
<TD>1994</TD>
<TD>1995</TD>
<TD>1996</TD>
<TD>1997</TD>
</TR>
<TR Style = "text-align:center">
<TD Style = "margin-left:20">Introduction to Cyberspace</TD>
<TD>330</TD>
<TD>426</TD>
<TD>567</TD>
<TD>823</TD>
</TR>
<TR Style = "text-align:center">
<TD Style = "margin-left:20">Using Cybertools</TD>
<TD>293</TD>
<TD>386</TD>
<TD>475</TD>
<TD>586</TD>
</TR>
<TR Style = "text-align:center">
<TD Style = "margin-left:20">Intermediate Cybernautics</TD>
<TD>353</TD>
<TD>517</TD>
<TD>603</TD>
<TD>719</TD>
</TR>
</TABLE>

<DIV Style = "Position:Absolute;Top:360;Left:550">
<P Class = "UofCyb">
<A Href = "E:\DHTML MTE\Skill 3\UofCyb.htm">
Home
</A>
</P>
</DIV>

</BODY>
</HTML>
```

Open it in IE to see the page in Figure 3.5. If you're feeling ambitious, use COLGROUP and COL to style some additional columns. If you're feeling *really* ambitious, script a couple of dynamic effects—like changing background colors, fonts, and border color as a result of mouse movement.

Summary

In Skills 2 and 3, you covered the basics of HTML, with the emphasis on style sheets and some new features in HTML 4.0. You learned about text, hypertext, graphics, and tables, and you added some dynamic effects. We've only scratched the surface, however. If you want to find out more—*much* more—about HTML 4.0, be sure to read *HTML 4.0: No experience required* by E. Stephen Mack and Janan Platt or *Mastering HTML 4.0* by Deborah S. Ray and Eric J. Ray, both published by Sybex.

In the next Skill, we'll explore style sheets more closely.

Have You Mastered the Essentials?

Now you can...

☑ Acquire a set of graphic images to work with

☑ Position graphics and text on your Web page

☑ Add simple dynamic effects to your graphics

☑ Work with tables and use new HTML 4.0 elements to style them

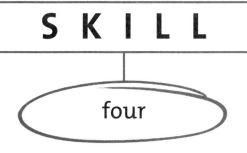

SKILL

four

Cascading Style Sheets

- ❏ Style sheet rules

- ❏ Styling a page

- ❏ Linking style sheets

- ❏ Exploring style properties

- ❏ Style sheets and positioning

In all the Skills up to this point, you've used style sheets. I wanted you to get accustomed to using style sheets, as they represent the future of HTML-related Web page development.

As the "M" in its name indicates, HTML was originally designed for marking up documents—for structuring paragraphs, headings, and so forth. It was not designed for setting up the presentation aspects of Web pages—like fonts, colors, and borders. Developers have used all kinds of elements and attributes as stop-gap measures for making Web pages look snazzy. Adding these elements to HTML, however, is much like adding extra rooms and wings to a house whose frame just wasn't made for the extra load: The extras may look good temporarily, but in the long run they detract from structural integrity and weaken the house.

So far, you've mostly used inline style sheets: You inserted the Style attribute into a tag and set it equal to a string that holds styling specifications, and those specifications applied only to that element. You've also used some style sheets that were more global in scope. In this Skill, we'll emphasize the global variety. Instead of placing the Style attribute inside a tag, you'll put a style sheet in the HEAD element, and use it to assign attribute values to elements in the body of the Web page. You make the style assignments once, at the beginning of the document, and the browser uses them as it renders the page. Once again, we'll use IE because of its strong support of Cascading Style Sheet standards.

Making Assignments

As we've seen before, the style assignment process starts with a <STYLE> tag and ends with a </STYLE> tag. The syntax for making the assignment is simple: Between <STYLE> and </STYLE>, you list the HTML tags to which you want to assign styles, and you follow each tag with a pair of curly brackets. Inside the brackets, you make the assignments for specific style attributes:

```
<STYLE Type = "css/text">
tag {attribute: value; attribute: value …}
.
.
.
</STYLE>
```

 NOTE In the <STYLE> tag, the expression "Type = text/css" indicates that the style sheet conforms to the CSS syntax.

In style sheet terminology, the `tag` is a *selector* and everything inside the curly brackets is a *declaration*. Note that just as in an inline style sheet, a declaration can encompass more than one assignment. A selector-declaration pair is called a *rule*. Thus, the style sheet consists of an opening <STYLE> tag, a set of selector-declaration rules, and a closing </STYLE> tag.

Here's an example of a selector-declaration rule:

```
H1 {color:crimson;font-family:Haettenschweiler}
```

This rule specifies that any H1 heading will have crimson as its font-color and Haettenschweiler (my favorite font-name) as its font-face.

This rule syntax is part of the *CSS1* language. CSS stands for "Cascading Style Sheets," and the "1" stands for "Level 1." Style sheets are said to *cascade* when they combine to specify the appearance of a page. You saw an example of this in Skill 1, and you'll see this in action in this Skill.

More on Selectors

It's possible for a selector to consist of more than one tag:

```
tag1,tag2 {attribute:value}
```

In this case, the rule assigns the attribute-value to both tags. For example, the rule

```
H1,EM {color:crimson}
```

assigns crimson as the color of all H1 headings and all EM (emphasized) elements.

If you use multiple tags and you don't include the comma, your browser interprets the rule in an entirely different way. The rule

```
H1 EM {color:crimson}
```

assigns crimson as the color of EM elements, but only those that appear in H1 headings. The type of selector in this rule is called a *contextual selector*.

More on Declarations

Some attributes, particularly font-related ones, have a special syntax for grouping style characteristics. You don't have to explicitly state each attribute-value pair in a semicolon-delineated list. Instead, you can create them in a more natural way.

Skill 4

For example, the rule

```
H1 {font-size:25pt; font-family:Haettenschweiler}
```

can also appear as

```
H1 {font: 25 pt Haettenschweiler}
```

Styling a Page

Let's jump into an example with a page you've already created. In your text editor, open WebAccessStats.htm from Skill 3. Save it as Stylized WebAccessStats.htm in Skill 4. Just to refresh your memory, Figure 4.1 shows that page rendered in IE.

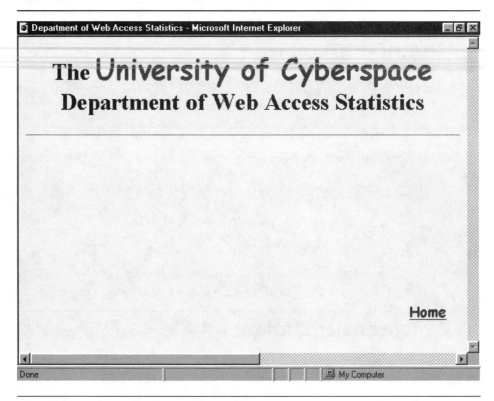

FIGURE 4.1: Stylized WebAccessStats.htm before you apply a new style sheet

This is the document that produces this page:

```
<HTML>
<HEAD>
<STYLE Type = "text/css">
.UofCyb{font-size:120%;color: green;font-weight:bold;font-family:cursive}

</STYLE>
<TITLE>Department of Web Access Statistics</TITLE>
</HEAD>
<BODY Style = "Background-Color:#FFFFCC">

<H1 Style = "Text-Align:Center">
The <A Class = "UofCyb">University of Cyberspace</A>
Department of Web Access Statistics
</H1>
<HR>

<DIV Style = "Position:Absolute;Top:90%;Left:90%">
<P Class = "UofCyb">
<A Href = "E:\DHTML MTE\Skill 2\UofCyb.htm">

Home
</A>
</P>
</DIV>
</BODY>
</HTML>
```

This page has a background color, an H1 heading, and a horizontal line. It already has some styling information in the HEAD element, a class called .UofCyb. We applied this style class whenever we used the phrase "University of Cyberspace." Here's an example:

```
The <A Class = "UofCyb">University of Cyberspace</A>
Department of Web Access Statistics
```

We also applied it to Home, which links back to the U of Cyb home page.

Next, we'll add a couple of paragraphs and a list, and then use a style sheet to specify the style of all these elements and dramatically change the appearance of the page. Right after the <HR> tag, add these paragraphs and the unordered list:

```
<P>Our Department focuses on research into the demographics of Web use.
<BR>
Who uses the Web? How Often? Why?
</P>
```

```
<P>Our coursework teaches the techniques for analyzing
Web-related demographic information.
<BR>
We teach statistics, statistical computing, survey analysis, and others.
</P>

<UL> Some of our courses are:
<LI> <A>Introductory Trend Analysis</A>
<LI> <A>Advanced Web Forecasting</A>
<LI> <A>Understanding Future Shlock</A>
<LI> <A>Online Survey Analysis</A>
</UL>
```

Be sure to include the <A> and </A> tags around each bulleted item, as we'll need them momentarily. Figure 4.2 shows the page with the added text.

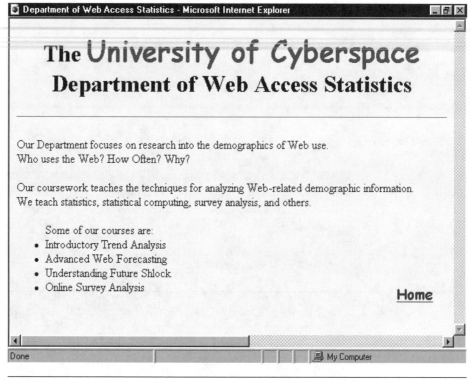

FIGURE 4.2: Stylized WebAccessStats.htm with added text

We'll begin with the header. Let's create a rule that specifies the font-size, font-face, and font-color for every H1 heading on the page. On the line after the `<STYLE type = "text/css">` tag, type

```
H1 {font: 25 pt Haettenschweiler; color: Crimson}
```

This rule specifies that in every H1 heading in this HTML document, the font will be 25 points, the face will be Haettenschweiler, and the color will be crimson. Only one H1 heading is on this page, of course, but if you created more of these headings, the browser would render them according to the rule you just created.

If you open the page in IE, you'll see the header altered, as shown in Figure 4.3.

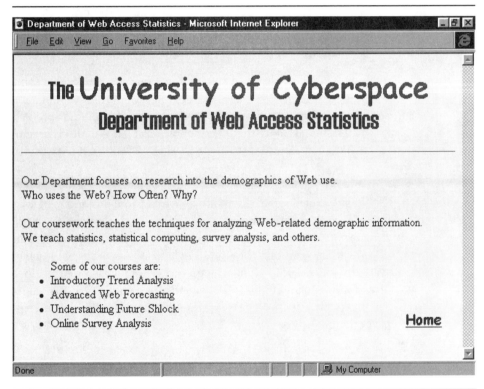

FIGURE 4.3: The appearance of `Stylized WebAccessStats.htm` after you apply a style sheet to the H1 header

Note that the "University of Cyberspace" still looks as it did before. Why? Within the header, the styles have combined, or cascaded, to produce the header's appearance. The rule for H1 produces the Crimson Haettenschweiler font, and the .UofCyb class (specified in the <A> tag within the header's text) produces the larger green cursive font within the header.

Adding to the *<STYLE>*

Let's add some rules. First, we'll work on the appearance of the horizontal line. It's now a nondescript two pixels high and it blends in with the background. Let's make it thicker and a different color. To change its appearance, insert a new line after the rule you just added. On that line, type

```
HR {height: 10; color: Blue}
```

The text in the body of this page is in a paragraph, and we can use a rule to change a paragraph's general appearance, too. We can change the size, face, and color of the font, and draw a border around every paragraph. While we're at it, we can also make sure that every paragraph has a wide right margin. To generate all these changes, add this rule to Stylized WebAccessStats.htm:

```
P {font: 15 pt; color: Green; margin-right: 1.5in; border: Solid}
```

The new rule, however, creates a bit of a problem for one of our on-screen items. Since Home (the link to our home page) is in a P element, the margin-right and border attribute values will put an unnecessarily large box around Home. How do we get around this? The solution is to take advantage of one of CSS's major features—the cascade I mentioned earlier. We'll cascade the global style sheet's rule for P with an inline style sheet attribute value: Override the margin-right setting in Home by setting its surrounding DIV's width to a value just large enough to accomodate Home—about 20 pixels. Add that value to the DIV's inline style sheet:

```
<DIV Style = "Position:Absolute;Top:90%;Left:90%;Width:20">
```

Figure 4.4 shows the results of all the rules you've created thus far.

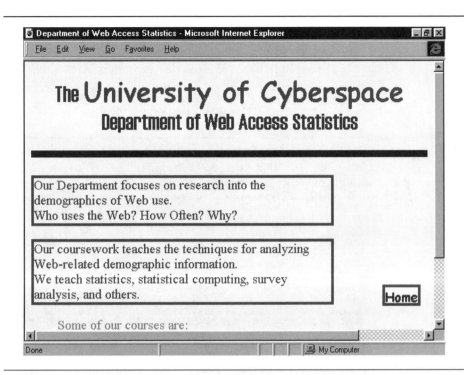

FIGURE 4.4: The result of assigning style attributes to the header, line, and paragraph of Stylized WebAccessStats.htm

A Touch of Class

As you've seen, Class is a useful feature. It enables you to specify the same style for a particular element each time it appears. If you make an element a member of a class by inserting Class = *ClassName* into its opening tag, it conforms to that class's specifications.

Let's use Class to build a rule that assigns style attributes to the appearance of bulleted text. In your document, <A> tags surround the bulleted text. Between <STYLE> and </STYLE>, add these lines to create the rules:

```
.listText {font: 15 pt; color:Darkorange}
```

In the <A> tag that precedes each bulleted item, add

```
Class = "listText"
```

Type that same expression in the <UL> tag, too. Note the usefulness and versatility of Class: Throughout the document, we use two classes of A elements (UofCyb and listText), and used one class (listText) in two different elements (A and UL).

While we're at it, let's add a rule for the bullets. Each bullet is an LI element, so we can add this rule to change each bullet's color and indentation:

```
LI {font: 15 pt;color:Magenta; text-indent: .5in}
```

 TIP   As a matter of practice, it's a good idea to insert this rule just after your rule for the P element. That way, you keep your tag rules separate from your class rules, although it's not necessary to do this.

Save the file and have a look in IE. Scroll down to see a page that looks like Figure 4.5.

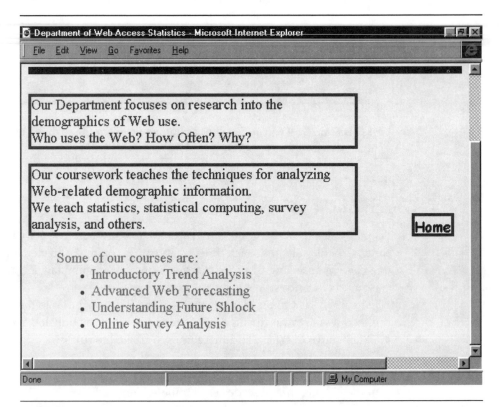

FIGURE 4.5: The bottom part of Stylized WebAccessStats.htm with all the rules in place

Adding *IDs*

ID is another feature of style sheets which helps you zero in on elements and add attribute values to them. It works something like the ID attribute you've seen before—you use it to assign a name to an element. In Skill 1, you assigned an ID to an element and then used that ID to refer to the element in a script. In a style sheet, you attach an ID to a rule. You then apply the rule to a specific element by assigning that ID to the element.

How do you attach an ID to a CSS rule? You precede it with a # sign. This turns the selector (the unbracketed part) into the "ID." If you then assign the selector as the value of the ID attribute in any element on the page, you apply the styling in the rule's declaration (the bracketed part).Let's add an ID to our STYLE element. Suppose you want to make a couple of the bulleted items stand out by coloring them black and making them 10% larger than the other bulleted items. Add this rule:

```
#largeBlackItem {color:black;font-size:110%}
```

Next, assign `largeBlackItem` as the ID for two of the bulleted items. Change

```
<LI> <A Class = "listText">Advanced Web Forecasting</A>
<LI> <A Class = "listText">Understanding Future Shlock</A>
```

to

```
<LI> <A Class = "listText" ID = "largeBlackItem">Advanced Web
Forecasting</A>
<LI> <A Class = "listText" ID = "largeBlackItem">Understanding Future
Shlock</A>
```

The lower half of `Stylized WebAccessStats.htm` should now look like Figure 4.6. In the second and third bulleted items, the `listText` class sets the font at 15 pts, and the `largeBlackItem` ID changes the color to black and increases the size by 10%.

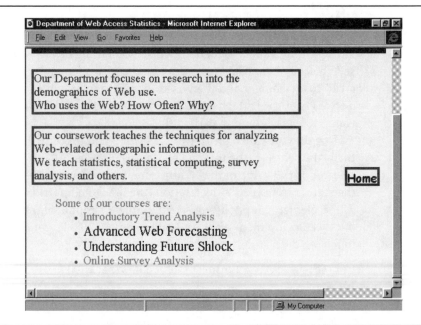

FIGURE 4.6: The lower half of Stylized WebAccessStats.htm after you add IDs to the second and third bulleted items. Adding the IDs applies the largeBlackItem style.

A Useful Element

SPAN is an HTML element that plays a prominent role in style sheets. In a rule, you use it in the selector as you would use any other HTML tag. In the body of the document, you use <SPAN> and </SPAN> to set the boundaries of the rule's styling specifications. You can use SPAN in conjunction with a class (as is the case for any other HTML element).

 NOTE   Although DIV and SPAN both set boundaries, they're two different types of elements. A DIV is a container for other elements. A SPAN is a way of rendering style information.

Here's an example. Many publications present at least part of the opening line of an article or a figure caption in uppercase text. Suppose you want to duplicate this effect in the first paragraph of your Web page. In the STYLE element for `Stylized WebAccessStats.htm`, add this rule:

```
SPAN.uppercase {text-transform: uppercase}
```

Let's also suppose you want to italicize some of the text on the page. Add this rule:

```
SPAN.italic {font-style: italic}
```

To apply these rules, change the document's first paragraph from

```
<P>Our Department focuses on research into the demographics of Web use.
<BR>
Who uses the Web? How Often? Why?
</P>
```

to

```
<P><SPAN Class = "uppercase">Our Department focuses on research</SPAN>
into the demographics of Web use.
<BR>
<SPAN Class = "italic">Who uses the Web? How Often? Why?</SPAN>
</P>
```

Applying the two SPAN rules makes the Web page look like Figure 4.7.

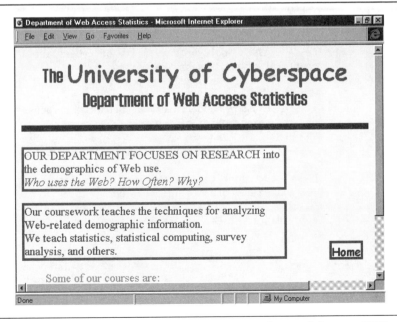

FIGURE 4.7: Stylized `WebAccessStats.htm` after applying two SPAN rules

The Big Finish

You'll never create a page that looks like this (it has too many colors, borders, font-sizes, and font-faces, and it's way too busy), but this exercise gives you an idea of the power of style sheets. When you use the STYLE element, style sheets set conventions for the way elements will look on your page.

Here's how the entire Stylized WebAccessStats.htm document should look:

 Stylized WebAccessStats.htm

```
<HTML>
<HEAD>
<STYLE Type = "text/css">
H1 {font: 25 pt Haettenschweiler; color: Crimson}
HR {height: 10; color: Blue}
P {font: 15 pt; color:Green; margin-right: 1.5in; border: Solid}
LI {font: 15 pt; color:Magenta; text-indent: .5in}
SPAN.uppercase {text-transform: uppercase}
SPAN.italic {font-style: italic}
.listText {font: 15 pt; color:Darkorange}
.UofCyb{font-size:120%;color:'green';font-weight:bold;font-family:cursive}
#largeBlackItem {color:black;font-size:110%}
</STYLE>
<TITLE>Department of Web Access Statistics</TITLE>
</HEAD>
<BODY Style = "Background-Color:#FFFFCC">
<H1 Style = "Text-Align:Center">
The <A Class = "UofCyb">University of Cyberspace</A>
Department of Web Access Statistics
</H1>
<HR>
<P><SPAN Class = "uppercase">Our Department focuses on research</SPAN>
into the demographics of Web use.
<BR>
<SPAN Class = "italic">Who uses the Web? How Often? Why?</SPAN>
</P>
<P>Our coursework teaches the techniques for analyzing
Web-related demographic information.
<BR>
We teach statistics, statistical computing, survey analysis, and others.
</P>
```

```
<UL Class = "listText"> Some of our courses are:
<LI> <A Class = "listText">Introductory Trend Analysis</A>
<LI> <A Class = "listText" ID = "largeBlackItem">Advanced Web
Forecasting</A>
<LI> <A Class = "listText" ID = "largeBlackItem">Understanding Future
Shlock</A>
<LI> <A Class = "listText">Online Survey Analysis</A>
</UL>
<DIV Style = "Position:Absolute;Top:90%;Left:90%;Width:20">
<P Class = "UofCyb">
<A Href = "E:\DHTML MTE\Skill 2\UofCyb.htm">
Home
</A>
</P>
</DIV>
</BODY>
</HTML>
```

Linking Style Sheets

For style sheet information to control a page's appearance, it's not necessary for that style sheet to appear on the page. Instead, you can put the style sheet in a separate document, and set a link to that document. You can then reuse the style sheet's information by linking it to other documents as well. This exercise will show you how to do this.

In your text editor, make sure you have the Stylized WebAccessStats.htm document open. Follow these steps:

1. Highlight everything between, and including, <STYLE> and </STYLE>.

2. Press Ctrl+X to cut the highlighted lines and place them on the Clipboard for pasting.

3. Open your Template file and save it as Styles in Skill 4.

4. In the new document, position your mouse cursor right after <HEAD>.

5. Paste the style information into this new document.

6. Give the new document the title Styles.

One more step is crucial. For reasons I haven't been able to fathom, a style sheet loses its first rule when another page links to it. To work around this "undocumented feature," place a dummy declaration—an open and close curly bracket—as the first "rule" after the <STYLE> tag in your newly created style sheet document. That way, the header rule becomes the second rule, and everything works out as planned.

Here's what this new file should look like:

```
<STYLE Type = "text/css">
{}
H1 {font: 25 pt Haettenschweiler; color: Crimson}
HR {height: 10; color: Blue}
P {font: 15 pt; color:Green; margin-right: 1.5in; border: Solid}
LI {font: 15 pt; color:Magenta; text-indent: .5in}
SPAN.uppercase {text-transform: uppercase}
SPAN.italic {font-style: italic}
.listText {font: 15 pt; color:Darkorange}
.UofCyb{font-size:120%;color:'green';font-weight:bold;font-family:
cursive}
#largeBlackItem {color:black;font-size:110%}
</STYLE>
```

Now we have to link our Web Access Statistics page to this style sheet document. In your Stylized WebAccessStats.htm document, create a new line just before the </HEAD> tag. (Style information should no longer be in this document.) On this new line, type

```
<LINK Rel = Stylesheet Type = "text/css"
HREF = "E:\DHTML MTE\Skill 4\Styles.htm" TITLE = "Styles">
```

Save the document and open the Stylized WebAccessStats.htm document in IE. It will look like Figure 4.7, even though no <STYLE> tags are in the document. If we linked all the pages in the U of Cyb Web site to this style sheet, we would see its styles appear on those pages, too. (You might try this as an exercise.) Thus, you can use style sheets to set conventions for the way elements should look throughout a Web site.

A STYLE SHEET FOR YOUR BROWSER

You can set up a style sheet for IE. As an experiment, select View ➤ Options... from the menu bar in IE. A set of tabbed pages appears. On the General tab, click the Accessibility button. In the Accessibility dialog box that opens, click the checkbox next to Format Documents Using My Style Sheet. Then click the Browse button and navigate until you find the style sheet in Skill 4 that you created for the last exercise. Click OK to close the dialog box and click OK to close the tab. Now try looking at one of your favorite Web sites. If it has bullets, paragraphs, or H1 headings, you'll find that it looks very much like the way-overdone Stylized Web Access Statistics page. Since you're unlikely to ever add a style sheet like this to your browser, why is this feature in IE? One reason is that setting an appropriate style sheet allows users with disabilites to change the way Web pages appear so they can see the pages more easily.

To return things to normal, retrace your steps and clear the check in the checkbox next to Format Documents Using My Style Sheet.

 NOTE   Jakob Nielsen, internationally known authority on software usability, believes that linked style sheets are the best way to use the style sheet concept. Linked style sheets ensure uniformity throughout a Web site, they're easy to maintain, and they offer a variety of other benefits. To read Nielsen's helpful comments, visit http://www.useit.com/alertbox/9707a.html.

The Elements of <*STYLE*>, The Style of Elements

Exactly what style attributes are available to you? I'll list them here, and then explore them more closely. You'll recognize some of them, as you've already worked with quite a few.

One category specifies characteristics of fonts:

```
font                        font-family

font-style                  font-weight

font-size
```

Another specifies the color and background of HTML elements:

```
color                       background

background-color            background-image

background-repeat           background-attachment

background-position
```

A third specifies properties of text inside an HTML document:

```
word-spacing                letter-spacing

text-decoration             vertical-align

text-transform              text-align

text-indent                 line-height
```

Still another deals with the characteristics of the (sometimes invisible) "boxes" that enclose HTML elements:

```
margin            margin-top        margin-right

margin-bottom     margin-left       padding

padding-top       padding-right     padding-bottom

padding-left      border-width      border-top-width
```

`border-right-width`	`border-bottom-width`	`border-left-width`
`border-color`	`border-style`	`border-top`
`border-right`	`border-bottom`	`border-left`
`border`	`width`	`height`
`float`		

Font Attributes

The exercises in this Skill emphasize an important use of style sheets—setting the characteristics of fonts. (If you follow the steps in the sidebar "A Style Sheet for Your Browser," you'll see a dramatic example of this.) The font attributes are `font-family`, `font-style`, `font-weight`, `font-size`, and (not surprisingly) `font`. That last one is a shorthand structure for setting several font characteristics at the same time. You used it in the CSS exercises to set the font of an `H1` heading.

Table 4.1 shows the possible values of the other font attributes. The first one, font-family, is unlike the others in that its value can be a list of font family names or generic fonts. As an author, you prioritize the list and the browser works with the first one it can render. Thus, if your preferred font isn't on a user's machine, you can still exercise some control over the font that his or her browser will render.

TABLE 4.1: CSS Font Attributes

Attribute	Possible Values
font-family	A comma-delimited sequence of font family names (e.g., gill or helvetica) and/or generic fonts (serif, sans-serif, cursive, fantasy, or monospace)
font-style	Normal, italic, or oblique
font-weight	Normal, bold, bolder, lighter, or one of nine numerical values (100, 200, 300, 400, 500, 600, 700, 800, or 900)
font-size	A term that denotes absolute size (xx-small, x-small, small, medium, large, x-large, xx-large), relative size (larger, smaller), a number (of pixels), or a percentage (of the parent element's size)

Skill 4

Color and Background Attributes

Attributes in this category specify the appearance of an element's foreground and background in terms of colors and images. The background attribute is, like font, a shorthand for setting several background attribute values at once. Table 4.2 shows most of the others.

TABLE 4.2: CSS Color and Background Attributes, What They Do, and Possible Values

Attribute	What It Does	Possible Values
Color	Sets an element's text-color (also called the "foreground color")	A color-name (as in Table 1.1) or a color code
Background-color	Specifies the color in an element's background	A color-name, a color-code, or transparent
Background-image	Sets the background image	A URL, or none
Background-repeat	With a background image specified, sets up how the image repeats throughout the page	Repeat-x (repeats horizontally) repeat-y (vertically), repeat (both), no-repeat
Background-attachment	Sets an element's behavior with respect to the rest of the page	Scroll (scrolls when the rest of the content scrolls), fixed (doesn't scroll)

The last attribute in this category is background-position. If you've specified a background image for an element, you use background-position to set a starting position for the image within that element. Its possible values can form numerous combinations, which is why I didn't put it in the table. You can combine either top, center, or bottom with either left, center, or right. Another possibility is to provide two numerical values, which can be percentages or lengths, measured in various units. For example, a value-pair of 0% 0% puts the image in the element's upper-left corner, while 100% 100% puts it in the lower-right corner.

Text Attributes

Text attributes provide the appearance of a page's text. They're pretty straight-forward, as Table 4.3 indicates.

T A B L E 4 . 3 : CSS Text Attributes, What They Do, and Possible Values

Attribute	What It Does	Possible Values
Word-spacing	Increases the default distance between consecutive words	Normal, or a length
Letter-spacing	Increases the default distance between consecutive letters	Normal, or a length
Text-decoration	Adds decoration to an element's text	None, or one or more of these terms: underline, overline, line-through, blink
Vertical-align	Determines an element's vertical positioning	Baseline, sub, super, top, text-top, middle, bottom, or text-bottom; can also be a percentage of the element's height
Text-transform	Applies a transformation to the text	Capitalize (puts the text into initial caps), uppercase, lowercase, or none
Text-align	Aligns text within the element	Left, right, center, or justify
Text-indent	Indents the first line of text	A percentage of the element's width, or a length
Line-height	Determines the distance between the baselines of consecutive lines of text	Normal, or a number, length, or percentage of the element's font size

Box Attributes

The attributes in this category refer to characteristics in CSS's *formatting model*, which treats each HTML element as if inside a box. Most of the time, the box is invisible, but as you saw in the exercise in this Skill, you can make a box visible by placing a border around it.

In the formatting model, the element's content is at the center of the box. *Padding* (empty space) can surround the content on all sides, and a usually invisible border surrounds the padding. To top it all off—and bottom, left, and right it off as well—

a margin surrounds the border. Most box attribute-names, then, begin with "margin," "border," or "padding."

The margin-related attributes are margin-top, margin-right, margin-left, and margin-bottom. Each one sets the value for its indicated side of the box. Possible values are a length or a percentage of the element's width. A shorthand attribute, margin, enables you to set values for all sides at the same time.

Padding-related attributes follow exactly the same pattern as margin-related attributes, including the possible values.

Some of the border-related attributes follow a similar pattern. Border-top-width, border-bottom-width, border-left-width, and border-right-width set the thickness of the border on the indicated box side. Possible values are thin, medium, thick, or a number that specifies the thickness. Border-width is a shorthand attribute that lets you set all the others at the same time.

Other border-related attributes are available. Border-color sets the color of a border, and border-style sets its appearance. The possible values for border-color are a color-name or a color-code. The possible border-styles are: dotted, dashed, solid, double, groove, ridge, inset, outset, or none. Border-top, border-bottom, border-left, and border-right enable you to set width, color, and style at the same time for the indicated side. A final attribute, border, allows you to set all the properties at once.

Four box attributes deal with the element at the core of the box. You've already worked with two of them, width and height. Width can be either a percentage or a numerical value. The percentage is a percentage of the width of the *parent element*—an element that contains the element in question. Most often, the parent element is the document, but, as you've seen, it can be a table-cell or a paragraph, or many other kinds of elements. Height is a numerical value.

The two other core-related attributes are Float and Clear. Float's possible values are Left, Right, or None. When the value is Left, the element moves to the left and text wraps around its right side. When the value is Right, the element moves to the right and text wraps around its left side. When the value is None, the browser renders the element where it appears in the text. Clear tells you where *floating elements* can appear with respect to an element. Its possible values are Left, Right, Both, or None. These values indicate where floating elements will not work. With Clear set to Right, for example, an element will move below any floating element on the right side. If Clear is set to None, floating elements can appear on all sides.

Classification Attributes

The attributes in this category have values that group elements in particular ways. The Display attribute determines how an element displays on a page. Its possible values are:

- Block—opens a new box for the element
- List-Item—also opens a new box and adds a list-item marker, like a bullet
- Inline—opens a box on the same line as previous content
- None—turns off the display of the element

The Whitespace attribute handles whitespace inside the element. Its possible values are:

- Normal—collapses whitespace
- Pre—treats whitespace as though rendered among letters in fixed-width type
- Nowrap

Remaining classification attributes deal with list-item elements, like the elements you find in bulleted lists. List-style-image specifies the image that serves as the list-item marker. Its value is a URL or None. List-style-type sets the appearance of the marker if List-item-marker is None or if the browser can't render the image in List-style-image's URL. List-style-type's possible values are Disc, Circle, Square, Decimal (1, 2, 3, …), Lower-Roman (i, ii, iii, iv, …), Upper-Roman, Lower-Alpha, Upper-Alpha, and None. List-style-position, whose possible values are Inside and Outside, specifies where the list-item-marker appears with respect to content. One other attribute, List-style, is a shorthand attribute that allows you to set the other three list-item attributes at the same time.

Style Sheets and Positioning

In Skills 1–3, you used inline style sheets to position elements. In every case, you used Position:Absolute, and you used both pixels and percentages in the values for Top and Left. Let's examine positioning a bit more closely.

Positioning Text

Figure 4.8 shows two lines of text. Line 1 has been positioned three line-breaks from the top edge of the window, and Line 2's position has been set via absolute positioning 50 pixels from the top edge of the window and 20 pixels from the left edge.

FIGURE 4.8: Line 1 has been positioned three line-breaks from the top of the browser window. Line 2 has been positioned via absolute positioning 50 pixels from the top and 20 pixels from the left.

Type this HTML into a new file called Positions.htm, and you'll see the display shown in Figure 4.8:

```
<HTML>
<HEAD>
<TITLE>Positions</TITLE>
</HEAD>
<BODY>
<BR><BR><BR>
```

```
This is Line 1.
<SPAN Style = "position:absolute;top:50;left:20">
This is Line 2 with absolute positioning.
</SPAN>
</BODY>
</HTML>
```

Now let's change the positioning of Line 2 from absolute to relative. Figure 4.9 shows the result.

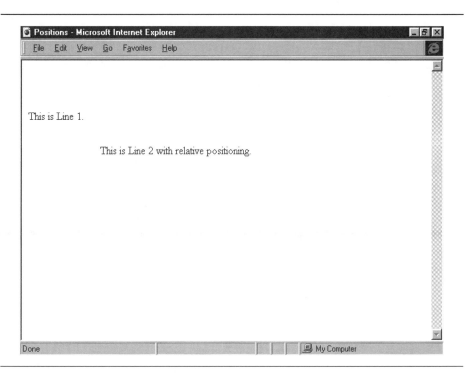

FIGURE 4.9: Changing the positioning of Line 2 from absolute to relative

A relatively positioned element is positioned relative to the element that precedes it in the HTML document. Thus, Line 2 is now offset 50 pixels down from Line 1 and 20 pixels to the right of the end of Line 1.

To see some more effects of relative positioning, we can change some of the characteristics of Line 1. Adding words to Line 1 and doubling the number of line-breaks that precede it results in a position-change for Line 2, as Figure 4.10 shows. Line 2 moves down the page and to the right.

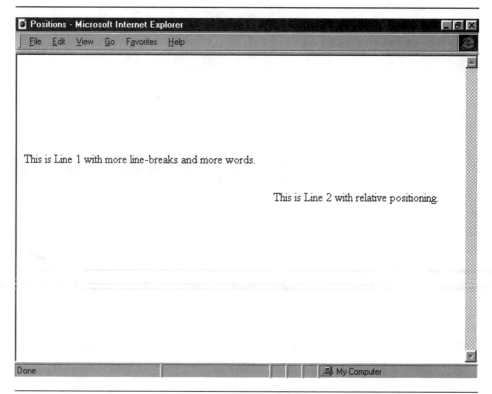

FIGURE 4.10: Adding words to Line 1 and moving it farther down the page causes Line 2 to move down and to the right.

Text, *SPANs*, and *DIVs*

We can liven things up a bit and learn some more positioning concepts by putting our text lines in separate DIVs and then positioning the DIVs. First, we return our HTML file to its original state, remove the line-breaks, and situate Line 2 via absolute positioning. Then, we put each line into a DIV. We'll add dimensions and a border to each DIV, so we can see what's happening:

```
<HTML>
<HEAD>
<TITLE>Positions</TITLE>
</HEAD>
<BODY>
```

```
<DIV Style = "width:100;height:100;border:solid">
This is Line 1.
</DIV>
<DIV Style = "width:150;height:100;border:solid">
<SPAN Style = "position:absolute;top:50;left:20">
This is Line 2 with absolute positioning.
</SPAN>
</DIV>
</BODY>
</HTML>
```

Figure 4.11 shows what happens, and indicates something quirky about SPANs and DIVs. The SPAN is inside the second DIV in the document, but appears outside the DIV on the page. You can see that Line 2 is part of the DIV because its width matches the width you specified for the DIV.

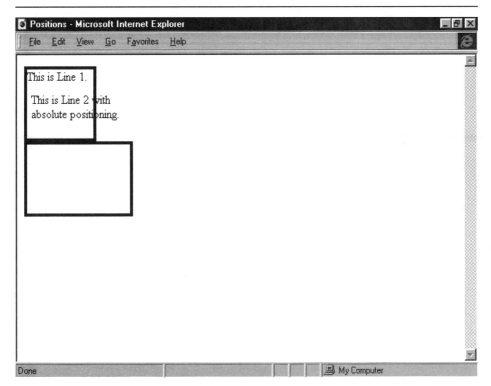

FIGURE 4.11: Putting the text lines in DIVs without setting positional information for the DIVs

Skill 4

The DIV is positioned according to defaults for DIVs (see Skill 1). The SPAN, however, is positioned according to its own Top and Left values relative to the top and left of the browser window. The reason is that we haven't specified any positional information in the DIV's inline style sheet. Adding a positional attribute pulls the SPAN inside the DIV:

```
<DIV Style =
"position:absolute;top:110;width:150;height:100;border:solid">
<SPAN Style = "position:absolute;top:50;left:20">
This is Line 2 with absolute positioning.
</SPAN>
</DIV>
```

Figure 4.12 shows this. We haven't moved the DIV, but the positional attribute changes the on-screen location of the SPAN.

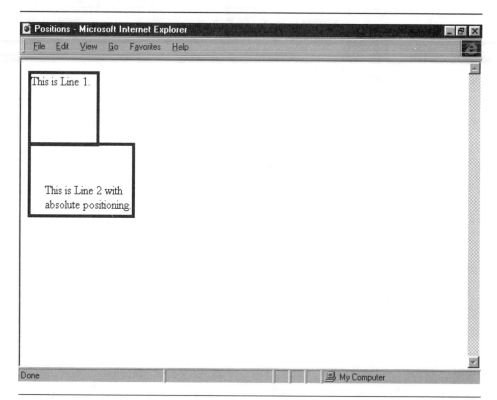

FIGURE 4.12: Adding a positional attribute to the DIV pulls the SPAN inside.

Just for good measure, let's change the second DIV's positioning to Relative. Figure 4.13 shows what happens. The second DIV is now offset 110 pixels from the bottom of the first DIV.

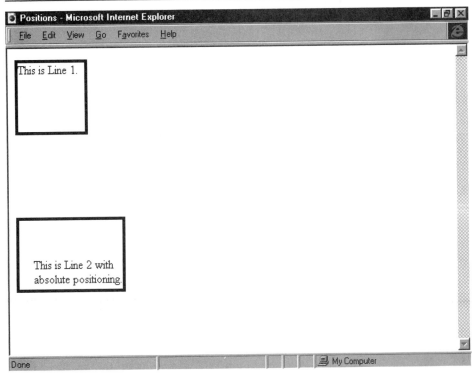

FIGURE 4.13: Changing the second DIV's positioning from Absolute to Relative offsets the second DIV relative to the first.

With the second DIV's positioning set to Relative, we can move the second DIV farther down the page by increasing the height of the first DIV, as Figure 4.14 illustrates.

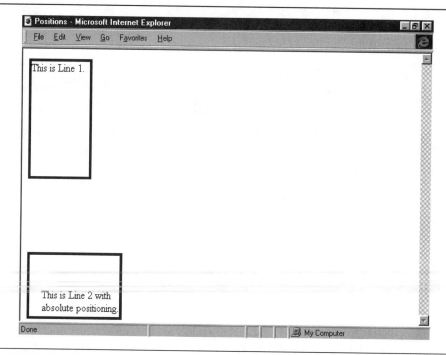

FIGURE 4.14: Because the second DIV is positioned relative to the first, we can move it farther down the page by increasing the first DIV's height.

After all the modifications, this is the HTML that produced Figure 4.14:

 Positions.htm

```
<HTML>
<HEAD>
<TITLE>Positions</TITLE>
</HEAD>
<BODY>
<DIV Style = "width:100;height:180;border:solid">
This is Line 1.
</DIV>
<DIV Style =
"position:relative;top:110;width:150;height:100;border:solid">
<SPAN Style = "position:absolute;top:50;left:20">
This is Line 2 with absolute positioning.
```

```
</SPAN>
</DIV>
</BODY>
</HTML>
```

Summary

Cascading style sheets are a powerful mechanism for Web page developers. They enable you to add flair to your work and efficiency to your code. Used correctly, they enforce standards and uniformity throughout a Web site, and they provide numerous attributes that you can script to create dynamic effects.

 NOTE   For all the information you'll ever need on style sheets and their attributes, read the document *Cascading Style Sheets, Level 1* by CSS creators Hakon Lie and Bert Bos. You'll find it at http://www.w3.org/TR/REC-CSS1.

In addition to Cascading Style Sheets, Navigator supports JavaScript Accessible Style Sheets (JASS). We'll examine JASS, but because the JASS depends on object-oriented concepts, we first have to get acquainted with object-oriented programming, which is the subject of Skill 5.

Have You Mastered the Essentials?

Now you can...

- ☑ Specify style sheets in CSS1 syntax
- ☑ Link a style sheet to an HTML document
- ☑ Understand CSS attributes and their possible values
- ☑ Work with classes, *ID*s, and *SPAN*s in style sheets
- ☑ Understand absolute and relative positioning

Skill 4

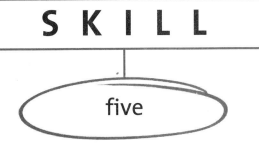

Orienting Toward Objects

- ❑ Objects in the real world

- ❑ Objects in HTML

- ❑ Objects in Dynamic HTML

- ❑ Objects in arrays

- ❑ Objects in style sheets

At the beginning of Skill 1, I pointed out that Dynamic HTML is a combination of HTML, Cascading Style Sheets, and scripts. So far, you've learned about HTML and Cascading Style Sheets. It's almost time to turn our attention to scripts, but because the two prominent scripting languages, VBScript and JavaScript (and JScript, the Microsoft version of JavaScript) work with *objects*, we must first focus on objects. We'll do that in this Skill, and then move into scripting in Skill 6.

We'll begin with general concepts about objects and then explore objects in a variety of contexts.

Objects in the Real World

The object-oriented way of creating software has come to prominence because it provides an efficient way to build large, complex systems. This approach is based on how we perceive the world around us. Object-oriented adherents believe that our thought processes typically focus on concrete objects in our world and on how they behave, rather than on the step-by-step nature of procedures.

To orient you toward objects, we won't worry about software development for the time being. Instead we'll concentrate on concrete objects and on how to think of them in object-oriented terms.

Classes, Subclasses, and Objects

Consider your home and all that's in it. Chances are that many of your hard-won worldly possessions fall into one of two categories—furniture or appliances. Let's focus on the appliances.

If you know something is an appliance, you can almost take for granted that it

- Runs on electricity

- Performs a service for you

- Has dials and gizmos that you adjust to help it perform its service

- Requires maintenance and occasional repair

- Has an ID number written on it somewhere

- Has an instruction manual that you've undoubtedly misplaced

While we could certainly come up with counterexamples that don't have one or more of these features, I think we'd agree that most of the features I listed categorize appliances. If I asked you to name some common appliances, a few would probably spring to mind more readily than others because they seem somehow more "appliance-like." All of this indicates that your ideas about appliances result from your *abstracting* their common features. Think of the appliance category as a *class*, and the features I listed as *properties*.

Let's delve into the appliance class a bit more deeply. We can divide this class into subclasses, name each subclass by its focus, and provide a few examples of each one:

- Food—refrigerator, stove, oven, toaster, blender, food processor

- Cleaning—washing machine, dishwasher

- Entertainment—radio, TV, stereo, VCR

- Information—telephone, computer

- Climate—air conditioner, space heater

You might come up with a different way to partition the world of appliances into subclasses, and you might derive a definition of appliances that eliminates some of the examples I've listed. By the way, each subclass is also a class. We can think of "food appliance" as a class, and "appliance" as its *superclass*. Another way to think about this relationship is that appliance is the *parent* and the food appliance is the *child*.

Keep in mind that each appliance is a class: "Refrigerator" is a class, and so is "radio." The particular refrigerator and radio in your house are *instances* of those classes. In the world of object orientation, an instance is also called an *object*. A class, in fact, is a sort of blueprint for creating an object.

Methods and Properties

Since all the items I listed are appliances, they all have the appliance properties I mentioned before. In object-oriented terminology, this is called *inheritance*. Each appliance also has its own particular set of properties. A refrigerator, for example, has a capacity, door, number of shelves, freezer, and other properties. A property, then, is an attribute of an object. It can be a concrete item (like a door), a number (shelves, capacity), or even another appliance (a freezer, for example).

In addition to its properties, each appliance has its own *method* of performing a service for you. A dishwasher has its method for cleaning dishes, and a washing machine has its method for cleaning clothes. Notice that the two methods perform the same function—they "clean"—even though the appliances implement the method in different ways. It's a good thing they do. If we tried to make the methods the same, we'd either have dirty clothes or broken dishes. In the object-oriented arena, this different implementation of similar methods is called *polymorphism*.

In general, we neither know nor care how an appliance, like a dishwasher, does what it does. All we usually know is that if we put some dirty dishes and some dishwashing detergent in the right places, we'll have a set of clean dishes. When an appliance hides its methods from us, that's called *encapsulation*.

To summarize, here are some of the main concepts of the object-oriented world:

- Inheritance

- Abstraction

- Polymorphism

- Encapsulation

The object-oriented approach to software development depends heavily on these concepts, and the scripting languages you use depend heavily on objects.

Notation

We can use object-oriented notation to describe our appliances, their properties, and their methods.

Let's refer to an instance of an appliance, like the particular dishwasher in your kitchen, as an *appliance object*. To distinguish each appliance object from every other one in the world, we'll give it a name. Our naming convention will be a short prefix that indicates the class, followed by an intercap descriptive word or phrase. (Sound familiar?) Here are a few examples: `rfgMyRefrigerator`, `radMyRadio`, `dshMyDishwasher`.

Now let's examine some properties. To indicate an object's property, we provide the object's name, a dot, and the name of the property. For example, the number of shelves in your dishwasher might be `dshMyDishwasher.numShelves`. Since it's an instance of the dishwasher class, which is in turn a subclass of the appliance class, the dishwasher has a serial number, `dshMyDishwasher.serialNumber`, and an instruction manual, `dshMyDishwasher.instructionManual`.

The same notation applies to methods. Your dishwasher's `clean` method would be `dshMyDishwasher.clean`. We might want to elaborate further on the `clean` method by noting that it works with dishes and detergent: `dshMyDishwasher.clean(dishesList, detergent)`. The items in parentheses are the `clean` method's arguments.

All of your appliances are located in your house. In a sense, your house is a *container* for your appliances. In object-oriented terms, we could refer to your refrigerator as `myHouse.myRefrigerator` and your dishwasher as `myHouse.myDishwasher`. We can go one step further. Think of the set of your appliances as a *collection*—a group of objects that you can index by assigning a number on the basis of when you put the object in the house. If your refrigerator was the first appliance in the house, we'll assign zero as its index in the collection. If your dishwasher was the second appliance you added to your abode, its index is 1, and so forth. In this terminology, your refrigerator is `myHouse.myAppliances(0)` and your dishwasher is `myHouse.myAppliances(1)`. We might expand this terminology and make it easier to understand by allowing these equivalences:

```
myHouse.appliances(0) = myHouse.appliances("myRefrigerator") =
myHouse.myRefrigerator
```

Objects in HTML: The *OBJECT* Element

Let's move from objects in your house to objects in HTML. Just as your house is a container for appliance objects and furniture objects, an HTML document is a container for objects. HTML provides an element that enables you to insert objects into Web pages. It's called, not surprisingly, `OBJECT`, and you can use it to embed a variety of items.

Java Applets

One widely used object is the Java *applet*. An applet is a small program that lives and works in a Web page. The recently deprecated APPLET element used to be the vehicle for embedding applets in HTML, but `OBJECT` has taken its place. You're about to go through an exercise that will give you some experience in using `OBJECT` to embed applets, but first you'll need some applets to embed.

The Sybex Web site is a great place to find them. As you probably know by now, you can find code from books in the *No experience required* series at this Web site. Right now, we're concerned with one of those books, Steven Holzner's *Visual J++ 1.1: No experience required*. In this book, Steve shows you how to use Microsoft's Java development environment to create Java code and compile the code into Java classes. The compiled classes are the applets. Follow these steps to download Steve's applets so we can use one of them in this exercise:

1. Point your browser to `http://www.sybex.com`. Figure 5.1 shows the Sybex home page.

2. In the Sybex home page, click on the No Experience Required button. As you can see in Figure 5.1, it's in the lower-left part of the page.

3. In the No Experience Required page, click the link for Visual J++ 1.1.

4. In the Visual J++ 1.1 page, click the Download button.

5. On the next page, scroll down and then click the Get Download button to open the File Download dialog box.

6. In that dialog box, make sure the option button next to Save This Program To Disk is selected and click OK to open the Save As dialog box.

7. In the Save As dialog box, select a directory for downloading the `instalvj` file and click Save.

8. When `instalvj` has downloaded, right-click its icon and select Open to open the WinZip Self-Extractor (`Instalvj.exe`) dialog box.

9. In that dialog box, specify a folder in the Unzip To Folder box or leave it as the default value (`C:\vj`), and click Unzip.

10. After the files have decompressed, your newly created `vj` folder has a separate folder for each applet Steve created. Find the folder labelled `dabbler` and open it.

11. Open `dabbler.htm` in either Navigator or IE.

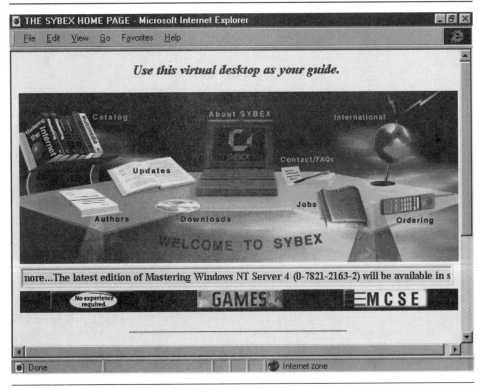

FIGURE 5.1: The Sybex home page

As Figure 5.2 shows, the dabbler applet is a kind of drawing tool. You can click one of four on-screen buttons to create a shape, or another to draw freehand, as I've done in the figure. The HTML for this file is:

dabbler.html

```
<HTML>
<HEAD>
<TITLE>dabbler</TITLE>
</HEAD>
<BODY>
<HR>
<APPLET Code=dabbler.class ID=dabbler Width=320 Height=240>
</APPLET>
<HR>
<A Href="dabbler.java">The source.</A>
</BODY>
</HTML>
```

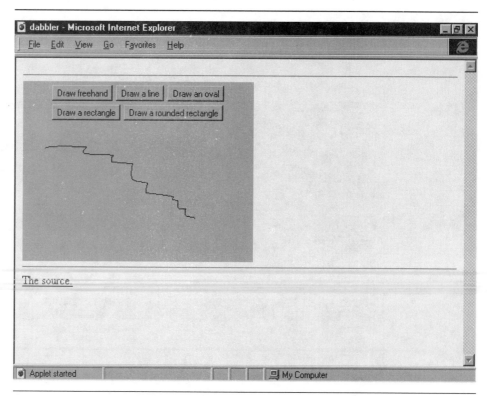

FIGURE 5.2: The dabbler applet

We'll use the OBJECT element to insert the applet into an HTML document. Create a new file called object-applet.htm and save it in Skill 5, then copy dabbler.class into Skill 5. Here's the HTML for object-applet.htm:

```
<HTML>
<HEAD>
<TITLE>Applet in an Object</TITLE>
</HEAD>
<BODY>
<OBJECT Classid="java:dabbler.class" Style = "width:320;height:240">
</OBJECT>
</BODY>
</HTML>
```

The Classid attribute identifies the dabbler.class file, and the Style attribute sets the dimensions of the applet. Open this document in Navigator to see a display that looks like Steve's original applet, as shown in Figure 5.3.

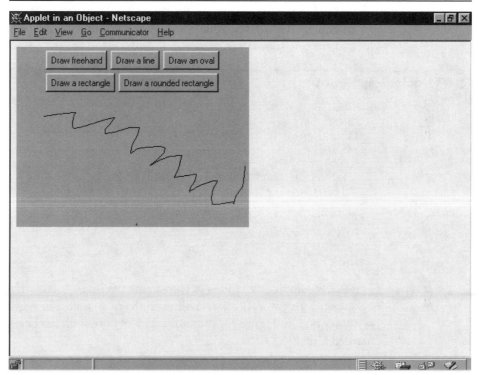

FIGURE 5.3: Object-applet.htm in Navigator

IE, on the other hand, is a bit quirky. If you open object-applet.htm in IE, you might see the button captions in enlarged font, and no background. The enlarged font makes it impossible to read the entire caption on any button. To modify the button captions in IE, select View ➢ Fonts ➢ Smaller from the IE menu bar. Refresh the display to see each caption in its entirety. When you close the page and reopen it, however, the original font size returns.

Another possibility is to make the applet bigger—say 600 pixels by 500 pixels. This expands the buttons and makes the captions legible, but it might mess up the layout of a multi-element Web page. In order to change the font permanently, we'd have to break into the Java source code, but that's beyond the scope of this book.

To provide a gray background, we can wrap the object in a DIV and give the DIV an inline Style that supplies the same dimensions as the OBJECT and provides a background color. Here's object-applet.htm with these modifications:

object-applet.htm

```
<HTML>
<HEAD>
<TITLE>Applet in an Object</TITLE>
</HEAD>
<BODY>
<DIV Style = "background:silver;width:320;height:240">
<OBJECT Classid="java:dabbler.class" Style = "width:320;height:240;
z-index:1">
</OBJECT>
</DIV>
</BODY>
</HTML>
```

Note that the applet's z-index is 1, ensuring that the applet is visible against the background. The modifications will open the page with a background in both Navigator and IE. Figure 5.4 shows the applet in IE with the background and the enlarged font.

TIP   To see a difference between Navigator and IE with respect to CSS attributes, add border:solid to the DIV's inline Style. Open the page in Navigator and IE. In IE, the border is contiguous with the background. In Navigator, it's not—a thin white line sits between the border and the background on all four sides.

NOTE   If you want to learn how to create the applets you downloaded, by all means read *Visual J++ 1.1: No experience required*. If you'd rather create Java applets without the Visual J++ environment, Steve's other book in the same series, *Java 1.1: No experience required*, will show you how.

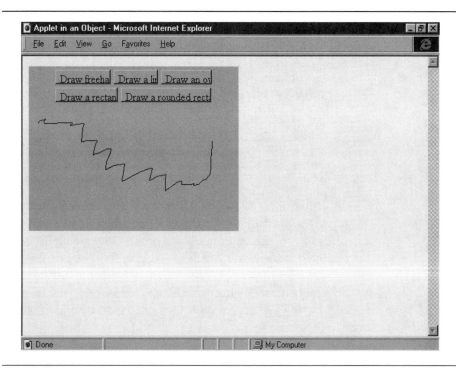

FIGURE 5.4:   Using the OBJECT element to embed the dabbler applet results in enlarged font on the applet's buttons when you render the page in IE.

ActiveX Controls

ActiveX controls are another type of object that developers insert in HTML documents. Promoted by Microsoft as a way of putting familiar looking components into Web pages, ActiveX controls come in many varieties: command buttons, checkboxes, combo boxes, and more. Third-party manufacturers seem to create new ones just about every week.

> **NOTE**   You'll work with some sophisticated ActiveX controls in Part II.

ActiveX controls live as .OCX files registered in your computer. When a Web page containing ActiveX controls appears in your browser, your browser uses the

.OCX files to render the controls. Here, for example, is an OBJECT element that causes IE to render an ActiveX command button:

```
<OBJECT ID="cmdbtnDemo" Style="Width:96;Height:32"
 CLASSID="CLSID:D7053240-CE69-11CD-A777-00DD01143C57">
    <PARAM NAME="Caption" VALUE="Click Me">
    <PARAM NAME="Size" VALUE="2540;846">
    <PARAM NAME="Accelerator" VALUE="67">
    <PARAM NAME="FontCharSet" VALUE="0">
    <PARAM NAME="FontPitchAndFamily" VALUE="2">
    <PARAM NAME="ParagraphAlign" VALUE="3">
    <PARAM NAME="FontWeight" VALUE="0">
</OBJECT>
```

Within the <OBJECT> tag, the ID attribute provides a name that scripts will use to refer to the button, Style provides dimensions, and CLASSID gives the unique identifier for this class of control. The control, along with its CLASSID value, has to be registered in the user's Windows Registry for the browser to render it. In case it's not, Web developers typically include a value for CODEBASE (not used here) that gives a URL from which the .OCX file downloads into the user's machine.

The PARAM elements give starting values for some of the control's properties, enabling the browser to render the control. For instance, the line

```
<PARAM NAME="Caption" VALUE="Click Me">
```

puts the phrase "Click Me" on the face of the button.

Images

In Skill 3, you used the IMG element to insert a graphic into a Web page. You can also use OBJECT to add an image, but you should be aware of some differences between the IMG element and the OBJECT element, as the next exercise illustrates.

Use your text editor to open Campus.htm from Skill 3, and then save it as ObjectCampus.htm in Skill 5. Find this part of the code,

```
<IMG Style = "position:absolute;top:12%;left:5%;"
Src = "E:\DHTML MTE\graphics\pictures\pine.gif"
Title = "Imaginary Tree">
```

and change it to

```
<OBJECT Style = "position:absolute;top:12%;left:5%;height:220;width:140"
Data = "E:\DHTML MTE\graphics\pictures\pine.gif"
Title = "Imaginary Tree">
</OBJECT>
```

You can see some differences immediately. First, with OBJECT you have to set a height and a width. You also have to include an </OBJECT> tag, and you have to substitute the Data attribute for Src. When you're done, and you open the page in IE, you'll be in for a bit of a surprise: You'll see the image in the OBJECT element, complete with horizontal and vertical scrollbars, as shown in Figure 5.5. You would have to expand the object's dimensions considerably, even beyond the height and width of the image, to eliminate the scrollbars. Another problem is that the tooltip specified by Title doesn't appear when you move the mouse into the object.

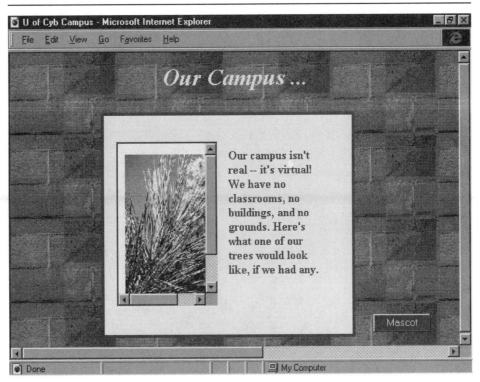

FIGURE 5.5: ObjectCampus.htm with its graphic in an OBJECT element rather than an IMG element

The W3C recommends the OBJECT element for embedding images. The IMG element, however, seems easier to use, less quirky, and more convenient.

Documents

Even with all the linking capabilities of HTML, it's sometimes useful to embed one HTML document in another and have it available for the user to see. The OBJECT element enables you to do this. You assign the embedded document's URL as the value for the Data attribute, and you're all set.

For example, the HTML code

```
<HTML>
<HEAD>
<TITLE>New Page</TITLE>
</HEAD>
<BODY>
Here's an example of an embedded document:
<OBJECT Data = "E:\DHTML MTE\Skill 3\Campus.htm"
Style = "Position:Absolute;Top:50;Left:100;Width:500;Height:300">
</OBJECT>
</BODY>
</HTML>
```

produces the display in Figure 5.6. The browser renders the embedded document complete with all its dynamic effects.

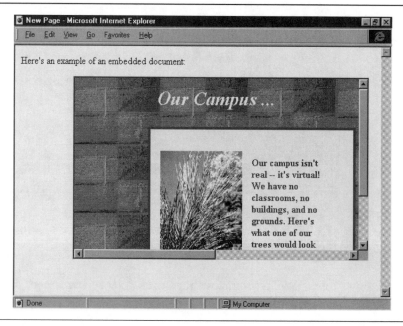

FIGURE 5.6: One HTML document embedded in another

The Attributes of *OBJECT*

The OBJECT element, as you've seen, is extremely versatile. You can use it to embed a variety of … well … objects into an HTML document. Table 5.1 explains its attributes.

TABLE 5.1: Attributes of the OBJECT Element

Attribute	What It Does
Accesskey	Specifies an accelerator key. Alt+Key selects the object in the browser.
Classid	Identifies the object's implementation. For ActiveX controls, the syntax is CLSID:class-identifier.
Code	Gives the name of the file that contains a compiled Java class
Codebase	Gives a URL for finding an object's implementation
Codetype	Specifies an Internet media type for code
Data	Gives a URL that references the object's data
ID	Provides an identifier for the object that scripts can use to refer to the object
Name	Specifies the name of a control or applet
Style	Specifies an inline style sheet for the object
Tabindex	Sets the object's tab index
Title	Provides advisory information rendered as a tooltip during an onMouseover event
Type	Specifies a MIME type for the data specified by the Data attribute

The OBJECT element has some other attributes that I didn't list in the table. One of these is Align, which specifies the object's alignment within the Web page, but it's been deprecated in favor of style sheets. Height and Width have also been deprecated. Two more attributes, Datafld and Datasrc, pertain to databound objects, which we'll deal with in Part II.

 **WARNING**

The OBJECT element, it seems, allows you to embed just about anything inside an HTML document. Do *not*, however, attempt to use OBJECT to embed a .WAV file into a Web page. That is, *don't* specify a path to a .WAV file as the value for Data in an OBJECT. You might mess up the way your browser renders fonts and colors.

Objects in Dynamic HTML

One of the strengths of DHTML, particularly the Microsoft version, is that it turns HTML elements into objects and their attributes into properties. The attributes we've worked with in previous chapters are attributes of Style, which apply to all the objects we've worked with. Style, itself an attribute, is also an object in this context, and its attributes become properties within DHTML.

IDs and Scripts

You provide an ID for an element so that you can refer to it as an object in scripts. You script user events to manipulate the properties of the objects, and as a result, create dynamic effects. In a similar way, the Netscape version turns the LAYER element into an object so that you can script events to alter its properties and create dynamic effects.

In Skill 1, you saw both these paradigms at work. In the Microsoft world, for example, the script snippet

```
Sub h1Header_onMouseOver
    h1Header.Style.Color = "Goldenrod"
    divMessage.Style.Visibility = "Visible"
    divReady.Style.Visibility = "Hidden"
    divStarted.Style.Visibility = "Visible"
End Sub
```

has the onMouseOver event change properties of four elements. In the Netscape world, the inline script snippet

```
onMouseOver = "layerMessage.visibility = 'show';
               layerHeader.visibility = 'hide';
               layerUnderHeader.visibility = 'show'"
```

has the onMouseOver event change properties in three LAYER elements.

A Little More about Layers

The LAYER element occupies center stage in Netscape's DHTML. In addition to the versatility this element displayed in Skill 1, it has another useful aspect: You can embed one layer inside another. The embedded layer is called the "child" and the embedding layer is the "parent," analogous to the parent/child relationship I described in the appliance world.

In addition to the visibility attribute in the script snippet, LAYER has a number of other attributes. Like visibility, they become properties of the LAYER object when you write them into scripts. Table 5.2 lists these attributes.

T A B L E   5 . 2 : Attributes of the LAYER Element

Attribute	What It Is
NAME	The name you assign to the layer
ID	Same as NAME, and the same as ID in IE
PAGEY	The layer's vertical position, in pixels, from the top edge of the page
PAGEX	The layer's horizontal position, in pixels, from the left edge of the page
TOP	The layer's vertical position, in pixels, from the top edge of its parent. If the layer is not embedded, TOP is equivalent to PAGEY.
LEFT	The layer's horizontal position, in pixels, from the left edge of its parent. If the layer is not embedded, LEFT is equivalent to PAGEX.
WIDTH	The layer's width, expressible in pixels or as a percentage of its parent's width
HEIGHT	The layer's height, expressible in pixels or as a percentage of its parent's height
ABOVE	Names the layer immediately above the one you're naming with the current layer tag
BELOW	Names the layer immediately below the one you're naming with the current layer tag
Z-INDEX	A number that specifies the layer's position in the "third" dimension
BGCOLOR	The layer's background color
BACKGROUND	The path to the file that holds the layer's background image
VISIBILITY	Specifies whether the layer is visible (show) or invisible (hide), or if it inherits the value of this property from its parent layer.
CLIP	Determines how much of the layer appears. You can make the layer expand or contract on its left, right, top, or bottom boundary.

Skill 5

The LAYER element also has methods, which appear in Table 5.3.

TABLE 5.3: Methods of the LAYER Element

Method	What It Does
moveBy	Moves the layer in the x-direction and the y-direction by a specified number of pixels
moveTo	Moves the layer so that its upper-left corner is at a specified x-y position in its container
moveToAbsolute	Moves the layer to a specified x-y position in the page
resizeBy	Resizes the layer horizontally and vertically by a specified number of pixels
resizeTo	Resizes the layer to a specified size in both x and y dimensions
moveAbove	Changes the layer's z-index so that the layer overlaps another element
moveBelow	Changes the layer's z-index so that the layer is overlapped by another element
load	Loads a file into a layer, and can change the layer's width

Visual Filters: Changing the Way Your Objects Look

Let's get back to the Microsoft world and continue with style properties. Like adding some shelves to your refrigerator or an ice cube maker to your freezer, you use CSS to add style properties to HTML elements, and, therefore, to DHTML objects.

We've already added style properties in numerous places, but let's take the opportunity to do it once more and introduce a property that you'll find useful for adding zip to your pages. The *filter* is a Microsoft extension to CSS. A filter dramatically alters an object's appearance. Figure 5.7 shows the application of filters to five DIVs. Each DIV holds a line of text that describes the filter's effects. The general style specifications for the DIVs are:

```
<STYLE>
DIV {height:80; width:400;Font-size:20pt}
</STYLE>
```

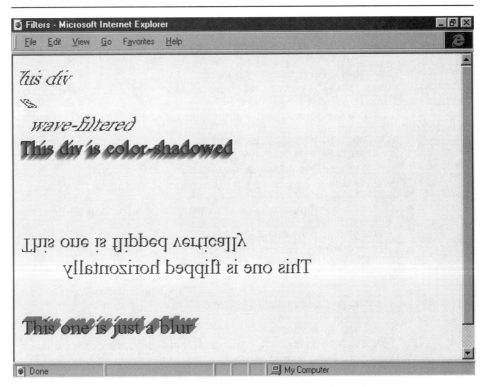

FIGURE 5.7: Applying five filters: The first is a wave filter, the second a shadow filter, the third a vertical flip, the fourth a horizontal flip, and the fifth a "blur."

The first filter applies a sine wave to the text. The sine wave appears in the vertical direction. You vary the appearance of the sine wave by varying parameters called add (1 = add the original image to the filtered image, 0 = don't add the original image), freq (number of waves in the filtered image), lightStrength (strength of the light on the wave effect), phase (offset of the start of the wave effect), and strength (something like the amplitude of the wave). The code for this filter is:

```
<DIV ID = divWave
Style ="filter:wave(add=0,freq=1,lightStrength=20,phase=50,strength=20)">
This div<BR> is<BR>wave-filtered
</DIV>
```

The second filter adds a shadow. Although you can't see it in Figure 5.7, the shadow is red:

```
<DIV ID = divColorShadow
Style ="filter:shadow(color=red)">
This div is color-shadowed
</DIV>
```

The third filter creates a mirror image of the text in the vertical direction:

```
<DIV ID = divFlipVertical
Style ="filter:FlipV">
This one is flipped vertically
</DIV>
```

The next filter creates a mirror image of the text in the horizontal direction:

```
<DIV ID = divFlipHorizontal
Style ="filter:FlipH">
This one is flipped horizontally
</DIV>
```

The last one applies a "blur":

```
<DIV ID = divBlur
Style ="filter:blur(add=1,direction=45,strength=10)">
This one is just a blur
</DIV>
```

The first parameter adds the original text to the filtered image, the second provides an orientation for the effect, and the third sets its strength.

At this point, filters.htm looks like this:

```
<HTML>
<HEAD>
<STYLE>
DIV {height:80; width:400;Font-size:20pt}
</STYLE>
<TITLE>Filters</TITLE>
</HEAD>
<BODY>
<DIV ID = divWave
```

```
Style ="filter:wave(add=0,freq=1,lightStrength=20,phase=50,strength=20)">
This div<BR> is<BR>wave-filtered
</DIV>
<DIV ID = divColorShadow
Style ="filter:shadow(color=red)">
This div is color-shadowed
</DIV>
<DIV ID = divFlipVertical
Style ="filter:FlipV">
This one is flipped vertically
</DIV>
<DIV ID = divFlipHorizontal
Style ="filter:FlipH">
This one is flipped horizontally
</DIV>
<DIV ID = divBlur
Style ="filter:blur(add=1,direction=45,strength=10)">
This one is just a blur
</DIV>
</BODY>
</HTML>
```

The filters can also dramatically change the appearance of images, not just text. To see this at work, save `filters.htm` as `dog-filters.htm` and for each line of displayed text, substitute an `IMG` element whose `Src` attribute is the path to the photo of Cyberdog:

```
<HTML>
<HEAD>
<STYLE>
DIV {height:80; width:400;Font-size:20pt}
</STYLE>
<TITLE>Dog-Filters</TITLE>
</HEAD>
<BODY>
<DIV ID = divWave
Style ="position:absolute;top:0;left:0;filter:wave(add=0,freq=1,
lightStrength=20,phase=50,strength=20)">
<IMG src = "E:\DHTML MTE\graphics\pictures\abi.gif">
</DIV>
<DIV ID = divColorShadow
```

```
Style ="position:absolute;top:0;left:250;filter:shadow(color=red)">
<IMG src = "E:\DHTML MTE\graphics\pictures\abi.gif">
</DIV>
<DIV ID = divFlipVertical
Style ="position:absolute;top:0;left:500;filter:FlipV">
<IMG src = "E:\DHTML MTE\graphics\pictures\abi.gif">
</DIV>
<DIV ID = divFlipHorizontal
Style ="position:absolute;top:300;left:0;filter:FlipH">
<IMG src = "E:\DHTML MTE\graphics\pictures\abi.gif">
</DIV>
<DIV ID = divBlur
Style ="position:absolute;top:300;left:450;filter:blur(add=1,
direction=45,strength=10)">
<IMG src = "E:\DHTML MTE\graphics\pictures\abi.gif">
</DIV>
</BODY>
</HTML>
```

Notice that I've also added some positioning information to the inline style sheets in order to place the images side by side. Figures 5.8 and 5.9 show the filters working on the photo of the dog.

FIGURE 5.8: The Wave, ColorShadow, and FlipVertical filters at work on an image

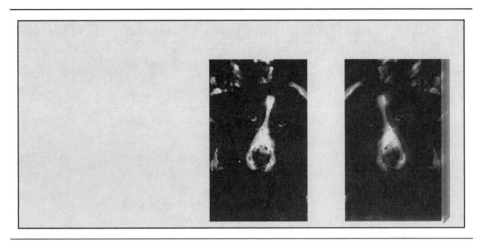

FIGURE 5.9: The `flipHorizontal` and `blur` filters applied to the image

You're probably interested in the whole set of filters and what they do. Take a look at Table 5.4.

TABLE 5.4: Visual Filters

Filter	What It Does	Parameters
Alpha	Sets level of opacity	Opacity, FinishOpacity, Style, StartX, StartY, FinishX, FinishY
Blur	Averages the object's pixels for a specified length and direction; gives the impression that the object is in high-speed motion	Add, Direction, Strength
Chroma	Renders a selected color to be transparent for an object	Color
DropShadow	Creates a solid silhouette of the object, offset in the specified direction	Color, OffX, OffY, Positive

TABLE 5.4 CONTINUED: Visual Filters

Filter	What It Does	Parameters
FlipH	Renders an object as a mirror image flipped along the horizontal plane	
FlipV	Renders an object as a mirror image flipped along the vertical plane	
Glow	Puts radiance around the outer edges of an object	Color, Strength
Gray	Omits color information, rendering the object in grayscale	
Invert	Reverses an object's hue, saturation, and brightness	
Light	Simulates projection of a light source onto the selected visual object	
Mask	For a selected object, paints the transparent pixels a specified color, and makes a transparent mask out of the nontransparent pixels	Color
Shadow	Puts a solid silhouette of the selected object along one of its edges, creating the illusion of a shadow around the object	Color, Direction
Wave	Creates a sine wave distortion of the object	Add, Freq, LightStrength, Phase, Strength
Xray	Changes the color depth of an object and renders the object in black and white	

Style Information: Where Is It?

A property called CSSText holds all the information about an object's style attributes. It's something like the technical specifications section of the instruction booklet that comes with an appliance. A little scripting will show this to be the case. We'll add a VBScript that displays a message box with all the CSS information on the DIVs in dog-filters.htm when you click your mouse on the wave-transformed image.

In dog-filters.htm, insert this script into the HEAD element:

```
<SCRIPT Language = VBS>
sub divWave_onClick
call Msgbox("divWave: " & divWave.style.CSSText & chr(13) _
& "divColorShadow: " & divColorShadow.style.CSSText & chr(13) _
& "divFlipVertical: " & divFlipVertical.style.CSSText & chr(13) _
& "divFlipHorizontal: " & divFlipHorizontal.style.CSSText & chr(13) _
& "divBlur: " & divBlur.style.CSSText,64,"Style Properties of the DIVs")
end sub
</SCRIPT>
```

In the very long first argument, the underscore at the end of each line is the VBS continuation character, and chr(13) provides the ASCII code for a new line. The second argument, 64, adds the information symbol to the message box. The third argument, "Style Properties of the DIVs", gives the message box its title. Figure 5.10 shows the Message Box with all the style information.

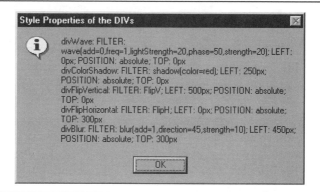

FIGURE 5.10: The Message Box with the style information for each DIV

Transition Filters: Changing the Way Your Objects Change

The *transition filter* is closely related to the filter. It sets up a style for making the transition from one visual object to another. Transition filters come in two varieties: *blend* and *reveal*. A blend transition makes an object gradually appear or disappear. A reveal transition makes an object visible or invisible in one of 24 ways. If you've ever set up transitions between Microsoft PowerPoint slides, you've seen the effect. When one slide disappears and the next appears, the transition can take all kinds of shapes—box in, box out, checkerboard, random dissolve, vertical blinds, and more.

The next exercise shows you how to work with this property and set up eye-catching transitions on your Web pages. To set up for this exercise, copy Campus .htm from Skill 3 to Skill 5. Rename the file filterCampus.htm and you're ready to start.

Open the page and click the button in the lower-right corner. It changes the central display from the tree to the dog, along with changes to the associated text. When you click the button, it changes the display back to the tree. The change, as you can see, is immediate. Our objective is to make the click-related change more dramatic by adding transition filters.

We start by adding a transition filter to the inline style sheet for divContainer1 and another to divContainer2. In the source code for this page, find this code:

```
<DIV ID = divContainer1 Style =
"position:absolute;left:125;top:80;width:350;height:300;
background-color:#FFFFCC;color:green;font-weight:bold;
border:solid;border-color:green;"
```

Additional code is in the <DIV> tag, but right now we're only concerned with the inline style sheet. To the inline style sheet, add

```
filter:revealTrans(Duration=0.8, Transition = 11);
```

The value of the first parameter specifies how long (in seconds) the transition will last. The value of the second parameter specifies the type of transition that occurs. In this case, the transition is a checkerboard pattern in a downward direction. A table at the end of this section tells you which number signifies which transition type.

Do almost the same for divContainer2. To divContainer2's inline style sheet, add

```
filter:revealTrans(Duration=0.8, Transition = 12);
```

This value of `Transition` specifies a "random dissolve."

Your two inline style sheets should now look something like this:

```
<DIV ID = divContainer1 Style =
"position:absolute;left:125;top:80;width:350;height:300;
background-color:#FFFFCC;color:green;font-
weight:bold;filter:revealTrans(Duration=0.8, Transition = 11);
border:solid;border-color:green;"
```

and

```
<DIV ID = divContainer2 Style =
"position:absolute;left:125;top:80;width:350;height:300;
background-color:#FFFFCC;color:green;font-
weight:bold;filter:revealTrans(Duration=0.8, Transition = 12);
border:solid;border-color:green;visibility:'hidden';"
```

You're not finished yet. In order to apply these transition filters to the DIVs and make them occur, we have to invoke a couple of filter methods. One is called *Apply*, and the other is *Play*. The first one applies the transition to the object and the second one starts the transition. In order to understand how to invoke these methods, you must first understand that filters are available to each DHTML object in the form of a collection. Just as your house can have a collection of appliances, a DHTML object can have a collection of filters. To refer to a filter, you use the syntax `objectName.filters(filternumber)`. To invoke the `Apply` method, the syntax is

```
objectName.filters(filternumber).Apply()
```

To invoke the `Play` method, the syntax is

```
objectName.filters(filternumber).Play()
```

Let's add the appropriate syntax to the `onClick` event for the button. The first part of the button's `if` statement makes `divContainer1` visible, so add the `Apply` and `Play` methods for `divContainer1` to the first part of the `if` statement:

```
divContainer1.filters(0).Apply();
divContainer1.filters(0).Play()
```

The second part of the `if` statement—the one that begins with `else`—makes `divContainer2` visible, so add the `Apply` and `Play` methods for `divContainer2`'s transition filter:

```
divContainer2.filters(0).Apply();
divContainer2.filters(0).Play();
```

After you make these changes, your onClick code should look like this:

```
onClick = "if (this.value == 'Tree') {
        this.value = 'Mascot';
        divContainer2.style.visibility = 'hidden';
        divContainer1.style.visibility = 'visible';
        divContainer1.filters(0).Apply();
        divContainer1.filters(0).Play()}
    else {
        this.value = 'Tree';
        divContainer2.style.visibility = 'visible';
        divContainer1.style.visibility = 'hidden';
        divContainer2.filters(0).Apply();
        divContainer2.filters(0).Play();
    }">
```

Try the new page. You'll see some fancy transitions when you click the button. Figures 5.11 and 5.12 show you the appearance of the two transitions you scripted about halfway through each transition.

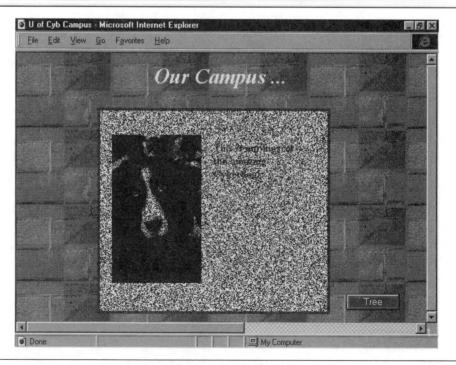

FIGURE 5.11: The "random dissolve" transition from the Tree to the Dog

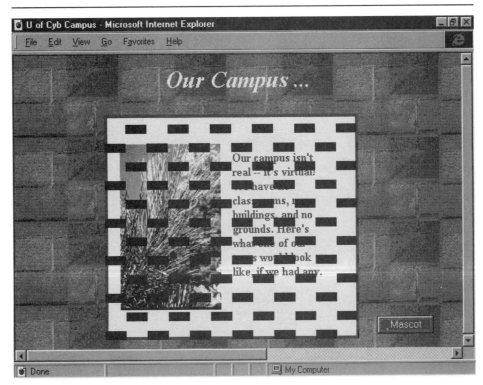

FIGURE 5.12: The "checkerboard down" transition from the Dog to the Tree

I'm sure you'll want to try out all the possibilities for the "reveal" transition, so Table 5.5 lists them for you.

TABLE 5.5: Types of Reveal Transition Filters

Type Number	What It Is
0	Box in
1	Box out
2	Circle in
3	Circle out
4	Wipe Up
5	Wipe down

TABLE 5.5 CONTINUED: Types of Reveal Transition Filters

Type Number	What It Is
6	Wipe right
7	Wipe left
8	Vertical blinds
9	Horizontal blinds
10	Checkerboard across
11	Checkerboard down
12	Random dissolve
13	Split vertical in
14	Split vertical out
15	Split horizontal in
16	Split horizontal out
17	Strips left down
18	Strips left up
19	Strips right down
20	Strips right up
21	Random bars horizontal
22	Random bars vertical
23	Random selection of all the preceding effects

The last type, "random selection," doesn't give you a different transition type each time you click the button. Instead, it gives a different type each time you refresh the page.

More on Transitions

The FilterCampus.htm file has several other events that we can augment with our transition filters. We can have the transitions occur when the mouse moves into the central display and when it moves out of the display. As you'll recall, the display exchanges its border color with its background color when the arrow moves in and out. If we add the transitions, they'll take place as the colors change, making for an attractive effect.

If you just add the `Apply` and `Play` statements to the `onMouseOver` and `onMouseOut` events, however, you'll generate scripting errors. The reason is that any mouse movements will cause the transition to start, and one transition will start while another is in progress. When this happens, an error results.

To get around this conflict, we must have a way of knowing when a transition has started. If it has, we won't begin a new transition. Fortunately, a property called *status* fits the bill. This property takes numerical values, and if the value is 2, the transition is in progress. (If the value is 0 the transition has stopped, and if it's 1, the transition has been applied.)

Accordingly, we write a function that proceeds with the transition if the value of status is not equal to 2, and we'll call that function from the `onMouseOver` and `onMouseOut` events. Somewhere in the HEAD of `FilterCampus.htm`, add this code:

```
<SCRIPT Language = "Javascript">
function filter_it(divname) {
    if(divname.filters(0).status != 2) {
        divname.filters(0).Apply();
        divname.filters(0).Play();
    }
}
</SCRIPT>
```

The `if` statement checks the status of the transition and starts the `Apply` and `Play` methods only if the transition hasn't already started. The argument enables us to use the same function for both `divContainer1` and `divContainer2`.

Now, in `divContainer1`, add the line

```
filter_it(divContainer1)
```

at the beginning of the code for `onMouseOver` and at the beginning of the code for `onMouseOut`. In `divContainer2`, add

```
filter_it(divContainer2)
```

at the beginning of `onMouseOver` and `onMouseOut`. It's important to add these lines at the beginning, rather than the end, so that the transitions occur while the colors are changing.

Here's the `FilterCampus.htm` file in its entirety:

 **FilterCampus.htm**

```
<HTML>
<HEAD>
<TITLE>U of Cyb Campus</TITLE>
<SCRIPT Language = "Javascript">
function filter_it(divname) {
     if(divname.filters(0).status != 2) {
             divname.filters(0).Apply();
             divname.filters(0).Play();
     }
}
</SCRIPT>
</HEAD>
<BODY Style = "background:url(E:\DHTML MTE\graphics\photobks\ltp16a.gif)">
<H1 Style = "text-align:center;color:#FFFFCC;font-style:italic;">Our Campus ...</H1>

<DIV ID = divContainer1 Style =
"position:absolute;left:125;top:80;width:350;height:300;
background-color:#FFFFCC;color:green;font-weight:bold;filter:revealTrans
(Duration=0.8, Transition = 11);
border:solid;border-color:green;"

onMouseOver = "filter_it(divContainer1);
             this.style.backgroundColor = 'green';
             this.style.borderColor = '#FFFFCC';
             this.style.color = '#FFFFCC';"

onMouseOut =  "filter_it(divContainer1);
             this.style.backgroundColor = '#FFFFCC';
             this.style.borderColor = 'green';
             this.style.color = 'green';">

<IMG Style = "position:absolute;top:12%;left:5%;"
Src = "E:\DHTML MTE\graphics\pictures\pine.gif"
Title = "Imaginary Tree">

<DIV Style = "position:absolute;left:50%;top:15%;width:40%;">
<P>Our campus isn't real - it's virtual! We have no classrooms,
no buildings, and no grounds. Here's what one of our trees would look
like, if we had any.</P>
</DIV>
</DIV>
```

```
<DIV ID = divContainer2 Style =
"position:absolute;left:125;top:80;width:350;height:300;
background-color:#FFFFCC;color:green;font-
weight:bold;filter:revealTrans(Duration=0.8, Transition = 12);
border:solid;border-color:green;visibility:'hidden';"

onMouseOver = "filter_it(divContainer2);
            this.style.backgroundColor = 'green';
            this.style.borderColor = '#FFFFCC';
            this.style.color = '#FFFFCC';"


onMouseOut = "filter_it(divContainer2);
            this.style.backgroundColor = '#FFFFCC';
            this.style.borderColor = 'green';
            this.style.color = 'green';">

<IMG Style = "position:absolute;top:12%;left:5%"
Src = "E:\DHTML MTE\graphics\pictures\abi.gif"
Title = "Cyberdog">

<DIV Style = "position:absolute;left:50%;top:15%;width:40%">
<P>This is our mascot – the amazing Cyberdog!</P>
</DIV>
</DIV>

<DIV Style = "position:absolute;left:500;top:350;">
<FORM>
<P><INPUT Type = button ID = inputButton Value = "Mascot"
style = "background-color:green;color:#FFFFCC;width:80"
onClick = "if (this.value == 'Tree') {
            this.value = 'Mascot';
            divContainer2.style.visibility = 'hidden';
            divContainer1.style.visibility = 'visible';
            divContainer1.filters(0).Apply();
            divContainer1.filters(0).Play()}
        else {
            this.value = 'Tree';
            divContainer2.style.visibility = 'visible';
            divContainer1.style.visibility = 'hidden';
            divContainer2.filters(0).Apply();
            divContainer2.filters(0).Play();
        }">
</P>
</FORM>
</DIV>

</BODY>
</HTML>
```

Open the file in IE and you'll see some nifty transitions when you move the mouse in and out of the central display, as well as when you click the on-screen button. For good measure, try a few of the other transitions in Table 5.3.

TIP   If you like, you can substitute the `filter_it` function (with the appropriate arguments) for the `Apply` and `Play` statements in the `onClick` event.

Objects in Arrays: Adding a Dimension

When you develop in DHTML, you use objects in all kinds of contexts. Sometimes you have to set up arrays, populate them with references to objects, and use objects in conjunction with array positions. In this exercise, you'll gain experience in handling objects within arrays, pick up some important scripting concepts, and work with the `z-index`. You'll write code in VBScript.

Save your template as `z-index.htm` in Skill 5, and create this code:

```
<HTML>
<HEAD>
<TITLE>Objects and the z-index</TITLE>
</HEAD>
<BODY Style = "background-color:Silver">
<H1 Style = "text-align:center">Using the Z-Index</H1>
<HR>
<DIV Style ="Width:225;Height:141; Position:Absolute; Top:100;
Left:180; z-index:0">
<IMG SRC = "E:\DHTML MTE\Graphics\Pictures\Pine1.gif">
</DIV>
</DIV>
</BODY>
</HTML>
```

Open the Web page in IE. It should look like Figure 5.13.

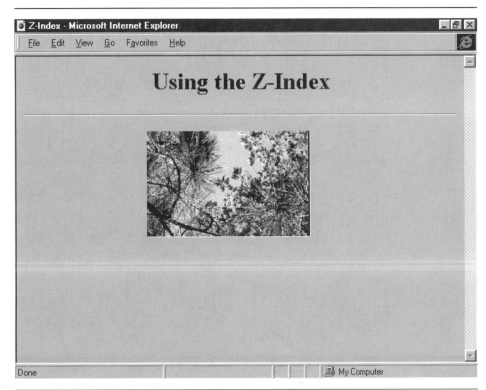

FIGURE 5.13: Your z-index.htm Web page in IE

Next, let's position another picture that's a bit lower, a bit farther to the right, and lying on top of the picture we just put on the page. Create this DIV on your Web page, right after the DIV:

```
<DIV Style ="Width:225;Height:141;Position:Absolute; Top:160; Left:255;
z-index:2">
<IMG Src = "E:\DHTML MTE\Graphics\Pictures\Forest.gif">
</DIV>
```

Notice that the value for Top is a little higher, which positions the new picture a little lower on the page, and the value for Left is a little higher, too, which positions the new picture a little farther to the right. The z-index value, 2, puts the new picture on top of the first one.

Open the page in IE to see a display like Figure 5.14.

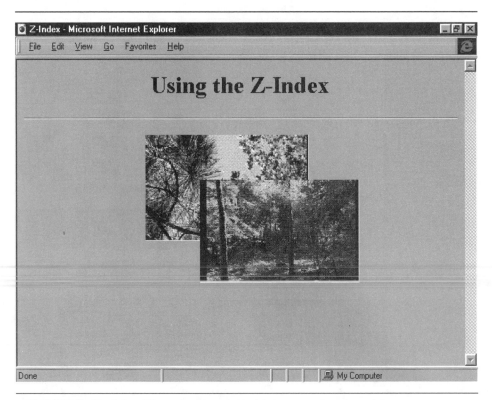

FIGURE 5.14: The z-index page with two overlapping pictures

Let's do one more. Create this DIV and you'll have three overlapping pictures:

```
<DIV Style ="Width:225;Height:141;Position:Absolute; Top:200; Left:330;
z-index:3">
<IMG Src = "E:\DHTML MTE\Graphics\Pictures\Pine2.gif">
</DIV>
```

The page should now look like Figure 5.15 when you open it in IE.

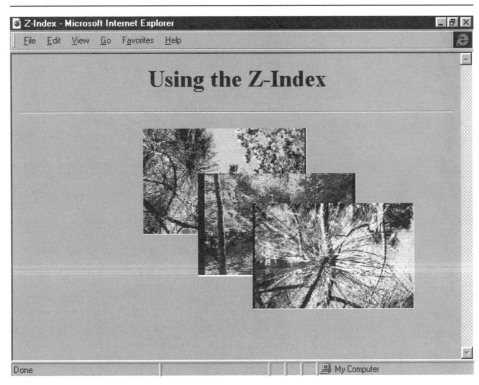

FIGURE 5.15: The z-index page with three overlapping pictures

Scripting the Third Dimension

Our objective is to write a script that changes the overlaps of the pictures when you click them. Obviously, we'll have to have onClick in our script, and each onClick event will change all the z-index values. We'll want the changes to occur systematically: When you click on a picture, it will come to the top, and the previous uppermost picture will move down one level. If you've clicked the bottom picture, both the others move down one level when the clicked one rises to the top.

Naming the Objects

We begin by naming the objects. Assign each division an ID that includes the name of its graphics file. The names should be divPine1, divForest, and divPine2. When you're finished, the part of your file that holds the <DIV> tags should look like this:

```
<DIV ID=divPine1 Style ="Width:225;Height:141; Position:Absolute;
Top:100; Left:180; z-index:1">
<IMG Src = "E:\DHTML MTE\Graphics\Pictures\Pine1.gif">
</DIV>
<DIV ID=divForest Style ="Width:225;Height:141;Position:Absolute;
Top:160; Left:255; z-index:2">
<IMG Src = "E:\DHTML MTE\Graphics\Pictures\Forest.gif">
</DIV>
<DIV ID=divPine2 Style ="Width:225;Height:141;Position:Absolute;
Top:200; Left:330; z-index:3">
<IMG Src = "E:\DHTML MTE\Graphics\Pictures\Pine2.gif">
</DIV>
```

Writing the Script

This exercise will show you a number of aspects of writing scripts for objects. We begin with a short analysis of our objectives:

- When you click on one of the pictures, you'll want it to rise to the top.

- Pictures that were formerly above the clicked picture should go back one slot closer to the "surface"—their z-indices should each decrease by one.

- Pictures that were formerly below the clicked picture should stay where they are—their z-indices should remain the same.

To handle these objectives, we'll work with an *array*. An array is like a table—a group of items that are so similar you can treat them all the same way. Putting them in an array groups them under one name and an index. You'll use an array to keep track of the picture objects and their z-indices. Your array will look like this:

```
divPine1
divForest
divPine2
```

When you click on, say, `divPine1` (whose `z-index` is 0), your script will:

- Check the `z-index` of each array-item against the `z-index` of `divPine1`.

- If the array-item's `z-index` is greater than `divPine1`'s `z-index`, decrease it by 1.

- Reset `divPine1`'s `z-index` to 2.

NOTE   Keep an object's `z-index` and its `array-index` separate in your mind. Coincidentally, each object's `z-index` and its `array-index` start out with the same value. The z-indices will change as the script executes; the array indices do not change.

The array is a *variable*—an entity whose value can change throughout the course of a script. VBScript has two kinds of variables. One kind, the *global* variable, is available to all the procedures in an HTML file. It's said to have a *global scope*. The other kind, the *local* variable, is available only to the procedure that contains it. Its scope is *local*. Let's make the array a global variable. That way, we can populate it in one procedure and use the populated values in another procedure. We'll use the prefix `glbl` to indicate the global scope. An appropriate name for this array is `glblDivArray`.

In VBScript, you can use a `dim` statement to name a variable, and you name global variables outside of any subroutines. In your `z-index.htm` file, create this code right after the `<HEAD>` tag:

```
<SCRIPT LANGUAGE="VBScript">
<!--
dim glblDivArray(2)
```

Notice the `(2)` after the name of the array. This tells VBS to make room for an array that has 3 rows. Remember, array indices start at zero. The first row is 0, the second is 1, and the third is 2.

Next, we have to populate the array. We'll want the array to populate whenever a window opens, so we'll use the `window_onload` event. Because the items in your array are objects, you have to handle them with care, and that's one of the main points of this exercise. In order to make a variable (like a row in an array) equal to an object, you have to use the VBS `set` command. The `set` command tells VBS to point to the memory location that holds a particular object.

Here, then, is the code for populating the array:

```
Sub window_onload()
set glblDivArray(0) = divPine1
set glblDivArray(1) = divForest
set glblDivArray(2) = divPine2
end sub
```

Next, script the subroutines for the onClick events for the three pictures. These subroutines are simple:

```
Sub divPine1_OnClick()
call ZIndexManager(divPine1)
end sub

Sub divPine2_OnClick()
call ZIndexManager(divPine2)
end sub

Sub divForest_OnClick()
call ZIndexManager(divForest)
end sub
```

As you can see, each one calls a subroutine named ZIndexManager to do the dirty work. And each one calls ZIndexManager with its own name as the subroutine's argument. Where does this subroutine come from? You're about to create it.

The subroutine you're about to build will manage z-index values, hence the name ZIndexManager. When one of the onClick subroutines calls ZIndexManager, ZIndexManager has to know which picture has been clicked and that information is passed to the subroutine in the Clicked argument. So, the first line of the subroutine should look like this:

```
Sub ZIndexManager(Clicked)
```

Since you'll be working with an array in this subroutine, you'll need a variable that acts as the array-index—i.e., a variable that keeps track of the array's rows. The name Row seems appropriate for this variable:

```
dim Row
```

You define this variable inside the subroutine. This makes it a local variable. After the subroutine finishes, the value of Row goes away. In other words, the value of Row doesn't carry over into any other subroutine in this script.

Now we have to get to the business end of this subroutine. Starting with the first object in the array, the subroutine has to:

1. Examine the z-index of this array-object and compare it to the clicked object's z-index.

2. If the array-object's z-index is greater, decrease it by one.

3. Move on to the next object in the array and start again at Step 1.

We can translate each of these steps into VBS code. Begin by setting up a structure that starts from the first element in the array and ends at the last. The structure is called for...next, and looks like this:

```
for counterVariable = beginning-value to end-value
.
.
.
next
```

Between for and next, you place the code that the script must execute. The value of counterVariable starts at beginning-value and increases by 1 each time the script gets to next. As long as the value of counterVariable doesn't exceed end-value, the script runs the code that sits between for and next. In our case, counterVariable is Row, beginning-value is 0 and end-value is 2 (to cover all the rows in our little array). So, our for...next structure is

```
for Row = 0 to 2
.
.
.
next
```

Now all we need is the code that sits in the middle. We have to compare the z-index of the object in each row with the z-index of the clicked object. We refer to an array object as glblDivArray(Row) and the clicked object as Clicked(the argument). An if statement performs the comparison:

```
If glblDivArray(Row).style.zindex > Clicked.style.zindex Then
```

If the array-object's z-index is greater, decrease its z-index by 1:

```
glblDivArray(Row).style.zindex = glblDivArray(Row).style.zindex - 1
```

Next, we must close the if statement:

```
end if
```

That's the code that sits inside the for...next structure. The whole for...next structure is:

```
for Row = 0 to 2
    If glblDivArray(Row).style.zindex > Clicked.style.zindex Then
      glblDivArray(Row).style.zindex = glblDivArray(Row).style.zindex - 1
    end if
next
```

One more line is necessary before you end the subroutine. You still have to assign 2 as the value of the z-index of the clicked object:

```
Clicked.style.zindex = 2
```

Here, then, is the code that you should create for ZIndexManager:

```
Sub ZIndexManager(Clicked)
dim Row

for Row = 0 to 2
    If glblDivArray(Row).style.zindex > Clicked.style.zindex Then
      glblDivArray(Row).style.zindex = glblDivArray(Row).style.zindex - 1
    end if
next

Clicked.style.zindex = 2
end sub
```

The whole z-index.htm file looks like this:

z-index.htm

```
<HTML>
<HEAD>
    <SCRIPT LANGUAGE="VBScript">
<!--
dim glblDivArray(2)

Sub window_onload()
set glblDivArray(0) = divPine1
set glblDivArray(1) = divForest
set glblDivArray(2) = divPine2
end sub
```

```
Sub divPine1_onClick()
call ZIndexManager(divPine1)
end sub

Sub divPine2_onClick()
call ZIndexManager(divPine2)
end sub

Sub divForest_onClick()
call ZIndexManager(divForest)
end sub

Sub ZIndexManager(Clicked)

dim Row

for Row = 0 to 2
    If glblDivArray(Row).style.zindex > Clicked.style.zindex Then
    glblDivArray(Row).style.zindex = glblDivArray(Row).style.zindex - 1
    end if
next

Clicked.style.zindex = 2
end sub

<TITLE>z-index</TITLE>
</HEAD>
<BODY BGCOLOR = "SILVER">
<H1><Center>Using the z-index</Center></H1>
<HR>
<DIV ID=divPine1 STYLE ="WIDTH:225;HEIGHT:141; POSITION:ABSOLUTE; TOP:100;
LEFT:180; Z-INDEX:1">
<IMG SRC = "E:\DHTML MTE\GRAPHICS\PICTURES\PINE1.GIF">
</DIV>
<DIV ID=divForest STYLE ="WIDTH:225;HEIGHT:141;POSITION:ABSOLUTE; TOP:160;
LEFT:255; Z-INDEX:2">
<IMG SRC = "E:\DHTML MTE\GRAPHICS\PICTURES\FOREST.GIF">
</DIV>
<DIV ID=divPine2 STYLE ="WIDTH:225;HEIGHT:141;POSITION:ABSOLUTE; TOP:200;
LEFT:330; Z-INDEX:3">
<IMG SRC = "E:\DHTML MTE\GRAPHICS\PICTURES\PINE2.GIF">
</DIV>
</BODY>
</HTML>
```

Skill 5

MAKING YOUR CODE MORE GENERAL

Our ZIndexManager works with a three-row array, but you can set it up to work with an array that has any amount of rows. How? Make the number of rows an argument, and build that argument into the subroutine. Then, you must use that argument whenever you call the subroutine. Here's how it would look:

```
Sub ZIndexManager(Clicked, LastRow)
dim Row
for Row = 0 to LastRow
If glblDivArray(Row).style.zindex > Clicked.style.zindex Then
        glblDivArray(Row).style.zindex =
        glblDivArray(Row).style.zindex - 1
end if
next

Clicked.style.zindex = LastRow
end sub
```

Within your script, here's an example of how you would call this subroutine:

```
call ZIndexManager(divForest, 2)
```

Save your work and open the page in IE. You should be able to form all possible overlap arrangements of the three photographs. Figure 5.16 shows what happens when you click divForest and then click divPine1. It's the reverse of Figure 5.15.

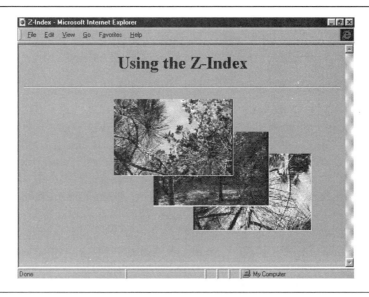

FIGURE 5.16: After you script onClick events for the pictures in z-index .htm, you can reverse the initial overlaps. (Compare with Figure 5.15.)

Objects in Style Sheets: JavaScript Accessible Style Sheets

As you learned in Skill 4, Cascading Style Sheets (CSS) provide a means for setting Web page styles in numerous ways. Recall that CSSs are written in the CSS1 language, a syntax that pairs selectors with declarations to form rules. Netscape has taken the concept in another direction. They used object-oriented concepts to create a new genre of style sheets. Dubbed *JavaScript Accessible Style Sheets* (JASS) or *JavaScript Style Sheets* (JSSS), these are style sheets that you write in object syntax. (JASS won't work on IE.)

Let's start by pointing out the differences between CSS and JASS. They accomplish similar objectives, but take different paths to achieve them. If you want to set a style for a paragraph in CSS, for example, you create a rule that looks like this:

```
P {margin-right:150;}
```

In this rule, P is the selector, everything inside the curly brackets is the declaration, and the whole line is the rule. This rule tells the browser to render every P element with a right margin of 150 pixels.

In JASS, you use object syntax to make the same specification:

```
document.tags.P.marginRight = 150
```

Aside from the cosmetic differences, what's the distinction? The first term, document, is the way we represent a Web page. Think of tags as a property of the Web page, P as a property of tags, and marginRight as a property of P. It's analogous to myHouse.myAppliances.myRefrigerator.freezerwidth. The line of CSS1 specifies a rule: The line of JavaScript sets the value of a property. By the way, we can leave out document and write that JASS line as

```
tags.P.marginRight = 150;
```

JavaScript allows a useful shorthand way of creating styles. Suppose you want to style a paragraph to have a particular right-hand margin, and bold, blue, italicized text. You could set all that up like this:

```
tags.P.marginRight = 150;
tags.P.color = "Blue";
tags.P.fontWeight = "Bold";
tags.P.fontStyle = "Italic";
```

or you could use this shorthand syntax:

```
with (tags.P) {
     margin-right = 150;
     color = "Blue";
     font-weight = "Bold";
     font-style = "Italic";
}
```

A few more points and we'll get into an example. As its name suggests, the tags property applies to a variety of HTML tags, not just <P>. You can use it to set properties for <BODY>, <H1>, and all the other levels of headings, to name a few. Also, tags isn't the only document property that you can use in JASS. You can use classes to create new styles, and IDs to create exceptions to styles. The next exercise will make this clearer.

An Example

Let's quickly create a Web page for another department at the University of Cyberspace, use a JASS to embellish it, and then open it in Navigator. We'll call this department "The Department of Web Feasibility Studies."

Here's the HTML for the document:

```
<HTML>
<HEAD>
<TITLE>Department of Web Feasibility</TITLE>
</HEAD>
<BODY>
<H1>
Department of Web Feasibility Studies</H1>
<HR>
<P>Does a particular business or organization need a Web site? If so,
how much benefit can they expect to derive? These questions and more
are the subjects of the work we do in this department.</P>
</BODY>
</HTML>
```

WebFeasibility.htm looks like Figure 5.17 when you open it in Navigator.

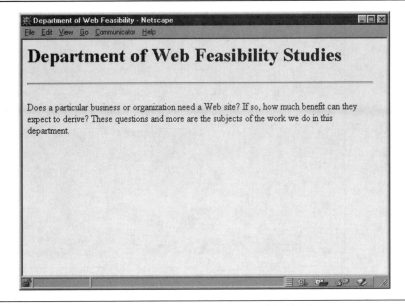

FIGURE 5.17: WebFeasibility.htm rendered in Navigator

Let's add JASS to spice things up. Before </HEAD>, use your text editor to add these tags:

```
<STYLE TYPE = "text/javascript">

</STYLE>
```

The TYPE attribute's value in the first tag tells the browser that a JASS sits between the two STYLE tags. The other possibility, of course, is a CSS. You'll place the styling information between these tags. Begin with the line from our example:

```
tags.P.marginRight = 150
```

Open the page in Navigator, and you'll see the wide right margin your JASS specifies, as shown in Figure 5.18.

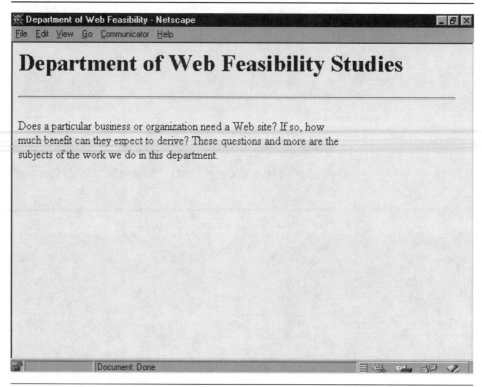

FIGURE 5.18: WebFeasibility.htm with your first JASS specification

Now add a statement that sets the background color of the page and the default color of the page's body:

```
tags.BODY.backgroundcolor = "silver"
tags.BODY.color = "green"
```

Add a paragraph to the body of the page:

```
<P>Coursework covers business analysis and statistical analysis. </P>
```

When you make these additions and open the page in Navigator, it looks like Figure 5.19.

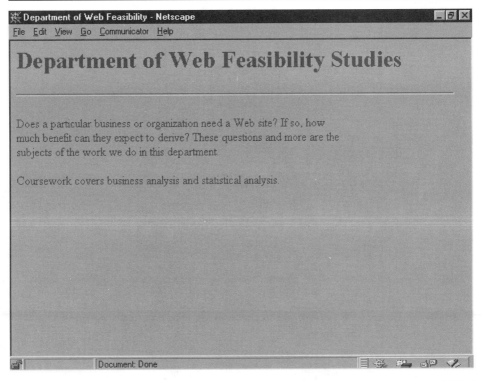

FIGURE 5.19: The Web Feasibility page with a style that specifies the color of the body, and an additional paragraph

As Figure 5.19 shows, the heading, the first paragraph, and the new paragraph conform to the latest addition to the JASS, and the background color has changed.

Now let's use the classes property to create a style. Suppose we want to achieve a distinctive look for some of the elements on our page: We might want to put text that's blue, bold, italic, and underlined on an orange background. If we give our style the name newstyle, here's how to do it:

```
classes.newstyle.all.color = "blue";
classes.newstyle.all.fontWeight = "bold";
classes.newstyle.all.fontStyle = "italic"
classes.newstyle.all.textDecoration = "underline"
classes.newstyle.all.backgroundColor = "orange"
```

Skill 5

Insert these lines into the JASS, and you've created the style.

 NOTE For an exceptionally annoying effect, set textDecoration to "blink". This setting makes the text blink on and off. It's even more irritating than a marquee!

How do you apply newstyle? Add a paragraph to the body, and in the <P> tag, insert CLASS = "NEWSTYLE":

```
<P CLASS = "NEWSTYLE">Most of the great Web site analysts are graduates
of our program. </P>
```

This puts all of newstyle's specifications to work, as in Figure 5.20.

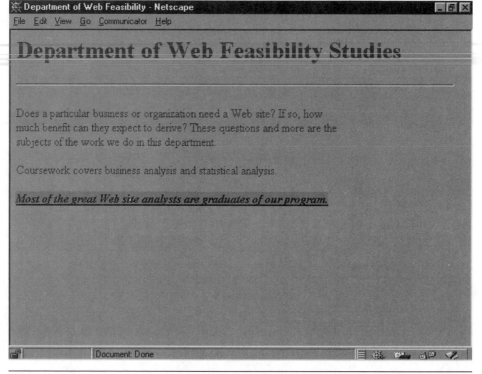

FIGURE 5.20: WebFeasibility.htm with newstyle at work

Suppose you want to use some of `newstyle`'s features, but change others? The IDs property does the trick. It enables you to override aspects of any style you use it with. If you insert these lines into the JASS

```
ids.standout.fontWeight = "normal"
ids.standout.Color = "white"
ids.standout.backgroundColor = "black"
```

you create an ID called `standout`, which specifies normal font, written in white on a black background. To apply standout to `newstyle`, add this paragraph to the page:

```
<P CLASS = "NEWSTYLE" ID = "STANDOUT">Check out our program today!</P>
```

Also, insert `ID = "STANDOUT"` into the `<P>` tag for the first paragraph to see how `standout` combines with that paragraph's styling specifications. The net result, in Navigator, is Figure 5.21. As you can see, `standout` combines with the existing features of each paragraph to produce two different appearances.

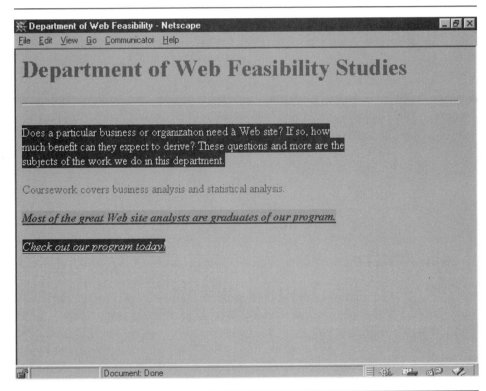

FIGURE 5.21: The Web Feasibility page with `standout` in the HTML document's JASS

Here's the entire `WebFeasibility.htm` file:

 WebFeasibility.htm

```
<HTML>
<HEAD>
<TITLE>Department of Web Feasibility</TITLE>
<STYLE TYPE = "text/javascript">
tags.P.marginRight = 150
tags.BODY.backgroundColor = "silver"
tags.BODY.color = "green"
classes.newstyle.all.color = "blue"
classes.newstyle.all.fontWeight = "bold"
classes.newstyle.all.fontStyle = "italic"
classes.newstyle.all.textDecoration = "underline"
classes.newstyle.all.backgroundColor = "orange"
ids.standout.fontWeight = "normal"
ids.standout.Color = "white"
ids.standout.backgroundColor = "black"
</STYLE>
</HEAD>
<BODY>
<H1>Department of Web Feasibility Studies</H1>
<HR>
<P ID = "Standout">Does a particular business or organization need
a Web site? If so, how much benefit can they expect to derive?
These questions and more are the subjects of the work we do in this
department.</P>
<P>Coursework covers business analysis and statistical analysis. </P>
<P Class = "Newstyle">Most of the great Web site analysts are graduates
of our program.</P>
<P Class = "Newstyle" ID = "Standout">Check out our program today!</P>
</BODY>
</HTML>
```

Summary

As in the rest of the software world, the object-oriented approach plays an integral role in contemporary Web page development. It forms the foundation for the scripting that turns Web pages into interactive applications.

In the Microsoft version of DHTML, HTML elements become objects whose properties and methods you can script. With Microsoft extensions to Cascading Style Sheets, you can dramatically alter the appearance of these objects. In the Netscape version, the LAYER element becomes a scriptable object. Netscape's JavaScript Accessible Style Sheets bring object-oriented syntax to style sheets.

NOTE For more information on JavaScript Accessible Style Sheets and other Netscape technologies, visit the Netscape site at http://developer.netscape.com. Follow the links to Library, and then to Documentation.

Have You Mastered the Essentials?

Now you can...

☑ Understand the object-oriented approach

☑ Use the HTML *OBJECT* element to embed Java applets, ActiveX controls, images, and HTML documents in Web pages

☑ Understand the properties of Netscape's *LAYER* element

☑ Use filters and transition filters to dramatically alter the appearance of objects in Microsoft's DHTML

☑ Work with objects in scripts

☑ Use Netscape's JavaScript Accessible Style Sheets

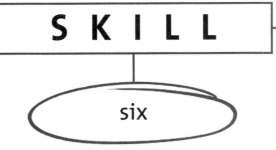

S K I L L

six

Getting into Scripting

- ❑ Overview

- ❑ Linking script files

- ❑ Events in IE

- ❑ Events in Navigator

- ❑ Using event objects

Now that you've learned about HTML, style sheets, and objects, it's time to turn your attention to scripting. Scripts breathe life into Web pages, turning static displays into interactive applications. Dynamic HTML moves scripting into the next dimension, by turning HTML elements into scriptable objects.

We begin with an overview of scripts. We'll touch on linking external script files to your Web pages, and then we'll examine how events work in both IE and Navigator.

Overview

Simply put, a script is a program that you can embed in an HTML document. You can also link a script to an HTML document, as you'll see later in this Skill. Scripts extend HTML capabilities in several ways:

- A script can execute as the document loads, and dynamically modify the document's content.

- A script can respond to events like mouse movements, clicks, and keystrokes.

- You can link a script to a form control (like a button) and create a graphical user interface element.

The *SCRIPT* Element

HTML provides the SCRIPT element, into which you write a script's code. SCRIPT has three attributes:

- Type—an Internet content type for a scripting language

- Language—a scripting language name

- Src—a URL for an externally linked script

Expect to see the Language attribute phase out as Type comes into greater use. For example, instead of

```
Language = "VBScript"
```

you can write

```
Type = "text/VBScript"
```

Linking a Script

You can link a script to an HTML document in much the same way you link a CSS to a document. You can link a script to a number of documents and thus save yourself some effort.

The next exercise will take you through the linking process. You can do this in both Navigator and IE. For this exercise, we'll use IE, since you've already created a document that lends itself to the exercise.

In your Skill 1 folder, use your text editor to open `First Dynamic IE.htm`. Save it to your Skill 6 folder. Cut the contents of the SCRIPT element out of this file and paste it into a new document called `Scriptfile.htm` (which you'll also keep in the Skill 6 folder). `First Dynamic IE.htm` should now look like this:

```
<HTML>
<HEAD>
<STYLE Type = "text/css">
.aquabox {background-color:aqua;
        color:aqua;
        text-align:center;
        width:120;
        height:60}
</STYLE>
<SCRIPT Language = "VBScript">
</SCRIPT>
<TITLE>My First Dynamic HTML Page</TITLE>
</HEAD>
.
.
.
</HTML>
```

In the <SCRIPT> tag, add

```
Src = "E:\DHTML No Exp Req\Skill 6\Scriptfile.htm"
```

Your `Scriptfile.htm` should now look like this:

Scriptfile.htm

```
Sub h1Header_onMouseOver
    h1Header.Style.Color = "Goldenrod"
    divMessage.Style.Visibility = "Visible"
    divReady.Style.Visibility = "Hidden"
    divStarted.Style.Visibility = "Visible"
End Sub

Sub h1Header_onMouseOut
    h1Header.Style.Color = "Black"
    divBox1.Style.Top = 180
    divBox1.Style.Left = 150
    divBox2.Style.Top = 180
    divBox2.Style.Left = 270
    divBox3.Style.Top = 240
    divBox3.Style.Left = 150
    divBox4.Style.Top = 240
    divBox4.Style.Left = 270
    divMessage.Style.Visibility = "Hidden"
    divReady.Style.Visibility = "Visible"
    divStarted.Style.Visibility = "Hidden"
End Sub

Sub h1Header_onClick
    pLearn.Style.Visibility = "Visible"
    Call MoveElementBy(divBox1,-20,-20)
    Call MoveElementBy(divBox2,20,-20)
    Call MoveElementBy(divBox3,-20,20)
    Call MoveElementBy(divBox4,20,20)
End Sub


Sub MoveElementBy(ElementID,LeftMovementAmount,TopMovementAmount)
    pPositionTop = InStr(ElementID.Style.Top,"px")
    pPositionLeft = InStr(ElementID.Style.Left,"px")
    ElementID.Style.Top = _
      CInt(Left(ElementID.Style.Top,pPositionTop-1)) + TopMovementAmount
    ElementID.Style.Left = _
      CInt(Left(ElementID.Style.Left,pPositionLeft-1)) + LeftMovementAmount
End Sub
```

Open the `First Dynamic IE.htm` file in IE, and you should see all the dynamic effects you saw in Skill 1.

Events

When you write a script, you connect it to an event. An event is usually an action initiated by a user, like a mouse-click, a mouse movement, or a keystroke. But an event can also be the opening or closing of a window, the change of a value in an on-screen control, a marquee bouncing off one side of the Web page, or numerous other possibilities.

Events take place all the time. If you connect a script to one, it means that you deem the event important enough for your Web page to react to it in some way by following the steps in your scripts. A script that goes into action as the result of an event is called an *event-handler*. Table 6.1 shows the types of events you can write event-handlers for in IE and Navigator scripts. The browsers are said to *expose* these events. Table 6.2 shows events exposed only in IE and Table 6.3 shows events exposed only in Navigator.

TABLE 6.1: Events Exposed in Both IE and Navigator

Event Name	Happens...
onabort	When the user aborts an image download
onblur	When a control loses focus
onchange	When an element's contents change
onclick	When the user clicks a mouse button
ondblclick	When the user double-clicks an element
onerror	In the event of an error during document loading (or during image loading in Navigator)
onfocus	When an element receives the focus
onkeydown	When the user presses a key
onkeypress	When the user presses a key
onkeyup	When the user releases a key
onload	After a page or element finishes loading
onmousedown	When the user presses a mouse button
onmousemove	When the mouse cursor moves
onmouseover	When the mouse cursor enters an element
onmouseout	When the mouse cursor exits an element
onmouseup	When the user releases a mouse button

Skill 6

TABLE 6.1 CONTINUED: Events Exposed in Both IE and Navigator

Event Name	Happens...
onreset	When the user clicks a reset button on a form
onresize	When the user resizes an object (in Navigator, when the Navigator window or a frame inside it is resized)
onselect	When the current selection in an element changes
onsubmit	When the user clicks a form's Submit button or a form is submitted
onunload	Just before a page unloads

TABLE 6.2: Events Exposed in IE Only

Event	Happens...
onafterupdate	When transfer of data from an element to a data provider is complete
onbeforeunload	Just before a page unloads, allowing databound controls to store their data
onbeforeupdate	Before transfer of changed data to the data provider when an element loses focus or the page unloads
onbounce	When a MARQUEE whose Behavior is set to Alternate reaches an edge of the page
ondataavailable	Periodically during the time data arrives from an asynchronous source
ondatasetchanged	When a dataset changes
ondatasetcomplete	Once all data are available from a data source object
ondragstart	When the user starts to drag an element
onerrorupdate	When an onbeforeupdate event cancels data updating, replacing an onafterupdate event
onfilterchange	When a filter changes state, or when a transition filter is complete
onfilterevent	When a specified transition finishes
onfinish	When a MARQUEE finishes looping
onhelp	When the user presses F1
onreadystatechange	When the readystate for an object changes
onrowenter	When data in the current row changes and new values are available

TABLE 6.2 CONTINUED: Events Exposed in IE Only

Event	Happens...
onrowexit	Before the data source changes data in the current row
onscroll	When the user scrolls a page
onselectstart	When the user starts to select an element's contents
onstart	In a MARQUEE when looping starts, or on a bounce when Alternate has been set as the value of Behavior

TABLE 6.3: Events Exposed in Navigator Only

Event	Happens...
ondragdrop	When the user drops a file or an object onto the browser window
onmove	When the browser window or a frame inside it is moved

Several of the events in Table 6.2 refer to data and data sources. If you're not familiar with some of the terminology in the event descriptions, don't be concerned. We'll discuss data-related Dynamic HTML elements in Skill 10.

The Secret Life of Events: The IE Way

When events occur, a lot happens behind the scenes. In IE, here's what goes on:

1. The user-initiated action or the browser condition associated with the event occurs.

2. A structure called the *event object* updates immediately, recording the event's conditions.

3. The event fires.

4. The event-handler associated with the *source element* is called. The source element is the element on the Web page from which the event was initiated (a command button that the user clicked, for example).

5. The event-handler goes through its scripted paces and returns.

6. A process called *event bubbling* takes place. I'll explain this in a moment.

7. If a final default action is called for, it takes place if an event-handler hasn't canceled it.

The event object and event bubbling are two main points that demand further explanation. The next two subsections tell you about them.

The *event* Object

The event object, new to both versions of Dynamic HTML, gives you a way to capture the parameters of an event as the event occurs. Since it's an object, it has properties, and these properties record the event's parameters. Table 6.4 shows the event object properties for the IE version.

TABLE 6.4: The IE event Object's Properties

Property	What It Provides
altKey	The state of the Alt key when the event occurs
button	The mouse button (if any) pressed to fire the event
cancelBubble	A setting to prevent the current event from bubbling
clientX	The x coordinate of the source element
clientY	The y coordinate of the source element
ctrlKey	The state of the Ctrl key when the event occurs
fromElement	The element from which the mouse cursor exits in an onmouseover or onmouseout event
keyCode	The ASCII code of a pressed key
offsetX	The x coordinate of the mouse cursor when the event occurs, in relation to the element that contains the mouse
offsetY	The y coordinate of the mouse cursor when the event occurs, in relation to the element that contains the mouse
reason	An indication that data transfer to an element was successful, or the reason it failed
returnValue	A specification for a return value for the event or for a dialog window
screenX	The x coordinate of the mouse cursor when the event occurs, in relation to the screen
screenY	The y coordinate of the mouse cursor when the event occurs, in relation to the screen
shiftKey	The state of the Shift key when the event occurs

TABLE 6.4 CONTINUED: The IE event Object's Properties

Property	What It Provides
srcElement	The element at the lowest level of the hierarchy over which the event occurs (related to event bubbling)
srcFilter	The filter that caused an element to produce an onfilterchange event
toElement	The element into which the mouse-cursor enters in an onmouseover or onmouseout event
type	A string that holds the name of the event (without the "on" prefix)
x	The x coordinate of the mouse cursor when the event occurs, in relation to a positioned parent or to the window
y	The y coordinate of the mouse cursor when the event occurs, in relation to a positioned parent or to the window

Event Bubbling

In the event bubbling process, the object associated with an event— i.e., the source element—receives the event first. Then, the event moves up to the source element's parent, then to the parent's parent, and so forth. Each object in the hierarchy has the opportunity to fire an event of the same type. It fires such an event if it has its own event-handler.

Suppose you've put a button on your page, and it's inside a form. In order to position the form, you've put it in a DIV. When you click the button, its onclick event-handler fires the onclick event and the button sends the event to its parent, the form. The form repeats the process: if you've scripted an onclick event for the form, it fires the event and sends it to the DIV. If the DIV, in turn, has an onclick event-handler, it fires the event and sends it to the BODY element, which follows the same process and sends it to the document. If at any point in the hierarchy an object doesn't have an event-handler for the event, it just sends the event on up the chain. This is particularly useful when your page contains a large amount of elements. Event bubbling frees you from having to write a separate event-handler for each element. You just write a document-level event-handler that checks the source of the event and reacts appropriately.

It's possible to stop the bubbling process. As Table 6.4 indicates, the event object has a property called cancelbubble. If you set it to True in any event-handler, the event stops bubbling after that event-handler does its work. You would do this when you want to handle an event at the element level rather than at the document level.

Skill 6

Handling Events

The exercises in this section will acquaint you with events, the event object, and event bubbling. We'll work in VBScript.

The *event* Object

I'll base the exercises on the Web page shown in Figure 6.1. The large text area in the center will display the event object's information. Rather than present the information in a message box that you have to close each time it opens, this page will show you the event's parameters in a continuously changing text area. The header, horizontal line, buttons, text area, and text all have IDs, as does the Web page's body element. The buttons and text box are form controls. The large text area is also a form control, but it's located in a different FORM element from the buttons and text. Create a file in Skill 6 called VBSEventObject.htm and we'll get started.

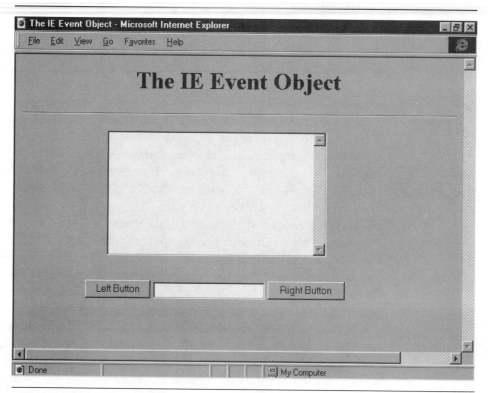

FIGURE 6.1: The IE Event Object Web page

Make the document's title The IE Event Object, set the body's ID to bodyPage, and put in the centered header and the horizontal line. Just for effect, add a silver background. Don't forget to include the ID for each element.

```
<TITLE>The Explorer Event Object</TITLE>
</HEAD>
<BODY ID = bodyPage Style = "background-color:silver">
<H1 ID = h1Header Style = "text-align:center">The IE Event Object</H1>
<HR ID = hrLine>
```

Next, create a DIV to hold the text area and its form.

```
<DIV Style = "position:absolute;top:100;left:130;width:100;height:75">
```

Now create the form and the text area:

```
<FORM ID = frmText>
<TEXTAREA ID = textareaEventInfo Rows = 10 Cols = 35>
</TEXTAREA>
```

and remember to close the form and the DIV:

```
</FORM>
</DIV>
```

Note that TEXTAREA is a separate element—not a value of the INPUT element's Type attribute, as is the case with the button and text controls. Its Rows and Cols attributes specify its size.

Finally, set up the other form and its controls, and wrap the form in a DIV:

```
<DIV ID = divForm Style = "position:absolute;top:300;left:100">
<FORM ID = frmControls>
<INPUT Type = Button Value = "Left Button" ID = btnLeft>
<INPUT Type = Text  ID = txtCenter >
<INPUT Type = Button Value = "Right Button" ID = btnRight>
</FORM>
</DIV>
```

Here's the whole file:

```
<HTML>
<HEAD>

<TITLE>The IE Event Object</TITLE>
</HEAD>
<BODY ID = bodyPage Style = "background-color:silver">
<H1 ID = h1Header Style = "text-align:center">The IE Event Object</H1>
<HR ID = hrLine>
```

Skill 6

```
<DIV Style = "position:absolute;top:100;left:130;width:100;height:75">
<FORM ID = frmText>
<TEXTAREA Name = textareaEventInfo Rows = 10 Cols = 35>
</TEXTAREA>
</FORM>
</DIV>

<DIV ID = divForm Style = "position:absolute;top:300;left:100">
<FORM ID = frmControls>
<INPUT Type = Button Value = "Left Button" ID = btnLeft>
<INPUT Type = Text  ID = txtCenter>
<INPUT Type = Button Value = "Right Button" ID = btnRight>
</FORM>
</DIV>

</BODY>
</HTML>
```

Now you're ready for some scripting. We'll work with the onmousemove event and capture the parameters of the event in the large text area as they occur.

Within the HEAD of this document, insert this code:

```
<SCRIPT LANGUAGE="VBScript">
<!--
Sub document_onmousemove
frmText.textAreaEventInfo.Value = "Source Element: " &
↪window.event.srcelement.id & chr(13) _
    & "OffsetX: " & window.event.offsetx & chr(13) _
    & "OffsetY: " & window.event.offsety & chr(13) _
    & "screenX: " & window.event.screenx & chr(13) _
    & "screenY: " & window.event.screeny & chr(13) _
    & "X: " & window.event.x & chr(13) _
    & "Y: " & window.event.y


End Sub
-->
</SCRIPT>
```

The opening <SCRIPT> tag sets the Language as VBScript and the expression Sub document_onmousemove identifies the beginning of the onmousemove event-handler.

Within the event-handler, we have to refer to the text area's content because that's what the event will modify. It will update that content with the event object's current property values. The text area's Value property is the one we'll update:

```
frmText.textAreaEventInfo.Value
```

Note that we have to specify the form (frmText) in the name of the text area. If we don't, the script won't work.

To update the content, we set frmText.textAreaEventInfo.Value to a string that holds the appropriate property values. To make the text area display look as nice as possible, we'll add a character after each property:

```
frmText.textAreaEventInfo.Value = "Source Element: " &
➥window.event.srcelement.id & chr(13) _
    & "OffsetX: " & window.event.offsetx & chr(13) _
    & "OffsetY: " & window.event.offsety & chr(13) _
    & "screenX: " & window.event.screenx & chr(13) _
    & "screenY: " & window.event.screeny & chr(13) _
    & "X: " & window.event.x & chr(13) _
    & "Y: " & window.event.y
```

We then end the Sub and supply a closing </SCRIPT> tag.

Here's the whole VBSEventObject.htm file:

VBSEventObject.htm

```
<HTML>
<HEAD>
<SCRIPT LANGUAGE="VBScript">
<!--
Sub document_onmousemove
frmText.textAreaEventInfo.Value = "Source Element: " &
➥ window.event.srcelement.id & chr(13) _
    & "OffsetX: " & window.event.offsetx & chr(13) _
    & "OffsetY: " & window.event.offsety & chr(13) _
    & "screenX: " & window.event.screenx & chr(13) _
    & "screenY: " & window.event.screeny & chr(13) _
    & "X: " & window.event.x & chr(13) _
    & "Y: " & window.event.y


End Sub
-->
</SCRIPT>
<TITLE>The IE Event Object</TITLE>
</HEAD>
<BODY ID = bodyPage Style = "background-color:silver">
<H1 ID = h1Header Style = "text-align:center">The IE Event Object</H1>
<HR ID = hrLine>

<DIV Style = "position:absolute;top:100;left:130;width:100;height:75">
<FORM ID = frmText>
<TEXTAREA Name = textareaEventInfo Rows = 10 Cols = 35>
</TEXTAREA>
```

Skill 6

```
</FORM>
</DIV>

<DIV ID = divForm Style = "position:absolute;top:300;left:100">
<FORM ID = frmControls>
<INPUT Type = Button Value = "Left Button" ID = btnLeft>
<INPUT Type = Text  ID = txtCenter>
<INPUT Type = Button Value = "Right Button" ID = btnRight>
</FORM>
</DIV>

</BODY>
</HTML>
```

If you open this file in IE, you'll see a page that looks like Figure 6.2. The text area displays continuous updates of the event object's properties and allows you to watch those updates as they occur. You'll see the source element and all the positioning information change as you move the mouse through the page. This is particularly helpful for tracking an event like onmousemove. You'd never use a display like this on a Web page, but it's a good trick to use when you're developing scripts and you have to know what the events are doing.

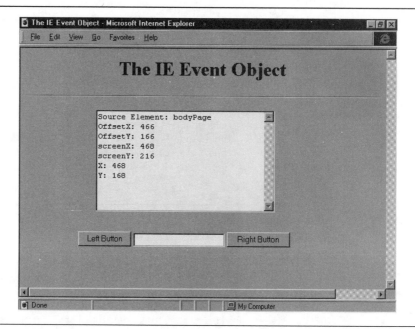

FIGURE 6.2: The IE Event Object page shows continuous updates to the event object as a result of the onmousemove event.

As an exercise, change the event-handler from onmousemove to something else, and substitute the appropriate properties in the text area display. Initiate that event on the page and watch the event's parameters change in the text display. It's a great way to understand how events work and to get to know the properties of the event object.

Event Bubbling

Now let's turn our attention to the process that moves events up the child–parent hierarchy of Web page elements. To study event bubbling, save the VBSObjectEvent.htm file as VBSBubble.htm in Skill 6. Delete the SCRIPT element, change the TITLE to IE Event Bubbling, and change the heading to IE Event Bubbling.

Our objective is to script onclick event-handlers for btnLeft, frmControls, divForm, bodyPage, and the document itself. Each event-handler will make its presence known by appending a message to a string, which we will display in the text area. That way, the string will keep a running record as the event bubbles up through the hierarchy of event-handlers. To make the display more informative, we'll update a counter each time an event-handler fires and include the counter's value in the display.

Each event-handler is simple. The general format is:

```
Sub id_onclick
    glblCount = glblCount + 1
    append("Event " & glblCount & ": " & me.id & " clicked!")

End Sub
```

where id represents an object's identifier, glblCount is the counter, and append is a subroutine that appends the event-handler's message to the string that becomes the value of the text area's Value attribute. Note the VBScript term me, which refers to the current object. It's similar to the JavaScript term this.

The one exception to the general format is the event-handler for the document object (the object that represents the HTML document):

```
Sub document_onclick
    glblCount = glblCount + 1
    append("Event " & glblCount & ": " & me.title & " clicked!")
End Sub
```

Can you see the exception? In the argument to append, this event-handler has me.title instead of me.id. The reason for the change is that the document object doesn't have an `id` property but it does have a `title`. That `title` is Event Bubbling—you set it when you created the page.

The code for `append` is:

```
Sub append(Message)
    frmText.textAreaEventInfo.Value =
    ➥ frmText.textAreaEventInfo.Value & Message & chr(13)
End Sub
```

We add `chr(13)`, the newline character, to display each message on a new row in the display.

To set up the counter, `dim glblCount` should appear in the SCRIPT element before any of the Sub statements. This will make the counter a global variable, available to all the subroutines. To initialize the counter and the text area, we'll write an event-handler for another event—the `onload` event of the `window` object. The `window` object represents the browser. When it opens, the `onload` event fires. Here's the event-handler:

```
Sub window_onload
    glblCount = 0
    frmText.textAreaEventInfo.Value = ""
End Sub
```

The code for `VBSBubble.htm` is:

 VBSBubble.htm

```
<HTML>
<HEAD>
<SCRIPT LANGUAGE="VBScript">
<!--
dim glblCount

Sub window_onload
    glblCount = 0
    frmText.textAreaEventInfo.Value = ""
End Sub

Sub divForm_onclick
    glblCount = glblCount + 1
    append("Event " & glblCount & ": " & me.id & " clicked!")
End Sub

Sub frmControls_onclick
    glblCount = glblCount + 1
    append("Event " & glblCount & ": " & me.id & " clicked!")
End Sub
```

```
Sub btnLeft_onclick
    glblCount = glblCount + 1
    append("Event " & glblCount & ": " & me.id & " clicked!")
    'window.event.cancelbubble = True
End Sub

Sub document_onclick
    glblCount = glblCount + 1
    append("Event " & glblCount & ": " & me.title & " clicked!")
End Sub

Sub bodyPage_onclick
    glblCount = glblCount + 1
    append("Event " & glblCount & ": " & me.id & " clicked!")
End Sub

Sub append(Message)
    frmText.textAreaEventInfo.Value =
    ➥frmText.textAreaEventInfo.Value & Message & chr(13)
End Sub
-->
</SCRIPT>
<TITLE>Event Bubbling</TITLE>
</HEAD>
<BODY ID = bodyPage Style = "background-color:silver">
<H1 ID = h1Header Style = "text-align:center">Event Bubbling</H1>
<HR ID = hrLine>

<DIV Style = "position:absolute;top:100;left:130;width:100;height:75">
<FORM ID = frmText>
<TEXTAREA Name = textareaEventInfo Rows = 10 Cols = 35>
</TEXTAREA>
</FORM>
</DIV>

<DIV ID = divForm Style = "position:absolute;top:300;left:100">
<FORM ID = frmControls>
<INPUT Type = Button Value = "Left Button" ID = btnLeft>
<INPUT Type = Text  ID = txtCenter>
<INPUT Type = Button Value = "Right Button" ID = btnRight>
</FORM>
</DIV>

</BODY>
</HTML>
```

The event-handlers are in no particular order. I did this to show you that they'll fire in the proper order regardless of where they appear in the document.

Open this file in IE, and click the Left button. The page will look like Figure 6.3.

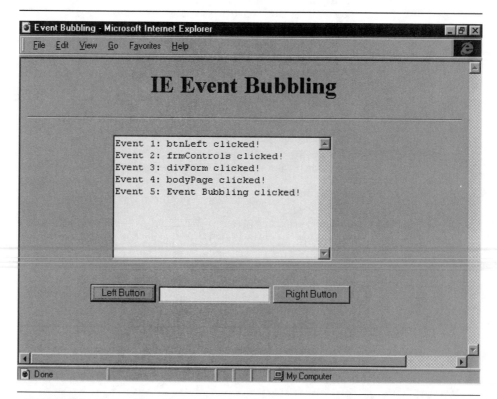

FIGURE 6.3: The display in VBSBubble.htm after you click the Left button

Let's take a closer look at the contents of the display:

```
Event 1: btnLeft clicked!
Event 2: frmControls clicked!
Event 3: divForm clicked!
Event 4: bodyPage clicked!
Event 5: Event Bubbling clicked!
```

The display shows that when the onclick event occurs with the cursor on the Left button, that button's event-handler is the first to fire. The button's form has an event-handler, and that one fires next. Then the event-handler for the form's DIV fires, followed by the BODY element's event-handler. Finally, the document object's event-handler fires, indicated by the document's title Event Bubbling.

If you refresh the page and click the Right button, the display shows

```
Event 1: frmControls clicked!
Event 2: divForm clicked!
Event 3: bodyPage clicked!
Event 4: Event Bubbling clicked!
```

Since the Right button does not have an event-handler, it passes the event along to frmControls, which, of course, does have an event-handler. The display shows the progress of the event bubbling.

If you want to keep experimenting, press F5 to refresh the page. The window's onload event resets glblCount to zero and blanks out the text area. Try and predict what the display will show when you click the page in areas other than the Left button or the Right button.

Bursting the Bubble

The event object allows you to stop the bubbling process. If you set its cancelbubble property to True, you'll stop the bubbling dead in its tracks. We can use our Event Bubbling page to illustrate this.

In VBSBubble.htm, find the event-handler for btnLeft. Insert this line into the event-handler:

```
window.event.cancelbubble = True
```

so that the event-handler is now

```
Sub btnLeft_onclick
    glblCount = glblCount + 1
    append("Event " & glblCount & ": " & me.id & " clicked!")
    window.event.cancelbubble = True
End Sub
```

Now when you open the document in IE and click the Left button, all you'll see in the text area is

```
Event 1: btnLeft clicked!
```

The Secret Life of Events: The Navigator Way

An event in Navigator kicks off a number of behind-the-scenes steps that are similar to those in IE. Unlike IE, however, Navigator events follow a process called *event capturing* rather than event bubbling.

Event Capturing

Event capturing proceeds in the reverse order from event bubbling. Events don't bubble up from the source element at the bottom of the hierarchy. Instead, events in Navigator originate at the top of the hierarchy and work their way down.

The window object, which represents the browser, is the first to see the event. The document object, which represents the Web page, sees it next, and so forth. The event's target element is the last to process the event before it falls off the bottom of the hierarchy and gets handled by a default event-handler (if one has been written).

The Navigator *event* Object

Just as IE has an event object that updates with each event, Navigator has one too. Table 6.5 presents its properties.

TABLE 6.5: The Navigator event Object's Properties

Property	What It Is
data	An array of strings that show the URLs of objects dropped onto the browser window
layerX	Horizontal location of the mouse cursor relative to the layer it's in
layerY	Vertical location of the mouse cursor relative to the layer it's in
modifiers	A number that indicates the modifier key or key combination pressed during a keypress event (Alt = 1, Ctrl = 2, Shift = 4; sums of these values represent combinations)
pageX	Horizontal location of the mouse cursor relative to the document window
pageY	Vertical location of the mouse cursor relative to the document window
screenX	Horizontal location of the mouse cursor on the screen when the event occurs
screenY	Vertical location of the mouse cursor on the screen when the event occurs
target	The name of the element to which the event was sent
type	A string that holds the type of event
which	ASCII code of a pressed key, or a value that indicates which mouse button was clicked

Handling Events

We'll do some exercises to acquaint you with the Navigator event object and event capturing.

Working with the *event* Object

In this exercise, we'll extract information about events and display it in a multi-line text area as we did previously. To start, create a file called NavEventObject .htm. We'll develop a page for Navigator that resembles the ones you created for the preceding exercises in IE (see Figure 6.4).

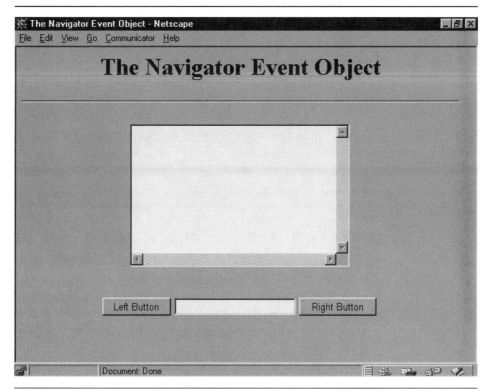

FIGURE 6.4: NavEventObject.htm opened in Navigator

Here's the code that sets up the page:

```
<HTML>
<HEAD>
<TITLE>The Navigator Event Object</TITLE>
</HEAD>
<BODY Style = "background-color:silver">
<H1 Style = "text-align:center">The Navigator Event Object</H1>
<HR>

<FORM name = frmText>
<CENTER>
<TEXTAREA name = textareaEventInfo Rows = 10 Cols = 35 Tabindex = 4>
</TEXTAREA>
</CENTER>
<BR><BR>
<CENTER>
<INPUT Type = Button Value = "Left Button" name = btnLeft tabindex = 1>
<INPUT Type = Text   name = txtCenter tabindex =2>
<INPUT Type = Button Value = "Right Button" name = btnRight tabindex = 3>
</HTML>
```

Note that we use the Name attribute to assign names to each control.

Now we'll add the opening tag of the SCRIPT element, along with some other important expressions that enable event capturing:

```
<SCRIPT Language = JavaScript1.2>
document.captureEvents(Event.MOUSEMOVE);
document.captureEvents(Event.MOUSEDOWN);
document.captureEvents(Event.KEYDOWN);
document.captureEvents(Event.KEYUP);
```

The Language attribute specifies the latest version of JavaScript. The next four statements are methods of the document object—the object that, in your script, represents the Web page. This object's captureEvents method works with the Navigator event object (analogous to the way your washing machine's clean method works with clothes). It allows the document to process the type of event indicated by uppercase letters in the argument. In addition to the uppercase letters, notice that the event names don't have the on prefix (it's an important wrinkle that you have to be aware of).

Next, we add the function that's similar to one we used before in the file VBSEventObject.htm. It adds the event's parameter information to the text area:

```
function info(e){
textArea = document.forms[0].elements["textareaEventInfo"];
```

```
textArea.value = "target: " + e.target.name + "\n"
    + "which: " + e.which + "\n"
    + "modifiers: " + e.modifiers + "\n"
    + "type: " + e.type + "\n"
    + "screenX: " + e.screenX + "\n"
    + "screenY: " + e.screenY + "\n"
    + "pageX: " + e.pageX + "\n"
    + "pageY: " + e.pageY;
}
```

The argument, which we have named e, is just a way of setting a reference to the event object. We could have called this argument anything we wanted.

The second line of the function is a bit more interesting. It sets a variable called textArea to the TEXTAREA element in our form. The expression

```
document.forms[0].elements["textareaEventInfo"]
```

is the Navigator way of referring to the TEXTAREA. Remember that the TEXTAREA element is in a form. The document has an array of forms—a collection with only one member in this case. The form, in turn, has an array of elements. The bracketed index [0] for the forms array indicates that we're referring to the first form (again, our only form on this page). The bracketed index ["textareaEventInfo"] for the elements array indicates the particular form element we want.

 NOTE   The expression that references the text area comes from the Navigator document object model. We'll discuss this model, along with the IE document object model, in Part 3.

The next expression, which extends over several lines, builds the string that holds the event information and assigns that information to the value property of the textArea variable. A couple of aspects of this expression are noteworthy:

- The JavaScript newline character is \n, and we have to surround it with double quotes

- Unlike VBS, JavaScript requires no line continuation character

By the way, we didn't have to define a new variable and set its value to the string. We could have done without the variable and assigned the string to

```
document.forms[0].elements["textareaEventInfo"].value
```

The variable just makes the code look nicer.

We close out the SCRIPT element by connecting the four types of captured events to the `info` function:

```
document.onmousemove = info;
document.onmousedown = info;
document.onkeydown = info;
document.onkeyup = info;
```

Your `NavEventObject.htm` file now looks like this:

 NavEventObject.htm

```
<HTML>
<HEAD>
<SCRIPT Language = JavaScript1.2>
document.captureEvents(Event.MOUSEMOVE);
document.captureEvents(Event.MOUSEDOWN);
document.captureEvents(Event.KEYDOWN);
document.captureEvents(Event.KEYUP);

function info(e){
textArea = document.forms[0].elements["textareaEventInfo"];
textArea.value = "target: " + e.target.name + "\n"
    + "which: " + e.which + "\n"
    + "modifiers: " + e.modifiers + "\n"
    + "type: " + e.type + "\n"
    + "screenX: " + e.screenX + "\n"
    + "screenY: " + e.screenY + "\n"
    + "pageX: " + e.pageX + "\n"
    + "pageY: " + e.pageY;
}

document.onmousemove = info;
document.onmousedown = info;
document.onkeydown = info;
document.onkeyup = info;


</SCRIPT>

<TITLE>The Navigator Event Object</TITLE>
</HEAD>
<BODY Style = "background-color:silver">

<H1 Style = "text-align:center">The Navigator Event Object</H1>
<HR>

<FORM name = frmText>
<CENTER>
```

```
<TEXTAREA name = textareaEventInfo Rows = 10 Cols = 35 Tabindex = 4>
</TEXTAREA>
</CENTER>
<BR><BR>
<CENTER>
<INPUT Type = Button Value = "Left Button" name = btnLeft tabindex = 1>
<INPUT Type = Text  name = txtCenter tabindex =2>
<INPUT Type = Button Value = "Right Button" name = btnRight tabindex = 3>
</CENTER>
</FORM>
</BODY>
</HTML>
```

Open it in Navigator and you'll have a display that enables you to continuously track mouse movements and mouse events as you move and click the mouse throughout the page. Figure 6.5 shows you this page with some information in the text area.

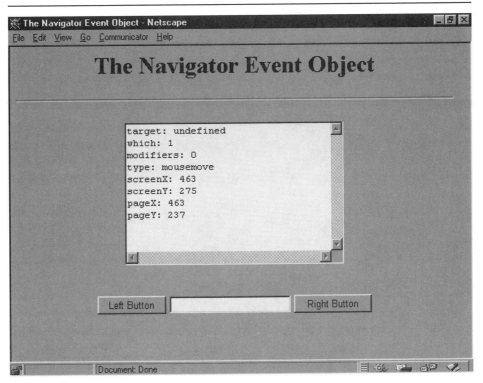

FIGURE 6.5: The completed Navigator Event Object page

Here's a typical display for the onmousemove event:

```
target: undefined
which: 1
modifiers: 0
type: mousemove
screenX: 348
screenY: 354
pageX: 348
pageY: 316
```

The undefined value for the target shows that the cursor is in the document, and not on any named control. If you move the cursor into a control, like the Left button, the display becomes:

```
target: textareaEventInfo
which: 1
modifiers: 0
type: mousemove
screenX: 162
screenY: 305
pageX: 162
pageY: 267
```

You can also track keyboard events. Here's what happens when you press Shift+G on your keyboard:

```
target: undefined
which: 71
modifiers: 4
type: keydown
screenX: 369
screenY: 361
pageX: 369
pageY: 323
```

I'll leave it to you to experiment further.

Scripting the Controls

Now let's add scripts for the form controls. We'll create simple event-handlers that connect the controls with our info function. Let's start with the TEXTAREA. We might be interested in what happens when the TEXTAREA element gets the focus and what happens when it loses the focus. To capture the relevant information, we script event-handlers for onfocus and onblur. In the TEXTAREA element, add

```
onfocus = "info(event)";
onblur = "info(event)"
```

Let's also add these event-handlers to the Text input control.

Now let's turn our attention to the buttons. Add an event-handler for onmousedown to the Left button:

```
onmousedown = "info(event)"
```

and an event-handler for onclick to the Right button:

```
onclick = "info(event)"
```

Here's how your form should now look:

```
<FORM name = frmText>
<CENTER>
<TEXTAREA name = textareaEventInfo Rows = 10 Cols = 35 Tabindex = 4
onfocus = "info(event)";
onblur = "info(event)">
</TEXTAREA>
</CENTER>
<BR><BR>
<CENTER>
<INPUT Type = Button Value = "Left Button" name = btnLeft tabindex = 1
onmousedown = "info(event)">
<INPUT Type = Text  name = txtCenter tabindex = 2
onfocus = "info(event)";
onblur = "info(event)">
<INPUT Type = Button Value = "Right Button" name = btnRight tabindex = 3
onclick = "info(event)">
</CENTER>
</FORM>
```

If you open this file in Navigator and start clicking and tabbing, you'll make all kinds of discoveries. For example, you'll find that the onclick event doesn't reveal positional information when you click the Right button, although onmousedown does when you click the Left button. If you connect onclick to the info function at the document level (by adding document.onclick = info to the SCRIPT element), you'll find that onclick does provide positional information in that context.

Other discoveries await you. If you give the focus to the text area and then click the Left button, the Left button's `onmousedown` event-handler doesn't fire. Instead, the text area's `onblur` event fires because the text area lost the focus when you clicked the Left button. An additional click is necessary for the `onmousedown` event to fire. On the other hand, clicking the Right button with the focus on the text area transfers the focus to the Right button and executes the Right button's `onclick` event.

Event Capturing

As I mentioned earlier, the Navigator event capturing process is the opposite of IE's event bubbling. Target elements see an event last, rather than first, as in the IE world.

This exercise will acquaint you with event capturing. Save your `NavEventObject`.htm file as `NavCapture.htm` in Skill 6. Then make the necessary changes and deletions to produce this code:

```
<HTML>
<HEAD>
<TITLE>Navigator Event Capturing</TITLE>
</HEAD>
<BODY ID Style = "background-color:silver">
<H1 Style = "text-align:center">Navigator Event Capturing</H1>
<HR>
<FORM name = frmText>
<CENTER>
<TEXTAREA name = textareaEventInfo Rows = 10 Cols = 35>
</TEXTAREA>
</CENTER>
<BR><BR>
<CENTER>
<INPUT Type = Button Value = "Window Capture" name = btnLeft>
<INPUT Type = Button Value = "Document Capture" name = btnCenter>
<INPUT Type = Button Value = "Right Button" name = btnRight>
</CENTER>
</FORM>
</BODY>
</HTML>
```

This gives you the `Navigator Event Capturing` page shown in Figure 6.6.

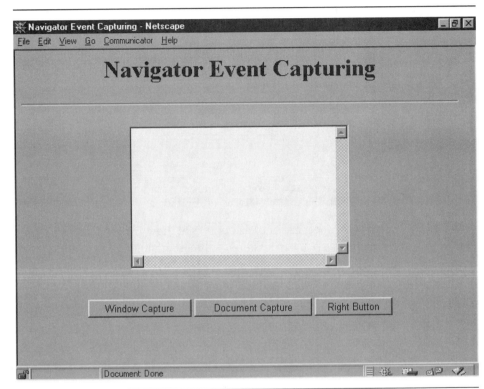

FIGURE 6.6: The Navigator Event Capturing page

We've replaced the text control between the two buttons with a third button, labeled Document Capture. We've also relabeled the Left button as Window Capture.

Our objective is to write some JavaScript that causes a mousedown on the Window Capture button to enable event capturing by the window object. (In your code, the window object represents the browser.) The mousedown also turns the Window Capture button into a Window Release button. A subsequent mousedown on this button causes the window object to release an event and change the label back to Window Capture. Releasing an event means that the processing of this event no longer takes place at the window level. The leftmost button, then, is a toggle between event capturing and event release.

The Document Capture button will work the same way, but at the document level. The Right button, as before, will have an event-handler for the `onclick` event. Our buttons for event capturing and event releasing will capture and release the `onclick` event. As in our previous exercises, the large text area will display the results and illuminate what's taking place.

Begin scripting by inserting the opening tag for the SCRIPT element with the Language attribute set appropriately:

```
<SCRIPT Language = JavaScript1.2>
```

Next, add these two expressions:

```
window.onclick = windowAppend;
document.onclick = documentAppend;
```

which connect the `onclick` events at the window and document levels to specific functions. Each expression produces a string that gets appended to the text area.

```
Now add the functions:function windowAppend() {
append("window");
}

function documentAppend() {
append("document");
}
```

Add another for the button level:

```
function buttonAppend() {
append("button");
}
```

The three functions you just added tell you that you'll need an append function, and here it is:

```
function append(strElementName){
textArea = document.forms[0].elements["textareaEventInfo"];
textArea.value = textArea.value + strElementName + " clicked!" + "\n"
          + "_____" + "\n";
}
```

This function adds messages to the text area. The messages indicate which level processed the `onclick` event. The function also adds a newline character, a dotted line (to make the text area display look a little nicer), and another newline character.

Let's move on to the code for the buttons that toggle between event capturing and event release. In order to toggle back and forth, each function uses a `switch` statement. A `switch` statement provides a way to do branching. Here's the code for the Window Capture button:

```
function winCaptureRelease(formButton) {
switch (formButton.value) {
    case "Window Capture" :
        formButton.value = "Window Release";
        window.captureEvents(Event.CLICK);
        break;
    case "Window Release" :
        formButton.value = "Window Capture";
        window.releaseEvents(Event.CLICK);
        break;
    default :
        alert("You should never see this");
    }
}
```

The general format of a `switch` statement is

```
switch (test expression) {
    case label :
        statement;
        statement;
        break;
    case label :
        statement;
        statement;
        break;
    case label :
        statement;
        statement;
        break;
    case label :
            .
            .
            .

    default :
        statement;
    }
```

If the test expression's value matches one of the labels, the statements beneath that label execute. If not, the statements below the default execute. It's a good idea to include the break statement in each branch. If you don't, you can get unpredictable results: Branches below the matching branch might execute their statements, even though their labels don't match the value of the test expression. Here's the code for the Document Capture button:

```
function docCaptureRelease(formButton) {
switch (formButton.value) {
    case "Document Capture" :
            formButton.value = "Document Release";
            document.captureEvents(Event.CLICK);
            break;
    case "Document Release" :
            formButton.value = "Document Capture";
            document.releaseEvents(Event.CLICK);
            break;
    default :
            alert("You should never see this");
    }
}
```

In both functions, if the Capture state is the active one, a mousedown on the button invokes the captureEvents method you saw in the previous Navigator-related events exercise. This time, the event in the argument is CLICK. If the Release state is active, a mousedown invokes the releaseEvents method which, as you might guess, releases the processing of events from a specified level.

You're almost finished. You still have to attach event-handlers to the three buttons. To the left-most button's HTML code, add

```
onmousedown = "winCaptureRelease(this)
```

To the center button's HTML add

```
onmousedown = "docCaptureRelease(this)"
```

 NOTE   Why specify an event-handler for onmousedown, and not onclick, for these two buttons? Think about it: If you specify onclick, and then click the left button to capture the onclick event at the window level, you can never click the left button to release the event. The window will capture the click you intended for the button!

To the Right button, add

```
onclick = "buttonAppend()"
```

The whole file should now look like this:

NavCapture.htm

```
<HTML>
<HEAD>
<SCRIPT Language = JavaScript1.2>

window.onclick = windowAppend;
document.onclick = documentAppend;


function windowAppend() {
append("window");
}

function documentAppend() {
append("document");
}

function buttonAppend() {
append("button");
}

function append(strElementName){
textArea = document.forms[0].elements["textareaEventInfo"];
textArea.value = textArea.value + strElementName + " clicked!" + "\n"
        + "_____" + "\n";
}

function winCaptureRelease(formButton) {
switch (formButton.value) {
    case "Window Capture" :
        formButton.value = "Window Release";
        window.captureEvents(Event.CLICK);
        break;
    case "Window Release" :
        formButton.value = "Window Capture";
        window.releaseEvents(Event.CLICK);
        break;
    default :
        alert("You should never see this");
    }
}
```

Skill 6

```
function docCaptureRelease(formButton) {
switch (formButton.value) {
    case "Document Capture" :
            formButton.value = "Document Release";
            document.captureEvents(Event.CLICK);
            break;
    case "Document Release" :
            formButton.value = "Document Capture";
            document.releaseEvents(Event.CLICK);
            break;
    default :
            alert("You should never see this");
    }
}

</SCRIPT>

<TITLE>Navigator Event Capturing</TITLE>
</HEAD>
<BODY Style = "background-color:silver">

<H1 Style = "text-align:center">Navigator Event Bubbling</H1>
<HR>

<FORM name = frmText>
<CENTER>
<TEXTAREA name = textareaEventInfo Rows = 10 Cols = 35 Tabindex = 4>
</TEXTAREA>
</CENTER>
<BR><BR>
<CENTER>
<INPUT Type = Button Value = "Window Capture" name = btnLeft
onmousedown = "winCaptureRelease(this)">
<INPUT Type = Button Value = "Document Capture"  name = btnCenter
onmousedown = "docCaptureRelease(this)">
<INPUT Type = Button Value = "Right Button" name = btnRight onclick =
"buttonAppend()";>
</CENTER>
</FORM>
</BODY>

</HTML>
```

Open the page in Navigator and click the Right button. Since event capturing hasn't been activated yet, the text area should say button clicked! Now move your mouse to the Window Capture button and click (actually, you're generating an onmousedown event). The button should change to Window Release and put a window clicked! message in the text area. Now when you click the Right button, you'll add another `window clicked!` message to the text area. Figure 6.7 shows this page after these actions.

Experiment with this page. Toggle back and forth between event capturing and releasing for both the window and the document levels, and see what the different combinations yield when you click the Right button.

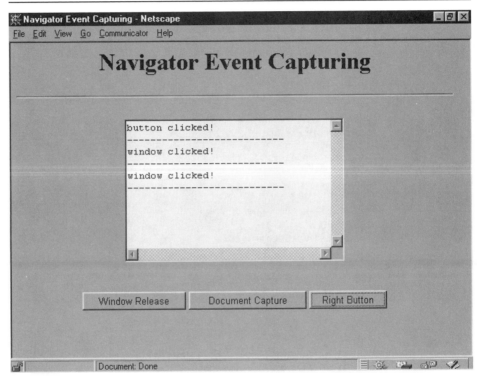

FIGURE 6.7: The `Navigator Event Capturing` page after clicking the Right button, generating an onmousedown event on the Window Capture button, and clicking the Right button again

Routing Events

One more scripting exercise will complete our look at events in the Netscape world. We've seen how a window and a document can capture events and release them. In Netscape's event capturing process, the window and the document can also route an event down to the next level in the hierarchy. They do this via the `routeEvent` method.

To see this happen, reopen your NavCapture.htm file. You're going to add a call to routeEvent in windowAppend and another in documentAppend. This method requires a reference to the event as its argument, so we'll have to add this reference as the argument to the two functions. Change the first line of windowAppend to

```
windowAppend(event)
```

and the first line of documentAppend to

```
documentAppend(event)
```

In windowAppend, add

```
window.routeEvent(event)
```

and in documentAppend, add

```
document.routeEvent(event)
```

The two functions should now look like this:

```
function windowAppend(event) {
append("window");
window.routeEvent(event);
}

function documentAppend(event) {
append("document");
document.routeEvent(event);
}
```

Just as before, it wasn't necessary to use event as the name of the argument. We could have used any term we wanted.

Save the changes and open the page in Navigator. Initiate a mousedown (notice I didn't say "click," although that's what you'll do) on the Window Capture button and on the Document Capture button. Messages appear in the text area, notifying you about these events. Move your mouse into the text area, drag and select those messages, and delete them.

Since those buttons ultimately connect to the two functions you just modified, you've activated event capturing and event routing by the window and by the document. This causes a click event on the Right button to be captured by the window, routed to the document, captured by the document, routed to the button, and processed by the button. Now, when you click the Right button, here's what you'll see in the text area:

```
window clicked!
_____
document clicked!
_____
button clicked!
_____
```

 NOTE We could have inserted another level in the hierarchy by embedding the FORM and its controls in a LAYER element.

Summary

Scripting is the third major component of Dynamic HTML. An exceptionally powerful tool, it enables you to make your pages interactive by creating responses to events. The two major scripting languages, VBScript and JavaScript (and Microsoft's version, JScript) offer numerous possibilities for your arsenal. Understanding how events work in IE and in Navigator will help you make maximum use of the potential that scripting provides.

You've come to the end of Part I. You've seen Dynamic HTML at work, and you've built a solid foundation in the fundamentals.

It's time to build on that foundation....

Have You Mastered the Essentials?

Now you can...

- ☑ **Link scripts from external files to your Web page**
- ☑ **Work with *event* objects and event-handlers in IE and Navigator**
- ☑ **Understand how event bubbling works in IE**
- ☑ **Understand how event capturing works in Navigator**
- ☑ **Use the JavaScript 1.2 *switch* statement**

PART II

Getting Dynamic

Now that you have a grasp of the foundations of Dynamic HTML, it's time to put the pieces together. In Part II, you'll apply your knowledge to creating animations, enhancing your pages with multimedia, incorporating drag-and-drop capabilities, building data-aware Web pages, and changing content on a downloaded page.

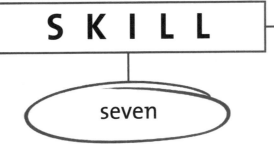

SKILL

seven

Adding Animation

- ❑ Animating your first DHTML pages
- ❑ Using time intervals
- ❑ Animation in IE and Navigator
- ❑ Randomizing object movements
- ❑ Using the z-index in animation effects
- ❑ Using visual filters with animation

Animation is one of the most eye-catching effects you can build into a Web page. Dynamic HTML is well suited to animation, as it enables you to write scripts that alter the size and position of objects. The animation effect occurs when your script resizes and repositions the objects in short, regular intervals of time. In this Skill, you'll learn how to do this in both browsers. You'll begin with IE, and then produce the same effects in Navigator.

Revisiting Your First Page

To get started, go back to your Skill 1 folder and open First Dynamic IE.htm. Save it as Animated Dynamic IE.htm in Skill 7, and change the title to My First Animated DHTML Page. With the change, the code for this file is

```
<HTML>
<HEAD>
<STYLE Type = "text/css">
.bluebox {background-color:blue;
     color:blue;
     text-align:center;
     width:120;
     height:60}
</STYLE>

<SCRIPT Language = "VBScript">

Sub h1Header_onMouseOver
    h1Header.Style.Color = "Goldenrod"
    divMessage.Style.Visibility = "Visible"
    divReady.Style.Visibility = "Hidden"
    divStarted.Style.Visibility = "Visible"
End Sub

Sub h1Header_onMouseOut
    h1Header.Style.Color = "Black"
    divBox1.Style.Top = 180
    divBox1.Style.Left = 150
    divBox2.Style.Top = 180
    divBox2.Style.Left = 270
    divBox3.Style.Top = 240
    divBox3.Style.Left = 150
    divBox4.Style.Top = 240
```

```
        divBox4.Style.Left = 270
        divMessage.Style.Visibility = "Hidden"
        divReady.Style.Visibility = "Visible"
        divStarted.Style.Visibility = "Hidden"
End Sub

Sub h1Header_onclick
        pLearn.Style.Visibility = "Visible"
        Call MoveElementBy(divBox1,-20,-20)
        Call MoveElementBy(divBox2,20,-20)
        Call MoveElementBy(divBox3,-20,20)
        Call MoveElementBy(divBox4,20,20)
End Sub


Sub MoveElementBy(ElementID,LeftMovementAmount,TopMovementAmount)
        pPositionTop = InStr(ElementID.Style.Top,"px")
        pPositionLeft = InStr(ElementID.Style.Left,"px")
        ElementID.Style.Top = _
          CInt(Left(ElementID.Style.Top,pPositionTop-1)) +
          ➥ TopMovementAmount
        ElementID.Style.Left = _
          CInt(Left(ElementID.Style.Left,pPositionLeft-1)) +
          ➥ LeftMovementAmount
End Sub

</SCRIPT>
<TITLE>My First Animated DHTML Page</TITLE>
</HEAD>
<BODY Style = "background-color:'Silver'">
<DIV Style = "Position:Absolute;Left:10;Top:0:Width:100%">
<H1 ID = h1Header Style = "text-align:center">Dynamic HTML: MTE</H1>
<HR>
</DIV>
<DIV ID = divMessage Style = "Position:Absolute;Left:5%;Top:10%;
Visibility:Hidden;z-index:-1;font-style:normal;font-weight:bold;
font-family:Normal;font-size:50;color:'White'">
<P> Topics in this book include
<UL>
<LI> Scripting
<LI> Cascading Style Sheets
<LI> Animation
<LI> ... And Many More!
</UL>
</P>
</DIV>
```

Skill 7

```
<DIV ID = divLearn Style="Position:Absolute;Left:180;Top:200;Width:210;
z-index:0;">
<P ID = pLearn Style = "font-family:cursive;font-size:15pt;
font-weight:bold">
Learn how to create striking effects on your Web pages.
</P>
</DIV>

<DIV ID = divBox1 Class = "bluebox"
Style="Position:Absolute;Left:150;Top:180;z-index:1">
</DIV>

<DIV ID = divBox2 Class = "bluebox"
Style="Position:Absolute;Left:270;Top:180;z-index:1">
</DIV>

<DIV ID = divBox3 Class = "bluebox"
Style="Position:Absolute;Left:150;Top:240;z-index:1">
</DIV>

<DIV ID = divBox4 Class = "bluebox"
STYLE="Position:Absolute;Left:270;Top:240;z-index:1">
</DIV>

<DIV ID = divReady Style =
"Position:Absolute;Top:70%;Left:80%;Width:10%;
z-index:1;Visibility:Visible">
<P Style = "text-align:center;font-family:cursive;Background-
Color:'Beige';Color:Chocolate">
Are<BR>You<BR>Ready?</P>
</DIV>

<DIV ID = divStarted Style =
"Position:Absolute;Top:70%;Left:80%;Width:10%;
z-index:0;Visibility:Hidden">
<P Style = "text-align:center;font-family:cursive;Background-
Color:'BlanchedAlmond';Color:Blue">
Let's<BR>Get<BR>Started</P>
</DIV>

</BODY>
</HTML>
```

When you first worked with this page in Skill 1, you probably noticed something that looked vaguely like animation each time you clicked the heading and the central boxes moved outward. The movement resulted from this code:

```
Sub h1Header_onclick
     pLearn.Style.Visibility = "Visible"
     Call MoveElementBy(divBox1,-20,-20)
     Call MoveElementBy(divBox2,20,-20)
     Call MoveElementBy(divBox3,-20,20)
     Call MoveElementBy(divBox4,20,20)
End Sub


Sub MoveElementBy(ElementID,LeftMovementAmount,TopMovementAmount)
     pPositionTop = InStr(ElementID.Style.Top,"px")
     pPositionLeft = InStr(ElementID.Style.Left,"px")
     ElementID.Style.Top = _
        CInt(Left(ElementID.Style.Top,pPositionTop-1)) +
TopMovementAmount
     ElementID.Style.Left = _
        CInt(Left(ElementID.Style.Left,pPositionLeft-1)) +
LeftMovementAmount
End Sub
```

To make this a true animation effect, we'll initiate what appears to be continuous movement after one click on the heading. We'll reset the boxes to their starting positions by moving the mouse out of the header, as we did in Skill 1.

A Matter of Timing

The window object—the object in your script that represents the browser—has methods for timing. You invoke a timing method, and you clear it when you're finished using it.

One method, setTimeout, is useful if you want to fire an event after a specified amount of time. It has a drawback, however: You have to reset this method whenever you use it. For animation, which requires repeated event firing, this can be inconvenient. Instead, we'll use setInterval, which fires whenever a specified time interval passes. To clear setInterval, you use another method, clearInterval.

To invoke the setInterval method, you set a variable equal to it, in this format:

```
variableName = window.setInterval("functionName", interval)
```

Skill 7

This tells `setInterval` to begin `"functionName"` after the number of milliseconds specified in `interval`.

We'll give our variable a global scope, so we can use it throughout the script. The statement

```
dim glblTimer
```

will be the first item in our code.

We need one more global variable, a flag that lets the script know that the animation has started:

```
dim glblAnimationStartedFlag
```

Initialize the variable:

```
glblAnimationStartedFlag = 0
```

In the script, we'll set this flag to 1 when we start the animation, and to 0 when we stop it. As you'll see, this will prevent unexpected results if you click the header while the animation is taking place.

The trick is to relocate the movement-related code from h1Header's `onclick` event into a new function which the `setInterval` method activates. Let's call our new function boxMovement. Cutting and pasting the relevant code from Sub h1Header_onclick gives us

```
Sub boxMovement
    Call MoveElementBy(divBox1,-20,-20)
    Call MoveElementBy(divBox2,20,-20)
    Call MoveElementBy(divBox3,-20,20)
    Call MoveElementBy(divBox4,20,20)
End Sub
```

Since we want to start this movement by clicking the header, we invoke `setInterval` from Sub h1Header_onclick:

```
Sub h1Header_onclick
    glblTimer = window.setInterval("boxMovement", 100)
End Sub
```

To prevent an `onclick` event from having any effect during the animation, we'll add a statement that examines `glblAnimationStartedFlag` and another that sets the flag. After these additions, the subroutine is:

```
Sub h1Header_onclick
    if glblAnimationStartedFlag = 0 Then
        glblTimer = window.setInterval("boxMovement", 100)
```

```
                 glblAnimationStartedFlag =1
         end if
End Sub
```

When you click the header, if the `glblAnimationStartedFlag` = 0, then the `setInterval` method will call the **boxMovement** procedure every 100 milliseconds. To turn the timer off and reset the `glblAnimationStartedFlag`, add the lines

```
clearInterval(glblTimer)
glblAnimationStartedFlag = 0
```

at the end of `Sub h1Header_onMouseOut`:

```
Sub h1Header_onMouseOut
    h1Header.Style.Color = "Black"
    divBox1.Style.Top = 180
    divBox1.Style.Left = 150
    divBox2.Style.Top = 180
    divBox2.Style.Left = 270
    divBox3.Style.Top = 240
    divBox3.Style.Left = 150
    divBox4.Style.Top = 240
    divBox4.Style.Left = 270
    divMessage.Style.Visibility = "Hidden"
    divReady.Style.Visibility = "Visible"
    divStarted.Style.Visibility = "Hidden"
    window.clearInterval(glblTimer)
      glblAnimationStartedFlag = 0
End Sub
```

If you open this page in IE, you'll find that clicking on the header starts the boxes moving outward, and moving the mouse out of the header resets the boxes.

NOTE   What would happen if we didn't include the flag? Try it and see. Comment out the statements that deal with the flag, save the file, and open the page in IE. Click on the header while the animation is in progress, and then move the mouse out of the header. The boxes will move toward the center, but then they'll move outward again. You won't be able to stop the animation, as you restarted the timer before you cleared it.

Skill 7

Randomizing the Movement

We don't have to confine ourselves to smooth, linear movement. Instead, we can randomize how far each box moves when boxMovement fires. The movement of the boxes won't be as smooth, but it might look more interesting to Web page users.

It's easy to add this capability to the script we've already written. All we have to do is use the VBScript rnd function, which randomly selects a number between 0 and 1. Multiply each numerical argument in MoveElementBy by rnd, and you'll generate a random number of pixels for the boxes to move each time boxMovement executes. Inserting rnd in the appropriate places makes boxMovement look like this:

```
Sub boxMovement
    Call MoveElementBy(divBox1,-20*rnd,-20*rnd)
    Call MoveElementBy(divBox2,20*rnd,-20*rnd)
    Call MoveElementBy(divBox3,-20*rnd,20*rnd)
    Call MoveElementBy(divBox4,20*rnd,20*rnd)
End Sub
```

One problem remains. Unless you do one more thing, rnd will always generate the same sequence of random numbers. Most randomization functions start from a *seed* number, and unless you change the seed, the sequence will remain the same. In order to change the seed before you invoke rnd, use VBS's built-in randomize function. Add a call to this function to Sub h1Header_onclick:

```
Sub h1Header_onclick
    if glblAnimationStartedFlag = 0 Then
        call randomize
        glblTimer = window.setInterval("boxMovement", 100)
        glblAnimationStartedFlag =1
    end if
End Sub
```

Open the page in IE, and click on the header. You'll see the boxes move outward at different rates from one another and along slightly different paths. Figure 7.1 shows where the boxes are after several of these moves.

We've instituted a kind of controlled randomness (how's that for an oxymoron?), as the boxes move in the same general directions as before. We've also put an upper bound on the amount of movement, and this upper bound is about the same as the previous amount of movement.

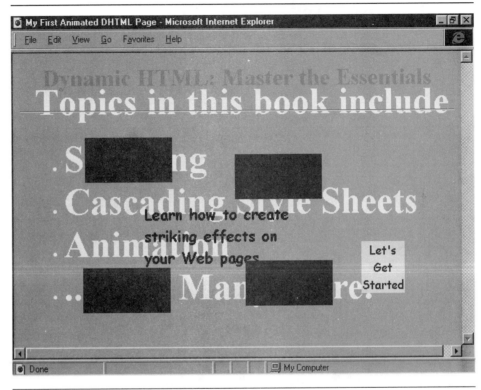

FIGURE 7.1: The First Animated DHTML page after the boxes have moved randomly outward

NOTE   If we wanted to randomly select a number between 1 and 20, we would use 21*rnd rather than 20*rnd.

We could change things drastically if we made the direction of the movement depend on the outcome of a random selection. On the other hand, we could dispense with randomization altogether and generate movement paths that depend on a rule or on the result of applying a mathematical function.

The Final Script

After all the changes and additions, your SCRIPT element for this page should look like this:

```vbscript
<SCRIPT Language = "VBScript">

dim glblTimer
dim glblAnimationStartedFlag
glblAnimationStartedFlag = 0

Sub h1Header_onMouseOver
    h1Header.Style.Color = "Goldenrod"
    divMessage.Style.Visibility = "Visible"
    divReady.Style.Visibility = "Hidden"
    divStarted.Style.Visibility = "Visible"
End Sub

Sub h1Header_onMouseOut
    h1Header.Style.Color = "Black"
    divBox1.Style.Top = 180
    divBox1.Style.Left = 150
    divBox2.Style.Top = 180
    divBox2.Style.Left = 270
    divBox3.Style.Top = 240
    divBox3.Style.Left = 150
    divBox4.Style.Top = 240
    divBox4.Style.Left = 270
    divMessage.Style.Visibility = "Hidden"
    divReady.Style.Visibility = "Visible"
    divStarted.Style.Visibility = "Hidden"
    window.clearInterval(glblTimer)
    glblAnimationStartedFlag = 0
End Sub

Sub h1Header_onclick
    if glblAnimationStartedFlag = 0 then
        call randomize
        glblTimer = window.setInterval("boxMovement", 100)
        glblAnimationStartedFlag = 1
    end if
End Sub

Sub boxMovement

        Call MoveElementBy(divBox1,-20*rnd,-20*rnd)
        Call MoveElementBy(divBox2,20*rnd,-20*rnd)
```

```
                    Call MoveElementBy(divBox3,-20*rnd,20*rnd)
                    Call MoveElementBy(divBox4,20*rnd,20*rnd)

         End Sub


         Sub MoveElementBy(ElementID,LeftMovementAmount,TopMovementAmount)
             pPositionTop = InStr(ElementID.Style.Top,"px")
             pPositionLeft = InStr(ElementID.Style.Left,"px")
             ElementID.Style.Top = _
                CInt(Left(ElementID.Style.Top,pPositionTop-1)) +
         TopMovementAmount
             ElementID.Style.Left = _
                CInt(Left(ElementID.Style.Left,pPositionLeft-1)) +
         LeftMovementAmount
         End Sub

         </SCRIPT>
```

Animating a Logo

If your organization's logo consists of several components, it's a good candidate for an animation effect that takes the components apart, moves some of them around the page, transforms them as they move, and then puts them back together again in their original form.

As we develop this effect in the next exercise, you'll begin to see concepts that build on the animation you just created. Specifically, you'll see a counter that keeps track of the in-progress animation, and you'll create filter effects that turn on and off during the animation and a transition filter that goes into effect after the animation concludes.

In your text editor, open the University of Cyberspace home page—UofCyb.htm in Skill 3. Save it as Animated UofCyb.htm in your Skill 7 folder. Here's the file:

Skill 7

UofCyb.htm

```
<HTML>
<HEAD>
<STYLE Type = "text/css">
.UofCyb{font-size:120%;color:'green';font-weight:bold;font-family:
cursive}
</STYLE>
```

```
<TITLE>The University of Cyberspace Home Page</TITLE>
</HEAD>
<BODY Style = "background-color:#FFFFCC">
<H1 Style = "text-align:center">Welcome to the <A Class =
"UofCyb">University of Cyberspace</A> Home Page!</H1>
<HR>

<P style = "margin-right:40%">At the
<A Class = "UofCyb">
University of Cyberspace</A>, we're proud of our faculty and
our students. Here are a few of our departments:

<UL>
    <LI><A Href = "E:\DHTML MTE\Skill 3\WebPageDesign.htm">
    Web Page Design</A></LI>
    <LI><A Href = "E:\DHTML MTE\Skill 3\WebAccessStats.htm">
    Web Access Statistics</A></LI>
    <LI><A Href = "E:\DHTML MTE\Skill 3\Cybereng.htm">
    Cyberengineering</A></LI>
</UL>
</P>
<P style = "margin-right:40%">
<A Class = "UofCyb">University of Cyberspace</A> departments
are known virtually all over the world.
</P>

<DIV style = "position:absolute;top:35%;left:65%;background-
color:'blue';
color:'white';width:150;height:120;z-index:0">
<P style = "font-weight:bold;font-size:20;text-align:center">Tops in
Virtual Education</P>
</DIV>

<DIV style = "position:absolute;top:50%;left:70%;background-
color:'green';
color:'white';width:150;height:120;z-index:1">
<P style = "font-weight:bold;font-size:20;text-align:center">
Number One Since 1994</P>
</DIV>

<DIV style = "position:absolute;top:65%;left:75%;background-
color:'goldenrod';
color:'white';width:150;height:120;z-index:2">
<P style = "font-weight:bold;font-size:20;text-align:center">
The Premier Educational Organization on the World-Wide Web!</P>
</DIV>
```

```
    </DIV>
    </BODY>
    </HTML>
```

Figure 7.2 shows this page in IE once again. In this exercise, you'll animate the three-box logo on the right side of the page.

FIGURE 7.2: The University of Cyberspace home page

Some Additions and Changes

The first thing to do is assign IDs to each of the boxes. Three appropriate ones are `divTops`, `divNumber`, and `divPremier`. In the same vein, assign `divInfo` as the ID for the `DIV` that contains the text about the university.

Next, we'll change the positioning of the three boxes from percentage-based to pixel-based. This will enable us to use our subroutine for moving the boxes, which works with pixel-based positioning rather than percentage-based positioning. With the IDs added and the position-values changed, the DIVs now look like this:

```
<DIV ID=divTops style = "position:absolute;top:130;left:390;
background-color:'blue';
color:'white';width:150;height:120;z-index:0">
<P style = "font-weight:bold;font-size:20;text-align:center">Tops in
Virtual Education</P>
</DIV>

<DIV ID=divNumber style = "position:absolute;top:190;left:420;
background-color:'green';
color:'white';width:150;height:120;z-index:1">
<P style = "font-weight:bold;font-size:20;text-align:center">
Number One Since 1994</P>
</DIV>

<DIV ID=divPremier style = "position:absolute;top:250;left:450;
background-color:'goldenrod';
color:'white';width:150;height:120;z-index:2">
<P style = "font-weight:bold;font-size:20;text-align:center">
The Premier Educational Organization on the World-Wide Web!</P>
</DIV>
```

Next, apply a transition filter that reveals some hidden text:

```
<DIV ID = divUnder Style = "position:absolute;top:150;left:10;
z-index:-1;visibility:hidden;
filter:revealTrans(Duration=0.8, Transition = 12)">
<P style = "margin-right:40%;font-size:35">
Enroll Now!<BR>
Start learning how to use today's techniques
and how to create tomorrow's technology.
</P>
</DIV>
```

The revealTrans filter is the "dissolve" effect you saw in Skill 5.

Writing the Script

Start by adding a SCRIPT element inside the file's HEAD element, and set the Language attribute in the <SCRIPT> tag to "VBScript".

Global Variables

For the exercise, you'll need a timer that moves two of the three components of the logo, another that applies filters during the animation, and another that alternately "unapplies" the filters during the animation. This means that you have to define three global variables. You'll also have to define a global variable that counts the number of times setInterval has activated. Put these lines in the beginning of your SCRIPT element:

```
dim glblTimer
dim glblFilterTimer
dim glblUnFilterTimer
dim glblCounter
```

Loading the Window

Initialize the variables in the window onload event:

```
Sub window_onload
    glblTimer = window.setInterval("boxMovement", 100)
    glblFilterTimer = window.setInterval("filterAction", 500)
    glblUnFilterTimer = window.setInterval("unfilterAction", 500)
    glblCounter = 0
End Sub
```

As you can see, the first line sets up a timer to call the boxMovement procedure every 100 milliseconds. The second one calls filterAction every 500 milliseconds, and the third calls unfilterAction every 500 milliseconds.

Movement and Filtering

The boxMovement procedure is the same as the one in the previous exercise, with changes to the arguments in MoveElementBy, and some necessary additional code:

```
Sub boxMovement
    Call MoveElementBy(divTops,-2,-1)
    Call MoveElementBy(divNumber,-2,0)
    glblCounter = glblCounter + 1
    if glblCounter = 130 then
            window.clearInterval(glblTimer)
            window.clearInterval(glblFilterTimer)
            window.clearInterval(glblUnFilterTimer)
            call reset
    end if

End Sub
```

Note that this subroutine only moves two of the components. The third one, divPremier, is close to the bottom of the page, so you'll transform it during the animation but you won't change its position, as it would soon move out of sight.

The third line of the subroutine updates glblCounter each time the boxes move. The if...then expression specifies what happens when the counter reaches 130 (a number I arrived at via a little tinkering). The script clears the three timers and calls a subroutine (reset) that puts all the boxes back where they started. MoveElementBy is the same as before:

```
Sub MoveElementBy(ElementID,LeftMovementAmount,TopMovementAmount)
    pPositionTop = InStr(ElementID.Style.Top,"px")
    pPositionLeft = InStr(ElementID.Style.Left,"px")
    ElementID.Style.Top = _
      CInt(Left(ElementID.Style.Top,pPositionTop-1)) +
      ➡ TopMovementAmount
    ElementID.Style.Left = _
      CInt(Left(ElementID.Style.Left,pPositionLeft-1)) +
      ➡ LeftMovementAmount
End Sub
```

For an explanation of this subroutine, see Skill 1.

Next, create filterAction. This subroutine will apply a wave filter to the first box (divTops), a flip-horizontal filter to the second (divNumber), and an invert filter to the third (divPremier). Since Filter is a Style attribute, the syntax is

```
objectName.Style.Filter = "filterName(arguments, enabled = 1)"
```

Note that the right side is a quoted string.

Of the three filters, the wave is the most complex:

```
divTops.Style.Filter = "wave(add=0,freq=1,lightStrength=20,phase=50,
strength=20,enabled=1)"
```

The others are straightforward:

```
divNumber.Style.Filter = "fliph(enabled=1)"
divPremier.Style.Filter = "invert(enabled=1)"
```

Precede those three lines with Sub filterAction, and follow them with End Sub.

The subroutine unfilterAction is very similar. The second and third filters are disabled (enabled = 0), while the wave filter is modified slightly to produce an oscillating effect during the movement of the boxes:

```
Sub unfilterAction
    divTops.Style.Filter = "wave(add=0,freq=1,lightStrength=20,
    ➡ phase=20,strength=20,enabled=1)"
```

```
        divNumber.Style.Filter = "fliph(enabled=0)"
        divPremier.Style.Filter = "invert(enabled=0)"
End Sub
```

The modification to the wave filter changes the phase from 50 to 20.

Resetting

The reset subroutine disables all the filters, returns all the components to their starting points, and applies a transition filter:

```
Sub reset

    divTops.Style.Filter =
        "wave(add=0,freq=1,lightStrength=20,phase=20,
        strength=20,enabled=0)"
    divNumber.Style.Filter = "fliph(enabled=0)"
    divPremier.Style.Filter = "invert(enabled=0)"
    divTops.Style.Top = 130
    divTops.Style.Left = 390
    divNumber.Style.Top = 190
    divNumber.Style.Left = 420
    divInfo.Style.Visibility = "hidden"
    divUnder.Filters(0).Apply
    divUnder.Style.Visibility ="visible"
    divUnder.Filters(0).Play

End Sub
```

The Whole File

With everything added and scripted, Animated UofCyb.htm looks like this:

Animated UofCyb.htm

```
<HTML>
<HEAD>
<STYLE Type = "text/css">
.UofCyb{font-size:120%;color:'green';font-weight:bold;font-family:
cursive}
</STYLE>
<SCRIPT Language = "VBScript">

dim glblTimer
dim glblFilterTimer
dim glblUnFilterTimer
dim glblCounter
```

```
Sub window_onload
      glblTimer = window.setInterval("boxMovement", 100)
      glblFilterTimer = window.setInterval("filterAction", 500)
      glblUnFilterTimer = window.setInterval("unfilterAction", 500)
      glblCounter = 0
End Sub
Sub boxMovement
      Call MoveElementBy(divTops,-2,-1)
      Call MoveElementBy(divNumber,-2,0)
      glblCounter = glblCounter + 1
      if glblCounter = 130 then
              window.clearInterval(glblTimer)
              window.clearInterval(glblFilterTimer)
              window.clearInterval(glblUnFilterTimer)
              call reset
      end if

End Sub


Sub filterAction
      divTops.Style.Filter = "wave(add=0,freq=1,lightStrength=20,
      ➡ phase=50,strength=20,enabled=1)"
      divNumber.Style.Filter = "fliph(enabled=1)"
      divPremier.Style.Filter = "invert(enabled=1)"
End Sub

Sub unfilterAction
      divTops.Style.Filter = "wave(add=0,freq=1,lightStrength=20,
      ➡ phase=20,strength=20,enabled=1)"
      divNumber.Style.Filter = "fliph(enabled=0)"
      divPremier.Style.Filter = "invert(enabled=0)"
End Sub

Sub MoveElementBy(ElementID,LeftMovementAmount,TopMovementAmount)
      pPositionTop = InStr(ElementID.Style.Top,"px")
      pPositionLeft = InStr(ElementID.Style.Left,"px")
      ElementID.Style.Top = _
        CInt(Left(ElementID.Style.Top,pPositionTop-1)) +
        ➡ TopMovementAmount
      ElementID.Style.Left = _
        CInt(Left(ElementID.Style.Left,pPositionLeft-1)) +
        ➡ LeftMovementAmount
End Sub
```

```
Sub reset

    divTops.Style.Filter = "wave(add=0,freq=1,lightStrength=20,
    ➥ phase=20,strength=20,enabled=0)"
    divNumber.Style.Filter = "fliph(enabled=0)"
    divPremier.Style.Filter = "invert(enabled=0)"
    divTops.Style.Top = 130
    divTops.Style.Left = 390
    divNumber.Style.Top = 190
    divNumber.Style.Left = 420
    divInfo.Style.Visibility = "hidden"
    divUnder.Filters(0).Apply
    divUnder.Style.Visibility ="visible"
    divUnder.Filters(0).Play

End Sub
</SCRIPT>
<TITLE>The University of Cyberspace Home Page</TITLE>
</HEAD>
<BODY Style = "background-color:#FFFFCC">
<H1 ID = h1Header Style = "text-align:center">Welcome to the <A Class =
"UofCyb">University of Cyberspace</A> Home Page!</H1>
<HR>

<DIV ID = divInfo Style = "position:absolute;top:150;left:10;
filter:revealTrans(Duration=0.8, Transition = 3)">
<P style = "margin-right:40%">At the
<A Class = "UofCyb">
University of Cyberspace</A>, we're proud of our faculty and
our students. Here are a few of our departments:

<UL>
    <LI><A Href = "E:\DHTML MTE\Skill 2\WebPageDesign.htm">
    Web Page Design</A></LI>
    <LI><A Href = "E:\DHTML MTE\Skill 2\WebAccessStats.htm">
    Web Access Statistics</A></LI>
    <LI><A Href = "E:\DHTML MTE\Skill 2\Cybereng.htm">
    Cyberengineering</A></LI>
</UL>
</P>
<P style = "margin-right:40%">
<A Class = "UofCyb">University of Cyberspace</A> departments
are known virtually all over the world.
</P>
</DIV>
```

Skill 7

```
<DIV ID = divUnder Style = "position:absolute;top:150;left:10;
z-index:-1;visibility:hidden;
filter:revealTrans(Duration=0.8, Transition = 12)">
<P style = "margin-right:40%;font-size:35">
Enroll Now!<BR>
Start learning how to use today's techniques
and how to create tomorrow's technology.
</P>
</DIV>

<DIV ID=divTops style = "position:absolute;top:130;left:390;
background-color:'blue';
color:'white';width:150;height:120;z-index:0">
<P style = "font-weight:bold;font-size:20;text-align:center">Tops in
Virtual Education</P>
</DIV>

<DIV ID=divNumber style = "position:absolute;top:190;left:420;
background-color:'green';
color:'white';width:150;height:120;z-index:1">
<P style = "font-weight:bold;font-size:20;text-align:center">
Number One Since 1994</P>
</DIV>

<DIV ID=divPremier style = "position:absolute;top:250;left:450;
background-color:'goldenrod';
color:'white';width:150;height:120;z-index:2">
<P style = "font-weight:bold;font-size:20;text-align:center">
The Premier Educational Organization on the World-Wide Web!</P>
</DIV>

</DIV>
</BODY>
</HTML>
```

Open the page in IE. You'll see two of the boxes in the three-box logo move toward the other side of the page. During the movement, the upper box undulates in a wave-like motion and the middle box's text alternates between normal and mirror-image. The lower box's text and background change color. Note that the invert filter doesn't exchange the text color with the background color. Figure 7.3 shows the animation in progress.

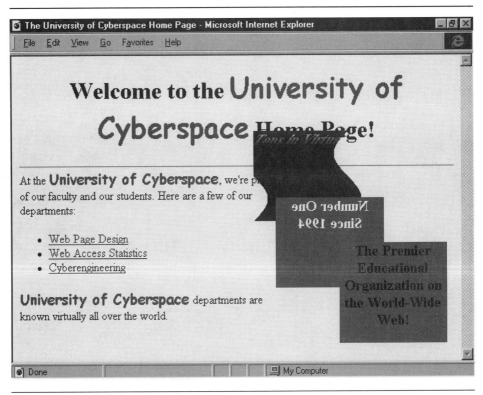

FIGURE 7.3: The Animated University of Cyberspace home page with the animation in progress

After the boxes have moved a considerable distance across the page, you'll see the animation stop and the boxes snap back to their original locations. A short time later, the text in the page will dissolve to reveal the hidden text in the DIV you added. Figure 7.4 shows the final state of the page.

FIGURE 7.4: The Animated University of Cyberspace home page after the animation has ended

Over and Under: Continuous Motion and the *z-index*

The z-index opens numerous possibilities for animation effects. We'll explore the z-index in this exercise, as we create continuously moving objects that seem to move over and under other objects on the page.

Use your text editor to create a file called Over and Under.htm and save it in Skill 7. We'll insert images that start on the left side of the screen, move toward the right, move over and under bars, and then turn back and move toward the left of the screen. When they reach the starting point, they turn back and repeat the process. Figure 7.5 shows what the page will look like when the animation starts.

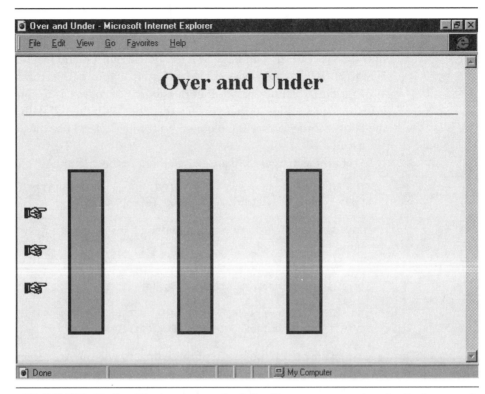

FIGURE 7.5: The images on the left will move over and under the bars, and then turn around and move back to their starting points.

Setting Up the Page

Title your new document Over and Under, and in the document's body, add a centered H1 heading that matches the title and add a horizontal line:

```
<HTML>
<HEAD>
<TITLE>Over and Under</TITLE>
</HEAD>
<BODY>
<H1 Style = "text-align:center">Over and Under </H1>
<HR>
```

Let's turn our attention to the animation objects. Up to now, the exercises applied animation to DIVs. In this one, we're using images. As Figure 7.5 shows, I've selected a right-pointing finger from the Lassen Technologies library. The file name is `ltb7.gif` and I keep it in my E: drive. On my machine, its path is `E:\DHTML MTE\graphics\small\ltb7.gif`. If your path is different, make the appropriate substitution. Another possibility, of course, is to copy the image file into the Skill 7 folder so that you can dispense with the full path when you set the `Src` attribute for the `IMG` element. In the exercises, I use the path to give you a sense of a URL.

To set up the images, add an `IMG` element to the document:

```
<IMG ID = imgFinger1 Src = "E:\DHTML MTE\graphics\small\ltb7.gif"
Style = "position:absolute;top:200;left:10">
```

Copy and paste to add two more, making sure that you adjust the IDs and **top** locations:

```
<IMG ID = imgFinger2 Src = "E:\DHTML MTE\graphics\small\ltb7.gif"
Style = "position:absolute;top:250;left:10">

<IMG ID = imgFinger3 Src = "E:\DHTML MTE\graphics\small\ltb7.gif"
Style = "position:absolute;top:300;left:10">
```

Now let's work on the bars that these fingers will move over and under. The easiest way to implement them is to set each one up as a separate `DIV` with filled color and a border. Here's one way to do this:

```
<DIV Style = "background-color:silver;border:solid;position:absolute;
top:150;left:70;
z-index:-1;width:50;height:220">
</DIV>
```

Most of the `Style` attributes, however, will repeat from `DIV` to `DIV`. The only ones that change are `left` and `z-index`. Copying and pasting make it trivial to do these repetitons, but we might as well create a STYLE element and take advantage of CSS capabilities:

```
<STYLE>
div {background-color:silver; border:solid;position:absolute;top:150;
z-index:-1;width:50;height:220}
</STYLE>
```

Now our DIVs can look like this:

```
<DIV Style = "left:70; z-index:-1">
</DIV>

<DIV Style = "left:220; z-index:1">
</DIV>

<DIV Style = "left:370; z-index:-1">
</DIV>
```

We don't assign IDs because we won't be scripting these objects.

At this point, here's how your HTML document should look:

```
<HTML>
<HEAD>
<STYLE>
div {background-color:silver; border:solid;position:absolute;top:150;
z-index:-1;width:50;height:220}
</STYLE>
<TITLE>Over and Under</TITLE>
</HEAD>
<BODY>
<H1 Style = "text-align:center">Over and Under </H1>
<HR>

<IMG ID = imgFinger1 Src = "E:\DHTML MTE\graphics\small\ltb7.gif"
Style = "position:absolute;top:200;left:10">

<IMG ID = imgFinger2 Src = "E:\DHTML MTE\graphics\small\ltb7.gif"
Style = "position:absolute;top:250;left:10">

<IMG ID = imgFinger3 Src = "E:\DHTML MTE\graphics\small\ltb7.gif"
Style = "position:absolute;top:300;left:10">

<DIV Style = "left:70; z-index:-1">
</DIV>

<DIV Style = "left:220; z-index:1">
</DIV>

<DIV Style = "left:370; z-index:-1">
</DIV>
</BODY>
</HTML>
```

The Script

In the HEAD element, insert a SCRIPT element with its Language attribute set to "VBScript".

Global Variables

Once again, we begin scripting by defining some global variables. We'll need a timer that moves the fingers from left to right, a timer that moves them back from right to left, and a counter:

```
dim glblTimer
dim glblBackTimer
dim glblCounter
```

Subroutines

We initialize two of the variables in the onload event:

```
Sub window_onload
    glblTimer = window.setInterval("fingerMovement", 100)
    glblCounter = 0
End Sub
```

The fingerMovement subroutine moves the images, updates the counter each time the images move, and takes some other actions when the counter reaches 240 (another value I arrived at by tinkering):

```
Sub fingerMovement
    Call MoveElementBy(imgFinger1, 2,0)
    Call MoveElementBy(imgFinger2, 2,0)
    Call MoveElementBy(imgFinger3, 2,0)
    glblCounter = glblCounter + 1
    if glblCounter = 240 then
            glblCounter = 0
            Call filterAction
            window.clearInterval(glblTimer)
            glblBackTimer = window.setInterval("backMovement", 100)

    end if
```

With the counter at 240, the subroutine resets the counter to zero, calls a subroutine that applies a filter to the images, stops the timer, and initializes the timer for moving the images back to their starting points.

The backMovement subroutine is very similar:

```
Sub backMovement
     Call MoveElementBy(imgFinger1, -2,0)
     Call MoveElementBy(imgFinger2, -2,0)
     Call MoveElementBy(imgFinger3, -2,0)
     glblCounter = glblCounter + 1
     if glblCounter = 240 then
             glblCounter = 0
             Call unfilterAction
             window.clearInterval(glblBackTimer)
             glblTimer = window.setInterval("fingerMovement",100)

     end if
End Sub
```

This subroutine moves the images to the left and updates the counter. When the counter reaches 240, the subroutine clears the timer that has been operating and restarts the original timer.

The filterAction subroutine applies the flip horizontal filter:

```
Sub filterAction
     imgFinger1.Style.Filter = "fliph(enabled=1)"
     imgFinger2.Style.Filter = "fliph(enabled=1)"
     imgFinger3.Style.Filter = "fliph(enabled=1)"
End Sub
```

The unfilterAction subroutine disables these filters:

```
Sub unfilterAction
     imgFinger1.Style.Filter = "fliph(enabled=0)"
     imgFinger2.Style.Filter = "fliph(enabled=0)"
     imgFinger3.Style.Filter = "fliph(enabled=0)"
End Sub
```

Finally, the MoveElementBy subroutine is the one we've been using:

```
Sub MoveElementBy(ElementID,LeftMovementAmount,TopMovementAmount)
     pPositionTop = InStr(ElementID.Style.Top,"px")
     pPositionLeft = InStr(ElementID.Style.Left,"px")
     ElementID.Style.Top = _
       CInt(Left(ElementID.Style.Top,pPositionTop-1)) +
       ➥ TopMovementAmount
     ElementID.Style.Left = _
       CInt(Left(ElementID.Style.Left,pPositionLeft-1)) +
       ➥ LeftMovementAmount
End Sub
```

The Whole Thing

Here's the entire Over and Under.htm file:

 Over and Under.htm

```
<HTML>
<HEAD>
<STYLE>

div {background-color:silver;border:solid;position:absolute;top:150;
z-index:-1;width:50;height:220}
</STYLE>

<SCRIPT Language = "VBScript">
dim glblTimer
dim glblBackTimer
dim glblCounter

Sub window_onload
      glblTimer = window.setInterval("fingerMovement", 100)
      glblCounter = 0
End Sub

Sub fingerMovement
      Call MoveElementBy(imgFinger1, 2,0)
      Call MoveElementBy(imgFinger2, 2,0)
      Call MoveElementBy(imgFinger3, 2,0)
      glblCounter = glblCounter + 1
      if glblCounter = 240 then
            glblCounter = 0
            Call filterAction
            window.clearInterval(glblTimer)
            glblBackTimer = window.setInterval("backMovement", 100)
            exit Sub
      end if

End Sub

Sub backMovement
      Call MoveElementBy(imgFinger1, -2,0)
      Call MoveElementBy(imgFinger2, -2,0)
      Call MoveElementBy(imgFinger3, -2,0)
      glblCounter = glblCounter + 1
      if glblCounter = 240 then
            glblCounter = 0
            Call unfilterAction
```

```
            window.clearInterval(glblBackTimer)
            glblTimer = window.setInterval("fingerMovement",100)
            exit Sub
     end if
End Sub

Sub filterAction
     imgFinger1.Style.Filter = "fliph(enabled=1)"
     imgFinger2.Style.Filter = "fliph(enabled=1)"
     imgFinger3.Style.Filter = "fliph(enabled=1)"
End Sub

Sub unfilterAction
     imgFinger1.Style.Filter = "fliph(enabled=0)"
     imgFinger2.Style.Filter = "fliph(enabled=0)"
     imgFinger3.Style.Filter = "fliph(enabled=0)"
End Sub

Sub MoveElementBy(ElementID,LeftMovementAmount,TopMovementAmount)
     pPositionTop = InStr(ElementID.Style.Top,"px")
     pPositionLeft = InStr(ElementID.Style.Left,"px")
     ElementID.Style.Top = _
       CInt(Left(ElementID.Style.Top,pPositionTop-1)) +
       ➡ TopMovementAmount
     ElementID.Style.Left = _
       CInt(Left(ElementID.Style.Left,pPositionLeft-1)) +
       ➡ LeftMovementAmount
End Sub
</SCRIPT>
<TITLE>Over and Under</TITLE>
</HEAD>
<BODY>
<H1 Style = "text-align:center">Over and Under </H1>
<HR>

<IMG ID = imgFinger1 Src = "E:\DHTML MTE\graphics\small\ltb7.gif"
Style = "position:absolute;top:200;left:10">

<IMG ID = imgFinger2 Src = "E:\DHTML MTE\graphics\small\ltb7.gif"
Style = "position:absolute;top:250;left:10">

<IMG ID = imgFinger3 Src = "E:\DHTML MTE\graphics\small\ltb7.gif"
Style = "position:absolute;top:300;left:10">

<DIV Style = "left:70; z-index:-1">
</DIV>
```

Skill 7

```
<DIV Style = "left:220; z-index:1">
</DIV>

<DIV Style = "left:370; z-index:-1">
</DIV>

</BODY>
</HTML>
```

Open this file in IE, and you'll see the fingers move toward the right, over the first gray bar, under the second, and over the third. After passing the third bar, they keep moving and then flip around, point to the left, and start moving to the left. When they reach their starting points, they flip around again and repeat the process. The way we've set it up, the process begins when you open the window and continues until you close it.

I've left you with numerous opportunities for exercises that embellish this page. You can use other images, build randomness into the movement (as we did in the first exercise), add objects that move from the bottom of the page to the top, and more.

Animation in Navigator

Let's go to Planet Netscape and implement the effects we just created in IE. Start by copying First Dynamic Nav.htm from your Skill 1 folder to your Skill 7 folder. Rename it Animated Dynamic Nav.htm and retitle it My First Animated DHTML Page.

We're going to use the same techniques we used to animate the IE page. We'll define a global variable, set it to setInterval, and use a function called boxMovement to initiate movement (instead of clicking the Outward button). We'll also set up a flag that keeps track of whether or not the animation has started.

The Script

Begin by adding a SCRIPT element to the document's HEAD. Set the SCRIPT's Language attribute to "JavaScript1.2". As we did in the IE page, define two global variables—one for the timer and one for the flag:

```
var glblTimer;
var glblAnimationStartedFlag = 0;
```

Next, we script the boxMovement function:

```
function boxMovement() {

        document.layers["layerBox1"].offset(-20,-20);
        document.layers["layerBox2"].offset(20,-20);
        document.layers["layerBox3"].offset(-20,20);
        document.layers["layerBox4"].offset(20,20);
        }
```

Cutting and pasting the code from the Outward button's onclick event will get most of the coding done. As you can see, however, inside the function, you have to refer to each layerBox by its full name within the document. This is the only function that we'll create within the SCRIPT element.

Let's move to the buttons, and make the necessary changes to their onclick events. For the Outward button, we have to put the code inside an if statement that checks the glblAnimationStartedFlag:

```
<INPUT Type = button Value = "Outward"
    onclick = "if (glblAnimationStartedFlag == 0) {
            glblTimer = setInterval('boxMovement()', 100);
            glblAnimationStartedFlag = 1;}">
```

This is analogous to what we did for the h1Header's onclick event in the IE page. If the flag's value is 0, setInterval goes into action, boxMovement gets started, and the flag's value is set to 1. Otherwise, nothing happens when you click the Outward button.

For the Inward button, we add statements that clear the timer and reset the flag's value to 0, just as we did with the h1Header's onMouseout event in the IE page:

```
<INPUT Type = button Value = "Inward"
    onclick = "layerBox1.moveTo(150,180);
            layerBox2.moveTo(270,180);
            layerBox3.moveTo(150,240);
            layerBox4.moveTo(270,240);
            clearInterval(glblTimer);
            glblAnimationStartedFlag = 0;">
```

If you save your work and open the page in Navigator, you'll find that clicking the Outward button starts the boxes moving toward the corners of the page, and clicking the Inward button brings them back. Clicking the Outward button during the movement has no effect.

Skill 7

Randomizing the Movement

Just as in IE, we can liven up the movement patterns by adding randomness. We'll use the JavaScript random() function to do this. A method of JavaScript's Math object, random() uses the time of day as its seed. For this reason, we don't have to call another function to set the seed. Also, since random() is a method of Math, the syntax is Math.random() whenever we refer to this function.

To randomize the movements, then, we change boxMovement():

```
function boxMovement() {

    document.layers["layerBox1"].offset(-20*Math.random(),
    ➥ -20*Math.random());
    document.layers["layerBox2"].offset(20*Math.random(),
    ➥ -20*Math.random());
    document.layers["layerBox3"].offset(-20*Math.random(),
    ➥ 20*Math.random());
    document.layers["layerBox4"].offset(20*Math.random(),
    ➥ 20*Math.random());
}
```

The Whole File

With all the changes and additions, here's the entire Animated Dynamic Nav.htm file:

 Animated Dynamic Nav.htm

```
<HTML>
<HEAD>
<SCRIPT Language = "JavaScript1.2">
var glblTimer;
var glblAnimationStartedFlag = 0;

function boxMovement() {

    document.layers["layerBox1"].offset(-20*Math.random(),
    ➥ -20*Math.random());
    document.layers["layerBox2"].offset(20*Math.random(),
    ➥ -20*Math.random());
    document.layers["layerBox3"].offset(-20*Math.random(),
    ➥ 20*Math.random());
    document.layers["layerBox4"].offset(20*Math.random(),
    ➥ 20*Math.random());
}
```

```
</SCRIPT>

</HEAD>
<BODY>
<TITLE>My First Animated DHTML Page</TITLE>
<BODY Bgcolor = "Silver">
<LAYER Name = layerHeader Left = 10 Top = 10 z-index = 0
onMouseOver = "layerMessage.visibility = 'show';
              layerHeader.visibility = 'hide';
              layerUnderHeader.visibility = 'show'"

onMouseOut = "layerMessage.visibility = 'hide';
              layerUnderHeader.visibility = 'hide'
              layerHeader.visibility = 'show'" >
<Center>
<H1>Dynamic HTML: MTE</H1></Center>
<HR>
</LAYER>

<LAYER Name = layerUnderHeader Left = 10 Top = 10 z-index = -1
Visibility = "hide">
<Center>
<H1 Style = "color:'khaki'">Dynamic HTML: MTE</H1></Center>
<HR>
</LAYER>
<Layer ID = layerMessage Left=10 Top=10
Visibility = "hide" z-index = -2 >

<P Style = "color:'green';  font-size:50px; font-weight:bold">Topics in
this book include
<UL Style = "color:'green';  font-size:50px; font-weight:bold">
<LI> Scripting
<LI> Cascading Style Sheets
<LI> Animation
<LI> ... And Many More!
</UL>
</P>
</LAYER>

<LAYER NAME = layerLearn LEFT = 180 TOP = 200 Width = 210 z-index  = 0>
<P  Style="font-family:Cursive;font-weight:bold;font-size:15pt">
Learn how to create striking effects on your Web pages.
</P>
</LAYER>

<LAYER NAME = layerBox1 Bgcolor = "Blue" LEFT = 150 TOP = 180 Width = 120
Height = 60 z-index = 1>
</LAYER>
```

```
<LAYER NAME = layerBox2 Bgcolor = "Blue" LEFT = 270 TOP = 180 Width = 120
Height = 60 z-index = 1>
</LAYER>

<LAYER NAME = layerBox3 Bgcolor = "Blue" LEFT = 150 TOP = 240 Width = 120
Height = 60 z-index = 1>
</LAYER>

<LAYER NAME = layerBox4 Bgcolor = "Blue" LEFT = 270 TOP = 240 Width = 120
Height = 60 z-index = 1>
</LAYER>

<LAYER Left = 450 Top = 350>
<FORM>
<INPUT Type = button Value = "Outward"
        onclick = "if (glblAnimationStartedFlag == 0) {
                glblTimer = setInterval('boxMovement()', 100);
                glblAnimationStartedFlag = 1;}">

<INPUT Type = button Value = "Inward"
        onclick = "layerBox1.moveTo(150,180);
                layerBox2.moveTo(270,180);
                layerBox3.moveTo(150,240);
                layerBox4.moveTo(270,240);
                clearInterval(glblTimer);
                glblAnimationStartedFlag = 0;">

</FORM>
</LAYER>
</BODY>
</HTML>
```

Open the file in Navigator, click the Outward button, and watch the boxes take different paths as they move toward the corners.

Here's an exercise for you: For this page and the equivalent IE page, make the window onload event initiate the randomized movement, and move the boxes inward on every 130th (or some other value) update of the counter. Don't use any flags, and don't clear the timer. You should see the boxes bounce in and out of the center for as long as the page is open.

Animating the Logo Revisited

Now we turn our attention to the three-part logo we animated in IE. Once again, copy the University of Cyberspace home page from Skill 3 to Skill 7. Rename the file `Nav UofCyb.htm`.

We won't be able to duplicate all the effects from the IE version, since Navigator doesn't support the filters we used. We can, however, animate the two boxes and replicate the movement we saw in IE.

Setting Up the Page

Let's start by changing some of the DIVs to LAYERs. For the boxes in the logo, change the code to:

```
<LAYER Name=layerTops Top=130 Left=390 bgcolor=blue
width=150 height=120 z-index=0>
<P Class = "box"> Tops in Virtual Education</P>
</LAYER>

<LAYER Name=layerNumber Top=190 Left=420 bgcolor=green
width=150 height=120 z-index=1>
<P Class = "box">
Number One Since 1994</P>
</LAYER>

<LAYER Name=layerPremier Top=250 left=450 Bgcolor='goldenrod';
Width=150 Height=120 z-index=2>
<P Class = "box">
The Premier Educational Organization on the World-Wide Web!</P>
</LAYER>
```

As the LAYER element doesn't support inline style sheets, we have to set the attributes the way I've shown them.

Note that I haven't set any style attributes for the P elements, but I have set a value for `Class`. Navigator supports CSS, so we can set the style for the P element by adding this rule to the STYLE element:

```
P.box {color:white;font-weight:bold;text-align:center}
```

We use the class in order to set style attributes for the P elements in our boxes, and not for the P elements in the main body of the page.

NOTE   My version of Navigator renders these rules correctly when they're in a STYLE element, but not when they're in an inline style sheet. See if your version behaves the same way.

TIP   In the CSS rule for UofCyb, remove the quote marks from green. If you don't, Navigator will render the UofCyb class in a lighter shade of green than you're accustomed to seeing.

Figure 7.6 shows the page opened in Navigator. Note that the font face for the UofCyb class doesn't appear as it did in IE.

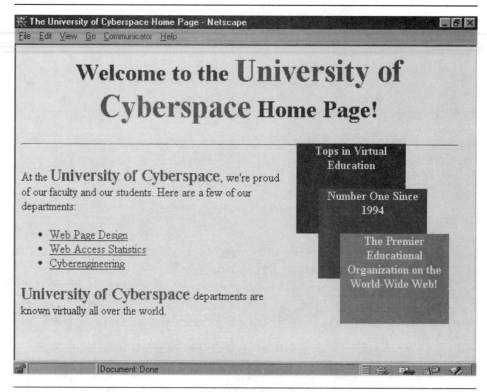

FIGURE 7.6: The Navigator version of the U of Cyb home page

Scripting the Animation

Add a SCRIPT element to the HEAD of the page, and set its Language attribute to "JavaScript1.2". First, we define our global variables and set one of them:

```
var glblTimer
var glblCounter;
glblCounter = 0;
```

We want the animation to start when the window opens, so create this function:

```
function windowLoad(){
    glblTimer = setInterval("layerMovement()", 100);

}
```

The layerMovement function is straightforward, and looks something like what you've already done in previous exercises:

```
function layerMovement(){
    document.layers["layerTops"].offset(-2,-1);
    document.layers["layerNumber"].offset(-2,0);
    glblCounter = glblCounter + 1;
    if (glblCounter == 130) {
            clearInterval(glblTimer);
            reset()
    }
}
```

We use the built-in offset method to move the layers, and each time we do, we increase the counter by 1. When the counter reaches 130, the function clears the timer and calls the reset function, which returns the layers to their starting points. Here's reset:

```
function reset(){

    document.layers["layerTops"].left = 390
    document.layers["layerTops"].top = 130
    document.layers["layerNumber"].left = 420
    document.layers["layerNumber"].top = 190
}
```

One more piece of coding will finish our work. To make the animation begin when the window opens, we have to add an onload event to the <BODY> tag and set it equal to our windowLoad function. Add the code, and the <BODY> tag will look like this:

```
<BODY onload = "windowLoad()" Style = "background-color:#FFFFCC">
```

The File

Here's the file with all the changes and JavaScript code:

 Nav UofCyb.htm

```html
<HTML>
<HEAD>
<STYLE Type = "text/css">
.UofCyb{font-size:120%;color:green;font-weight:bold;font-family:cursive}
P.box {color:white;font-weight:bold;text-align:center}
</STYLE>
<SCRIPT Language = "JavaScript1.2">

var glblTimer
var glblCounter;
glblCounter = 0;

function windowLoad(){
        glblTimer = setInterval("layerMovement()", 100);

}

function layerMovement(){
    document.layers["layerTops"].offset(-2,-1);
    document.layers["layerNumber"].offset(-2,0);
    glblCounter = glblCounter + 1;
    if (glblCounter == 130) {
            clearInterval(glblTimer);
            reset()
    }
}

function reset(){

    document.layers["layerTops"].left = 390
    document.layers["layerTops"].top = 130
    document.layers["layerNumber"].left = 420
    document.layers["layerNumber"].top = 190
}

</SCRIPT>

<TITLE>The University of Cyberspace Home Page</TITLE>
</HEAD>
<BODY onload = "windowLoad()" Style = "background-color:#FFFFCC">
```

```
<H1 Style = "text-align:center">Welcome to the <A Class =
"UofCyb">University of Cyberspace</A> Home Page!</H1>
<HR>


<P style = "margin-right:40%">At the
<A Class = "UofCyb">
University of Cyberspace</A>, we're proud of our faculty and
our students. Here are a few of our departments:

<UL>
    <LI><A Href = "E:\DHTML MTE\Skill 3\WebPageDesign.htm">
    Web Page Design</A></LI>
    <LI><A Href = "E:\DHTML MTE\Skill 3\WebAccessStats.htm">
    Web Access Statistics</A></LI>
    <LI><A Href = "E:\DHTML MTE\Skill 3\Cybereng.htm">
    Cyberengineering</A></LI>
</UL>
</P>
<P style = "margin-right:40%">
<A Class = "UofCyb">University of Cyberspace</A> departments
are known virtually all over the world.
</P>

<LAYER Name=layerTops Top=130 Left=390 bgcolor=blue
width=150 height=120 z-index=0>
<P Class = "box"> Tops in Virtual Education</P>
</LAYER>

<LAYER Name=layerNumber Top=190 Left=420 bgcolor=green
width=150 height=120 z-index=1>
<P Class = "box">
Number One Since 1994</P>
</LAYER>

<LAYER Name=layerPremier Top=250 left=450 Bgcolor='goldenrod';
Width=150 Height=120 z-index=2>
<P Class = "box">
The Premier Educational Organization on the World-Wide Web!</P>
</LAYER>

</BODY>
</HTML>
```

Open the page in Navigator to see the two boxes move and then snap back into their original positions.

The Moving Fingers in Navigator

We continue our exercises with a replication of some of the effects in the Over and Under.htm page that we constructed for IE. Again, since Navigator doesn't support the visual filtering we used, we won't be able to replicate all the effects. Specifically, the fingers will not turn and point leftward after moving a distance toward the right.

Setting Up the Page

As in the previous two exercises, we have to convert some of the HTML to set up the page for Navigator. Open Over and Under.htm and save it as Nav Over and Under.htm. Retitle the new document Navigator Over and Under.

First, we'll convert the HTML elements to LAYERs. Change the moving images to

```
<LAYER Name = "layerFinger1" Top = 200 Left = 10 z-index = 2>
<IMG Src = "file:///E|/DHTML MTE/graphics/small/ltb7.gif">
</LAYER>

<LAYER Name = "layerFinger2" Top = 250 Left = 10 z-index = 2>
<IMG Src = "file:///E|/DHTML MTE/graphics/small/ltb7.gif">
</LAYER>

<LAYER Name = "layerFinger3" Top = 300 Left = 10 z-index = 2>
<IMG Src = "file:///E|/DHTML MTE/graphics/small/ltb7.gif">
</LAYER>
```

Note the format for specifying file paths in Navigator—it's different from the way it's done in IE. Note also that the z-indices are set to 2. The z-index in Navigator is somewhat different from the z-index in IE. The values we used for the IE version won't produce the desired effect in Navigator, as some of those values are negative.

The bars that the fingers pass over and under are

```
<LAYER Bgcolor = silver Top=150 Left=70
z-index=1 Width=50 Height=220>
</LAYER>

<LAYER Bgcolor = silver Top=150 Left=220
z-index=3 Width=50 Height=220>
</LAYER>
```

```
<LAYER Bgcolor = silver Top=150 Left=370
z-index=1 Width=50 Height=220>
</LAYER>
```

The z-index is 2 for the bars that the fingers pass over, and the z-index is 3 for the bar that the fingers pass under.

The Script

Insert a SCRIPT element into the HEAD and once again, set its Language attribute to "JavaScript1.2". We'll need global variables for the timer that moves the fingers rightward, for the timer that moves them back, and for the counter. We'll initialize the counter to 0:

```
var glblTimer;
var glblBackTimer;
var glblCounter;
glblCounter = 0;
```

As in the preceding exercise, a windowLoad function starts things off:

```
function windowLoad(){
    glblTimer = setInterval("fingerMovement()", 100)
}
```

The logic for the fingerMovement and backMovement functions resembles the logic in the equivalent functions in the IE VBScript version:

```
function fingerMovement() {
    document.layers["layerFinger1"].offset(2,0);
    document.layers["layerFinger2"].offset(2,0);
    document.layers["layerFinger3"].offset(2,0);
    glblCounter = glblCounter + 1;
    if (glblCounter == 240) {
        glblCounter = 0;
        clearInterval(glblTimer);
        glblBackTimer = setInterval("backMovement()",100);
    }

}

function backMovement(){
    document.layers["layerFinger1"].offset(-2,0);
    document.layers["layerFinger2"].offset(-2,0);
    document.layers["layerFinger3"].offset(-2,0);
    glblCounter = glblCounter + 1
    if (glblCounter == 240) {
```

```
            glblCounter = 0;
            clearInterval(glblBackTimer);
            glblTimer = setInterval("fingerMovement()",100);
        }
    }
```

In each function, the counter updates after every movement. When it reaches the specified value, the functions reset it at zero, clear the appropriate timer, and each function calls the other to start the movement in the opposite direction.

The Entire Over and Under File

The whole file looks like this:

 Nav Over and Under.htm

```
<HTML>
<HEAD>
<SCRIPT Language = "JavaScript1.2">
var glblTimer
var glblBackTimer
var glblCounter
glblCounter = 0

function windowLoad(){
    glblTimer = setInterval("fingerMovement()", 100)
}


function fingerMovement() {
    document.layers["layerFinger1"].offset(2,0);
    document.layers["layerFinger2"].offset(2,0);
    document.layers["layerFinger3"].offset(2,0);
    glblCounter = glblCounter + 1;
    if (glblCounter == 240) {
            glblCounter = 0;
            clearInterval(glblTimer);
            glblBackTimer = setInterval("backMovement()",100);
    }

}

function backMovement(){
    document.layers["layerFinger1"].offset(-2,0);
    document.layers["layerFinger2"].offset(-2,0);
    document.layers["layerFinger3"].offset(-2,0);
    glblCounter = glblCounter + 1
```

```
        if (glblCounter == 240) {
                glblCounter = 0;
                clearInterval(glblBackTimer);
                glblTimer = setInterval("fingerMovement()",100);
        }
}


</SCRIPT>

<TITLE>Navigator Over and Under</TITLE>
</HEAD>
<BODY OnLoad = "windowLoad()">
<H1 Style = "text-align:center">Over and Under </H1>
<HR>

<LAYER Name = "layerFinger1" Top = 200 Left = 10 z-index = 2>
<IMG Src = "file:///E|/DHTML MTE/graphics/small/ltb7.gif">
</LAYER>

<LAYER Name = "layerFinger2" Top = 250 Left = 10 z-index = 2>
<IMG Src = "file:///E|/DHTML MTE/graphics/small/ltb7.gif">
</LAYER>

<LAYER Name = "layerFinger3" Top = 300 Left = 10 z-index = 2>
<IMG Src = "file:///E|/DHTML MTE/graphics/small/ltb7.gif">
</LAYER>

<LAYER Bgcolor = silver Top=150 Left=70
z-index=1 Width=50 Height=220>
</LAYER>

<LAYER Bgcolor = silver Top=150 Left=220
z-index=3 Width=50 Height=220>
</LAYER>

<LAYER Bgcolor = silver Top=150 Left=370
z-index=1 Width=50 Height=220>
</LAYER>

</BODY>
</HTML>
```

Open the page in Navigator to see the over and under effect. It won't look quite the same as the IE version, because the fingers won't appear to flip around when they change direction. The important thing is to understand the concepts that generate the animation.

NOTE   The Over and Under page is similar to a demonstration that you'll find at the Netscape site at `http://developer.netscape.com/library/documentation/communicator/dynhtml/fish1.htm`. In this demonstration, animation begins with a button-click. Unlike our button-click animations, however, this one doesn't protect against button-clicks during the animation. Visit the site, check out the animation (it's a nice effect), click the button during the movement of the object, and note what happens.

Pushing the Envelope

With version 4.0 of IE, Microsoft has added some ActiveX controls that expand your ability to include multimedia animations in your Web pages. Dubbed DirectAnimation Controls, they enable you to add impressive effects to your Web pages without long download times. This set of controls consists of:

- Path Control—Moves objects around a page over time in paths that you can set, with control over the speed of movement

- Sequencer Control—Creates complex sequences of actions

- Sprite Control—Adds still and animated images to the Web page

- Structured Graphics Control—Adds graphics that you can scale and rotate in three dimensions, and applies colors, patterns, and gradient fills to the graphics

DirectAnimation Multimedia encompasses a rich set of methods, techniques, and possibilities, and demands a much more detailed treatment than we can provide here. We will, however, go through an example to whet your appetite.

 NOTE   To learn more about DirectAnimation, visit `http://www.microsoft.com/msdn/sdk/inetsdk/help/dxm/da/default.htm`.

Structured Graphics

In this exercise, we'll use the Structured Graphics control to develop a Web page. The page will show three "UofCyb" strings rotating in three dimensions. Figure 7.7 shows how the finished page will look.

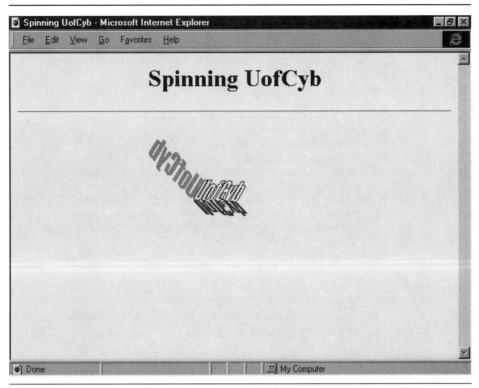

FIGURE 7.7: A Web page developed with the DirectAnimation Structured Graphics control. The page has been caught in mid-rotation.

Although three UofCybs appear to be rotating, we're going to develop four. One will serve as an outline for another. Each one requires a separate structured graphic control, and each control is an OBJECT element on the Web page.

Setting the Stage

Create a document called SpinningUofCyb.htm. Give it that name as a title and as an H1 heading followed by an HR. Give the body a background color of lightyellow or some other light color, and we'll get started.

We're going to put four OBJECT elements in the same place on the page and give them the same height and width, so in the HEAD element, create this CSS:

```
<STYLE>
Object {Position:Absolute;Left:25%;Top:25%;Height:200;Width:200}
</STYLE>
```

Let's create the first structured graphic control. This one will render UofCyb in white. In the body of the page, add this code:

```
<OBJECT ID=structgWhite
Style="z-index:0"
CLASSID = "CLSID:369303C2-D7AC-11D0-89D5-00A0C90833E6">
<PARAM NAME="Line0001" VALUE="SetLineStyle(0)">
<PARAM NAME="Line0002" VALUE="SetFillColor(255, 255, 255)">
<PARAM NAME="Line0003" VALUE="SetFillStyle(1)">
<PARAM NAME="Line0004" VALUE="SetFont('Haettenschweiler', 100,
700, 0, 0, 0)">
<PARAM NAME="Line0005" VALUE="Text('UofCyb', 0, 0)">
</OBJECT>
```

The ID sets an identifier that we'll use in a VBS script. The Style puts the control's z-index at the level of the page. CLASSID identifies the OBJECT as a structured graphics control (make sure you type it in *exactly* as it appears). The PARAM values specify aspects of the graphic's appearance.

- SetLineStyle—Specifies the type of line that surrounds the graphic (0 = None, 1= Solid, 2 = Dash)

- SetFillColor—Provides a color in RGB format

- SetFillStyle—Sets the type of fill (0 = None, 1 = Solid, 3 through 8 specify types of hatching, 9 through 14 specify types of gradients)

- SetFont—Provides a font for our UofCyb string. The arguments are name, height in points, weight (700 = heavy bold), isItalic, isUnderline, isStrikethrough (the zeros in our code indicate that we won't use any of these effects); I used my favorite font name here—you can use a different one if you like.

- Text—Creates a string using the current font and color; the arguments are the string to be created and the x and y positions for the baseline of the first character in the string. You can add another optional argument that sets the amount of rotation (in degrees) from the 0 degrees position.

This object renders a white string. Now we'll create an OBJECT that renders a black outline for this string:

```
<OBJECT id=structgOutline
Style="z-index:0"
CLASSID = "CLSID:369303C2-D7AC-11D0-89D5-00A0C90833E6">
<PARAM NAME="Line0001" VALUE="SetLineStyle(1)">
<PARAM NAME="Line0002" VALUE="SetLineColor(0, 0, 0)">
<PARAM NAME="Line0003" VALUE="SetFillStyle(0)">
<PARAM NAME="Line0004" VALUE="SetFont('Haettenschweiler', 100,
700, 0, 0, 0)">
<PARAM NAME="Line0005" VALUE="Text('UofCyb', 0, 0)">
</OBJECT>
```

In this one, we set the line style to 1, the line color to black, and we don't fill the string.

Two more, and we're done with the OBJECTs. The first one creates a green string:

```
<OBJECT id=structgGreen
Style="z-index:1"
CLASSID = "CLSID:369303C2-D7AC-11D0-89D5-00A0C90833E6">
<PARAM NAME="Line0001" VALUE="SetLineStyle(0)">
<PARAM NAME="Line0002" VALUE="SetFillColor(0, 255, 0)">
<PARAM NAME="Line0003" VALUE="SetFillStyle(1)">
<PARAM NAME="Line0004" VALUE="SetFont('Haettenschweiler', 100,
700, 0, 0, 0)">
<PARAM NAME="Line0005" VALUE="Text('UofCyb', 0, 0)">
</OBJECT>
```

The second creates a red one:

```
<OBJECT id=structgRed
Style="z-index:2"
CLASSID ="CLSID:369303C2-D7AC-11D0-89D5-00A0C90833E6">
<PARAM NAME="Line0001" VALUE="SetLineStyle(0)">
<PARAM NAME="Line0002" VALUE="SetFillColor(255, 0, 0)">
<PARAM NAME="Line0003" VALUE="SetFillStyle(1)">
<PARAM NAME="Line0004" VALUE="SetFont('Haettenschweiler', 100,
700, 0, 0, 0)">
<PARAM NAME="Line0005" VALUE="Text('UofCyb', 0, 0)">
</OBJECT>
```

Note that we give them z-indices of 1 and 2. This will add a nice three-dimensional effect to our rotation.

Writing the Script

Two subroutines will handle the rotation. They rely on two of the structured graphic control's built-in methods, Scale and Rotate. The first subroutine goes into action when the window opens, and sets the starting positions of the strings. It also calls the window timing method you've used before, setInterval:

```
Sub Window_OnLoad()
      call structgOutline.Scale(0.50, 0.50, 0.50)
      call structgRed.Scale(0.50, 0.50, 0.50)
      call structgGreen.Scale(0.50, 0.50, 0.50)
      call structgWhite.Scale(0.50, 0.50, 0.50)
      call structgOutline.Rotate(0, 0, 0)
      call structgWhite.Rotate(0,0,0)
      call structgRed.Rotate(90, 0, 0)
      call structgGreen.Rotate(0, 90, 0)
      call Window.setInterval("rotationMovement", 10)
end sub
```

The Scale method shrinks the strings along the x, y, and z axes to make them fit into the dimensions of the OBJECTs. The Rotate method sets starting positions for the strings so that they are rotated with respect to the x, y, and z axes by the indicated number of degrees. setInterval fires repeatedly. Its first argument is the subroutine, rotationMovement, that activates whenever setInterval fires; its second argument is the number of milliseconds between firings.

This is rotationMovement:

```
Sub rotationMovement
      Call structgOutline.Rotate(4,6,2)
      Call structgRed.Rotate(4,6,2)
      Call structgGreen.Rotate(4,6,2)
      Call structgWhite.Rotate(4,6,2)
      Movement = Window.SetTimeout("Call Rotation", 10, "VBSCript")
End Sub
```

As in the first subroutine, this subroutine uses the Rotate method to rotate the controls around the x, y, and z axes. Because it activates every 10 milliseconds—thanks to setInterval—it generates the continuous movement of the strings.

The Whole Document

Here's the entire `SpinningUofCyb.htm` file:

SpinningUofCyb.htm

```
<HTML>
<HEAD>
<TITLE>Spinning UofCyb</TITLE>
<STYLE>
Object {Position:Absolute;Left:25%;Top:25%;Height:200;Width:200}
</STYLE>

<SCRIPT LANGUAGE="VBScript">

Sub Window_OnLoad()
    call structgOutline.Scale(0.50, 0.50, 0.50)
    call structgRed.Scale(0.50, 0.50, 0.50)
    call structgGreen.Scale(0.50, 0.50, 0.50)
    call structgWhite.Scale(0.50, 0.50, 0.50)
    call structgOutline.Rotate(0, 0, 0)
    call structgWhite.Rotate(0,0,0)
    call structgRed.Rotate(90, 0, 0)
    call structgGreen.Rotate(0, 90, 0)
    call Window.setInterval("rotationMovement", 10)
end sub

Sub rotationMovement
    Call structgOutline.Rotate(4,6,2)
    Call structgRed.Rotate(4,6,2)
    Call structgGreen.Rotate(4,6,2)
    Call structgWhite.Rotate(4,6,2)
End Sub

</SCRIPT>

</HEAD>
<BODY style = "background-color:lightyellow">
<H1 Style = "text-align:center">Spinning UofCyb</H1>
<HR>

<OBJECT id=structgWhite
Style="z-index:0"
CLASSID = "CLSID:369303C2-D7AC-11D0-89D5-00A0C90833E6">
<PARAM NAME="Line0001" VALUE="SetLineStyle(0)">
<PARAM NAME="Line0002" VALUE="SetFillColor(255, 255, 255)">
<PARAM NAME="Line0003" VALUE="SetFillStyle(1)">
```

```
<PARAM NAME="Line0004" VALUE="SetFont('Haettenschweiler', 100,
700, 0, 0, 0)">
<PARAM NAME="Line0005" VALUE="Text('UofCyb', 0, 0)">
</OBJECT>

<OBJECT id=structgOutline
Style="z-index:0"
CLASSID = "CLSID:369303C2-D7AC-11D0-89D5-00A0C90833E6">
<PARAM NAME="Line0001" VALUE="SetLineStyle(1)">
<PARAM NAME="Line0002" VALUE="SetLineColor(0, 0, 0)">
<PARAM NAME="Line0003" VALUE="SetFillStyle(0)">
<PARAM NAME="Line0004" VALUE="SetFont('Haettenschweiler', 100,
700, 0, 0, 0)">
<PARAM NAME="Line0005" VALUE="Text('UofCyb', 0, 0)">
</OBJECT>

<OBJECT id=structgGreen
Style="z-index:1"
CLASSID = "CLSID:369303C2-D7AC-11D0-89D5-00A0C90833E6">
<PARAM NAME="Line0001" VALUE="SetLineStyle(0)">
<PARAM NAME="Line0002" VALUE="SetFillColor(0, 255, 0)">
<PARAM NAME="Line0003" VALUE="SetFillStyle(1)">
<PARAM NAME="Line0004" VALUE="SetFont('Haettenschweiler', 100,
700, 0, 0, 0)">
<PARAM NAME="Line0005" VALUE="Text('UofCyb', 0, 0)">
</OBJECT>

<OBJECT id=structgRed
Style="z-index:2"
CLASSID ="CLSID:369303C2-D7AC-11D0-89D5-00A0C90833E6">
<PARAM NAME="Line0001" VALUE="SetLineStyle(0)">
<PARAM NAME="Line0002" VALUE="SetFillColor(255, 0, 0)">
<PARAM NAME="Line0003" VALUE="SetFillStyle(1)">
<PARAM NAME="Line0004" VALUE="SetFont('Haettenschweiler', 100,
700, 0, 0, 0)">
<PARAM NAME="Line0005" VALUE="Text('UofCyb', 0, 0)">
</OBJECT>

</BODY>
</HTML>
```

Open it in IE, and watch the UofCyb strings rotate. To help yourself understand how the structured graphic control works, make a copy of this file and substitute different values in the script and in the HTML.

Summary

Animation adds another dimension to Web pages. The illusion of motion can attract attention and make a page memorable. Generating an animation is straightforward: It involves setting an interval and connecting it to a procedure that changes the location of a set of objects. The quality of the animation depends on the amount of change and the length of the interval.

VBScript and JavaScript make it easy to build animations. It's important, however, to keep in mind some of the important differences between IE and Navigator. In IE, every element in the HTML document is a scriptable object, and, hence, capable of animation. The set of scriptable objects in Navigator is considerably narrower. LAYER elements are scriptable and can act as containers for other elements. For this reason, you put objects into LAYER elements if you want to animate them in Navigator.

Have You Mastered the Essentials?

Now you can...

☑ Use the window *setInterval* method to create animations in IE and in Navigator

☑ Develop animations that activate when the user initiates an event and stop when the user initiates an event

☑ Develop animations that activate when the browser window opens

☑ Create animations that start and end automatically

☑ Create animations that stay in effect as long as the Web page stays open

☑ Create animations that incorporate visual filtering effects

☑ Use randomization functions in VBScript and JavaScript to add variety to objects' movement paths

☑ Work with the Netscape *LAYER* element to produce animations

Skill 7

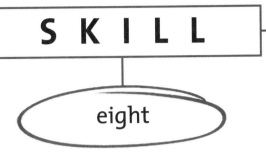

S K I L L

eight

Multiplying the Media

❑ Multimedia in Navigator and IE

❑ Adding sound to an animation

❑ Working with Navigator plug-ins and ActiveX controls

❑ Adding video to a Web page

❑ Working with the Microsoft DirectAnimation
Multimedia structured graphic control

8

Images, graphics, and animations add to the excitement of surfing the Web. Adding sounds, video, and music pump up the volume even more. Both Navigator and IE hold the potential for building intriguing multimedia presentations, and this Skill will show you how to realize this potential. For the exercises in this Skill, you'll need a sound card and speakers installed in your computer. You'll also have to have your Windows 95 CD in your CD-ROM drive.

We'll begin by examining multimedia in Navigator, and then move on to IE.

Multimedia in Navigator

Each browser implements multimedia in a different way. Navigator uses *plug-ins* to get the job done. A plug-in is a software package that extends Navigator's capabilities. Navigator can recognize and work with .GIF, .JPEG, and HTML files, but it can't recognize other important formats (like .WAV and .AVI, for example). Beginning with Navigator 2.0, third-party software developers have worked with Netscape to build plug-ins that enable Navigator to work with these other formats directly inside the browser window. When you activate a plug-in, you're still in Navigator. Other than plug-ins, *helper* applications extend Navigator's reach, but are external to the browser. When you activate a helper, the helper's window opens and proceeds with the task at hand.

In this section, we'll be concerned with the LiveAudio plug-in and the NPAVI32 plug-in. The first one works with sound in a number of file formats, the second with video in .AVI format.

Sounds

We'll start our multimedia exercises with sounds, which we'll use in a couple of ways. First, we'll add sound to an animation we created in Skill 7. Then, we'll look more closely at the element that allows us to put a sound file into an HTML document.

Adding Sound to an Animation

To form a bridge between what you did in Skill 7 and what's coming up in Skill 8, we'll start with the Over and Under page you just developed. That's the one where the fingers moved from the left of the page to the right and then came back to the left side of the page. Along the way, they went over and under a sequence of rectangular shapes.

In this exercise, you'll add sound. When the fingers arrive at their destination on the right, a noise will occur. It will sound like an object striking a wall. Then the fingers will move back to the left, and when they get to their starting point, the sound will occur again just before the fingers move to the right. The process will repeat until you close the window.

Copy Nav Over and Under.htm from your Skill 7 folder to Skill 8. Open it in your text editor, and you'll see

```
<HTML>
<HEAD>
<SCRIPT Language = "JavaScript1.2">
var glblTimer;
var glblBackTimer;
var glblCounter;
glblCounter = 0;

function windowLoad(){
    glblTimer = setInterval("fingerMovement()", 100)
}


function fingerMovement() {
    document.layers["layerFinger1"].offset(2,0);
    document.layers["layerFinger2"].offset(2,0);
    document.layers["layerFinger3"].offset(2,0);
    glblCounter = glblCounter + 1;
    if (glblCounter == 240) {
        glblCounter = 0;
        clearInterval(glblTimer);
        glblBackTimer = setInterval("backMovement()",100);
    }

}

function backMovement(){
    document.layers["layerFinger1"].offset(-2,0);
    document.layers["layerFinger2"].offset(-2,0);
    document.layers["layerFinger3"].offset(-2,0);
    glblCounter = glblCounter + 1
    if (glblCounter == 240) {
        glblCounter = 0;
        clearInterval(glblBackTimer);
        glblTimer = setInterval("fingerMovement()",100);
    }
}
```

Skill 8

```
</SCRIPT>

<TITLE>Navigator Over and Under</TITLE>
</HEAD>
<BODY OnLoad = "windowLoad()">
<H1 Style = "text-align:center">Over and Under </H1>
<HR>

<LAYER Name = "layerFinger1" Top = 200 Left = 10 z-index = 2>
<IMG Src = "file:///E|/DHTML MTE/graphics/small/ltb7.gif">
</LAYER>

<LAYER Name = "layerFinger2" Top = 250 Left = 10 z-index = 2>
<IMG Src = "file:///E|/DHTML MTE/graphics/small/ltb7.gif">
</LAYER>

<LAYER Name = "layerFinger3" Top = 300 Left = 10 z-index = 2>
<IMG Src = "file:///E|/DHTML MTE/graphics/small/ltb7.gif">
</LAYER>

<LAYER Bgcolor = silver Top=150 Left=70
z-index=1 Width=50 Height=220>
</LAYER>

<LAYER Bgcolor = silver Top=150 Left=220
z-index=3 Width=50 Height=220>
</LAYER>

<LAYER Bgcolor = silver Top=150 Left=370
z-index=1 Width=50 Height=220>
</LAYER>

</BODY>
</HTML>
```

The first thing we have to do is find the sound we want to use, and then we have to embed it in the document. Here's where your Windows 95 CD comes in handy. Open it and find the folder funstuff\hover\sounds\mixed. This is a set of sounds for the game "Hover," which comes with Windows 95. The one we're interested in is hit_wall.wav. To embed this sound in your animation, you use, appropriately enough, the EMBED element.

Designed by Netscape for adding multimedia to HTML, EMBED works very much like the OBJECT element we looked at in Skill 5. There's one important difference, however: If you use a .WAV file as the source for EMBED, you won't mess up some of your browser's abilities to render fonts and colors. (Remember the warning in Skill 5?)

Here's how to use the EMBED element. After the last LAYER, and before </BODY>, insert

```
<EMBED Src = "file:///J|funstuff/hover/sounds/mixed/hit_wall.wav"
Autostart = "false" Name = "embedWall" Volume = 20 MASTERSOUND
Hidden = "true">
```

> **TIP** My CD drive happens to be my J: drive. Remember to substitute the appropriate letter for your CD drive, or copy the file into your Skill 8 folder and just use the file name as the value of the Src attribute.

Note Navigator's format for the file path to hit_wall.wav, and how it differs from the format you're probably used to. Autostart = "false" keeps the sound file from playing as soon as the page opens in Navigator. The Name attribute establishes an identifier (embedWall) that we can use in a script to refer to this element. The Volume attribute, a number between 0 and 100, initializes the volume for the sound. MASTERSOUND is an attribute (without a value) that has to be present for a script to work with the sound, and Hidden = "true" makes the EMBED element invisible.

To generate the sound, we invoke the element's play method like this:

```
document.embedWall.play(false);
```

The false argument specifies that the sound only plays once. If the argument is true, the sound plays repeatedly after the first time you hear it.

To play the sound when the fingers reach their destination on the right side of the page, add that line to the if statement in the function that moves the fingers to the right:

```
function fingerMovement() {
    document.layers["layerFinger1"].offset(2,0);
    document.layers["layerFinger2"].offset(2,0);
    document.layers["layerFinger3"].offset(2,0);
    glblCounter = glblCounter + 1;
    if (glblCounter == 240) {
        glblCounter = 0;
        document.embedWall.play(false);
        clearInterval(glblTimer);
        glblBackTimer = setInterval("backMovement()",100);
    }
```

Skill 8

Do the same in the function that moves the fingers to the left:

```
function backMovement(){
    document.layers["layerFinger1"].offset(-2,0);
    document.layers["layerFinger2"].offset(-2,0);
    document.layers["layerFinger3"].offset(-2,0);
    glblCounter = glblCounter + 1
    if (glblCounter == 240) {
        glblCounter = 0;
        document.embedWall.play(false);
        clearInterval(glblBackTimer);
        glblTimer = setInterval("fingerMovement()",100);
    }
}
```

You've added sound to your animation. Open the page in Navigator and listen to the sounds as you watch the fingers fly to their destinations.

A Sound Bite

Let's examine the LiveAudio plug-in a bit more closely. In order to do so, we'll need a sound that lasts a few seconds. I've recorded a message, `welcome.wav`, that you can download from the Sybex Web site and use with the pages you're about to develop. Store the message in your Skill 8 folder.

 NOTE

If you'd rather not listen to my voice (and quite frankly, I wouldn't blame you), use the Windows sound recorder to record a message of your own. You'll need a microphone connected to your sound card to make it happen. Your sound recorder is probably at `C:\Windows\SNDREC32.exe`.

Create this page in your text editor, and call it `NavSound.htm`:

 NavSound.htm

```
<HTML>
<HEAD>
<TITLE>Sound in Navigator</TITLE>
</HEAD>
<BODY>
<H1 Style = "text-align:center">Sound in Navigator</H1>
<HR>
<EMBED Src = "welcome.wav" Width = 144 Height = 60
Controls = Console Volume = 50>
</BODY>
</HTML>
```

Width and Height set the dimensions, Control = Console specifies the type of display, and Volume sets a starting volume.

Open the file in Navigator. LiveAudio may take a few moments to load, and then you'll see a page that looks like Figure 8.1.

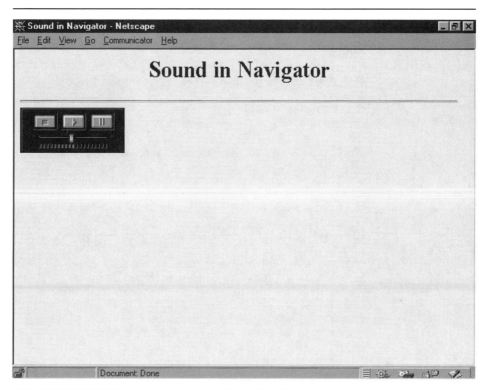

FIGURE 8.1: The NavSound.htm page in Navigator

Click on the middle button to begin playing the file, on the left button to stop playing (and reset to the beginning), and on the right button to pause. The slider is the volume control, but I didn't notice any change in volume when I moved it.

Right-clicking on the display opens a pop-up menu with five choices. The first three enable you to play, pause, and stop the message. The fourth allows you to save the message file, and the fifth opens an information box about the plug-in.

Scripting a Console

The EMBED element enables you to show as much or as little of the console as you like. In the first exercise, you hid the element. In the second, you showed the entire console. In this exercise, you'll hide the element and create buttons that use scripts to control the playing of the message.

Create a file in Skill 8 called NavConsole.htm, and make it look like this:

```
<HTML>
<HEAD>
<TITLE>A Console in Navigator</TITLE>
</HEAD>
<BODY Bgcolor = "Silver">
<H1 style = "text-align:center"> A Console in Navigator</H1>
<HR>
<P> Click "Play" to hear an overly histrionic message from the author.
</P>
<P> Click "Pause" to temporarily stop the histrionics
</P>
<P> Click "Pump It Up!" or "Lower It!" to adjust the volume
</P>
<P> Click "Stop" to put this sound bite out of its misery
</P>
<EMBED Src = "welcome.wav" Name = "embedWelcome"
Volume = 30 MASTERSOUND Hidden = "true" Autostart = "false">
<FORM>
<INPUT Type = button Value = Play>
<INPUT Type = button Value = Pause>
<INPUT Type = button Value = "Pump It Up!">
<INPUT Type = button Value = "Lower It!">
<INPUT Type = button Value = Stop>

</FORM>
</BODY>
</HTML>
```

Opened in Navigator, the file looks like Figure 8.2.

Next, attach functionality to the buttons. LiveAudio has built-in methods that you can invoke. From the first exercise, you already know about play(). Script this method for the first button's onClick event:

```
<INPUT Type = button
    onClick = "embedWelcome.play(false)"
    Value = Play>
```

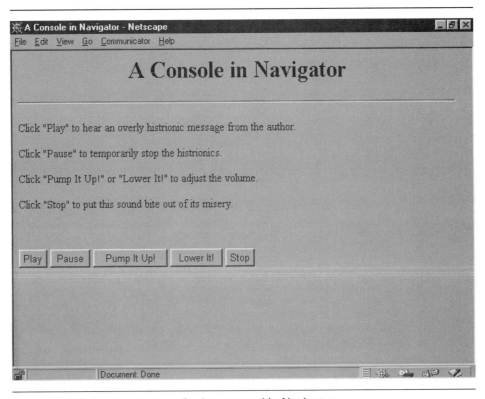

FIGURE 8.2: NavConsole.htm opened in Navigator

 NOTE   Remember that false means to play the sound only once.

You'll notice a difference between the way we refer to the EMBED element inline from the onClick event, and the way we refer to it from a function in the SCRIPT element. You'll see this difference at work again here. In Netscape's implementation, items in the SCRIPT element are in a different *namespace* from items in other elements on the page. For this reason, a function in the SCRIPT element can't refer to an object the same way that an inline function call in the BODY can. A function in the SCRIPT element has to refer to the EMBED element as document.embedWelcome. In the inline call, the shorter name, embedWelcome, is sufficient.

Add pause() and stop() to the appropriate buttons:

```
<INPUT Type = button
       onClick = "embedWelcome.pause()"
       Value = Pause>
    .
    .
    .
<INPUT Type = button
       onClick = "embedWelcome.stop()"
       Value = Stop>
```

Now we'll turn our attention to the buttons that adjust the volume. Here's how the HTML for these buttons should look:

```
<INPUT Type = button
       onClick = "increaseVolume()"
       Value = "Pump It Up!">
<INPUT Type = button
       onClick = "decreaseVolume()"
       Value = "Lower It!">
```

Of course, we have to create increaseVolume() and decreaseVolume(). Let's first put the framework together. In the HEAD element, add

```
<SCRIPT Language = "JavaScript1.2">
function increaseVolume() {
}

function decreaseVolume() {
}
</SCRIPT>
```

The volume is a number that can vary from 0 to 100. First, we'll use the built-in GetVolume method to set the current volume:

```
currentVolume = document.embedWelcome.GetVolume();
```

 NOTE   Notice the reference document.embedWelcome.

In the increaseVolume() function, we'll change the volume by 10 each time we click one of the volume buttons. So, the next line of increaseVolume() should be

```
updatedVolume = currentVolume + 10;
```

Now we have to be aware of three possibilities:

- If the current volume is already 100, we don't want to increase it. We will, however, inform the user that the volume is already maxed out.

- If the updated volume is between 90 and 100, we'll increase the volume to 100. We'll use the built-in method setvol to set the volume.

- If the updated volume is less than 90, we'll use setvol to set the volume to the updated volume.

We'll create if statements to handle these possibilities:

```
if (currentVolume == 100) {
        alert("Volume is already at maximum level");
    }

    if ((updatedVolume <= 100) && (updatedVolume >= 90)) {
        document.embedWelcome.setvol(100);
    }
    else {
        if (updatedVolume < 90) {
                document.embedWelcome.setvol(updatedVolume);
        }
    }
```

That takes care of the increaseVolume() function.
The other function, decreaseVolume(), works the same way:

```
function decreaseVolume() {
    currentVolume = document.embedWelcome.GetVolume();
    updatedVolume = currentVolume - 10;
    if (currentVolume == 0) {
            alert("Volume is already at minimum level");
    }

    if ((updatedVolume >= 0) && (updatedVolume <= 10)) {
        document.embedWelcome.setvol(0);
    }
    else {
        if (updatedVolume > 10) {
                document.embedWelcome.setvol(updatedVolume);
        }
    }
}
```

In this case, the if statements handle these possibilities:

- If the current volume is already 0, don't lower it more, and inform the user that the volume is already at the minimum level.

- If the current volume is between 0 and 10, use setvol to lower the volume to 0.

- If the current volume is greater than 10, use setvol to lower the volume to the updated volume.

Here's the entire NavConsole.htm file:

NavConsole.htm

```
<HTML>
<HEAD>
<SCRIPT Language = "JavaScript1.2">
function increaseVolume() {
    currentVolume = document.embedWelcome.GetVolume();
    updatedVolume = currentVolume + 10;
    if (currentVolume == 100) {
        alert("Volume is already at maximum level");
    }

    if ((updatedVolume <= 100) && (updatedVolume > 90)) {
        document.embedWelcome.setvol(100);
    }
    else {
        if (updatedVolume < 90) {
            document.embedWelcome.setvol(updatedVolume);
        }
    }
}

function decreaseVolume() {
    currentVolume = document.embedWelcome.GetVolume();
    updatedVolume = currentVolume - 10;
    if (currentVolume == 0) {
        alert("Volume is already at minimum level");
    }

    if ((updatedVolume >= 0) && (updatedVolume < 10)) {
        document.embedWelcome.setvol(0);
    }
```

```
        else {
                if (updatedVolume > 10) {
                        document.embedWelcome.setvol(updatedVolume);
                }
        }
}
</SCRIPT>


<TITLE>A Console in Navigator</TITLE>
</HEAD>
<BODY Bgcolor = "Silver">
<H1 style = "text-align:center"> A Console in Navigator</H1>
<HR>
<P> Click "Play" to hear an overly histrionic message from the author.
</P>
<P> Click "Pause" to temporarily stop the histrionics
</P>
<P> Click "Pump It Up!" or "Lower It!" to adjust the volume
</P>
<P> Click "Stop" to put this sound bite out of its misery
</P>
<EMBED Src = "welcome.wav" Name = "embedWelcome"
Volume = 30 MASTERSOUND Hidden = "true" Autostart = "false">
<FORM>
<INPUT Type = button
      onClick = "embedWelcome.play(false)"
      Value = Play>
<INPUT Type = button
      onClick = "embedWelcome.pause()"
      Value = Pause>
<INPUT Type = button
      onClick = "increaseVolume()"
      Value = "Pump It Up!">
<INPUT Type = button
      onClick = "decreaseVolume()"
      Value = "Lower It!">
<INPUT Type = button
      onClick = "embedWelcome.stop()"
      Value = Stop>

</FORM>
</BODY>
</HTML>
```

Open it in Navigator and use the buttons to control the sound bite.

NOTE   In my system, the on-screen buttons, like the slider in the previous exercise, had no effect on the volume. Perhaps in your system the results will be different.

Table 8.1 presents the attributes for the EMBED element when you use it with the Navigator LiveAudio plug-in.

T A B L E   8 . 1 : The EMBED Element's Attributes When Used with LiveAudio

Attribute	What It Does
Src	Specifies the file to play. Can be in .WAV, .AU, .AIFF, or .MIDI format.
Height	Specifies the height of the console or console element in pixels
Width	Specifies the width of the console or console element in pixels
Controls	Customizes the LiveAudio plug-in's display
	Possible values:
	Console—A full console display with Play, Pause, Stop, and Volume Control
	SmallConsole—Play, Stop, and Volume Control (with this value, an audio file autostarts by default)
	PlayButton—Starts the audio
	PauseButton—Pauses the audio
	StopButton—Stops and unloads the audio
	VolumeLever—Volume Control slider
Autostart	"True" begins playing the audio when the page loads. "False" defers playing until the user clicks the Play button.
Loop	"True" plays the sound continuously until the user clicks the Stop button or closes the page. "False" plays the sound only once. "Integer" repeats the sound the designated number of times.
Starttime	In minutes:seconds sets a point in the file for the audio to start playing.
Endtime	In minutes:seconds sets a point in the file for the audio to stop playing.
Volume	Specifies the volume of the sound as a number from 0 to 100
Hidden	"True" hides the plug-in display.
Mastersound	Enables you to script controls to manipulate the audio
Name	Sets a unique identifier that you can use in a script

Movies

The EMBED element enables you to add video as well as audio to your Web page. Netscape's built-in video plug-in works with video files in the .AVI format. We'll use goodtimes.avi for this exercise, one of the video files on your Windows 95 CD. To give you some experience with the methods that EMBED gives you, we'll put some buttons on the page and script them to control the playback.

Create a file called NavMovie.htm, and title it Movies in Navigator. Give it the centered H1 heading Let's Go To The Movies in Navigator! Follow the heading with an HR element, give the body a background color of silver, and your file should look like this:

```
<HTML>
<HEAD>
<TITLE>Movies in Navigator</TITLE>
</HEAD>
<BODY BGcolor = "Silver">
<H1 style = "text-align:center"> Let's Go To The Movies in Navigator!
</H1>
<HR>
</BODY>
</HTML>
```

Now for the video: After the <HR> tag and before </BODY>, insert an EMBED element with the goodtime.avi file as the source:

```
<EMBED Name = "embedGoodtime"
Src="file:///J|funstuff/videos/highperf/goodtime.avi"
Width = 320 Height = 240>
```

Follow this with a form that contains a set of input buttons whose onClick events are scripted to invoke methods for controlling the video:

```
<FORM>
<INPUT Type = button
    Onclick = "embedGoodtime.play(false)"
    Value = Play>
<INPUT Type = button
    Onclick = "embedGoodtime.rewind(false)"
    Value = Rewind>
<INPUT Type = button
    Onclick = "embedGoodtime.stop(false)"
    Value = Stop>
<INPUT Type = button
    Onclick = "embedGoodtime.forward(false)"
    Value = Forward>
```

Skill 8

```
<INPUT Type = button
    Onclick = "embedGoodtime.frameForward(false)"
    Value = "Frame Forward">
<INPUT Type = button
    Onclick = "embedGoodtime.frameBack(false)"
    Value = "Frame Back">
<BR><BR>
<INPUT Name = editSeek Type = text Value = 0 Size = 10>
<INPUT Type = button
    Onclick="embedGoodtime.seek(false,parseInt(form.editSeek.value))"
    Value = Seek>
</FORM>
```

The last two input controls enable you to move the video to a specific frame. The value of the text input is part of the argument to the Seek button's onClick event. Since it's a string, we'll use the built-in function parseInt to turn that value into an integer.

Open this file in Navigator, hit the Play button, and the page will look like Figure 8.3.

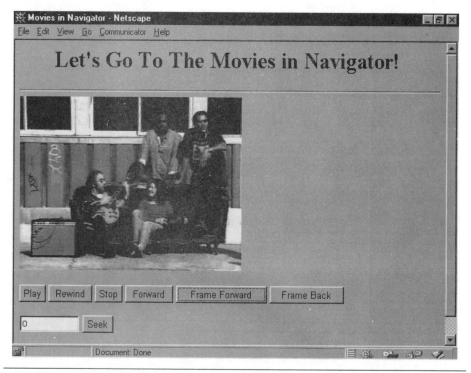

FIGURE 8.3: NavMovie.htm, with the "Goodtime" video in progress

Experiment with the other buttons, and you'll see that you can stop the video (this one is like "pause"), advance it forward or backward one frame at a time, rewind it back to the beginning, or forward it all the way to the end. Use the text box and the Seek button to move to a specific frame.

The attributes with the EMBED tag for video are a subset of the ones for audio: Src, Autostart, Loop, Width, and Height. See Table 8.1 for the details.

Multimedia in IE

In contrast with Netscape plug-ins, Microsoft extends the functionality of IE with ActiveX controls. I mentioned ActiveX controls in Skill 5 when we examined the OBJECT element.

ActiveX controls live as .OCX files in your computer and are represented as OBJECT elements in HTML documents. A Web page that specifies ActiveX controls in its HTML calls these controls into action when it downloads into your machine. If the specified controls aren't registered on your machine, the document can use the OBJECT element's Codebase attribute to download and register them. Your computer can then use them when future Web pages specify them.

To get a quick take on the number of ActiveX controls in your computer, select Start ➤ Find and search for *.OCX. You'll find a number of them in your C:\Windows\System folder. Some of them downloaded when you installed IE. For this section, we're interested in one of them—the Active Movie control. This control enables you to hear audio and watch video in IE.

 NOTE   The field of ActiveX is so rich and varied that I could write a whole book on that subject alone. In fact, I *did* write a book about it, so here's a shameless plug: If you're interested in harnessing the power of ActiveX for your Web pages, take a look at *ActiveX: No experience required*, also published by Sybex.

Sounds

Surprisingly, you can access the Active Movie control in IE through the EMBED element, just as you can use this element to access multimedia plug-ins in Navigator. Other methods are available, but first we'll go through the <EMBED> tag.

Adding Sound to an Animation

As we did with Navigator, let's start by adding sound to an animation. Copy Over and Under.htm from Skill 7 into Skill 8, and rename it Over and Under Sound.htm. Here's the file:

Over and Under Sound.htm

```
<HTML>
<HEAD>
<STYLE>
div {background-color:silver;border:solid;position:absolute;top:150;
z-index:-1;width:50;height:220}
</STYLE>

<SCRIPT Language = "VBScript">
dim glblTimer
dim glblBackTimer
dim glblCounter

Sub window_onload
    glblTimer = window.setInterval("fingerMovement", 100)
    glblCounter = 0
End Sub

Sub fingerMovement
    Call MoveElementBy(imgFinger1, 2,0)
    Call MoveElementBy(imgFinger2, 2,0)
    Call MoveElementBy(imgFinger3, 2,0)
    glblCounter = glblCounter + 1
    if glblCounter = 240 then
            glblCounter = 0
            Call filterAction
            window.clearInterval(glblTimer)
            glblBackTimer = window.setInterval("backMovement", 100)
        end if

End Sub

Sub backMovement
    Call MoveElementBy(imgFinger1, -2,0)
    Call MoveElementBy(imgFinger2, -2,0)
    Call MoveElementBy(imgFinger3, -2,0)
    glblCounter = glblCounter + 1
    if glblCounter = 240 then
            glblCounter = 0
            Call unfilterAction
```

```
                window.clearInterval(glblBackTimer)
                glblTimer = window.setInterval("fingerMovement",100)
        end if
End Sub

Sub filterAction
        imgFinger1.Style.Filter = "fliph(enabled=1)"
        imgFinger2.Style.Filter = "fliph(enabled=1)"
        imgFinger3.Style.Filter = "fliph(enabled=1)"
End Sub

Sub unfilterAction
        imgFinger1.Style.Filter = "fliph(enabled=0)"
        imgFinger2.Style.Filter = "fliph(enabled=0)"
        imgFinger3.Style.Filter = "fliph(enabled=0)"
End Sub

Sub MoveElementBy(ElementID,LeftMovementAmount,TopMovementAmount)
        pPositionTop = InStr(ElementID.Style.Top,"px")
        pPositionLeft = InStr(ElementID.Style.Left,"px")
        ElementID.Style.Top = _
          CInt(Left(ElementID.Style.Top,pPositionTop-1)) +
TopMovementAmount
        ElementID.Style.Left = _
          CInt(Left(ElementID.Style.Left,pPositionLeft-1)) +
LeftMovementAmount
End Sub
</SCRIPT>

<TITLE>Over and Under</TITLE>
</HEAD>
<BODY>
<H1 Style = "text-align:center">Over and Under with Sound </H1>
<HR>

<IMG ID = imgFinger1 Src = "E:\DHTML MTE\graphics\small\ltb7.gif"
Style = "position:absolute;top:200;left:10">

<IMG ID = imgFinger2 Src = "E:\DHTML MTE\graphics\small\ltb7.gif"
Style = "position:absolute;top:250;left:10">

<IMG ID = imgFinger3 Src = "E:\DHTML MTE\graphics\small\ltb7.gif"
Style = "position:absolute;top:300;left:10">

<DIV Style = "left:70; z-index:-1">
</DIV>

<DIV Style = "left:220; z-index:1">
</DIV>
```

Skill 8

```
<DIV Style = "left:370; z-index:-1">
</DIV>

</BODY>
</HTML>
```

To add the audio, insert this code between the last </DIV> and </BODY>:

```
<EMBED ID = "embedWall" Src =
"J:\funstuff\hover\sounds\mixed\hit_wall.wav"
Hidden = "true" Autostart = "false">
```

NOTE   In the Microsoft version, you don't add the Mastersound attribute to the EMBED element.

To play the .WAV file, add this code to the if statement in the fingerMovement subroutine and to the if statement in the backMovement subroutine:

```
embedWall.Run
```

TIP   In VBScript, notice that you can use the ID you specified in the <EMBED> tag. In the Microsoft world, items in the SCRIPT element are in the same namespace as items in the rest of the document. You'll find this to be the case in JScript as well.

Open this page in IE, and you'll see the fingers make that "hit-the-wall" noise when they reach the right side of the page and again when they make it back to their starting points.

A Sound Bite

Let's have a look at the Active Movie control. Create this file:

IESound.htm

```
<HTML>
<HEAD>
<TITLE>Sound in IE</TITLE>
</HEAD>
<BODY>
<H1 Style = "text-align:center">Sound in IE</H1>
<HR>
<EMBED Src = "welcome.wav" Hidden = "false" Autostart = "false">
</BODY>
</HTML>
```

Save the file as IESound.htm. As you can see, it's almost exactly the same as the NavSound.htm file you created for Navigator. Although the HTML is virtually the same, Figure 8.4 shows that the page is different from the page in Figure 8.1. In NavSound.htm, you were accessing a Navigator plug-in. Here, you're accessing an ActiveX control.

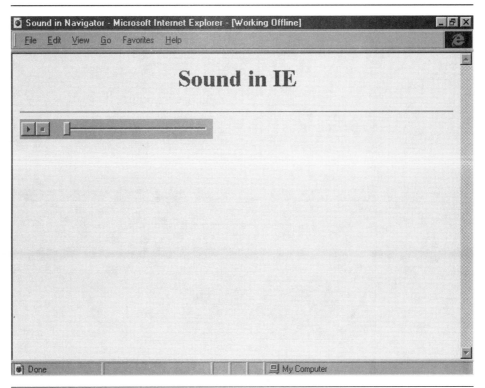

FIGURE 8.4: The IESound.htm file opened in IE. (Compare with Figure 8.1.)

If you right-click on the control and select Properties from the pop-up menu, you'll see a set of tabbed Properties pages that allow you to set properties of the control, even while the sound is playing (see Figure 8.5).

If you select the Controls tab and click the Display panel checkbox, for example, the Active Movie control will appear, as in Figure 8.6. (You can also make this visible by clicking Display on the pop-up menu.)

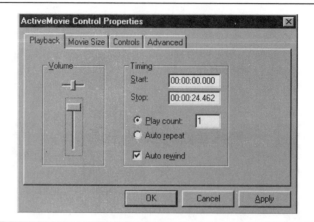

FIGURE 8.5: The tabbed Properties pages of the Active Movie control

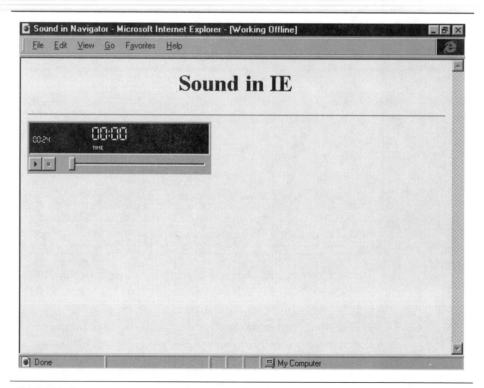

FIGURE 8.6: The Active Movie control with its Display panel visible

Scripting a Console

To get some experience with the Active Movie control's methods, let's script some buttons that will manipulate some of the control's properties. We'll adapt the JavaScript that we wrote for the similar page in Navigator, and you'll see some of the differences between JavaScript 1.2 and Microsoft's JScript.

Create a file called IEConsole.htm. Reuse the NavConsole.htm file if you like, at least to set up the text, the embedded .WAV file, and the buttons. Except for the header, it will look exactly like NavConsole.htm when you open it in IE. Here's how the file should look before we do any scripting:

```
<HTML>
<HEAD>
<TITLE>A Console in IE</TITLE>
</HEAD>
<BODY Style = "background-color:silver">
<H1 style = "text-align:center"> A Console in IE</H1>
<HR>
<P> Click "Play" to hear an overly histrionic message from the author.
</P>
<P> Click "Pause" to temporarily stop the histrionics.
</P>
<P> Click "Pump It Up!" or "Lower It!" to adjust the volume.
</P>
<P> Click "Stop" to put this sound bite out of its misery.
</P>
<EMBED Src = "welcome.wav" ID = "embedWelcome"
Hidden = "true" Autostart = "false">
<FORM>
<INPUT Type = button Value = Play>
<INPUT Type = button Value = Pause>
<INPUT Type = button Value = "Pump It Up!">
<INPUT Type = button Value = "Lower It!">
<INPUT Type = button Value = Stop>
</FORM>
</BODY>
</HTML>
```

As we did in the Navigator version, add functionality to the buttons:

```
<INPUT Type = button
    onClick = "embedWelcome.Run()"
    Value = Play>
<INPUT Type = button
    onClick = "embedWelcome.Pause()"
    Value = Pause>
<INPUT Type = button
    onClick = "increaseVolume()"
    Value = "Pump It Up!">
```

Skill 8

```
<INPUT Type = button
    onClick = "decreaseVolume()"
    Value = "Lower It!">
<INPUT Type = button
    onClick = "embedWelcome.Stop()"
    Value = Stop>
```

In the Microsoft version, Run is the name of the method that starts playing the file.

Now we have to construct the increaseVolume() and decreaseVolume() functions. Volume in the Active Movie control is somewhat different from volume in the Navigator plug-in. Instead of a number that varies from 0 to 100, the volume is a number—in hundredths of decibels— that varies from –10,000 (no volume) to 0 (maximum volume). Given these constraints, we can adapt the code we wrote for the Navigator version, but with some important differences:

- Again, since the items in the SCRIPT element share the same namespace as items in the rest of the document, we can use the ID we assigned to the EMBED element inside the functions.

- Instead of GetVolume() and setvol methods, the Active Movie control has the Volume property. We use this property to retrieve the current volume.

- Since the numerical difference between no volume and maximum volume is so large, we'll write the script to change the volume by 1,000 each time we click one of the volume buttons.

The functions are:

```
<SCRIPT Language = "JavaScript">
function increaseVolume() {
    currentVolume = embedWelcome.Volume;
    updatedVolume = currentVolume + 1000;
    if (currentVolume == 0) {
        alert("Volume is already at maximum level");
    }
    if ((updatedVolume < 0) && (updatedVolume >= -1000)) {
        embedWelcome.Volume = 0;
    }
    else {
        if (updatedVolume < -1000) {
            embedWelcome.Volume = updatedVolume;
        }
    }
}

function decreaseVolume() {
    currentVolume = embedWelcome.Volume;
    updatedVolume = currentVolume - 1000;
```

```
if (currentVolume == -10000) {
        alert("Volume is already at minimum level");
}
if ((updatedVolume > -10000) && (updatedVolume <= -9000)) {
        embedWelcome.Volume = -10000;
}
else {
        if (updatedVolume > -9000) {
                embedWelcome.Volume = updatedVolume;
        }
}
}
</SCRIPT>
```

NOTE We don't use "1.2" after "JavaScript" in the value for the Language attribute. That only applies to the Navigator version.

Open this page in IE, and experiment with the buttons. For one thing, you'll find that the volume buttons do adjust the volume (at least they do on my system). For another, you'll find that no matter how you set a Volume attribute in the <EMBED> tag, the volume always comes up at maximum level when you refresh the page.

Movies

As its name strongly suggests, the Active Movie control enables you to add video to your Web pages. This code (I saved it as IEMovie.htm) presents the "Goodtime" video:

```
<HTML>
<HEAD>
<TITLE>Movies in IE</TITLE>
</HEAD>
<BODY BGcolor = "Silver">
<H1 style = "text-align:center"> Let's Go To The Movies in IE </H1>
<HR>
<EMBED Autostart = "false" ID = "goodtime" ShowDisplay = 1
Src="J:\funstuff\videos\highperf\goodtime.avi"
Width = 320 Height = 240>

</BODY>
</HTML>
```

Notice that the ShowDisplay attribute is set to -1. This causes IE to render the display shown in Figure 8.7.

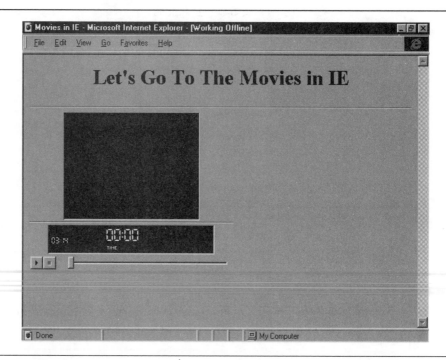

FIGURE 8.7: IEMovie.htm in IE. Setting the ShowDisplay attribute to –1 causes the time display to appear.

Using the *OBJECT* Element

Although the EMBED element is useful for adding sound and video, you can also use the OBJECT element when you work with multimedia in IE. If you're going to work with ActiveX controls, it's a good idea to get accustomed to the OBJECT element.

Wait a minute! Haven't I warned you a couple of times about the potential danger to your browser if you use the OBJECT element with .WAV files? The warning still holds: If you just set up an OBJECT and try to use a .WAV file as the DataSrc, you'll be in big trouble. With multimedia, the idea is to use the OBJECT element to represent the Active Movie control.

Just how do you do that?

Every ActiveX control is assigned a unique ID called a CLASSID, which is an attribute of the OBJECT element. The properties of the control are values in PARAM elements. Here's how to use the OBJECT element to code the Active Movie control in our last exercise:

```
<OBJECT ID="actvmvGoodTime" WIDTH=320 HEIGHT=240
CLASSID="CLSID:05589FA1-C356-11CE-BF01-00AA0055595A">
<PARAM Name = "ShowDisplay" Value = "-1">
<PARAM Name = "FileName" Value = "J:\funstuff\videos\highperf\
goodtime.avi">
<PARAM Name = "Autostart" Value = "0">
</OBJECT>
```

This code renders the display in Figure 8.8:

```
<OBJECT ID="actvmvGoodTime" WIDTH=320 HEIGHT=240
CLASSID="CLSID:05589FA1-C356-11CE-BF01-00AA0055595A">
<PARAM Name = "ShowDisplay" Value = "-1">
<PARAM Name = "ShowControls" Value = "-1">
<PARAM Name = "ShowPositionControls" Value = "-1">
<PARAM Name = "ShowSelectionControls" Value = "-1">
<PARAM Name = "FileName" Value = "J:\funstuff\videos\highperf\
goodtime.avi">
<PARAM Name = "Autostart" Value = "0">
</OBJECT>
```

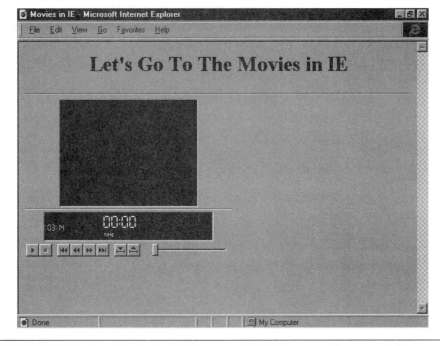

FIGURE 8.8: The Active Movie control with its control buttons visible

ABOUT THAT ID...

The ID actvmvGoodTime for the OBJECT element might strike you as strange. According to our naming convention, shouldn't we have used something like objectGoodTime?

When we use an ActiveX control, we'll start the ID with a lowercase abbreviation of the control's class—in this case, actvmv for Active Movie. So many ActiveX controls are available that this will help you keep track when you script them.

The Active Movie control properties in the preceding code snippet are a subset of all the available ones. Table 8.2 presents a more complete picture.

TABLE 8.2: Properties of the Active Movie Control

Property	What It Does
AllowChangeDisplayMode	Indicates if the end-user can change the display mode at run time between seconds and frames*
AllowHideControls	Indicates if the end-user can hide the control panel at run time*
AllowHideDisplay	Indicates if the end-user can hide the display at run time*
Appearance	Sets the appearance of the display panel's border (1 = An inset border, giving the appearance of depth; 0 = No border)
AutoRewind	Specifies whether or not to automatically rewind when the file stops playing*
AutoStart	Specifies whether or not to start playing when the Web page opens*
Balance	Specifies the stereo's balance (0 = Sound perfectly balanced between both speakers; -10,000 = All sound to left speaker; 10,000 = All sound to right speaker)
BorderStyle	Sets the control's border style (0 = No border; 1 = Fixed, single-line border)
CurrentPosition	Gives the current position in the playback file, in seconds
CurrentState	Gives the player's current state: stopped, running, or paused (0 = Stopped; 1 = Paused; 2 = Running)
DisplayBackColor	Specifies the display panel's background color
DisplayForeColor	Specifies the display panel's foreground color

TABLE 8.2 CONTINUED: Properties of the Active Movie Control

Property	What It Does
DisplayMode	Indicates whether the display panel shows the current position in seconds or in frames (0 = seconds; 1 = frames)
EnableContextMenu	Indicates whether or not to enable the shortcut menu*
Enabled	Specifies if the control is enabled*
EnablePositionControls	Indicates whether or not to show the position buttons in the controls panel*
EnableSelectionControls	Indicates whether or not to show the selection buttons in the controls panel*
EnableTracker	Indicates whether or not to show the trackbar control in the controls panel*
FileName	Specifies the multimedia file to be played
FullScreenMode	Expands the video display to fill the entire screen*
MovieWindowSize	Sets the size of the playback panel (0 = Authored (original) size; 1 = Twice the authored size; 2 = One-sixteenth the size of the screen; 3 = One-fourth the size of the screen; 4 = One-half the size of the screen)
PlayCount	Sets the number of times to play the file
Rate	Sets the playback rate (1.0 = Original (default) rate)
ReadyState	Gives the state of readiness for the Active Movie control, based on how completely the source file has loaded (0 = Control is loading a file; 1 = FileName has not been initialized; 3 = Control has loaded a file, and has downloaded enough data to play the file, but hasn't yet received all the data; 4 = all data are downloaded)
SelectionEnd	Sets the ending position in seconds from the beginning of the file
SelectionStart	Sets the starting position in seconds from the beginning of the file
ShowControls	Specifies if the controls panel is visible*
ShowDisplay	Specifies if the display panel is visible*
ShowPositionControls	Specifies if the position controls are visible*
ShowSelectionControls	Specifies if the selection controls are visible*
ShowTracker	Specifies if the trackbar is visible*
Volume	Sets the volume in hundredths of decibels

Skill 8

An asterisk (*) indicates that the possible values are –1 ("true") and 0 ("false").

NOTE I didn't include `FilterGraph` and `FilterGraphDispatch`, two properties relevant to software components that process the multimedia file.

Summary

Because multimedia stimulates the eyes and ears, it can bring new dimensions to your Web pages. It's easy to add multimedia, as Navigator plug-ins and ActiveX controls have become sophisticated and developer-friendly. Microsoft now provides a rich set of DirectAnimation Multimedia controls to help you with the development process.

Sounds and video, already an integral part of the Web, will become even more prevalent as high-speed connections become more common, and new standards and formats emerge.

Have You Mastered the Essentials?

Now you can...

- ☑ Use the *EMBED* element to add sounds and video to Web pages for both IE and Navigator
- ☑ Use the *OBJECT* element to add multimedia to Web pages for IE
- ☑ Work with multimedia-related Navigator plug-ins
- ☑ Work with multimedia-related ActiveX controls
- ☑ Work with some of the features of Microsoft's DirectAnimation Multimedia structured graphic control

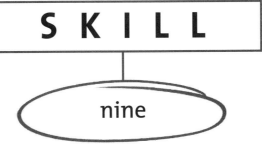

Adding Interactivity: Dragging and Dropping

❏ Dragging and dropping in IE

❏ Dragging and dropping in Navigator

❏ A game application

One of the major attractions of Dynamic HTML is the opportunity it presents for forms of interactivity that haven't appeared on Web pages before. Dragging and dropping, a standby in the world of everyday software, is now available for the Web. People have become so accustomed to using a mouse that this technique is now almost a necessity. It's a good idea to build drag-and-drop into Web pages, and this Skill will show you how.

We'll begin by examining drag-and-drop in IE, then move on to Navigator, and conclude with an application of this capability.

Dragging and Dropping in IE

As we progress, you'll see that the drag-and-drop capability is heavily dependent on the event models we discussed in Skill 6. A drag-and-drop consists of three events:

- Mousedown
- Mousemove
- Mouseup

We have to track the mouse's location during each event, and move the clicked object to the mouse's location as the mouse moves.

Let's start with a page that has a few image files. We'll develop VBScript for moving the files around, and as we did in Skill 6, we'll include a text area that continuously tracks events and mouse locations. The items we'll put in the text area will help you understand the events and the variables involved in dragging and dropping. The finished page will look like Figure 9.1.

Create a new page entitled Dragging and Dropping in VBS. Within the HEAD element, add a SCRIPT element and set its Language attribute to "VBScript".

We'll begin by adding a heading, a horizontal line, and the three objects that we're going to drag and drop. One is an image of a small blue ball, the second is an image of a telephone, and the third is the image of a book. Create this code in the BODY element:

```
<H1 style = "text-align:center">Dragging and Dropping in IE </H1>
<HR>
<IMG id = "imgBall" Src = "E:\DHTML MTE\graphics\small\ltblbal.gif"
Style = "position:absolute;top:350;left:175">
```

```
<IMG id = "imgPhone" Src = "E:\DHTML MTE\graphics\small\ltb4.gif"
Style = "position:absolute;top:350;left:275">

<IMG id = "imgBook" Src = "E:\DHTML MTE\graphics\small\ltb26.gif"
Style = "position:absolute;top:350;left:425">
```

We'll also need a text area to display the values of our variables as we move the mouse around, so create this code in the BODY element as well:

```
<CENTER>
<FORM ID = frmText>
<TEXTAREA ID = textareaEventInfo Rows = 14 Cols = 35>
</TEXTAREA>
</FORM>
</CENTER>
```

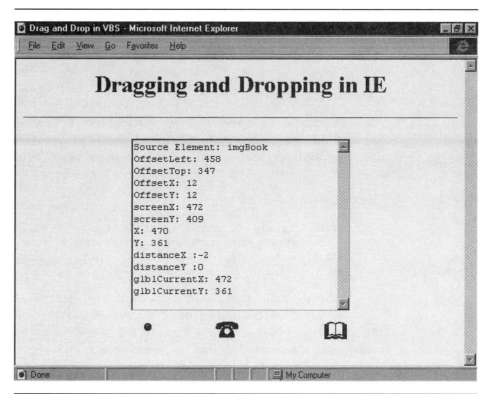

FIGURE 9.1: Your drag-and-drop page in IE

Starting the Script

The first thing you'll notice about the script is that the event-handlers we write all pertain to the document, rather than to individual on-screen elements. This is the beauty of an event-model: it frees us from having to write separate event-handlers for every on-screen element. Instead, we write one set of event-handlers for the document and code these event-handlers to work with the on-screen elements.

To begin, we'll create three global variables. One of these variables will point to the object we'll drag and drop, and the other two will track its position. In the SCRIPT element, add this code:

```
dim glblSelectedObject
dim glblCurrentX
dim glblCurrentY
```

As you can see, we precede each one with glbl, to indicate that the variable is global.

Next, we initialize the tracking variables:

```
glblCurrentX = 0
glblCurrentY = 0
```

Before we turn our attention to onmousedown, onmousemove, and onmouseup, the events that constitute a drag-and-drop, let's add a helpful effect. We'll create a subroutine that changes the cursor when the mouse is over a draggable object:

```
sub document_onmouseover

    if InStr(window.event.srcElement.ID,"img") > 0 Then
            window.event.srcElement.style.cursor = "move"
    end if
end sub
```

The subroutine examines the ID of the "moused-over" element, and if it contains "img", the cursor changes into a symbol that indicates the element is movable. Notice that we use the built-in VBS function InStr as we did in Skill 1. This function returns 0 if the substring "img" isn't in window.event.srcElement.ID.

The *onmousedown* Event

Now we'll build an event-handler for onmousedown. This event-handler's major task is to provide accurate information on the selected element's position. Here's the subroutine:

```
sub document_onmousedown
    set glblSelectedObject = window.event.srcElement

    if InStr(glblSelectedObject.ID,"img") = 0 then
            glblSelectedObject = null
            exit sub
    end if

    glblSelectedObject.style.pixelLeft = glblSelectedObject.offsetLeft
    glblSelectedObject.style.pixelTop = glblSelectedObject.offsetTop

    glblCurrentX = window.event.clientX + document.body.scrollLeft
    glblCurrentY = window.event.clientY + document.body.scrollTop
end sub
```

The first line uses the VBS set operator (remember Skill 5?) to point the variable glblSelectedObject to the source element of the onmousedown event.

T   TIP   If you're a little shaky on the "source element" concept, go back and read Skill 6.

The script in the if statement executes if the ID doesn't contain "img". It sets glblSelectedObject to null, a built-in VBScript keyword that indicates the variable contains no data. We're about to develop an event-handler for the onmousemove event, and we'll have to let that event-handler know if nothing is selected. If this is the case, the next statement exits the subroutine.

The next two lines

```
glblSelectedObject.style.pixelLeft = glblSelectedObject.offsetLeft
glblSelectedObject.style.pixelTop = glblSelectedObject.offsetTop
```

take care of some chores regarding the selected element's position. They deal with pixelLeft and pixelTop—two properties we haven't worked with before. In Skill 1, we wrote a procedure that converted style.top and style.left from strings to numbers so that we could move on-screen objects. I told you then that a way around this was possible, and this is one way: `pixelLeft` and `pixelTop` give the positioning information as numbers rather than strings. We set these properties to the selected object's `offsetLeft` and `offsetTop` properties, respectively.

Why do we do this? Every element is positioned from the top and left of the element that contains it, and every element has `offsetLeft` and `offsetTop` properties that hold this information. These properties are read-only. (You can write a script that reads them, but you can't write a script that changes them.) The `pixelLeft` and `pixelTop` properties are generated during the user's interaction with the document and may not be completely accurate. Usually they're right on the money, but just in case they're not, the subroutine does the appropriate updating. We'll use `pixelLeft` and `pixelTop` later in the script, so we want to make sure they contain the correct information.

TIP   Don't confuse `offsetLeft` and `offsetTop` (which we use here for the first time) with `offsetX` and `offsetY` (which you've seen before in Skill 6). `offsetLeft` and `offsetTop` give the coordinates of an element relative to the element that contains it. `offsetX` and `offsetY` give the coordinates of the mouse relative to the element in which the mouse is positioned.

The next two lines

```
glblCurrentX = window.event.clientX + document.body.scrollLeft
glblCurrentY = window.event.clientY + document.body.scrollTop
```

set the current position. The event's `clientX` and `clientY` properties give the page position excluding scrollbars. For accuracy, therefore, we add the document body's `scrollLeft` and `scrollTop` properties.

The *onmousemove* Event

Now that we've selected an object, the event-handler for `onmousemove` will take care of the dragging:

```
sub document_onmousemove
    on error resume next
    if glblSelectedObject = null then
            exit sub
    end if

    newX = window.event.clientX + document.body.scrollLeft
    newY = window.event.clientY + document.body.scrollTop
    distanceX = newX - glblCurrentX
    distanceY = newY - glblCurrentY
```

```
glblCurrentX = newX
glblCurrentY = newY

glblSelectedObject.style.pixelLeft =
➥ glblSelectedObject.style.pixelLeft + distanceX
glblSelectedObject.style.pixelTop =
➥ glblSelectedObject.style.pixelTop + distanceY
window.event.returnValue = false

frmText.textAreaEventInfo.Value = "Source Element: " &
➥ window.event.srcelement.id & chr(13) _
& "OffsetLeft: " & glblSelectedObject.offsetLeft & chr(13) _
& "OffsetTop: " & glblSelectedObject.offsetTop & chr(13) _
& "OffsetX: " & window.event.offsetx & chr(13) _
& "OffsetY: " & window.event.offsety & chr(13) _
& "screenX: " & window.event.screenx & chr(13) _
& "screenY: " & window.event.screeny & chr(13) _
& "X: " & window.event.x & chr(13) _
& "Y: " & window.event.y & chr(13) _
& "distanceX :" & distanceX & chr(13) _
& "distanceY :" & distanceY & chr(13) _
& "glblCurrentX: " & glblCurrentX & chr(13) _
& "glblCurrentY: " & glblCurrentY

end sub
```

As you can see, this one is fairly involved, so let's break it into chunks.

On Error...What's That?!?

The first line of this subroutine

```
on error resume next
```

may strike you as a bit cryptic. After all, if our code contains an error, shouldn't we debug it?

This is a built-in VBS way of protecting your script from crashing and burning when it encounters inconsistencies. Without this line, we'll get an error message when the page opens. Why? When the page opens, this event-handler activates as soon as you move your mouse. The subroutine's if statement immediately checks the value of glblSelectedObject. Because the window just opened, this variable doesn't have a value yet. That causes the error message. It's a system inconsistency that irons itself out very quickly if we can just get around it. We do just that by using the on error resume next expression, which tells IE's VBScript interpreter to ignore the inconsistency and pass control to the next statement.

A Graceful Exit

The if...then structure takes us out of the event-handler if glblSelectedObject isn't pointing to anything. In other words, if no object is selected, there's nothing to drag, and the subroutine is finished.

```
if glblSelectedObject = null then
        exit sub
end if
```

Getting the Distance

The next group of statements calculates the distance to move the selected object and then updates glblCurrentX and glblCurrentY with the new positioning information. In the first two lines

```
newX = window.event.clientX + document.body.scrollLeft
newY = window.event.clientY + document.body.scrollTop
```

two local variables, newX and newY, store the new position of the mouse.

The next two lines

```
distanceX = newX - glblCurrentX
distanceY = newY - glblCurrentY
```

show you why we made glblCurrentX and glblCurrentY global variables. Their values were set in the onmousedown event-handler, and we have to use them in this event-handler to calculate the distance to move the selected object.

Finally, we update those two global variables by assigning them the values for the two local ones:

```
glblCurrentX = newX
glblCurrentY = newY
```

Going the Distance

The remaining task is to move the object, and this part gets it done:

```
glblSelectedObject.style.pixelLeft =
➥ glblSelectedObject.style.pixelLeft + distanceX
glblSelectedObject.style.pixelTop =
➥ glblSelectedObject.style.pixelTop + distanceY
window.event.returnValue = false
```

The first two lines set the position for the selected object in terms of its `pixelLeft` and `pixelTop` properties.

The third line is important. It returns a value of `false` for the event, cancelling any other actions that might be taking place. In so doing, it makes the whole process proceed more smoothly. After you've coded the whole script, comment this line out and watch what happens.

 NOTE   Apparently, "dragging and dropping" is really "selecting–moving–catching–up–and–releasing," but that's not as catchy.

Recording It All

Finally, we come to the device we used in Skill 6—a text area that tracks the values of variables so that you can understand what's happening. This long, long structure is, believe it or not, one line of code:

```
frmText.textAreaEventInfo.Value = "Source Element: " &
➥window.event.srcelement.id & chr(13) _
    & "OffsetLeft: " & glblSelectedObject.offsetLeft & chr(13) _
    & "OffsetTop: " & glblSelectedObject.offsetTop & chr(13) _
    & "OffsetX: " & window.event.offsetx & chr(13) _
    & "OffsetY: " & window.event.offsety & chr(13) _
    & "screenX: " & window.event.screenx & chr(13) _
    & "screenY: " & window.event.screeny & chr(13) _
    & "X: " & window.event.x & chr(13) _
    & "Y: " & window.event.y & chr(13) _
    & "distanceX :" & distanceX & chr(13) _
    & "distanceY :" & distanceY & chr(13) _
    & "glblCurrentX: " & glblCurrentX & chr(13) _
    & "glblCurrentY: " & glblCurrentY

end sub
```

This line continuously updates the text area as the mouse moves.

 NOTE   In this text area, I've included offsetX and offsetY along with offsetLeft and offsetRight, so that you understand the difference between these similarly named properties.

The *onmouseup* Event

This one is easy. Since the onmouseup event drops the object, this event-handler's job is to release glblSelectedObject from pointing to the formerly selected element:

```
sub document_onmouseup

        glblSelectedObject = null

end sub
```

The Whole File

Here's the entire Drag and Drop in VBS.htm file:

 Drag and Drop in VBS.htm

```
<HTML>
<HEAD>
<SCRIPT Language = "VBScript">

dim glblSelectedObject
dim glblCurrentX
dim glblCurrentY

glblCurrentX = 0
glblCurrentY = 0


sub document_onmouseover

    if InStr(window.event.srcElement.ID,"img") > 0 Then
            window.event.srcElement.style.cursor = "move"
    end if
end sub

sub document_onmousedown
    set glblSelectedObject = window.event.srcElement

    if InStr(glblSelectedObject.ID,"img") = 0 then
            glblSelectedObject = null
            exit sub
    end if

    glblSelectedObject.style.pixelLeft = glblSelectedObject.offsetLeft
    glblSelectedObject.style.pixelTop = glblSelectedObject.offsetTop
```

```
        glblCurrentX = window.event.clientX + document.body.scrollLeft
        glblCurrentY = window.event.clientY + document.body.scrollTop
end sub


sub document_onmousemove
    on error resume next
    if glblSelectedObject = null then
            exit sub
    end if

    newX = window.event.clientX + document.body.scrollLeft
    newY = window.event.clientY + document.body.scrollTop
    distanceX = newX - glblCurrentX
    distanceY = newY - glblCurrentY
    glblCurrentX = newX
    glblCurrentY = newY

    glblSelectedObject.style.pixelLeft =
    ➥ glblSelectedObject.style.pixelLeft + distanceX
    glblSelectedObject.style.pixelTop =
    ➥ glblSelectedObject.style.pixelTop + distanceY
    window.event.returnValue = false


frmText.textAreaEventInfo.Value = "Source Element: " &
➥ window.event.srcelement.id & chr(13) _
    & "OffsetLeft: " & glblSelectedObject.offsetLeft & chr(13) _
    & "OffsetTop: " & glblSelectedObject.offsetTop & chr(13) _
    & "OffsetX: " & window.event.offsetx & chr(13) _
    & "OffsetY: " & window.event.offsety & chr(13) _
    & "screenX: " & window.event.screenx & chr(13) _
    & "screenY: " & window.event.screeny & chr(13) _
    & "X: " & window.event.x & chr(13) _
    & "Y: " & window.event.y & chr(13) _
    & "distanceX :" & distanceX & chr(13) _
    & "distanceY :" & distanceY & chr(13) _
    & "glblCurrentX: " & glblCurrentX & chr(13) _
    & "glblCurrentY: " & glblCurrentY

end sub

sub document_onmouseup

    glblSelectedObject = null

end sub

</SCRIPT>
```

```
<TITLE>New Page</TITLE>
</HEAD>
<BODY>

<IMG id = "imgBall" Src = "E:\DHTML MTE\graphics\small\ltblbal.gif"
Style = "position:absolute;top:350;left:175">

<IMG id = "imgPhone" Src = "E:\DHTML MTE\graphics\small\ltb4.gif"
Style = "position:absolute;top:350;left:275">

<IMG id = "imgBook" Src = "E:\DHTML MTE\graphics\small\ltb26.gif"
Style = "position:absolute;top:350;left:425">

<CENTER>
<FORM ID = frmText>
<TEXTAREA ID = textareaEventInfo Rows = 14 Cols = 35>
</TEXTAREA>
</FORM>
</CENTER>
```

```
</BODY>
</HTML>
```

If you open it in IE, you'll see a page that looks just like Figure 9.1. Drag the images around, and note the values in the text area as they change. In particular, note the differences between `offsetX` and `offsetLeft`, and between `offsetY` and `offsetTop`.

As part of your explorations, make sure you drag an object up to the menu bar. Take careful note of what happens, as we'll revisit this issue later in this Skill.

Dragging and Dropping in Navigator

Now we'll take a look at dragging and dropping on Planet Netscape. Once again, you'll see an event model come into play, as our code will work at the document level. When you finish coding, your page will resemble the one from the previous exercise, and will look like Figure 9.2.

Create a file called `Drag and Drop in Nav.htm`. In the BODY element, create the H1 heading `Dragging and Dropping in Navigator` and follow it with a horizontal line:

```
<BODY>
<H1 style = "text-align:center"> Dragging and Dropping in Navigator</H1>
<HR>
<FORM name = frmText>
```

Next, create the text area that will hold the continuously updated information:

```
<CENTER>
<TEXTAREA name = textareaEventInfo Rows = 9 Cols = 35>
</TEXTAREA>
</CENTER>
</FORM>
```

One major difference between IE and Navigator is that in IE, we could embed the images into the document and drag the IMG elements. In Navigator, we have to put the IMG elements in LAYER containers and drag the LAYERs. Compare Figure 9.1 with Figure 9.2, and you'll see what I mean.

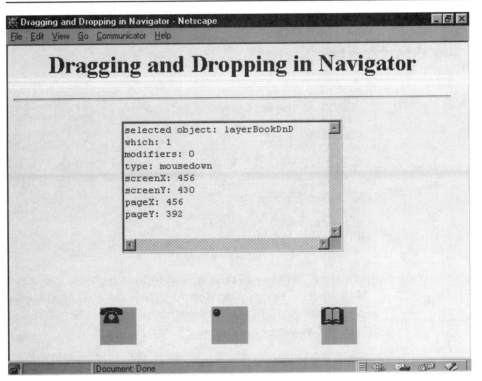

FIGURE 9.2: Your page for dragging and dropping in Navigator

We have three images to drag, so we'll use three layers:

```
<LAYER ID = "layerPhoneDnD" Top = 350 Left = 125 Bgcolor = silver
Height = 50 Width = 50>
<IMG  Src = "file:///E|/DHTML MTE/graphics/small/ltb4.gif">
```

```
</LAYER>

<LAYER ID = "layerBallDnD" Top = 350 Left = 275 Bgcolor = silver
Height = 50 Width = 50>
<IMG  Src = "file:///E|/DHTML MTE/graphics/small/ltblbal.gif">
</LAYER>

<LAYER ID = "layerBookDnD" Top = 350 Left = 425 Bgcolor = silver
Height = 50 Width = 50 >
<IMG  Src = "file:///E|/DHTML MTE/graphics/small/ltb26.gif">
</LAYER>
```

Notice the DnD at the end of each ID. This indicates that a LAYER is draggable. We'll write our script so that LAYERs with DnD in their IDs will be draggable, and LAYERs without DnD will not.

Starting the Script

In the HEAD element, begin creating the script:

```
<SCRIPT Language = "JavaScript1.2">

</SCRIPT>
```

As in the IE exercise, we'll create three global variables. One will be set to the selected element, and the other two will hold position information. Inside the SCRIPT element, add

```
glblSelectedObject = null;
glblCurrentX = 0;
glblCurrentY = 0;
```

Again, we prefix the variables with glbl to indicate their global scope.

Now we have to set up the document to handle the onmousedown and onmouseup events. First, we have to make the document capture those events, as per the Netscape event capturing model:

```
document.captureEvents(Event.MOUSEDOWN | Event.MOUSEUP);
```

Then we connect the document's events to functions that we're about to write:

```
document.onmousedown = selectTheObject;
document.onmouseup = dropTheObject;
```

What happened to onmousemove? The selectTheObject function will call an event-handler for that one.

Now all we have to do is write the functions.

Selecting the Object

Our strategy for selectTheObject is to get the position of the mouse cursor when it's clicked, and then see if it's over a drag-and-droppable object. That is, we'll see if DnD is in the object's ID. If it's not, the function won't do anything. If it is, we'll set our glblSelectedObject to the object that the cursor is over, set the values of glblCurrentX and glblCurrentY, and move on to the dragTheObject function.

Here's selectTheObject:

```
function selectTheObject(e) {
    var workObject;
    cursorX = e.pageX;
    cursorY = e.pageY;

    for(i=0; i < document.layers.length; i++) {
        workObject = document.layers[i];
        if (workObject.id.indexOf("DnD") == -1) {continue}
        if ((cursorX > workObject.left) &&
            (cursorX < (workObject.left + workObject.clip.width)) &&
            (cursorY > workObject.top) &&
            (cursorY < (workObject.top + workObject.clip.height)))
            {glblSelectedObject = workObject;}
    }

    if (glblSelectedObject == null) {return};

    glblCurrentX = e.pageX;
    glblCurrentY = e.pageY;
    info(e);
    document.captureEvents(Event.MOUSEMOVE);
    document.onmousemove = dragTheObject;
    }
```

As in the IE version, let's take this in easy stages.

In the Beginning

Let's look at the first four lines:

```
function selectTheObject(e) {
    var workObject;
    cursorX = e.pageX;
    cursorY = e.pageY;
```

The e in the function's argument is a generic reference to an event—the event that calls the function. If you look back at the beginning of the script, you'll see that this function is called by the document's onmousedown event. Thus, the e in this function refers to onmousedown.

The next three lines create local variables. workObject is the variable we'll use when we examine the object that the mouse cursor is over. (var is the JavaScript equivalent of the VBS dim.) cursorX and cursorY store the location of the mouse when the event occurs. That information is in e.pageX and e.pageY. pageX gives the horizontal position with respect to the window, and pageY gives the vertical position with respect to the window.

Checking the *ID*

Now we have to see if the clicked object has DnD in its ID. To do this, we have to access the document's layers array, which we've encountered before. This is an indexed set of all the LAYER elements on the page.

We use a for loop to find our object in this collection:

```
for(i=0; i < document.layers.length; i++) {
        workObject = document.layers[i];
        if (workObject.id.indexOf("DnD") == -1) {continue}
        if ((cursorX > workObject.left) &&
            (cursorX < (workObject.left + workObject.clip.width)) &&
            (cursorY > workObject.top) &&
            (cursorY < (workObject.top + workObject.clip.height)))
        {glblSelectedObject = workObject;}
}
```

The for loop starts at the first (in other words, the zeroth) item in the array and works its way to the last (denoted by document.layers.length), one item at a time (denoted by i++). workObject is the variable that works through the array, and we use the indexOf method to check the ID. indexOf is the JavaScript equivalent of VBScript's inStr. If DnD isn't in the ID, indexOf returns –1, and the loop continues—that is, i gets incremented and the loop repeats for the new value of i. If DnD is in the ID, the next if statement checks to see if the cursor is within the visible boundaries (clip.height and clip.width) of the object.

TIP   The clip property is the key here. Intuitively, you might think workObject.width and workObject.height would be sufficient, but they're not. Go figure.

If the cursor is inside those boundaries, the element is assigned to glblSelectedObject.

TIP   Notice that JavaScript doesn't use a set expression.

It's possible that all the cycling through the loop will reveal that the mouse wasn't clicked over a drag-and-droppable object. For this reason, we have to test the value of `glblSelectedObject`, and if it's `null`, the function returns

```
if (glblSelectedObject == null) {return};
```

Positioning and Moving On

The rest of the function sets `glblCurrentX` and `glblCurrentY` to the onmouse-down event's location,

```
glblCurrentX = e.pageX;
glblCurrentY = e.pageY;
```

updates the information in the text area,

```
info(e);
```

sets up the document to capture the ensuing onmousemove event,

```
document.captureEvents(Event.MOUSEMOVE);
```

and calls `dragTheObject` when the mouse moves:

```
document.onmousemove = dragTheObject;
```

Dragging the Object

The function for dragging the object is fairly straightforward:

```
function dragTheObject(e) {
    distanceX = (e.pageX - glblCurrentX);
    distanceY = (e.pageY - glblCurrentY);
    glblCurrentX = e.pageX;
    glblCurrentY = e.pageY;
    if (glblSelectedObject == null) {return};
    glblSelectedObject.moveBy(distanceX,distanceY);
    info(e);
}
```

As in the IE version, we find the distance to move the object by subtracting `glblCurrentX` from the mouse's new horizontal location (given by `e.pageX`) and `glblCurrentY` from the mouse's new vertical location (`e.pageY`).

TIP   Remember, e now refers to the onmousemove event, so e.pageX and e.pageY hold the mouse's new position after the move.

Then we update glblCurrentX and glblCurrentY by assigning them the values of e.pageX and e.pageY, respectively.

If glblSelectedObject isn't pointing to anything, as is the case right after you drop an object, the check for a null value causes the function to return. This is somewhat similar to the way we used on error resume next in the IE version.

Otherwise, the moveBy method moves the object the required distance, and info(e) records the whole thing in the text area.

Dropping the Object

As we've seen before, this function is easy to write:

```
function dropTheObject(e) {
    releaseEvents(Event.MOUSEMOVE);
    glblSelectedObject = null;
    info(e);
}
```

First, it releases the onmousemove event, and then it sets glblSelectedObject to null. Again, info(e) updates the text area.

Recording the Transaction

This one is almost an exact copy of the text area update function we used in Skill 6. I've added a couple of lines to adapt it to this script:

```
function info(event){
    var selection;
    if (glblSelectedObject != null) {selection =
            glblSelectedObject.id}
    else {selection = "released"}
    textArea = document.forms[0].elements["textareaEventInfo"];
    textArea.value = "selected object: " + selection + "\n"
            + "which: " + event.which + "\n"
            + "modifiers: " + event.modifiers + "\n"
            + "type: " + event.type + "\n"
            + "screenX: " + event.screenX + "\n"
            + "screenY: " + event.screenY + "\n"
            + "pageX: " + event.pageX + "\n"
            + "pageY: " + event.pageY;
}
```

The local variable `selection` helps us work with `glblSelectedObject`. If `glblSelectedObject` is not `null`, selection holds the object's ID. If it is `null`, selection holds the string `"released"`. This enables us to create an informative message about the selected object in the text area.

The Whole File

Here's `Drag and Drop in Nav.htm`:

 Drag and Drop in Nav.htm

```
<HTML>
<HEAD>
<SCRIPT Language = "JavaScript1.2">

glblSelectedObject = null;
glblCurrentX = 0;
glblCurrentY = 0;

document.captureEvents(Event.MOUSEDOWN | Event.MOUSEUP);
document.onmousedown = selectTheObject;
document.onmouseup = dropTheObject;

function selectTheObject(e) {
        var workObject;
        cursorX = e.pageX;
        cursorY = e.pageY;
        for(i=0; i < document.layers.length; i++) {
                workObject = document.layers[i];
                if (workObject.id.indexOf("DnD") == -1) {continue}
                if ((cursorX > workObject.left) &&
                    (cursorX < (workObject.left + workObject.clip.width)) &&
                    (cursorY > workObject.top) &&
                    (cursorY < (workObject.top + workObject.clip.height)))
                {glblSelectedObject = workObject;}
        }
        if (glblSelectedObject == null) {return};
        glblCurrentX = e.pageX;
        glblCurrentY = e.pageY;
        info(e);
        document.captureEvents(Event.MOUSEMOVE);
        document.onmousemove = dragTheObject;
        }
```

```
function dragTheObject(e) {
        distanceX = (e.pageX - glblCurrentX);
        distanceY = (e.pageY - glblCurrentY);
        glblCurrentX = e.pageX;
        glblCurrentY = e.pageY;
        if (glblSelectedObject == null) {return};
        glblSelectedObject.moveBy(distanceX,distanceY);
        info(e);
}

function dropTheObject(e) {
        releaseEvents(Event.MOUSEMOVE);
        glblSelectedObject = null;
        info(e);
}

function info(event){
        var selection;
        if (glblSelectedObject != null) {selection = glblSelectedObject.id}
        else {selection = "released"}
        textArea = document.forms[0].elements["textareaEventInfo"];
        textArea.value = "selected object: " + selection + "\n"
                + "which: " + event.which + "\n"
                + "modifiers: " + event.modifiers + "\n"
                + "type: " + event.type + "\n"
                + "screenX: " + event.screenX + "\n"
                + "screenY: " + event.screenY + "\n"
                + "pageX: " + event.pageX + "\n"
                + "pageY: " + event.pageY;
}

</SCRIPT>
<TITLE>Dragging and Dropping in Navigator</TITLE>
</HEAD>
<BODY>
<H1 style = "text-align:center"> Dragging and Dropping in Navigator</H1>
<HR>
<FORM name = frmText>
<CENTER>
<TEXTAREA name = textareaEventInfo Rows = 9 Cols = 35>
</TEXTAREA>
</CENTER>
</FORM>

<LAYER ID = "layerPhoneDnD" Top = 350 Left = 125 Bgcolor = silver Height = 50
Width = 50>
<IMG  Src = "file:///E|/DHTML MTE/graphics/small/ltb4.gif">
</LAYER>
```

```
<LAYER ID = "layerBallDnD" Top = 350 Left = 275 Bgcolor = silver Height = 50
Width = 50>
<IMG  Src = "file:///E|/DHTML MTE/graphics/small/ltblbal.gif">
</LAYER>

<LAYER ID = "layerBookDnD" Top = 350 Left = 425 Bgcolor = silver Height = 50
Width = 50>
<IMG  Src = "file:///E|/DHTML MTE/graphics/small/ltb26.gif">
</LAYER>

</BODY>

</HTML>
```

Open it in Navigator to see a page that looks like Figure 9.2. Drag and drop the images and note what happens in the text area.

You'll find that dragging and dropping works fine, except when you click on the image itself and try to drag it, rather than on other parts of the containing layer. (The coordination breaks down between the drag and the drop.) You'll also see that when you drag a layer into the text area, it goes under the area. In IE, it goes over the text area. Increasing a LAYER's z-index has no effect on this.

A Drag-and-Drop Application

Dragging and dropping is a terrific technique for user interfaces. Once a user learns how to maneuver a mouse, dragging and dropping becomes almost second nature. You can use it on Web pages where users have to arrange items, like furniture on a floor plan, or elements of a computer network.

To show you how to harness this technique, I've used the VBScript code we wrote earlier in this Skill to develop a Web page version of a familiar game. Known in some circles as "peg solitaire," this game has been around for hundreds of years.

The name comes from a version that uses pegs on a board with holes. Thirty-three holes are on the board, and each hole has a peg, except for the hole in the center. Each move is a "jump," as in checkers. When one peg jumps over another, the jumped piece is removed from the board. Unlike checkers, however, diagonal jumps aren't allowed. The objective is to leave exactly one peg on the board, in the center hole. Figure 9.3 shows the finished Web page for this game.

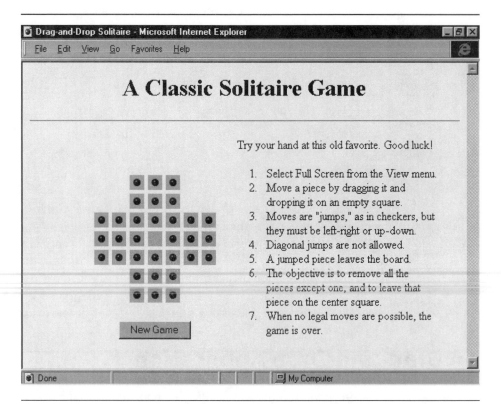

FIGURE 9.3: Solitare.htm in IE, a Web page version of a centuries-old game

In this section, we'll build the Solitaire Web page in VBScript.

Getting Started

Begin by making a copy of Drag and Drop in VBS.htm. Rename this file Soltaire.htm. Remove the FORM, the Textarea, and the three IMG elements. We'll add code to this file in several places.

The "board" that you see in Figure 9.3 is a two-dimensional array of DIVs. The pieces on the board squares are 32 instances of a particular image, ltlblbal.gif, from the Lassen Technologies library. This one is the blue ball we used in the previous two exercises. If you have some other appropriately sized .GIF that you prefer to use, by all means do so.

The DIVs are styled to be small gray squares. The easiest way to arrange 33 of them as shown in Figure 9.3 is to start with a 7 × 7 array, and designate 16 of the squares as "unused." In other words, in each corner, we'll format four cells so that they're not visible. Cascading Style Sheets give us a convenient way to do this. Create a STYLE element in the HEAD of your newly named file and add these two rules:

```
div {background-color:silver;width:20;height:20;position:absolute}
div.unused {background-color:white}
```

With these rules, we can create the board. The first rule sets the dimensions and the color of each square. The second specifies that the "unused" class of squares will be white and, therefore, invisible.

Add this rule to the STYLE element, to help position the pieces on the board:

```
img {position:absolute}
```

The Board and the Pieces

Putting the DIVs and the .GIF images into the document is a little tedious, but copying and pasting will get you through it pretty quickly. (Downloading the source code from the Sybex Web site will get you through it even more quickly.) First, create the HTML that puts the images into the document:

```
<IMG id = "imgBall02" Src = "ltblbal.gif">
<IMG id = "imgBall03" Src = "ltblbal.gif">
<IMG id = "imgBall04" Src = "ltblbal.gif">
<IMG id = "imgBall12" Src = "ltblbal.gif">
<IMG id = "imgBall13" Src = "ltblbal.gif">
<IMG id = "imgBall14" Src = "ltblbal.gif">
<IMG id = "imgBall20" Src = "ltblbal.gif">
<IMG id = "imgBall21" Src = "ltblbal.gif">
<IMG id = "imgBall22" Src = "ltblbal.gif">
<IMG id = "imgBall23" Src = "ltblbal.gif">
<IMG id = "imgBall24" Src = "ltblbal.gif">
<IMG id = "imgBall25" Src = "ltblbal.gif">
<IMG id = "imgBall26" Src = "ltblbal.gif">
<IMG id = "imgBall30" Src = "ltblbal.gif">
<IMG id = "imgBall31" Src = "ltblbal.gif">
<IMG id = "imgBall32" Src = "ltblbal.gif">
<IMG id = "imgBall34" Src = "ltblbal.gif">
<IMG id = "imgBall35" Src = "ltblbal.gif">
<IMG id = "imgBall36" Src = "ltblbal.gif">
<IMG id = "imgBall40" Src = "ltblbal.gif">
<IMG id = "imgBall41" Src = "ltblbal.gif">
<IMG id = "imgBall42" Src = "ltblbal.gif">
<IMG id = "imgBall43" Src = "ltblbal.gif">
<IMG id = "imgBall44" Src = "ltblbal.gif">
<IMG id = "imgBall45" Src = "ltblbal.gif">
<IMG id = "imgBall46" Src = "ltblbal.gif">
```

Skill 9

```
<IMG id = "imgBall52" Src = "ltblbal.gif">
<IMG id = "imgBall53" Src = "ltblbal.gif">
<IMG id = "imgBall54" Src = "ltblbal.gif">
<IMG id = "imgBall62" Src = "ltblbal.gif">
<IMG id = "imgBall63" Src = "ltblbal.gif">
<IMG id = "imgBall64" Src = "ltblbal.gif">
```

For expediency's sake, I'm assuming that you've copied the .GIF into your Skill 9 folder. Make sure you enter the IDs exactly as I have. They correspond to the starting row and column positions of the pieces on the board. The piece whose ID is imgBall54, for example, is in row 5 and column 4. You'll notice that we don't create images for unused squares. You won't see an imgBall33, for example, as no image occupies the center square (row 3, column 3).

Let's take a moment to discuss our row and column numbering scheme. We'll denote a square in row x, column y with (x,y). The top row is row 0, the bottom row is row 6. The left-most column is column 0, and the right-most column is column 6. The 16 unused squares figure into our numbering. They are (0,0), (0,1), (0,5), (0,6), (1,0), (1,1), (1,5), (1,6), (5,0), (5,1), (5,5), (5,6), (6,0), (6,1), (6,5), and (6,6).

Apply this scheme to the IDs for the DIVs, and enter them into the BODY of the file:

```
<DIV ID = div00 Class = "unused"></DIV>
<DIV ID = div01 Class = "unused"></DIV>
<DIV ID = div02></DIV>
<DIV ID = div03></DIV>
<DIV ID = div04></DIV>
<DIV ID = div05 Class = "unused"></DIV>
<DIV ID = div06 Class = "unused"></DIV>
<DIV ID = div10 Class = "unused"></DIV>
<DIV ID = div11 Class = "unused"></DIV>
<DIV ID = div12></DIV>
<DIV ID = div13></DIV>
<DIV ID = div14></DIV>
<DIV ID = div15 Class = "unused"></DIV>
<DIV ID = div16 Class = "unused"></DIV>
<DIV ID = div20></DIV>
<DIV ID = div21></DIV>
<DIV ID = div22></DIV>
<DIV ID = div23></DIV>
<DIV ID = div24></DIV>
<DIV ID = div25></DIV>
<DIV ID = div26></DIV>
<DIV ID = div30></DIV>
<DIV ID = div31></DIV>
<DIV ID = div32></DIV>
<DIV ID = div33></DIV>
```

```
<DIV ID = div34></DIV>
<DIV ID = div35></DIV>
<DIV ID = div36></DIV>
<DIV ID = div40></DIV>
<DIV ID = div41></DIV>
<DIV ID = div42></DIV>
<DIV ID = div43></DIV>
<DIV ID = div44></DIV>
<DIV ID = div45></DIV>
<DIV ID = div46></DIV>
<DIV ID = div50 Class = "unused"></DIV>
<DIV ID = div51 Class = "unused"></DIV>
<DIV ID = div52></DIV>
<DIV ID = div53></DIV>
<DIV ID = div54></DIV>
<DIV ID = div55 Class = "unused"></DIV>
<DIV ID = div56 Class = "unused"></DIV>
<DIV ID = div60 Class = "unused"></DIV>
<DIV ID = div61 Class = "unused"></DIV>
<DIV ID = div62></DIV>
<DIV ID = div63></DIV>
<DIV ID = div64></DIV>
<DIV ID = div65 Class = "unused"></DIV>
<DIV ID = div66 Class = "unused"></DIV>
```

Be sure you mark the appropriate DIVs "unused," as I've indicated.

Before we move on to the scripting, let's finish the BODY. Add the heading, the horizontal line, and the wording that you see in Figure 9.3, as well as the New Game button:

```
<H1 Style = "text-align:center">A Classic Solitaire Game</H1> <HR>
<DIV Style = "position:absolute;top:100;left:300;
background-color:white;
height:50;width:280">
Try your hand at this old favorite. Good luck!<BR>
<OL>
<LI> Select Full Screen from the View menu.
<LI> Move a piece by dragging it and dropping it on an empty square.
<LI> Moves are "jumps," as in checkers, but they must be left-right or
up-down.
<LI> Diagonal jumps are not allowed.
<LI> A jumped piece leaves the board.
<LI> The objective is to remove all the pieces except one, and to leave
that piece on the center square.
<LI> When no legal moves are possible, the game is over.
</OL>
</DIV>
```

Skill 9

```
<DIV Style = "position:absolute; top:345; left: 135;
background-color:white">
<FORM ID = "frmButton">
<INPUT Type = Button ID = "btnNewgame" Value = "New Game"
Style="height:25:width:75">
</FORM>
</DIV>
```

Note the use of the OL (ordered list) element along with the LI elements. OL produces the numbered items along the right side of the Solitaire page. Had we used UL (unordered list) instead of OL, the LIs would have been rendered as bulleted items.

The Script

A lot of the code from the first exercise in this Skill will remain intact. I'll reproduce it for you and bold the new code for this exercise so you can see how it fits in.

Global Variables and Arrays

At the beginning of the SCRIPT element, we have to add some global variables that deal with rows and columns on our game board, and we have to define some global arrays:

```
dim glblSelectedObject
dim glblCurrentX
dim glblCurrentY
dim glblRowValue
dim glblColValue
dim glblBoardArray(6,6)
dim glblBallArray(31)

glblCurrentX = 0
glblCurrentY = 0

dim glblCurrentRow
dim glblCurrentColumn

dim glblNewRow
dim glblNewColumn

dim glblDivArray(6, 6)
```

glblBoardArray will keep track of which piece is on which square.
glblBallArray will index the images. glblDivArray will help us set up the
board. The new variables for rows and columns track the movements of the
pieces among the rows and columns of the board.

Opening the Page

We'll need an onload event-handler to get the ball rolling when the page opens.
This subroutine will initialize all our arrays and call a subroutine that sets up a
new game. Add this code to your SCRIPT element (yes there's a lot, but copying
and pasting will ease the strain):

```
Sub window_onload
    set glblDivArray(0,0)=div00
    set glblDivArray(0,1)=div01
    set glblDivArray(0,2)=div02
    set glblDivArray(0,3)=div03
    set glblDivArray(0,4)=div04
    set glblDivArray(0,5)=div05
    set glblDivArray(0,6)=div06
    set glblDivArray(1,0)=div10
    set glblDivArray(1,1)=div11
    set glblDivArray(1,2)=div12
    set glblDivArray(1,3)=div13
    set glblDivArray(1,4)=div14
    set glblDivArray(1,5)=div15
    set glblDivArray(1,6)=div16
    set glblDivArray(2,0)=div20
    set glblDivArray(2,1)=div21
    set glblDivArray(2,2)=div22
    set glblDivArray(2,3)=div23
    set glblDivArray(2,4)=div24
    set glblDivArray(2,5)=div25
    set glblDivArray(2,6)=div26
    set glblDivArray(3,0)=div30
    set glblDivArray(3,1)=div31
    set glblDivArray(3,2)=div32
    set glblDivArray(3,3)=div33
    set glblDivArray(3,4)=div34
    set glblDivArray(3,5)=div35
    set glblDivArray(3,6)=div36
    set glblDivArray(4,0)=div40
    set glblDivArray(4,1)=div41
    set glblDivArray(4,2)=div42
```

```
set glblDivArray(4,3)=div43
set glblDivArray(4,4)=div44
set glblDivArray(4,5)=div45
set glblDivArray(4,6)=div46
set glblDivArray(5,0)=div50
set glblDivArray(5,1)=div51
set glblDivArray(5,2)=div52
set glblDivArray(5,3)=div53
set glblDivArray(5,4)=div54
set glblDivArray(5,5)=div55
set glblDivArray(5,6)=div56
set glblDivArray(6,0)=div60
set glblDivArray(6,1)=div61
set glblDivArray(6,2)=div62
set glblDivArray(6,3)=div63
set glblDivArray(6,4)=div64
set glblDivArray(6,5)=div65
set glblDivArray(6,6)=div66
for i = 0 to 6
        for j = 0 to 6
                glblDivArray(i,j).style.left = 100 + j*25
                glblDivArray(i,j).style.top = 150 + i*25
        next
next

for i = 0 to 6
        for j = 0 to 6
                glblBoardArray(i,j) = null
        next
next


set glblBallArray(0) = imgBall02
set glblBallArray(1) = imgBall03
set glblBallArray(2) = imgBall04
set glblBallArray(3) = imgBall12
set glblBallArray(4) = imgBall13
set glblBallArray(5) = imgBall14
set glblBallArray(6) = imgBall20
set glblBallArray(7) = imgBall21
set glblBallArray(8) = imgBall22
set glblBallArray(9) = imgBall23
set glblBallArray(10) = imgBall24
set glblBallArray(11) = imgBall25
set glblBallArray(12) = imgBall26
set glblBallArray(13) = imgBall30
```

```
set glblBallArray(14) = imgBall31
set glblBallArray(15) = imgBall32
set glblBallArray(16) = imgBall34
set glblBallArray(17) = imgBall35
set glblBallArray(18) = imgBall36
set glblBallArray(19) = imgBall40
set glblBallArray(20) = imgBall41
set glblBallArray(21) = imgBall42
set glblBallArray(22) = imgBall43
set glblBallArray(23) = imgBall44
set glblBallArray(24) = imgBall45
set glblBallArray(25) = imgBall46
set glblBallArray(26) = imgBall52
set glblBallArray(27) = imgBall53
set glblBallArray(28) = imgBall54
set glblBallArray(29) = imgBall62
set glblBallArray(30) = imgBall63
set glblBallArray(31) = imgBall64

    newGame

End Sub
```

The first set of `for` loops

```
for i = 0 to 6
    for j = 0 to 6
        glblDivArray(i,j).style.left = 100 + j*25
        glblDivArray(i,j).style.top = 150 + i*25
    next
next
```

positions the DIVs on the screen, starting 100 pixels from the left edge of the window and 150 pixels from the top. Each DIV is 20 pixels × 20 pixels. Allowing 5 pixels between consecutive DIVs gives the 25 as the multiplier for i and j.

The second set of `for` loops

```
for i = 0 to 6
    for j = 0 to 6
        glblBoardArray(i,j) = null
    next
next
```

gives us an empty board on which to position the pieces. "Positioning a piece" means to set a cell in this array to point to an object which represents the piece. The newGame subroutine in the next subsection takes care of this.

Starting a New Game

After `window_onload` finishes initializing the variables and arrays, it calls this subroutine:

```
Sub newGame

    for i = 0 To 31
            intID = CInt(Right(glblBallArray(i).id, 2))
            rowNum = intID\10
            colNum = intID mod 10
            glblBallArray(i).style.pixelTop = 150 + rowNum*25 + 3
            glblBallArray(i).style.pixelLeft = 100 + colNum*25 + 3
            glblBallArray(i).style.zIndex = 1
            set glblBoardArray(rowNum, colNum) = glblBallArray(i)
    next

End Sub
```

newGame goes through the array of images (glblBallArray). It implements a couple of tricks that use the images' IDs to position them on the screen and in glblBoardArray. The first trick is to take an IMG element's ID, like imgBall34, and parse it to get the two-digit string at the end and turn it into a two-digit integer. The built-in VBS function Right gets the last two digits and CInt converts them into an integer that is stored in the local variable intID.

The next trick turns the two-digit intID into a row number and a column number. The first digit is the row number, the second is the column number. To get the first integer, we integer-divide intID by 10, as indicated by the backslash in intID\10. The expression 34\10, for example, gives a result of 3. To get the second integer, we use the VBS mod operator, which gives the remainder of a division: 34 mod 10 is equal to 4. (We'll mention these operators again in Skill 13.)

The next two lines position the images on the screen in the corresponding DIVs. The 3 at the end of each line centers an image within a DIV. We set the z-index to 1 to superimpose the image on the board. The subroutine finishes by setting the appropriate entry in glblBoardArray to point to the IMG element we just processed.

Enter this subroutine into your SCRIPT element and we'll move on to mouse movement event-handlers.

Mouse Movement Event-Handlers

The document_onmouseover subroutine is the same as before, so I won't present it again here. We add a few new expressions to document_onmousedown, indicated by the bold items:

```
sub document_onmousedown
    set glblSelectedObject = window.event.srcElement

    if InStr(glblSelectedObject.ID,"img") = 0 then
        glblSelectedObject = null
        exit sub
    end if

    glblSelectedObject.style.pixelLeft = glblSelectedObject.offsetLeft
    glblSelectedObject.style.pixelTop = glblSelectedObject.offsetTop

    glblCurrentX = window.event.clientX + document.body.scrollLeft
    glblCurrentY = window.event.clientY + document.body.scrollTop

    glblCurrentRow = (window.event.y - 150)\25
    glblCurrentColumn = (window.event.x - 100)\25

end sub
```

The new expressions take the x and y locations of the mouse during the onmousedown event and turn them into column and row positions. To do this, they subtract the starting position and divide the difference by the distance between the beginning of one DIV and the beginning of another.

The document_onmousemove subroutine is unchanged, as you might expect. The rules of our Solitaire game, however, necessitate several additions to document_onmouseup: After a user has dragged a piece and dropped it on a square, the script has to decide whether the move is legal:

```
sub document_onmouseup
    on error resume next

    if InStr(glblSelectedObject.ID,"img") = 0 then
        glblSelectedObject = null
        exit sub
    end if

    glblNewRow = (window.event.y - 150)\25
```

```
glblNewColumn = (window.event.x - 100)\25
call checkForLegalMove(glblCurrentRow,glblCurrentColumn,
➥ glblNewRow,glblNewColumn)
glblSelectedObject = null

end sub
```

As you can see, most of the code is new. The on error resume next protects against crashing and burning if a user decides to click the mouse on a page location that's not on the game board, such as the New Game button. The if...then prevents the program from doing anything with an object that isn't an image.

Of the last three new lines of code, the first turns the y location of the onmouseup event into a row and stores it in glblNewRow, the second turns the x location of the onmouseup event into a column and stores it in glblNewColumn, and the third calls a subroutine that checks the legality of the move from (glblCurrentRow, glblCurrentColumn) to (glblNewRow, glblNewColumn).

Add the new code to document_onmouseup, and we'll examine the subroutine that checks the legality of moves.

Checking for Legal Moves

This is the subroutine that deals with the essence of the game. Add it to your SCRIPT element and we'll dissect it step by step:

```
sub checkForLegalMove(startRow,startColumn,targetRow,targetColumn)

    if (startRow = targetRow) and (startColumn = targetColumn) then
        glblSelectedObject.style.pixelTop = 150 + targetRow*25 + 3
        glblSelectedObject.style.pixelLeft = 100 + targetColumn*25
        ➥ + 3
        exit sub
    end if

    if (targetRow > 6) or (targetColumn > 6) or _
       (targetRow < 0) or (targetColumn < 0) then
        call notifyIllegalMove(startRow,startColumn,
        ➥ targetRow,targetColumn)
        exit sub
    end if

    if isUnused(targetRow, targetColumn) then
        call notifyIllegalMove(startRow,startColumn,
        ➥ targetRow,targetColumn)
        exit sub
    end if
```

```
if isObject(glblBoardArray(targetRow, targetColumn)) then
      call notifyIllegalMove(startRow,startColumn,
      ➥ targetRow,targetColumn)
      exit sub
end if

if (abs(startRow - targetRow) = 1) or
➥ (abs(startRow - targetRow) > 2) then
      call notifyIllegalMove(startRow,startColumn,
      ➥ targetRow,targetColumn)
      exit sub
end if

if (abs(startColumn - targetColumn) = 1) or
➥ (abs(startColumn - targetColumn) > 2) then
      call notifyIllegalMove(startRow,startColumn,
      ➥ targetRow,targetColumn)
      exit sub
end if

if(abs(startColumn - targetColumn) = 2) and
➥ (abs(startRow - targetRow)) = 2 then
      call notifyIllegalMove(startRow,startColumn,
      ➥ targetRow,targetColumn)
      exit sub
end if

if not isObject((glblBoardArray(between(startRow, targetRow),
➥ between(startColumn, targetColumn)))) then
      call notifyIllegalMove(startRow,startColumn,
      ➥ targetRow,targetColumn)
      exit sub
end if

    call
completeLegalMove(startRow,startColumn,targetRow,targetColumn)
end sub
```

Each if...then looks for a specific condition, reacts accordingly if that condition has occurred, and exits the subroutine after it reacts.

The first if...then checks to see if the user dragged the piece around and decided to drop it back on the square it was dragged from:

```
if (startRow = targetRow) and (startColumn = targetColumn) then
      glblSelectedObject.style.pixelTop = 150 + targetRow*25 + 3
      glblSelectedObject.style.pixelLeft = 100 + targetColumn*25
      ➥ + 3
      exit sub
end if
```

This is legal. The steps after the then statement reposition the piece on its original square.

The remaining if...thens check for a variety of illegal moves and calls the notifyIllegalMove subroutine if necessary. Specifically, they check for:

1. Dropping a piece in an area of the page that's not on the board

2. Dropping a piece in one of the unused DIVs (this one calls isUnused, a function we have to write)

3. Dropping a piece onto a DIV that another piece is currently occupying (note the use of the built-in VBS function isObject, which checks to see if a variable is pointing to an object)

4. Moving a piece onto a DIV in a row that's too close or too far

5. Moving a piece onto a DIV in a column that's too close or too far

6. Attempting a diagonal jump

7. Attempting to jump over a DIV that's not occupied

In the if...thens that correspond to 4, 5, and 6, note the use of abs, a VBS function that returns the absolute value of an expression. In 7, we use not along with isObject to determine if a DIV is unoccupied. We also use between, a function that we have to write. The between function supplies the DIV between the DIV where a move starts and the DIV where it ends.

 TIP   Remember that usage of not along with isObject to test whether a variable is pointing to an object. The expression variable = null won't work.

If none of the illegal conditions have occurred, the subroutine calls completeLegalMove, which we'll look at next.

Completing a Legal Move

This subroutine takes care of the housekeeping on the board when a piece legally moves from one board position to another:

```
sub completeLegalMove(startRow,startColumn,targetRow,targetColumn)
    glblBoardArray(startRow,startColumn) = null
    set glblBoardArray(targetRow,targetColumn) = glblSelectedObject
```

```
        glblBoardArray(between(startRow,targetRow),
        ➥ between(startColumn,targetColumn)).style.zIndex = -1
        glblBoardArray(between(startRow,targetRow),
        ➥ between(startColumn,targetColumn)) = null
        glblSelectedObject.style.pixelTop = 150 + targetRow*25 + 3
        glblSelectedObject.style.pixelLeft = 100 + targetColumn*25 + 3
    end sub
```

Here's how the subroutine works:

1. It starts with the `glblBoardArray` position that the piece moved from, and sets it to `null`.

2. It then sets the moved-to `glblBoardArray` position to point to the moved piece.

3. Next, it removes the jumped-over piece from the board. It does this by setting its `z-index` to −1, effectively putting that piece under the board.

4. It sets the jumped-over piece's `glblBoardArray` position to `null`.

5. It finishes by centering the moved piece within the DIV it now occupies.

Notification of Illegal Moves

This subroutine covers a multitude of illegalities:

```
    sub notifyIllegalMove(startRow,startColumn,targetRow,targetColumn)
        MsgBox "Illegal Move"
        set glblBoardArray(startRow, startColumn) = glblSelectedObject
        glblSelectedObject.style.pixelTop = 150 + startRow*25 + 3
        glblSelectedObject.style.pixelLeft = 100 + startColumn*25 + 3
    end sub
```

After the subject clicks OK on the "Illegal Move" Message Box, the subroutine sets the dropped piece's starting `glblBoardArray` position to point to that piece, moves the piece back to its starting position on the board, and centers it within the DIV.

Other Procedures

Here are two functions that other subroutines call, along with an `onclick` event handler for the New Game button.

The isUnused function performs some arithmetic on its arguments to see if they consitute the row and column of a square in the unused areas of the board:

```
function isUnused(targetRow, targetColumn)
    rowColumnNumber = 10*targetRow + targetColumn
    if (rowColumnNumber = 0) or (rowColumnNumber = 1) or _
       (rowColumnNumber = 5) or (rowColumnNumber = 6) or _
       (rowColumnNumber = 10) or (rowColumnNumber = 11) or _
       (rowColumnNumber = 15) or (rowColumnNumber = 16) or _
       (rowColumnNumber = 50) or (rowColumnNumber = 51) or _
       (rowColumnNumber = 55) or (rowColumnNumber = 56) or _
       (rowColumnNumber = 60) or (rowColumnNumber = 61) or _
       (rowColumnNumber = 65) or (rowColumnNumber = 66)   then
            isUnused = true
    else
            isUnused = false
    end if
end function
```

The next function does some arithmetic on its arguments to give either a row number or a column number for the board position between the starting position and the ending position of a move. This is important, because we have to test the in-between square for occupancy by a piece:

```
function between(a, b)
    between = a + (.5 * (b - a))
end function
```

This subroutine calls the same subroutine that window_onload calls to position the pieces on the board:

```
sub btnNewgame_onclick
    newGame
End Sub
```

The Whole Megillah

Here's Solitaire.htm in all its glory:

 Solitaire.htm

```
<HTML>
<HEAD>
<STYLE>
div {background-color:silver;width:20;height:20;position:absolute}
div.unused {background-color:white}
```

```
img {position:absolute}
</STYLE>

<SCRIPT Language = "VBScript">
dim glblCurrentX
dim glblCurrentY
dim glblSelectedObject
dim glblRowValue
dim glblColValue
dim glblBoardArray(6,6)
dim glblBallArray(31)

glblCurrentX = 0
glblCurrentY = 0

dim glblCurrentRow
dim glblCurrentColumn

dim glblNewRow
dim glblNewColumn

dim glblDivArray(6, 6)

Sub window_onload
    set glblDivArray(0,0)=div00
    set glblDivArray(0,1)=div01
    set glblDivArray(0,2)=div02
    set glblDivArray(0,3)=div03
    set glblDivArray(0,4)=div04
    set glblDivArray(0,5)=div05
    set glblDivArray(0,6)=div06
    set glblDivArray(1,0)=div10
    set glblDivArray(1,1)=div11
    set glblDivArray(1,2)=div12
    set glblDivArray(1,3)=div13
    set glblDivArray(1,4)=div14
    set glblDivArray(1,5)=div15
    set glblDivArray(1,6)=div16
    set glblDivArray(2,0)=div20
    set glblDivArray(2,1)=div21
    set glblDivArray(2,2)=div22
    set glblDivArray(2,3)=div23
    set glblDivArray(2,4)=div24
    set glblDivArray(2,5)=div25
    set glblDivArray(2,6)=div26
    set glblDivArray(3,0)=div30
    set glblDivArray(3,1)=div31
    set glblDivArray(3,2)=div32
```

Skill 9

```
set glblDivArray(3,3)=div33
set glblDivArray(3,4)=div34
set glblDivArray(3,5)=div35
set glblDivArray(3,6)=div36
set glblDivArray(4,0)=div40
set glblDivArray(4,1)=div41
set glblDivArray(4,2)=div42
set glblDivArray(4,3)=div43
set glblDivArray(4,4)=div44
set glblDivArray(4,5)=div45
set glblDivArray(4,6)=div46
set glblDivArray(5,0)=div50
set glblDivArray(5,1)=div51
set glblDivArray(5,2)=div52
set glblDivArray(5,3)=div53
set glblDivArray(5,4)=div54
set glblDivArray(5,5)=div55
set glblDivArray(5,6)=div56
set glblDivArray(6,0)=div60
set glblDivArray(6,1)=div61
set glblDivArray(6,2)=div62
set glblDivArray(6,3)=div63
set glblDivArray(6,4)=div64
set glblDivArray(6,5)=div65
set glblDivArray(6,6)=div66

for i = 0 to 6
        for j = 0 to 6
                glblDivArray(i,j).style.left = 100 + j*25
                glblDivArray(i,j).style.top = 150 + i*25
        next
next


for i = 0 to 6
        for j = 0 to 6
                glblBoardArray(i,j) = null
        next
next


set glblBallArray(0) = imgBall02
set glblBallArray(1) = imgBall03
set glblBallArray(2) = imgBall04
set glblBallArray(3) = imgBall12
set glblBallArray(4) = imgBall13
set glblBallArray(5) = imgBall14
set glblBallArray(6) = imgBall20
set glblBallArray(7) = imgBall21
set glblBallArray(8) = imgBall22
```

```
        set glblBallArray(9) = imgBall23
        set glblBallArray(10) = imgBall24
        set glblBallArray(11) = imgBall25
        set glblBallArray(12) = imgBall26
        set glblBallArray(13) = imgBall30
        set glblBallArray(14) = imgBall31
        set glblBallArray(15) = imgBall32
        set glblBallArray(16) = imgBall34
        set glblBallArray(17) = imgBall35
        set glblBallArray(18) = imgBall36
        set glblBallArray(19) = imgBall40
        set glblBallArray(20) = imgBall41
        set glblBallArray(21) = imgBall42
        set glblBallArray(22) = imgBall43
        set glblBallArray(23) = imgBall44
        set glblBallArray(24) = imgBall45
        set glblBallArray(25) = imgBall46
        set glblBallArray(26) = imgBall52
        set glblBallArray(27) = imgBall53
        set glblBallArray(28) = imgBall54
        set glblBallArray(29) = imgBall62
        set glblBallArray(30) = imgBall63
        set glblBallArray(31) = imgBall64

        newGame

End Sub

Sub newGame

    for i = 0 To 31
            intID = CInt(Right(glblBallArray(i).id, 2))
            rowNum = intID\10
            colNum = intID mod 10
            glblBallArray(i).style.pixelTop = 150 + rowNum*25 + 3
            glblBallArray(i).style.pixelLeft = 100 + colNum*25 + 3
            glblBallArray(i).style.zIndex = 1
            set glblBoardArray(rowNum, colNum) = glblBallArray(i)
    next

End Sub

sub document_onmouseover

    if InStr(window.event.srcElement.ID,"img") > 0 Then
            window.event.srcElement.style.cursor = "move"
    end if

end sub
```

Skill 9

```
sub document_onmousedown
     set glblSelectedObject = window.event.srcElement

     if InStr(glblSelectedObject.ID,"img") = 0 then
          glblSelectedObject = null
          exit sub
     end if

     glblSelectedObject.style.pixelLeft = glblSelectedObject.offsetLeft
     glblSelectedObject.style.pixelTop = glblSelectedObject.offsetTop

     glblCurrentX = window.event.clientX + document.body.scrollLeft
     glblCurrentY = window.event.clientY + document.body.scrollTop

     glblCurrentRow = (window.event.y - 150)\25
     glblCurrentColumn = (window.event.x - 100)\25

end sub


sub document_onmousemove

     on error resume next
     if glblSelectedObject = null then
          exit sub
     end if

     newX = window.event.clientX + document.body.scrollLeft
     newY = window.event.clientY + document.body.scrollTop
     distanceX = newX - glblCurrentX
     distanceY = newY - glblCurrentY
     glblCurrentX = newX
     glblCurrentY = newY

     glblSelectedObject.style.pixelLeft =
  ➥ glblSelectedObject.style.pixelLeft + distanceX
     glblSelectedObject.style.pixelTop =
  ➥ glblSelectedObject.style.pixelTop + distanceY
     window.event.returnValue = false

end sub

sub document_onmouseup
     on error resume next

     if InStr(glblSelectedObject.ID,"img") = 0 then
          glblSelectedObject = null
          exit sub
```

```
            end if

            glblNewRow = (window.event.y - 150)\25
            glblNewColumn = (window.event.x - 100)\25
            call checkForLegalMove(glblCurrentRow,glblCurrentColumn,
            ➥ glblNewRow,glblNewColumn)
            glblSelectedObject = null

end sub

sub checkForLegalMove(startRow,startColumn,targetRow,targetColumn)

        if (startRow = targetRow) and (startColumn = targetColumn) then
                glblSelectedObject.style.pixelTop = 150 + targetRow*25 + 3
                glblSelectedObject.style.pixelLeft = 100 + targetColumn*25
                ➥ + 3
                exit sub
        end if

        if (targetRow > 6) or (targetColumn > 6) or _
           (targetRow < 0) or (targetColumn < 0) then
                call notifyIllegalMove(startRow,startColumn,
                ➥ targetRow,targetColumn)
                exit sub
        end if

        if isUnused(targetRow, targetColumn) then
                call notifyIllegalMove(startRow,startColumn,
                ➥ targetRow,targetColumn)
                exit sub
        end if

        if isObject(glblBoardArray(targetRow, targetColumn)) then
                call notifyIllegalMove(startRow,startColumn,
                ➥ targetRow,targetColumn)
                exit sub
        end if

        if (abs(startRow - targetRow) = 1) or
        ➥ (abs(startRow - targetRow) > 2) then
                call
notifyIllegalMove(startRow,startColumn,targetRow,targetColumn)
                exit sub
        end if
```

Skill 9

```
        if (abs(startColumn - targetColumn) = 1) or
    ➥ (abs(startColumn - targetColumn) > 2) then
            call notifyIllegalMove(startRow,startColumn,
            ➥ targetRow,targetColumn)
            exit sub
        end if

        if(abs(startColumn - targetColumn) = 2) and
    ➥ (abs(startRow - targetRow)) = 2 then
            call notifyIllegalMove(startRow,startColumn,
            ➥ targetRow,targetColumn)
            exit sub
        end if

        if not isObject((glblBoardArray(between(startRow, targetRow),
    ➥ between(startColumn, targetColumn)))) then
            call notifyIllegalMove(startRow,startColumn,
            ➥ targetRow,targetColumn)
            exit sub
        end if

        call
completeLegalMove(startRow,startColumn,targetRow,targetColumn)
end sub

sub completeLegalMove(startRow,startColumn,targetRow,targetColumn)
    glblBoardArray(startRow,startColumn) = null
    set glblBoardArray(targetRow,targetColumn) = glblSelectedObject
    glblBoardArray(between(startRow,targetRow),
    ➥ between(startColumn,targetColumn)).style.zIndex = -1
    glblBoardArray(between(startRow,targetRow),
    ➥ between(startColumn,targetColumn)) = null
    glblSelectedObject.style.pixelTop = 150 + targetRow*25 + 3
    glblSelectedObject.style.pixelLeft = 100 + targetColumn*25 + 3
end sub

sub notifyIllegalMove(startRow,startColumn,targetRow,targetColumn)
    MsgBox "Illegal Move"
    set glblBoardArray(startRow, startColumn) = glblSelectedObject
    glblSelectedObject.style.pixelTop = 150 + startRow*25 + 3
    glblSelectedObject.style.pixelLeft = 100 + startColumn*25 + 3
end sub

function isUnused(targetRow, targetColumn)
    rowColumnNumber = 10*targetRow + targetColumn
    if (rowColumnNumber = 0) or (rowColumnNumber = 1) or _
       (rowColumnNumber = 5) or (rowColumnNumber = 6) or _
       (rowColumnNumber = 10) or (rowColumnNumber = 11) or _
```

```
                (rowColumnNumber = 15) or (rowColumnNumber = 16) or _
                (rowColumnNumber = 50) or (rowColumnNumber = 51) or _
                (rowColumnNumber = 55) or (rowColumnNumber = 56) or _
                (rowColumnNumber = 60) or (rowColumnNumber = 61) or _
                (rowColumnNumber = 65) or (rowColumnNumber = 66)   then
                    isUnused = true
        else
                    isUnused = false
        end if
end function

function between(a, b)
        between = a + (.5 * (b - a))
end function

sub btnNewgame_onclick
        newGame
End Sub

</SCRIPT>
<TITLE>Drag-and-Drop Solitaire</TITLE>
</HEAD>
<BODY>

<IMG id = "imgBall02" Src = "ltblbal.gif">
<IMG id = "imgBall03" Src = "ltblbal.gif">
<IMG id = "imgBall04" Src = "ltblbal.gif">
<IMG id = "imgBall12" Src = "ltblbal.gif">
<IMG id = "imgBall13" Src = "ltblbal.gif">
<IMG id = "imgBall14" Src = "ltblbal.gif">
<IMG id = "imgBall20" Src = "ltblbal.gif">
<IMG id = "imgBall21" Src = "ltblbal.gif">
<IMG id = "imgBall22" Src = "ltblbal.gif">
<IMG id = "imgBall23" Src = "ltblbal.gif">
<IMG id = "imgBall24" Src = "ltblbal.gif">
<IMG id = "imgBall25" Src = "ltblbal.gif">
<IMG id = "imgBall26" Src = "ltblbal.gif">
<IMG id = "imgBall30" Src = "ltblbal.gif">
<IMG id = "imgBall31" Src = "ltblbal.gif">
<IMG id = "imgBall32" Src = "ltblbal.gif">
<IMG id = "imgBall34" Src = "ltblbal.gif">
<IMG id = "imgBall35" Src = "ltblbal.gif">
<IMG id = "imgBall36" Src = "ltblbal.gif">
<IMG id = "imgBall40" Src = "ltblbal.gif">
<IMG id = "imgBall41" Src = "ltblbal.gif">
<IMG id = "imgBall42" Src = "ltblbal.gif">
<IMG id = "imgBall43" Src = "ltblbal.gif">
<IMG id = "imgBall44" Src = "ltblbal.gif">
```

Skill 9

```
<IMG id = "imgBall45" Src = "ltblbal.gif">
<IMG id = "imgBall46" Src = "ltblbal.gif">
<IMG id = "imgBall52" Src = "ltblbal.gif">
<IMG id = "imgBall53" Src = "ltblbal.gif">
<IMG id = "imgBall54" Src = "ltblbal.gif">
<IMG id = "imgBall62" Src = "ltblbal.gif">
<IMG id = "imgBall63" Src = "ltblbal.gif">
<IMG id = "imgBall64" Src = "ltblbal.gif">
<DIV ID = div00 Class = "unused"></DIV>
<DIV ID = div01 Class = "unused"></DIV>
<DIV ID = div02></DIV>
<DIV ID = div03></DIV>
<DIV ID = div04></DIV>
<DIV ID = div05 Class = "unused"></DIV>
<DIV ID = div06 Class = "unused"></DIV>
<DIV ID = div10 Class = "unused"></DIV>
<DIV ID = div11 Class = "unused"></DIV>
<DIV ID = div12></DIV>
<DIV ID = div13></DIV>
<DIV ID = div14></DIV>
<DIV ID = div15 Class = "unused"></DIV>
<DIV ID = div16 Class = "unused"></DIV>
<DIV ID = div20></DIV>
<DIV ID = div21></DIV>
<DIV ID = div22></DIV>
<DIV ID = div23></DIV>
<DIV ID = div24></DIV>
<DIV ID = div25></DIV>
<DIV ID = div26></DIV>
<DIV ID = div30></DIV>
<DIV ID = div31></DIV>
<DIV ID = div32></DIV>
<DIV ID = div33></DIV>
<DIV ID = div34></DIV>
<DIV ID = div35></DIV>
<DIV ID = div36></DIV>
<DIV ID = div40></DIV>
<DIV ID = div41></DIV>
<DIV ID = div42></DIV>
<DIV ID = div43></DIV>
<DIV ID = div44></DIV>
<DIV ID = div45></DIV>
<DIV ID = div46></DIV>
<DIV ID = div50 Class = "unused"></DIV>
<DIV ID = div51 Class = "unused"></DIV>
<DIV ID = div52></DIV>
<DIV ID = div53></DIV>
<DIV ID = div54></DIV>
```

```
<DIV ID = div55 Class = "unused"></DIV>
<DIV ID = div56 Class = "unused"></DIV>
<DIV ID = div60 Class = "unused"></DIV>
<DIV ID = div61 Class = "unused"></DIV>
<DIV ID = div62></DIV>
<DIV ID = div63></DIV>
<DIV ID = div64></DIV>
<DIV ID = div65 Class = "unused"></DIV>
<DIV ID = div66 Class = "unused"></DIV>

<H1 Style = "text-align:center">A Classic Solitaire Game</H1> <HR>
<DIV Style = "position:absolute;top:100;left:300;
background-color:white;height:50;width:280">
Try your hand at this old favorite. Good luck!<BR>
<OL>
<LI> Select Full Screen from the View menu.
<LI> Move a piece by dragging it and dropping it on an empty square.
<LI> Moves are "jumps," as in checkers, but they must be left-right
or up-down.
<LI> Diagonal jumps are not allowed.
<LI> A jumped piece leaves the board.
<LI> The objective is to remove all the pieces except one, and to leave
that piece on the center square.
<LI> When no legal moves are possible, the game is over.
</OL>
</DIV>

<DIV Style = "position:absolute; top:345; left: 135;
background-color:white">
<FORM ID = "frmButton">
<INPUT Type = Button ID = "btnNewgame" Value = "New Game"
Style="height:25:width:75">
</FORM>
</DIV>
</BODY>
</HTML>
```

Open this file in IE and spend many happy hours playing a classic Solitaire game. Notice the first rule about putting the browser in full-screen view. This gets at the issue that I mentioned at the end of the first exercise in this Skill. When you drag an object up to the menu bar (and other bars at the top of the window), funny things happen. The dragging and dropping become discombobulated, and this has bad effects on the Solitaire game. Putting the browser in full-screen view eliminates this problem by hiding the bars at the top and side of the window.

You can add to this application in several ways:

- In its present form, the program doesn't recognize multiple-jump moves as legal. They're legal by the rules of the game, but the script doesn't deal with them. You might try to add code that deals with multiple jumps.

- It's possible to apply some of the knowledge you acquired in Skill 8 and make this game a multimedia experience. Embed a short sound in the document and have the program play it whenever a legal move is completed.

- Create a button that gives the user the option of allowing diagonal jumps. To make this happen, you'll have to work with the code in the `checkForLegalMove` subroutine.

- At present, the game doesn't have a move counter. Add one to the program so that you can keep track of how few moves it takes you to beat the game. You might also consider adding code that automatically detects when a game is over and notifies the user.

- The "Illegal Move" Message Box isn't informative. Think of ways to use it as a coaching device to help the user. One possibility is to move the Message Box out of the `notifyIllegalMove` subroutine and put a different Message Box inside each `if...then` in `checkForLegalMove`.

- Some variations of the game start with fewer than the 32 pieces in the standard version. The pieces are arranged in patterns and the objective is the same: to leave one piece in the center square. Our script can only set up a game in the standard way. Perhaps you can create code that gives the user the option of setting up the game any way that he or she wants to.

If you want to read more about this game, take a look at "Peg Solitaire," an article in *The Unexpected Hanging and Other Mathematical Diversions* by Martin Gardner (published by The University of Chicago Press). This book is one of several collections of Gardner's wonderful "Mathematical Games" columns that appeared in *Scientific American* every month for more than 30 years. For the absolute definitive work on peg solitaire, read *The Ins and Outs of Peg Solitaire* by John Beasley (published by Oxford University Press).

TIP When you're developing a board game, it's helpful to have an on-screen TEXTAREA (as in many of our exercises) that continuously monitors information about the mouse. Key pieces of information are the mouse position in terms of x and y location, the mouse position in terms of row and column, and the element the mouse is positioned in. This will help your thought process as you decide on position parameters for the subroutines in your script. When you're finished creating the game, you remove the TEXTAREA from the screen.

Summary

Dragging and dropping is ideal for a variety of applications, including Web pages. Users will appreciate the freedom it gives them to interact with your Web-based creations, especially since this is a technique they use every day. Dynamic HTML gives you the tools to easily implement this capability.

Have You Mastered the Essentials?

Now you can...

- ☑ Implement dragging and dropping in VBScript in IE

- ☑ Implement dragging and dropping in JavaScript in Navigator

- ☑ Understand some of the differences between the two browsers with respect to dragging and dropping

- ☑ Understand the value of an event model

- ☑ Use VBScript to build a game that incorporates dragging and dropping

- ☑ Understand some of the requirements for programming the display and movement of pieces in a board game

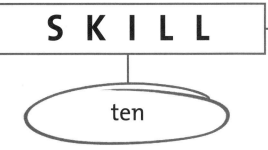

S K I L L

ten

Working with Data
and Dialog Boxes

- ❑ Introducing the Tabular Data Control
- ❑ Working with tables
- ❑ Filtering data
- ❑ Sorting data
- ❑ Dynamic filtering and sorting
- ❑ Moving through a recordset
- ❑ Working with a dialog box

When you install IE 4.0, you install a set of useful ActiveX controls along with it. I've already mentioned some of them—the DirectAnimation controls. In Skill 7, you worked through an exercise that hinted at their potential.

This Skill explores another ActiveX control that comes with IE. Dubbed the Tabular Data Control (TDC), this control enables you to work with data in ways that formerly required tedious round-trips between your machine and a server. Before this control was available, if you downloaded data from a server and wanted to change how the data looked on-screen, or if you changed your mind about which data values you wanted to see, you were in for a potentially long wait. Your machine had to send a request to a server, and the server had to process the request and then send a reply. If the whole transaction took place over a slow modem connection, you probably experienced frustration along with the delay.

The TDC changes all that, and not a moment too soon. This control reads data from a text file. Its properties and methods enable users to view and interact with the data to change the way it appears on-screen, after the data has down-loaded. The server doesn't control the interaction: Everything takes place in the user's machine.

In this Skill, you'll work through a series of exercises to learn how to harness the capabilities of the TDC.

 NOTE   Microsoft also provides Remote Data Services (RDS), designed for accessing and updating data in a database management system that complies with ODBC (a standard programming language interface that connects with a variety of data sources). With the TDC, the user can view the data. With RDS, the user can view, edit, and update live data. We'll only cover the TDC in this Skill.

Tabling the TDC

You'll start learning about the TDC by seeing how it works with HTML's TABLE element, which is designed for presenting data. In Skill 3, you built a table for the University of Cyberspace's Department of Cyberengineering. Copy Cybereng.htm, the file that holds this table, into your Skill 10 folder. Figure 10.1 shows this page rendered in IE.

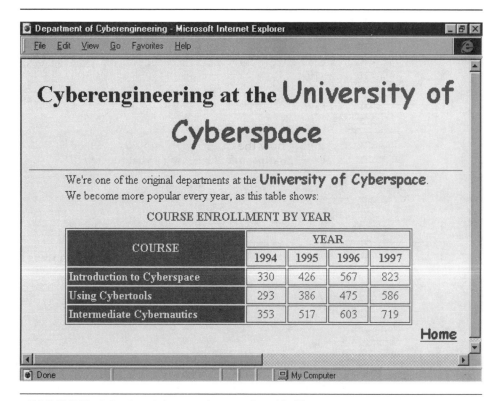

FIGURE 10.1: Cybereng.htm rendered in IE

Here's the code that creates the table:

```
<TABLE Style = "Position:Absolute;Top:200;Left:60;Width:480;
Color:'green';font-weight:normal"
Cols = 5 Border Bordercolor = "green">
<CAPTION Style = "font-weight:bold">COURSE ENROLLMENT BY YEAR</CAPTION>
<COLGROUP>
<COL Style = "background-color:'green';color:#FFFFCC;
text-align:left;font-weight:bold;width:240">
<TR Style = "text-align:center;font-weight:bold">
<TD Rowspan = 2 Style = "text-align:center">COURSE</TD>
<TD Colspan = 4>YEAR</TD>
</TR>
<TR Style = "text-align:center;font-weight:bold">
<TD>1994</TD>
<TD>1995</TD>
```

```
<TD>1996</TD>
<TD>1997</TD>
</TR>
<TR Style = "text-align:center">
<TD Style = "margin-left:20">Introduction to Cyberspace</TD>
<TD>330</TD>
<TD>426</TD>
<TD>567</TD>
<TD>823</TD>
</TR>
<TR Style = "text-align:center">
<TD Style = "margin-left:20">Using Cybertools</TD>
<TD>293</TD>
<TD>386</TD>
<TD>475</TD>
<TD>586</TD>
</TR>
<TR Style = "text-align:center">
<TD Style = "margin-left:20">Intermediate Cybernautics</TD>
<TD>353</TD>
<TD>517</TD>
<TD>603</TD>
<TD>719</TD>
</TR>
</TABLE>
```

Although it's fairly straightforward, this approach has a major disadvantage: The data is hard-coded in HTML, and if you want to use the data again in another page, you have to rewrite it all in another file.

A more efficient approach would be to store the data in a file that you could use by just referring to it in code. Then you could put it into as many pages as you like without rewriting any of it.

With the TDC, you can do just that. In your text editor, create this text file:

```
Course,1994,1995,1996,1997
Introduction to Cyberspace,330,426,567,823
Using Cybertools,293,386,475,586
Intermediate Cybernautics,353,517,603,719
```

As you can see, this code captures all the data from the table in Figure 10.1. The first line represents the table headings. Subsequent lines represent rows of the table. A comma separates adjacent values, and for this reason the file is said to be *comma-delimited*. Carriage returns separate consecutive rows. Save the file as cyberstats.txt in your Skill 10 folder.

 NOTE   Make sure you press Enter at the end of each line. This sets up the carriage return character as the *row delimiter*.

The Head and the Body

Now you're in business. In your `Cybereng.htm` file, find the TABLE element. Before you use the TDC to connect `cyberstats.txt` to the TABLE, you're going to add a couple of elements. The first is THEAD, which marks off the head of the table. Right after the COL element, add <THEAD>. Then, right after the TR element that follows the TD that specifies the 1997 header, add </THEAD>.

Next, add an attribute to the <TABLE> tag. The attribute, `Datasrc`, will specify an ID that you'll assign to the TDC. In the <TABLE> tag, add

```
Datasrc = #tdcCyberdata
```

 NOTE   Make sure you include the # sign.

At this point, the first part of your TABLE element should look like this:

```
<TABLE Datasrc = #tdcCyberdata Style =
"Position:Absolute;Top:200;Left:60;Width:480;
Color:'green';font-weight:normal"
Cols = 5 Border Bordercolor = "green">
<CAPTION Style = "font-weight:bold">COURSE ENROLLMENT BY YEAR</CAPTION>
<COLGROUP>
<COL Style = "background-color:'green';color:#FFFFCC;
text-align:left;font-weight:bold;width:240">
<THEAD>
<TR Style = "text-align:center;font-weight:bold">
<TD Rowspan = 2 Style = "text-align:center">COURSE</TD>
<TD Colspan = 4>YEAR</TD>
</TR>
<TR Style = "text-align:center;font-weight:bold">
<TD>1994</TD>
<TD>1995</TD>
<TD>1996</TD>
<TD>1997</TD>
</TR>
</THEAD>
```

On the next line, add <TBODY>, the opening tag of an element that delineates the table's body. Just before </TABLE>, add </TBODY>. Here, in abbreviated form, is the rest of your TABLE element after the changes:

```
<TBODY>
<TR Style = "text-align:center">
<TD Style = "margin-left:20">Introduction to Cyberspace</TD>
<TD>330</TD>
<TD>426</TD>
<TD>567</TD>
```

```
<TD>823</TD>
</TR>
    .
    .
    .
<TD>603</TD>
<TD>719</TD>
</TR></TBODY>
</TABLE>
```

The Heart and the Soul

Now it's time for the TDC. Just before the </BODY> tag, add this code:

```
<OBJECT id=tdcCyberdata
CLASSID="clsid:333C7BC4-460F-11D0-BC04-0080C7055A83">
    <PARAM NAME="DataURL" VALUE="cyberstats.txt">
    <PARAM NAME="UseHeader" VALUE="True">
</OBJECT>
```

NOTE   Make sure you type the value of CLASSID exactly as I wrote it. You might consider creating in your text editor a bare-bones template of this OBJECT element with the CLASSID typed in. This will save you some typing when you have to insert a TDC in future Web pages.

NOTE   Delete the DIV that contains the link back to the U of Cyb home page. We won't use it in this exercise.

The OBJECT element is in a format that specifies an ActiveX control, and the CLASSID tells your machine which control is specified. The ID, tdcCyberdata, gives the control a name. The PARAM elements set specific properties of the TDC. The first property gives the name of the file to draw data from, and the second indicates that the first row of that file contains headers rather than a data record.

What does this enable you to do? You can now delete all the TDs that hold the hard-coded data. You can make it easy on yourself by only deleting the second and third rows of data. (You'll just make some substitutions in the first row.) In your cybereng.htm file, delete

```
<TR Style = "text-align:center">
<TD Style = "margin-left:20">Using Cybertools</TD>
<TD>293</TD>
<TD>386</TD>
```

```
<TD>475</TD>
<TD>586</TD>
</TR>
<TR Style = "text-align:center">
<TD Style = "margin-left:20">Intermediate Cybernautics</TD>
<TD>353</TD>
<TD>517</TD>
<TD>603</TD>
<TD>719</TD>
</TR>
```

Find the first row of data (the one you didn't delete):

```
<TR Style = "text-align:center">
<TD Style = "margin-left:20">Introduction to Cyberspace</TD>
<TD>330</TD>
<TD>426</TD>
<TD>567</TD>
<TD>823</TD>
</TR>
```

In place of the hard-coded data, substitute references to the data file. Start with the second line:

```
<TD Style = "margin-left:20">Introduction to Cyberspace</TD>
```

For the course title Introduction to Cyberspace, substitute a reference to the appropriate column (or *field*) in cyberstats.txt. That reference will be the value of Datafld, an attribute of a DIV or a SPAN element. Insert the reference like this:

```
<TD Style = "margin-left:20"><DIV Datafld = "Course"></DIV></TD>
```

This tells the browser to use the data in the Course column in cyberstats.txt as the data for the corresponding column in the TABLE.

Make similar substitutions in the remaining lines so that you use five Dataflds to specify five column-names. When you're finished, that part of your TABLE element should look like this:

```
<TR Style = "text-align:center">
<TD Style = "margin-left:20"><DIV Datafld = "Course"></DIV></TD>
<TD><DIV Datafld = "1994"></DIV></TD>
<TD><DIV Datafld = "1995"></DIV></TD>
<TD><DIV Datafld = "1996"></DIV></TD>
<TD><DIV Datafld = "1997"></DIV></TD>
</TR>
```

In place of hard-coded data, you're using references to columns in cyberstats.txt.

Here's the entire Cybereng.htm file with all the hard-coded data removed:

Cybereng.htm

```
<HTML>
<HEAD>
<STYLE Type = "text/css">
.UofCyb{font-size:120%;color:'green';font-weight:bold;font-family:cursive}
</STYLE>
<TITLE>Department of Cyberengineering</TITLE>
</HEAD>
<BODY Style = "Background-Color:#FFFFCC">
<H1 Style = "Text-Align:Center">
Cyberengineering at
the <A Class = "UofCyb">University of Cyberspace</A>
</H1>
<HR>
<DIV Style = "Position:Absolute;Top:145;Left:60;Width:576">
<P> We're one of the original departments at the
<A Class = "UofCyb">University of Cyberspace</A>.<BR>We become
more popular every year, as this table shows:
</P>
</DIV>
<TABLE datasrc = #tdcCyberdata Style =
"Position:Absolute;Top:200;Left:60;Width:480;
Color:'green';font-weight:normal"
Cols = 5 Border Bordercolor = "green">
<CAPTION Style = "font-weight:bold">COURSE ENROLLMENT BY YEAR</CAPTION>
<COLGROUP>
<COL Style = "background-color:'green';color:#FFFFCC;
text-align:left;font-weight:bold;width:240">
<THEAD>
<TR Style = "text-align:center;font-weight:bold">
<TD Rowspan = 2 Style = "text-align:center">COURSE</TD>
<TD Colspan = 4>YEAR</TD>
</TR>
<TR Style = "text-align:center;font-weight:bold">
<TD>1994</TD>
<TD>1995</TD>
<TD>1996</TD>
<TD>1997</TD>
</TR>
</THEAD>
<TBODY>
<TR Style = "text-align:center">
<TD Style = "margin-left:20"><DIV datafld = "Course"></DIV></TD>
```

```
<TD><DIV datafld = "1994"></DIV></TD>
<TD><DIV datafld = "1995"></DIV></TD>
<TD><DIV datafld = "1996"></DIV></TD>
<TD><DIV datafld = "1997"></DIV></TD>
</TR></TBODY>
</TABLE>

<OBJECT id=tdcCyberdata
CLASSID="clsid:333C7BC4-460F-11D0-BC04-0080C7055A83">
    <PARAM NAME="DataURL" VALUE="cyberstats.txt">
    <PARAM NAME="UseHeader" VALUE="True">
</OBJECT>
</BODY>
</HTML>
```

If you open this document in IE, you'll see a page that looks just like Figure 10.1 (without the link to the U of Cyb home page). The new page has all the tabulated values with no values hard-coded in the file.

Filtering the Data

The preceding exercise suggests what the TDC can do. The net savings, however, was just a few lines of code. The next exercise will give you a greater understanding of the TDC's benefits.

Suppose you have to set up an intranet and you want to build pages that present your organization's data. Suppose, also, that different pages (and different pieces of data) have to go to different groups within the organization. Do you have to set up separate data files for each group? With the TDC, you can use one data file and send customized information to different groups by appropriately *filtering* the data for different pages.

In this exercise, you're going to use one comma-delimited text file to hold all the enrollment data for three departments at the University of Cyberspace, and apply three filters to the data in the text file to build three different tables for three different department pages. That is, you'll manipulate the data so that you only show part of it on any page.

NOTE   For this exercise, you'll use your text editor to create the data file. In real-life applications, you probably wouldn't create a file like this by hand: You would most likely export it from a spreadsheet or a database.

Use your text editor to create this file with one header row and twelve rows of data:

```
Department,Course,1994:INT,1995:INT,1996:INT,1997:INT
Cyberengineering,Introduction to Cyberspace,330,426,567,823
Cyberengineering,Using Cybertools,293,386,475,586
Cyberengineering,Intermediate Cybernautics,353,517,603,719
Web Page Design,Graphic User Interfaces,457,678,579,607
Web Page Design,Page Layouts,559,403,525,609
Web Page Design,Text and Graphics,554,463,323,492
Web Page Design,Art in the Cyberage,449,501,556,608
Web Page Design,Graphic File Formats,303,357,389,409
Web Access Statistics,Surveys on the Web,211,256,290,301
Web Access Statistics,Analysis and Design,201,205,234,245
Web Access Statistics,Introductory Statistics,199,209,287,302
Web Access Statistics,Intermediate Statistics,103,199,209,287
```

The :INT after four of the headers in the first line indicates that the entries in those columns are integers, and the TDC should treat them that way when it reads the data from the file. This is important when you have numerical data. Without this specification, the TDC would interpret the numerical data as strings, and filtering and sorting would be inaccurate. Make sure you hit Return at the end of every line. Save the file as UCybData.txt in Skill 10. It will serve as the setting for the TDC DataURL property for the rest of the exercises.

NOTE   Since it's a reference to a URL, the DataURL property can point to a file in another server.

Let's start by using this file to build a page like the one shown in Figure 10.1. To do this, all you have to do is make a couple of changes to the OBJECT element in cybereng.htm. Obviously, you have to change the DataURL to UCybData.txt. The other change is to add a PARAM element that specifies the filter. Here's how the OBJECT element should look:

```
<OBJECT id=tdcCyberstats
CLASSID="clsid:333C7BC4-460F-11D0-BC04-0080C7055A83">
    <PARAM NAME="DataURL" VALUE="UCybData.txt">
    <PARAM NAME="UseHeader" VALUE="True">
    <PARAM NAME=Filter VALUE= "Department = Cyberengineering">

</OBJECT>
```

This will produce the page for the Department of Cyberengineering.

Similarly, this OBJECT—along with the proper table specifications—produces the data for a page for the Department of Web Page Design (Figure 10.2):

```
<OBJECT id=tdcCyberdata
CLASSID="clsid:333C7BC4-460F-11D0-BC04-0080C7055A83">
    <PARAM NAME="DataURL" VALUE="UCybData.txt">
    <PARAM NAME="UseHeader" VALUE="True">
    <PARAM NAME=Filter VALUE= "Department = Web Page Design">

</OBJECT>
```

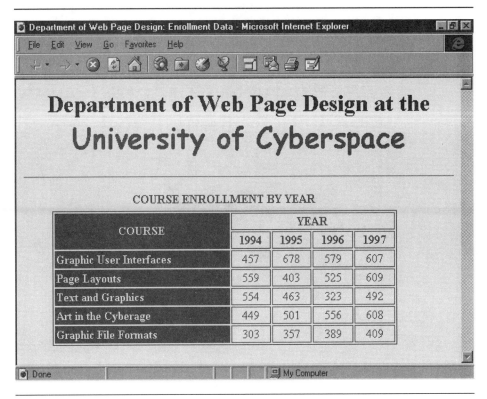

FIGURE 10.2: A page for the Department of Web Page Design. The data are filtered from the UCybData.txt file.

This OBJECT

```
<OBJECT id=tdcCyberdata
CLASSID="clsid:333C7BC4-460F-11D0-BC04-0080C7055A83">
```

```
<PARAM NAME="DataURL" VALUE="UCybData.txt">
<PARAM NAME="UseHeader" VALUE="True">
<PARAM NAME=Filter VALUE= "Department = Web Access Statistics">

</OBJECT>
```

produces the data for a page for the Department of Web Access Statistics (Figure 10.3).

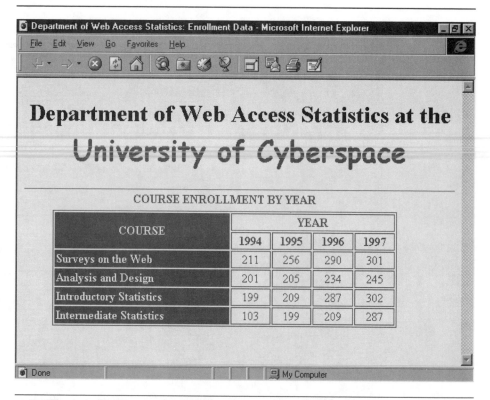

FIGURE 10.3: A page for the Department of Web Access Statistics, also filtered from UCybData.txt

More on Filtering

The TDC allows you to filter your data in a variety of ways. You can combine filters to get informative views of your data. Suppose, for example, you were interested in the enrollment figures for the Department of Web Page Design.

Perhaps you want to only see the data for courses in that department whose enrollment was more than 450 in 1994. Here's what the OBJECT element would look like:

```
<OBJECT id=tdcCyberdata CLASSID="clsid:333C7BC4-460F-11D0-BC04-0080C7055A83">
      <PARAM NAME="DataURL" VALUE="UCybData.txt">
      <PARAM NAME="UseHeader" VALUE="True">
      <PARAM NAME=Filter VALUE= "Department = Web Page Design & 1994 > 450">

</OBJECT>
```

Figure 10.4 shows the result of applying this compound filter.

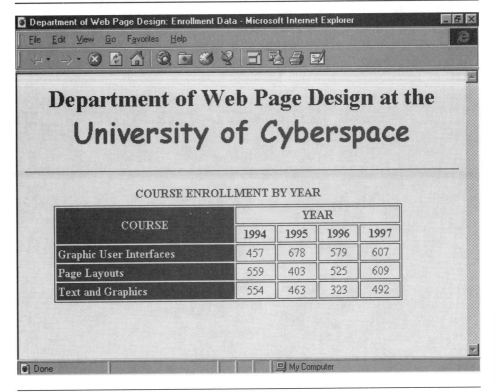

FIGURE 10.4: Enrollment figures for the Department of Web Page Design, for courses with more than 450 students in 1994 (compare with Figure 10.2)

Sorting the Data

In addition to filtering the data, TDC allows you to *sort* data entries—in other words, to arrange them in some fashion that you specify. For example, if you were interested in seeing a department's courses in alphabetical order, or in increasing order of the number of students enrolled, you would sort the data.

SortColumn is the TDC property that sorts data. Here's how to set it to arrange the courses in alphabetical order for the Department of Web Access Statistics:

```
<OBJECT id=tdcCyberdata
CLASSID="clsid:333C7BC4-460F-11D0-BC04-0080C7055A83">
    <PARAM NAME="DataURL" VALUE="UCybData.txt">
    <PARAM NAME="UseHeader" VALUE="True">
    <PARAM NAME=Filter VALUE= "Department = Web Access Statistics">
    <PARAM NAME=SortColumn VALUE = "Course">
```

Figure 10.5 shows the result.

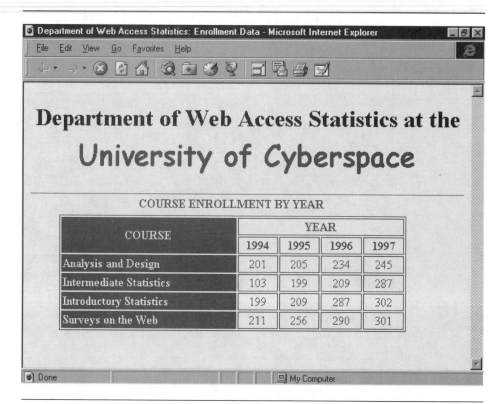

FIGURE 10.5: Enrollment data for the Department of Web Access Statistics, sorted by course title (compare with Figure 10.3)

Dynamic Filtering and Sorting

Filtering and sorting are terrific capabilities. They enable you to craft a set of data to present information in a variety of ways.

You can, however, go one step further and allow your users to filter and sort the data dynamically. That is, you can present data on a Web page and provide filtering and sorting capabilities so that users can decide which information they want to see. This eliminates the tedious round-trips to the server I mentioned earlier.

Figure 10.6 shows an example of filtering and sorting dynamically. (I selected View ➢ Full Screen to make sure the whole table is visible.) The table presents all the data in `UCybData.txt`. The drop-down listbox at the top enables filtering by department. Clicking on a column-header sorts the dataset by that column. For example, if you click on Department, the TDC arranges the data according to the alphabetical order of the department names. If you click on Course, the TDC arranges the data according to the alphabetical order of the course titles. If you click on a year, the TDC arranges the data in the numerical order of the entries in that column.

Creating the Document

Let's create the file that generates the page shown in Figure 10.6. Create a new file, save it as `Filtering and Sorting.htm`, and enter this HTML:

```
<HTML>
<HEAD><TITLE>Filtering and Sorting the Enrollment Data</TITLE>
<STYLE>
.headers {color:green;font-size:20;font-weight:bold}
</STYLE>
</HEAD>
<BODY Style = "Background-color:#FFFFCC">
<H1 ID = h1Header Style = "text-align:center">Filtering and Sorting
the Enrollment Data</H1>
<HR>
</BODY>
</HTML>
```

The rule in the STYLE element will determine the appearance of the `Filter` label and the column-headers.

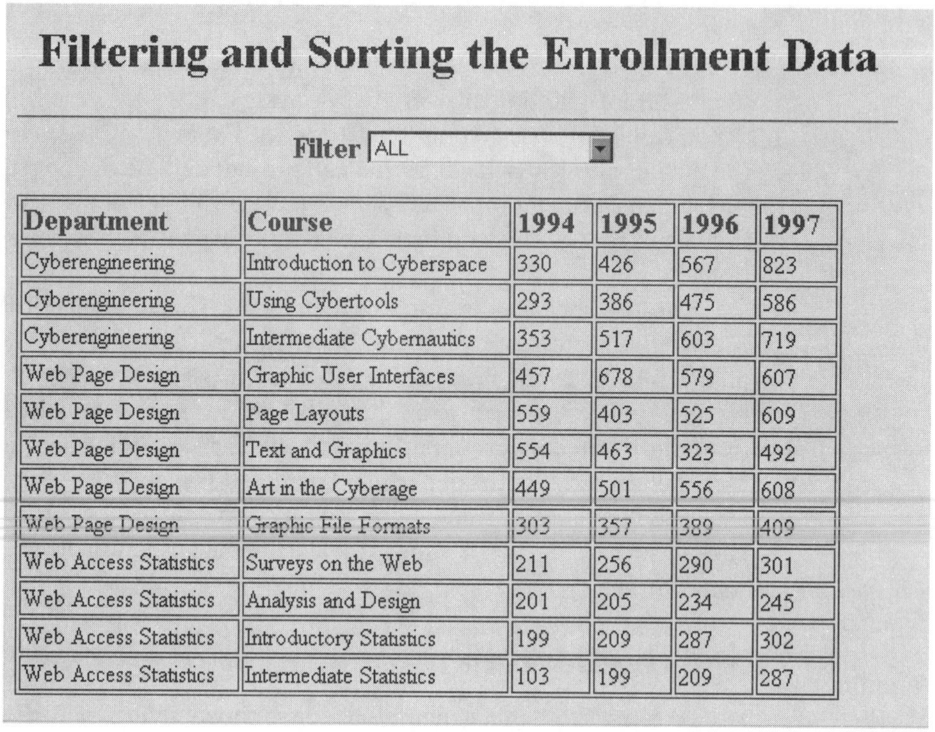

Filtering and Sorting the Enrollment Data

Filter [ALL ▼]

Department	Course	1994	1995	1996	1997
Cyberengineering	Introduction to Cyberspace	330	426	567	823
Cyberengineering	Using Cybertools	293	386	475	586
Cyberengineering	Intermediate Cybernautics	353	517	603	719
Web Page Design	Graphic User Interfaces	457	678	579	607
Web Page Design	Page Layouts	559	403	525	609
Web Page Design	Text and Graphics	554	463	323	492
Web Page Design	Art in the Cyberage	449	501	556	608
Web Page Design	Graphic File Formats	303	357	389	409
Web Access Statistics	Surveys on the Web	211	256	290	301
Web Access Statistics	Analysis and Design	201	205	234	245
Web Access Statistics	Introductory Statistics	199	209	287	302
Web Access Statistics	Intermediate Statistics	103	199	209	287

FIGURE 10.6: This page (in Full Screen view) allows you to dynamically filter and sort the data in UCybData.txt.

The Listbox

Now you'll add the listbox. This is a SELECT element—an *intrinsic* control built into HTML. In the BODY, add this HTML code:

```
<SELECT Style = "width:170" ID=selectDept>
<OPTION Selected VALUE=ALL>ALL
<OPTION Value=1>Cyberengineering
<OPTION Value=2>Web Page Design
<OPTION Value=3>Web Access Statistics
</SELECT>
```

The ID gives the SELECT control a name you can use to refer to the control in script. The OPTION elements specify the entries in the listbox. The Selected attribute designates the first OPTION as the default—the value displayed in the control when the page first appears.

Let's use an HTML LABEL element to assign a label to the listbox. Just before the SELECT element, add:

```
<LABEL Class = "headers" FOR=selectDept>Filter </LABEL>
```

Finally, center the label and the listbox by adding a <CENTER> tag before <LABEL> and a </CENTER> tag after </SELECT>.

Next, add the TDC:

```
<OBJECT id=tdcCyberdata
CLASSID="clsid:333C7BC4-460F-11D0-BC04-0080C7055A83">
    <PARAM NAME="DataURL" VALUE="UCybData.txt">
    <PARAM NAME="UseHeader" VALUE="True">
</OBJECT>
```

As you can see, you haven't added any filtering or sorting PARAMs. The user will filter and sort directly on the page in the browser.

Setting the Table

The TABLE is the last element to add to the BODY. Add a <TABLE> tag and give it a Datasrc attribute that connects to the TDC. In this tag, include Style attributes that position the TABLE, along with Border and Bordercolor attributes that set the TABLE's borders:

```
<TABLE ID=tblEnrollment Datasrc=#tdcCyberdata
Style = "Position:Absolute;Top:130;Left:10"
Border Bordercolor = "green">
```

Next, add the THEAD element that holds the top row. In this element, place the TDs that specify the column-headers and include each header in a DIV:

```
<THEAD>
<TD class = "headers" style = "width:150">
<DIV ID=tdDepartment>Department</DIV></TD>
<TD class = "headers" style = "width:180">
<DIV ID=tdCourse>Course</DIV></TD>
<TD class = "headers" style = "width:50">
<DIV ID=td1994>1994</DIV></TD>
<TD class = "headers" style = "width:50">
<DIV ID=td1995>1995</DIV></TD>
<TD class = "headers" style = "width:50">
<DIV ID=td1996>1996</DIV></TD>
```

Skill 10

```
<TD class = "headers" style = "width:50">
<DIV ID=td1997>1997</DIV></TD>
</THEAD>
```

Now, put the remainder of the TABLE in a TBODY element, and include the TDs that hold the DataFld for each column. Place each DataFld attribute inside a SPAN:

```
<TBODY>
<TR>
<TD><SPAN DataFld="Department"></SPAN></TD>
<TD><SPAN DataFld="Course"></SPAN></TD>
<TD><SPAN DataFld="1994"></SPAN></TD>
<TD><SPAN DataFld="1995"></SPAN></TD>
<TD><SPAN DataFld="1996"></SPAN></TD>
<TD><SPAN DataFld="1997"></SPAN></TD>
</TR>
</TBODY>
</TABLE>
```

Writing the Script

Begin a SCRIPT element in the HEAD of the document, and set the Language attribute to "VBScript". The script consists of one subroutine for the listbox and one for each column header. Let's tackle the one for the listbox first.

You want to select a department name from the listbox and have filtering occur as soon as you make the selection. This requires an onclick event-handler for the listbox. The event-handler will sort the data according to your selection. Similar to the filtering statement that appears in a TDC's HTML specification, the event-handler will send the TDC a message that looks like this:

```
"Department = DepartmentName"
```

To do this, the subroutine will set three TDC properties—FilterColumn, FilterCriterion, and FilterValue. The first statement deals with the first property:

```
sub selectDept_onclick()
  tdcCyberdata.FilterColumn = "Department"
```

The listbox selection will determine which department's data appears on-screen as the result of filtering. We refer to a selection by its index within the listbox. (The item in the top row has an index of 0.) An if...then structure with an embedded select case will deal with the selection process.

```
if selectDept.selectedIndex = 0 then
   tdcCyberdata.FilterCriterion = "<>"
   tdcCyberdata.FilterValue = "no value"
else
   tdcCyberdata.FilterCriterion = "="
    select case selectDept.selectedIndex
          case 1
                  tdcCyberdata.FilterValue = "Cyberengineering"
          case 2
                  tdcCyberdata.FilterValue = "Web Page Design"
          case 3
                  tdcCyberdata.FilterValue = "Web Access Statistics"
          case else
                  MsgBox "Make a selection"
     end select

end if
```

The first part of the if...then structure tells the TDC to filter on department names that are not equal to "no value". This specifies that no filtering will take place when the user selects All from the listbox. In the event of any other selection, else sets the TDC's FilterCriterion to "=", and the select case sets the FilterValue accordingly.

You're not quite done with the subroutine. After you programmatically set the constraints of a filtering operation or a sorting operation, you have to tell the TDC to reset according to the new constraints. You do that by invoking the TDC's Reset method:

```
tdcCyberdata.Reset()
```

End the subroutine with an end sub statement to move on to the column-header event-handlers.

Clicking on a column-header will sort the data according to the entries in that column. Each click will set a value for the TDC's SortColumn property. One way to script this is to create a separate event-handler for each header.

Instead, we can take advantage of IE's event-bubbling model. We can create one event-handler for the onclick event at the document level, have that subroutine examine the source element of the onclick, and sort the data appropriately:

```
sub document_onclick

     Select Case window.event.srcElement.id

          Case "tdDepartment"
                tdcCyberdata.SortColumn = "Department"
```

```
                        Case "tdCourse"
                                tdcCyberdata.SortColumn = "Course"

                        Case "td1994"
                                tdcCyberdata.SortColumn = "1994"

                        Case "td1995"
                                tdcCyberdata.SortColumn = "1995"

                        Case "td1996"
                                tdcCyberdata.SortColumn = "1996"

                        Case "td1997"
                                tdcCyberdata.SortColumn = "1997"

                        Case else
                                exit sub

                End Select

                tdcCyberdata.Reset()

        End sub
```

That finishes the scripting.

The Entire File

Here's the whole Filtering and Sorting.htm file:

 Filtering and Sorting.htm

```
<HTML>
<HEAD><TITLE>Filtering and Sorting the Enrollment Data</TITLE>
<STYLE>
.headers {color:green;font-size:20;font-weight:bold}
</STYLE>
<SCRIPT LANGUAGE=VBSCRIPT>

sub selectDept_onclick()
  tdcCyberdata.FilterColumn = "Department"
  if selectDept.selectedIndex = 0 then
    tdcCyberdata.FilterCriterion = "<>"
    tdcCyberdata.FilterValue = "no value"
  else
    tdcCyberdata.FilterCriterion = "="
     select case selectDept.selectedIndex
            case 1
                tdcCyberdata.FilterValue = "Cyberengineering"
```

```
                    case 2
                        tdcCyberdata.FilterValue = "Web Page Design"
                    case 3
                        tdcCyberdata.FilterValue = "Web Access Statistics"
                    case else
                        MsgBox "Make a selection"
            end select

    end if

    tdcCyberdata.Reset()

end sub

sub document_onclick

        Select Case window.event.srcElement.id

                Case "tdDepartment"
                    tdcCyberdata.SortColumn = "Department"

                Case "tdCourse"
                    tdcCyberdata.SortColumn = "Course"

                Case "td1994"
                    tdcCyberdata.SortColumn = "1994"

                Case "td1995"
                    tdcCyberdata.SortColumn = "1995"

                Case "td1996"
                    tdcCyberdata.SortColumn = "1996"

                Case "td1997"
                    tdcCyberdata.SortColumn = "1997"

                Case else
                    exit sub

        End Select

        tdcCyberdata.Reset()

End sub

</SCRIPT>
</HEAD>
<BODY Style = "Background-color:#FFFFCC">
<H1 ID = h1Header Style = "text-align:center">Filtering and Sorting
the Enrollment Data</H1>
<HR>
```

```
<OBJECT id=tdcCyberdata CLASSID="clsid:333C7BC4-460F-11D0-BC04-
0080C7055A83">
    <PARAM NAME="DataURL" VALUE="UCybData.txt">
    <PARAM NAME="UseHeader" VALUE="True">
</OBJECT>

<CENTER>
<LABEL Class = "headers" FOR=selectDept>Filter </LABEL>

<SELECT Style = "width:170" ID=selectDept>
<OPTION Selected Value=ALL>ALL
<OPTION Value=1>Cyberengineering
<OPTION Value=2>Web Page Design
<OPTION Value=3>Web Access Statistics
</SELECT>
</CENTER>


<TABLE ID=tblEnrollment datasrc=#tdcCyberdata Style =
"Position:Absolute;Top:130;Left:10"
Border Bordercolor = "green">
<THEAD>
<TD class = "headers" style = "width:150">
<DIV ID=tdDepartment>Department</DIV></TD>
<TD class = "headers" style = "width:180">
<DIV ID=tdCourse>Course</DIV></TD>
<TD class = "headers" style = "width:50"><DIV ID=td1994>1994</DIV></TD>
<TD class = "headers" style = "width:50"><DIV ID=td1995>1995</DIV></TD>
<TD class = "headers" style = "width:50"><DIV ID=td1996>1996</DIV></TD>
<TD class = "headers" style = "width:50"><DIV ID=td1997>1997</DIV></TD>
</THEAD>
<TBODY>
<TR>
<TD><SPAN Datafld="Department"></SPAN></TD>
<TD><SPAN Datafld="Course"></SPAN></TD>
<TD><SPAN Datafld="1994"></SPAN></TD>
<TD><SPAN Datafld="1995"></SPAN></TD>
<TD><SPAN Datafld="1996"></SPAN></TD>
<TD><SPAN Datafld="1997"></SPAN></TD>
</TR>
</TBODY>
</TABLE>

</BODY>
</HTML>
```

Open this file in IE, and you'll see the page shown in Figure 10.6. Experiment with the filtering and sorting capabilities, and you'll go a long way toward understanding the TDC.

Examining the Data

Many of today's data-based applications have graphical user interface (GUI) front-ends. They typically present users with a screen that looks like Figure 10.7. The one in Figure 10.7 is a front-end for the data in UCybData.txt.

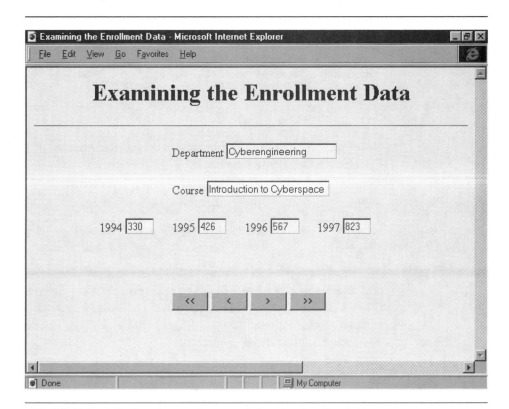

FIGURE 10.7: A page for examining the data in UCybData.txt

On a graphical screen like this, a user can examine each record in a set of records. The text boxes display the values for each field in a record. The buttons at the bottom of the screen let you navigate through the records. Clicking the left-most button displays the first record. Clicking the right-most button displays the last record. Clicking the button with the left-pointing arrow displays the previous record. Clicking the button with the right-pointing arrow displays the next record.

The Page

To put this page together, create a file called `Examining.htm` and save it in Skill 10. First, you'll develop the HTML that appears at the beginning of most of your pages:

```
<HTML>
<HEAD>
<TITLE>Examining the Enrollment Data</TITLE>
</HEAD>
<BODY Style = "Background-Color:#FFFFCC">
<H1 Style = "Text-Align:Center">
Examining the Enrollment Data
</H1>
<HR>
```

Now you'll create the code that labels and positions the text boxes. Here's the HTML for the Department text box:

```
<DIV Style = "Position:absolute;top:100;left:200">
<LABEL>
Department
<INPUT TYPE = TEXT DataSrc = #tdcCyberdata Datafld = "Department">
</LABEL>
</DIV>
```

Notice that the text box has a `DataSrc` attribute that connects it to the TDC (which you haven't put on the page yet) and a `Datafld` that connects it to the appropriate column in `UCybData.txt` (which the TDC will reference).

The remaining text boxes are similar:

```
<DIV Style = "Position:absolute;top:150;left:200">
<LABEL>
Course
<INPUT Style = "width: 170" TYPE = TEXT DataSrc = #tdcCyberdata
Datafld = "Course">
</LABEL>
</DIV>

<DIV Style = "Position:absolute;top:200;left:100">
<LABEL>
1994
<INPUT Class = "textbox" Style = "width: 40" TYPE = TEXT
DataSrc = #tdcCyberdata Datafld = "1994">
</LABEL>
</DIV>
```

```
<DIV Style = "Position:absolute;top:200;left:200">
<LABEL>
1995
<INPUT Style = "width: 40" TYPE = TEXT DataSrc = #tdcCyberdata
Datafld = "1995">
</LABEL>
</DIV>

<DIV Style = "Position:absolute;top:200;left:300">
<LABEL>
1996
<INPUT Style = "width: 40" TYPE = TEXT DataSrc = #tdcCyberdata
Datafld = "1996">
</LABEL>
</DIV>

<DIV Style = "Position:absolute;top:200;left:400">
<LABEL>
1997
<INPUT Style = "width: 40" TYPE = TEXT DataSrc = #tdcCyberdata
Datafld = "1997">
</LABEL>
</DIV>
```

Now let's create the record navigation buttons. You'll put them in a FORM, and put the FORM inside a DIV so that you can position the FORM. The HTML for the left-most button looks like this:

```
<DIV Style = "Position:absolute;top:300;left:200">
<FORM>
<INPUT Type = "Button" Style = "width:50" ID = buttonFirstRecord
Value = "<<"
Title = "Go to the first Record">
```

The Title attribute provides a Tool Tip that appears when the mouse cursor is over the button.

The HTML for the remaining buttons in the FORM is similar:

```
<INPUT Type = "Button" Style = "width:50" ID = buttonPreviousRecord
Value = "<"
Title = "Go back one record">

<INPUT Type = "Button" Style = "width:50" ID = buttonNextRecord
Value = ">"
Title = "Move forward one record">
```

```
<INPUT Type = "Button" Style = "width:50" ID = buttonLastRecord
Value = ">>"
Title = "Go to the last record">

</FORM>
</DIV>
```

Finish the HTML by putting the TDC on the page:

```
<OBJECT id = tdcCyberdata
CLASSID="clsid:333C7BC4-460F-11D0-BC04-0080C7055A83">
    <PARAM NAME="DataURL" VALUE="UCybData.txt">
    <PARAM NAME="UseHeader" VALUE="True">
</OBJECT>
```

The Script

To start the script, create a SCRIPT element whose Language attribute is set to
"VBScript".

You'll write an onclick event-handler for each button. These event-handlers
will enable you to move through the rows of UCybData.txt. In database terms,
the rows of this file constitute a *recordset*, and this is the name of the TDC property that we refer to in the event-handlers. The recordset property returns a
reference to a recordset object, and this object provides methods for moving
through the recordset: moveFirst, movePrevious, moveNext, and moveLast.
They work just as their names suggest. We'll also use two other recordset properties, AbsolutePosition (which gives the index of the currently displayed
row) and RecordCount (which gives the number of rows in the recordset).

To script the buttons, we once again take advantage of the event-bubbling
model and develop one onclick event-handler for the document. In this event-
handler, we'll have a Select Case structure that executes appropriate code
depending on the source element of the onclick event. The beginning of the
subroutine is:

```
Sub document_onclick

    Select case window.event.srcElement.id

        Case "buttonFirstRecord"
            tdcCyberdata.recordset.moveFirst
```

If the source element is `buttonNextRecord`, this `Case` will handle it:

```
Case "buttonPreviousRecord"
        if tdcCyberdata.recordset.AbsolutePosition > 1 then
            tdcCyberdata.recordset.movePrevious
        else MsgBox "Already at first record",64,"
        ➥ University of Cyberspace"
        end if
```

The first part of the `if...then` moves back one record if the currently displayed record is not the first one in the recordset. If it is the first one, an informative message box appears.

NOTE   The 64 in MsgBox's second argument causes an information symbol to appear in the Message Box. The third argument is the Message Box's title.

Likewise, the `Case` that handles `buttonNextRecord` is

```
Case "buttonNextRecord"
        if tdcCyberdata.recordset.AbsolutePosition <>
        ➥ tdcCyberdata.recordset.RecordCount then
                tdcCyberdata.recordset.moveNext
        else MsgBox "Already at last record",64,"University
        ➥ of Cyberspace"
        end if
```

This one advances one record unless the current record is the last one in the recordset, in which case a message box appears.

The next case handles "buttonLastRecord":

```
Case "buttonLastRecord"
        tdcCyberdata.recordset.moveLast
```

Finally, for good programming practice, we include one more case:

```
Case Else
        exit sub
```

Then we end the `select`, and end the subroutine:

```
End select

End Sub
```

Skill 10

The Whole File

The entire Examining.htm file looks like this:

 Examining.htm

```
<HTML>
<HEAD>

<SCRIPT Language = "VBScript">

Sub document_onclick

    Select case window.event.srcElement.id

        Case "buttonFirstRecord"
            tdcCyberdata.recordset.moveFirst

        Case "buttonPreviousRecord"
            if tdcCyberdata.recordset.AbsolutePosition > 1 then
                    tdcCyberdata.recordset.movePrevious
            else MsgBox "Already at first record",64,
            ➡ "University of Cyberspace"
            end if

        Case "buttonNextRecord"
            if tdcCyberdata.recordset.AbsolutePosition <>
            ➡ tdcCyberdata.recordset.RecordCount then
                    tdcCyberdata.recordset.moveNext
            else MsgBox "Already at last record",64,
            ➡ "Universityof Cyberspace"
            end if

        Case "buttonLastRecord"
            tdcCyberdata.recordset.moveLast

        Case Else
            exit sub

    End select

End Sub
</SCRIPT>
<TITLE>Examining the Enrollment Data</TITLE>
</HEAD>
<BODY Style = "Background-Color:#FFFFCC">
<H1 Style = "Text-Align:Center">
Examining the Enrollment Data
</H1>
```

```
<HR>
<DIV Style = "Position:absolute;top:100;left:200">
<LABEL>
Department
<INPUT TYPE = TEXT DataSrc = #tdcCyberdata Datafld = "Department">
</LABEL>
</DIV>

<DIV Style = "Position:absolute;top:150;left:200">
<LABEL>
Course
<INPUT Style = "width: 170" TYPE = TEXT DataSrc = #tdcCyberdata
Datafld = "Course">
</LABEL>
</DIV>

<DIV Style = "Position:absolute;top:200;left:100">
<LABEL>
1994
<INPUT Class = "textbox" Style = "width: 40" TYPE = TEXT
DataSrc = #tdcCyberdata Datafld = "1994">
</LABEL>
</DIV>

<DIV Style = "Position:absolute;top:200;left:200">
<LABEL>
1995
<INPUT Style = "width: 40" TYPE = TEXT DataSrc = #tdcCyberdata
Datafld = "1995">
</LABEL>
</DIV>

<DIV Style = "Position:absolute;top:200;left:300">
<LABEL>
1996
<INPUT Style = "width: 40" TYPE = TEXT DataSrc = #tdcCyberdata
Datafld = "1996">
</LABEL>
</DIV>

<DIV Style = "Position:absolute;top:200;left:400">
<LABEL>
1997
<INPUT Style = "width: 40" TYPE = TEXT DataSrc = #tdcCyberdata
Datafld = "1997">
</LABEL>
</DIV>

<DIV Style = "Position:absolute;top:300;left:200">
<FORM>
<INPUT Type = "Button" Style = "width:50" ID = buttonFirstRecord
```

```
Value = "<<"
Title = "Go to the first Record">
<INPUT Type = "Button" Style = "width:50" ID = buttonPreviousRecord
Value = "<"
Title = "Go back one record">
<INPUT Type = "Button" Style = "width:50" ID = buttonNextRecord
Value = ">"
Title = "Move forward one record">
<INPUT Type = "Button" Style = "width:50" ID = buttonLastRecord
Value = ">>"
Title = "Go to the last record">
</FORM>
</DIV>

<OBJECT id = tdcCyberdata
CLASSID="clsid:333C7BC4-460F-11D0-BC04-0080C7055A83">
    <PARAM NAME="DataURL" VALUE="UCybData.txt">
    <PARAM NAME="UseHeader" VALUE="True">

</OBJECT>

</BODY>
</HTML>
```

Open this page in IE and go through the records in UCybData.txt. If you have to develop a Web page or an intranet site that presents data, consider adding the navigational capabilities in this exercise.

Working with Dialog Boxes

In most applications, the user has to enter some information. In those cases, it's often helpful to open a *dialog box*. The user enters the information, the dialog box closes, and the application continues. Dialog boxes are also a good idea when the application presents information that the user has to acknowledge before continuing.

For information entry, a dialog box is often *modal*. That is, it maintains the focus until the user finishes entering information and closes it. In this exercise, you'll learn how to create a dialog box that gets information from the user and passes it back to the main window. In the process, you'll learn about manipulating the Filter property of the TDC. You're going to construct a dialog box that enables a user to enter filtering expressions and immediately see the results of those expressions.

Figure 10.8 shows the page you're going to build. It looks very much like Figure 10.6 except that the listbox is missing. For demonstration purposes, a Filter button is in its place. (In real-world applications, you'd probably call this button something like "Search" or "Find.") I've also changed the heading to distinguish it somewhat from the page in the earlier exercise.

Filtering and Sorting

Filter

Department	Course	1994	1995	1996	1997
Cyberengineering	Introduction to Cyberspace	330	426	567	823
Cyberengineering	Using Cybertools	293	386	475	586
Cyberengineering	Intermediate Cybernautics	353	517	603	719
Web Page Design	Graphic User Interfaces	457	678	579	607
Web Page Design	Page Layouts	559	403	525	609
Web Page Design	Text and Graphics	554	463	323	492
Web Page Design	Art in the Cyberage	449	501	556	608
Web Page Design	Graphic File Formats	303	357	389	409
Web Access Statistics	Surveys on the Web	211	256	290	301
Web Access Statistics	Analysis and Design	201	205	234	245
Web Access Statistics	Introductory Statistics	199	209	287	302
Web Access Statistics	Intermediate Statistics	103	199	209	287

FIGURE 10.8: Another page for filtering and sorting. Clicking the Filter button opens a modal dialog box.

Clicking the Filter button opens the modal dialog box shown in Figure 10.9. The dialog box contains a text box for entering filtering expressions like

```
Department = C*
```

or

```
Department = Web * & Course = *I* & 1994 > 350
```

Skill 10

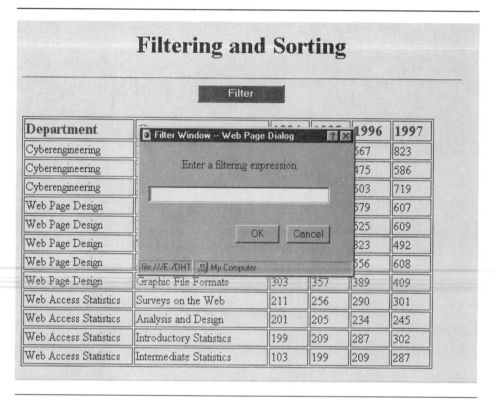

FIGURE 10.9: The modal dialog box that opens when you click the Filter button in Figure 10.8

When the user closes the dialog box, the filtered data will appear in the main page.

NOTE To be totally bulletproof, this code should have some mechanisms for validating user input—in other words, for parsing the input and making sure that the user has entered valid data values, and for checking case sensitivity (e.g. "I" vs. "i"). These capabilities are beyond our scope, however. The exercise *will* familiarize you with dialog boxes.

Building the Dialog Box

To create this page, the first order of business is to create the dialog box. In HTML, a dialog box is a separate page that the showModalDialog box method displays in a separate window. Our dialog box will be an HTML document that we'll call `Filter Window.htm`. First, create the code that positions the elements:

```
<HTML>
<HEAD>
<TITLE>Filter Window</TITLE>
</HEAD>
<BODY style = "background-color:silver">
<BR>
<P style = "text-align:center">Enter a filtering expression:</P>
<CENTER>
<INPUT ID = textFilter Type = text Style = "width:90%">
</CENTER>
<BUTTON style = "Position:absolute;top:70%;left:48%;width:60"
onclick = "doOK()">OK</BUTTON>
<BUTTON style = "Position:absolute;top:70%;left:73%;width:60"
onclick = "doCancel()">Cancel</BUTTON>
</BODY>
</HTML>
```

Just to use a new feature of HTML 4.0, we'll use a BUTTON element instead of a FORM with an INPUT whose Type is `"button"`. The style attribute values make the dialog box look like Figure 10.8. Each button's `onclick` event makes an in-line call to a function, and you'll now code those functions.

Add a SCRIPT element in the document's HEAD. Set its Language attribute to `"JScript"`. Each function sets a value for a window property called `returnValue`. This is a string that the dialog box sends back to the main window. The first function sets `returnValue` to the value of the text box; the second sets `returnValue` to an empty string. Both functions close the dialog box:

```
<SCRIPT Language = "JScript">

function doOK() {
    window.returnValue = textFilter.value;
    window.close();

}

function doCancel() {
    window.returnValue = "";
    window.close();
}
</SCRIPT>
```

TIP   At this point, you're probably wondering why I used JavaScript instead of VBScript. The reason is that the expression `window.returnValue` causes an error in VBScript.

Invoking the Dialog Box

Now turn your attention to the main page. The easiest way to start is to make a copy of `Filtering and Sorting.htm`. Rename it `Filtering with a Dialog box.htm`. In your newly named file, delete the `SELECT` element and the subroutine for its `onclick` event.

In place of the `SELECT`, add this centered `BUTTON` element:

```
<CENTER>
<BUTTON Style = "font-weight:bold;width:120;background-
color:green;color:#FFFFCC" ID = buttonFilter Title = "Click to enter
Filter statements">Filter</BUTTON>
</CENTER>
```

Note the `Title` attribute that gives a helpful Tool Tip. Note also that the button's colors are consistent with the U of Cyb motif.

In place of the `SELECT`'s `onclick` event-handler, add an event-handler that opens the dialog box and uses the value the user types:

```
sub buttonFilter_onclick()
    strDialog boxValue = window.showModalDialog box("Filter
Window.htm",null,"dialog boxWidth:300px;dialog boxHeight:200px")
    if Len(strDialog boxValue) = 0 Then
            exit sub
    end if
    tdcCyberdata.Filter = strDialog boxValue
    tdcCyberdata.Reset()
end sub
```

The first line of this subroutine uses the window `showModalDialog box` method to open the dialog box. The first argument for this method is the dialog box's file name. The second argument—unused here—passes a value from the main window to the dialog box. The third is a string that sets style attributes for the dialog box. Setting a variable, `strDialog boxValue`, equal to `window.showModalDialog box` gets around VBScript's troublesome `window.returnValue` problem. Another way would have been to write this as a JavaScript function. (You can mix the two programming languages in an HTML document that IE will render.)

When a value comes back from the dialog box, the `if…then` uses the built-in VBS `Len` function to see if the dialog box has returned a string of zero length, and if it has (meaning the user has clicked Cancel or has clicked OK without entering anything), `exit sub` exits the subroutine. If not, you set the TDC's `Filter` property equal to the returned value, and then reset the TDC so that it adheres to the constraints specified in the string.

That's all there is to it.

Using the Dialog Box

Open `Filtering with a Dialog box.htm` in IE and start experimenting with different filtering expressions. In addition to learning about dialog boxes, you'll see that this is a great device for learning the kinds of expressions the TDC filter accepts. You can create complex expressions and you can even use a wildcard character (*).

 NOTE   If you enter an invalid expression and click OK, no filtering occurs and the entire data set appears in the main window. As I pointed out earlier, data validation would make this bulletproof, but that's beyond our scope. The upside is that an invalid entry doesn't break anything. The downside? Since an invalid entry causes all rows of data to be displayed, a user might think that all these rows match the criteria specified by the invalid entry.

Figure 10.10 shows one expression. It specifies that you want to only see records from departments whose names contain an "s" and only those records where 1995 enrollment figures are greater than 250.

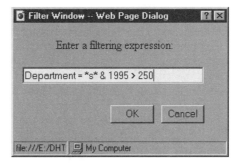

FIGURE 10.10:   In this dialog box, the expression asks for records from departments whose names contain an "s" and whose courses have 1995 enrollment figures that exceed 250.

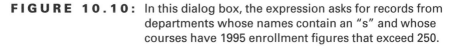

Figure 10.11 shows the result of applying the expression. By the way, after you apply the expression, you can still click on a column-header to sort the data by the entries in that column.

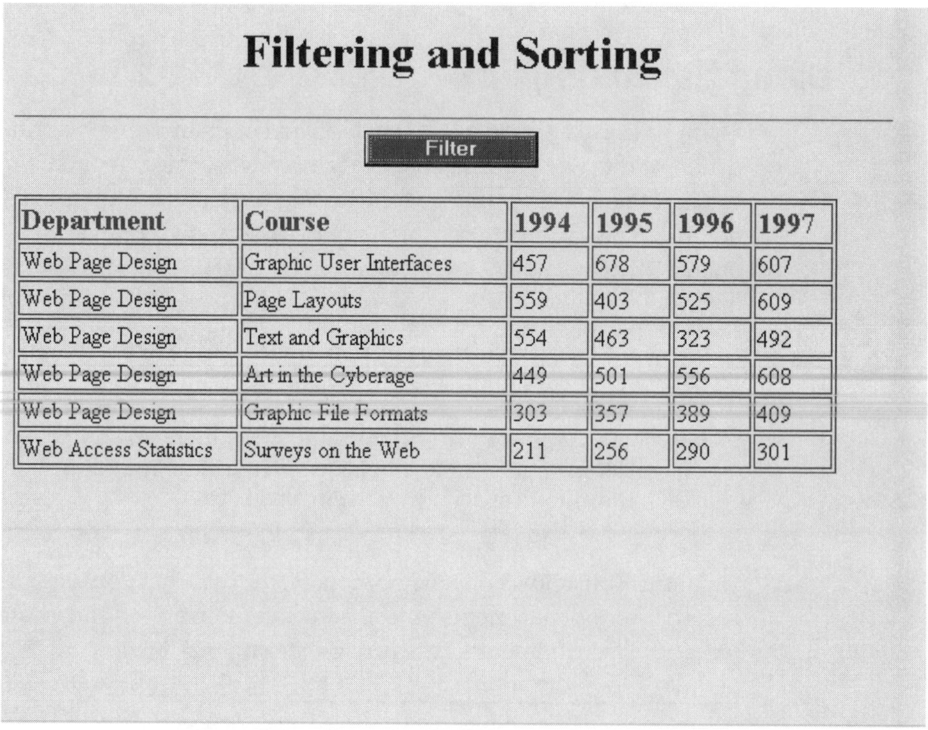

Filtering and Sorting

Filter

Department	Course	1994	1995	1996	1997
Web Page Design	Graphic User Interfaces	457	678	579	607
Web Page Design	Page Layouts	559	403	525	609
Web Page Design	Text and Graphics	554	463	323	492
Web Page Design	Art in the Cyberage	449	501	556	608
Web Page Design	Graphic File Formats	303	357	389	409
Web Access Statistics	Surveys on the Web	211	256	290	301

FIGURE 10.11: The result of applying the expression in Figure 10.10

Summary

The Tabular Data Control (TDC) presents numerous opportunities for displaying data and allowing users to sort and filter that data. This used to be a tedious affair, involving repeated round-trips between a user's machine and a server. An ActiveX control, the TDC resides on a user's machine. The TDC reads the data from a text file, and its properties and methods allow the user to manipulate those data.

Filtering and sorting are the ways you manipulate static data provided by the TDC. You can use these techniques to create different tables from the same data and thus tailor the information you present to different groups.

You can write scripts that enable users to filter and sort the data after it downloads. You can also create a graphical user interface that allows users to easily navigate through all the records in a set of downloaded data. Finally, you can build a dialog box that lets users specify how they want to filter or sort the data.

All these capabilities are particularly useful for corporate intranets that send different data from the same table to different groups.

 NOTE   To find out more about the TDC, visit `http://www.microsoft.com/msdn/sdk/` `inetsdk/help/complib/tabdata/overview.htm TDC_/USE.`

Have You Mastered the Essentials?

Now you can...

☑ **Use the Tabular Data Control in conjunction with the HTML *TABLE* element**

☑ **Use filtering to create different tables from the same data**

☑ **Use sorting to order the data in a table**

☑ **Enable users to filter and sort data that has downloaded**

☑ **Build a graphical user interface that allows users to easily navigate through data records**

☑ **Create a Web page that behaves like a modal dialog box**

☑ **Use the dialog box to learn about the kinds of expressions the Tabular Data Control's *Filter* accepts**

Skill 10

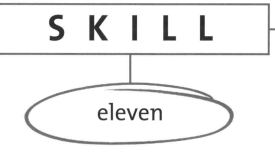

Working with Text:
Dynamically Changing Content

- ❑ Introducing textRanges

- ❑ Moving through text

- ❑ Searching for text

- ❑ Replacing text

- ❑ Tracking content properties

- ❑ Changing content properties

- ❑ Inserting content

In previous Skills, you've worked through exercises that show some of the power of Dynamic HTML. You've learned techniques, like animation and drag-and-drop, that change the location and appearance of objects on a page after the page has downloaded. The IE version of DHTML doesn't end there: In addition to changing a downloaded element's style, you can change its content, as the exercises in this Skill will show.

Introducing *textRanges*

The textRange object is an IE structure that enables you to refer to a particular part of a document. You can create a textRange object that encompasses part of a page. The text within that part of the page is then a property of that object—a property you can manipulate via scripts and events to perform useful tasks like finding and replacing specific words and phrases.

Here's an exercise to acquaint you with this concept. Figure 11.1 shows the page you're about to build. Based on a file called Buttons and Text.htm, it includes two buttons, a text area, and a text input. The text in these elements will change as a result of event-handlers that you'll script.

Start by creating the file in your text editor, and save it as Buttons and Text.htm in your Skill 11 folder. Here's how the HTML should look:

```
<HTML>
<HEAD>
<TITLE>Dynamic Content: Buttons and Text</TITLE>

<BODY>
<H1 Style = "text-align:center">
Changing Text!
</H1>
<HR>
<CENTER>
<BR>

<BUTTON>
Hello!
</BUTTON>
<BR><BR>

<BUTTON>
How are you?
```

```
</BUTTON>
<BR><BR>
<TEXTAREA Rows = 5>
For a dramatic demonstration,
roll the mouse over this text area
</TEXTAREA>

<FORM>
<INPUT Type = Text Value = "Starting Text">
</FORM>

</CENTER>

</BODY>
</HTML>
```

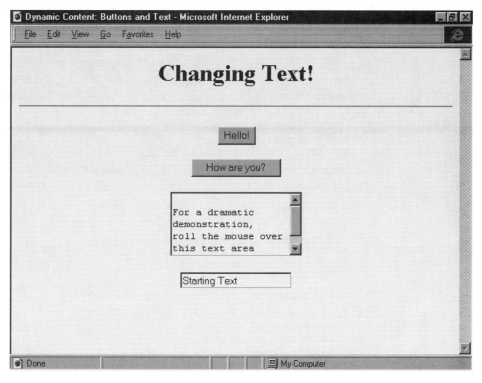

FIGURE 11.1: Buttons and Text.htm, a page that illustrates the textRange concept

We'll write newText, a JScript function that provides new text for each element. An element will call the function, with the new text as one of its arguments. The function will create a textRange on that element and then set the textRange's text to that argument.

In the HEAD, create a SCRIPT element. Since we'll be writing a JScript function (every JavaScript procedure is a function), we can omit the Language attribute. As always, the first line of the function provides the name and the arguments, along with an opening curly bracket to start things off:

```
function newText(ScreenElement,NewCaption) {
```

The ScreenElement argument will refer to the on-screen element calling the function as a result of an event, and the NewCaption argument will contain the new text.

Now we'll create the textRange object. To do this, we invoke the createTextRange method, which is only available on BUTTON, TEXT input, TEXT AREA, and BODY elements. For our function, the code is

```
r = ScreenElement.createTextRange();
```

The final step is to set the text property of the newly created textRange object to the new caption we want to display. The function's second argument supplies the new caption:

```
r.text = NewCaption;
```

Close with a right curly bracket, and you're done.

Now we have to call this function from an event associated with each element. For the buttons, we can call it as a result of a click or a double-click, for the other two as a result of a mouseover event. (Other combinations are possible, of course.) In the opening tag for the first button, add

```
onclick = "newText(this,'Clicked')"
```

The JavaScript keyword this refers to the current object.

In the opening tag for the second button, add

```
onclick = "newText(this,'I am fine')"
ondblclick = "newText(this,'')"
```

In <TEXTAREA>, add

```
onmouseover = "newText(this,'I Have Changed!')"
```

and in the TEXT input,

```
onmouseover = "newText(this,'Finishing Text')"
```

The entire Buttons and Text.htm file should look like this:

Buttons and Text.htm

```
<HTML>
<HEAD>
<TITLE>Dynamic Content: Buttons and Text</TITLE>
<SCRIPT>
function newText(ScreenElement,NewCaption) {
r = ScreenElement.createTextRange();
r.text = NewCaption;

}
</SCRIPT>
<BODY>
<H1 Style = "text-align:center">
Changing Text!
</H1>
<HR>
<CENTER>
<BR>

<BUTTON onclick = "newText(this,'Clicked')">
Hello!
</BUTTON>
<BR><BR>

<BUTTON onclick = "newText(this,'I am fine')"
ondblclick = "newText(this,'')">
How are you?
</BUTTON>
<BR><BR>

<TEXTAREA Rows = 5 onmouseover = "newText(this,'I Have Changed!')">
For a dramatic demonstration,
roll the mouse over this text area
</TEXTAREA>

<FORM>
<INPUT Type = Text Value = "Starting Text"
onmouseover = "newText(this,'Finishing Text')">
</FORM>

</CENTER>

</BODY>
</HTML>
```

After you open the page in IE, click the buttons, and move your mouse over the other two elements, it will look like Figure 11.2.

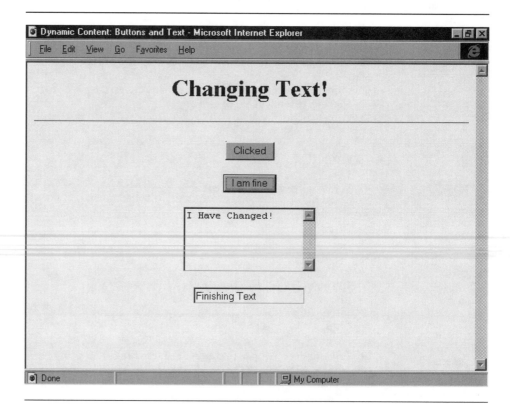

FIGURE 11.2: Buttons and Text.htm after you click the buttons and move the mouse over the text area and the text input

If you double-click on the second button, you'll see it shrink as a result of passing an empty string as the second argument to newText for the double-click event. Click again and I am fine returns.

Here's some behavior to note. After you've changed the text in all four controls, press F5 to refresh the page. You'll find that the original button captions return, but the original text lines in the other two elements do not. Select View ➢ Source and then select File ➢ Save in your text editor. Return to the page, press F5, and all the original values come back. Using the createTextRange method to alter text on buttons produces a different result than using it to alter text in text inputs and text areas.

Moving Through Text

Let's move on to another level of complexity. textRanges have a number of
methods, and we'll use some of them in the next exercise to move through a document's BODY. As we do, we'll track the values of some textRange properties.
Figure 11.3 shows the page we'll create:

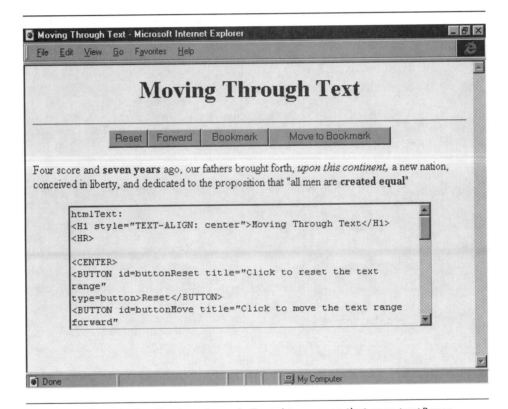

FIGURE 11.3: Moving through Text.htm, a page that uses textRange
methods and tracks textRange properties

Lay out the page according to this HTML code:

```
<HTML>
<HEAD>
<TITLE>Moving Through Text</TITLE>
</HEAD>
<BODY ID = bodyDocument>
```

```
<H1 style = "text-align:center">Moving Through Text</H1>
<HR>
<CENTER>
<BUTTON ID = buttonReset Title = "Click to reset the
textRange">Reset</BUTTON>
<BUTTON ID = buttonMove Title = "Click to move the textRange
forward">Forward</BUTTON>
<BUTTON ID = buttonBookmark Title = "Click to set a
bookmark">Bookmark</BUTTON>
<BUTTON ID = buttonMoveToBookmark Title = "Click to move to a
bookmark">Move to Bookmark</BUTTON>
</CENTER>
<BR>
<P ID = pGettysburg>Four score and <B ID = boldPhrase>seven years</B>
ago, our fathers brought forth,
<I ID = italicPhrase>upon this continent,</I> a new nation,
<SPAN ID = spanLiberty>conceived in liberty,</SPAN> and dedicated to
the proposition that "all men are <B ID = boldCreated>created
equal</B>"</P>
```

```
<CENTER>
<TEXTAREA ID = textareaRangeTracker Rows = 10 Cols = 60>
</TEXTAREA>

</BODY>
</HTML>
```

We'll use a technique you've seen before, a continuously updated multiline text area, to track property values as we weave our way through the BODY. As the file and Figure 11.3 show, a famous sentence will serve as our testbed. Note the tags in that sentence:

```
<P ID = pGettysburg>Four score and <B ID = boldPhrase>seven years</B>
ago, our fathers brought forth,
<I ID = italicPhrase>upon this continent,</I> a new nation,
<SPAN ID = spanLiberty>conceived in liberty,</SPAN> and dedicated to the
proposition that "all men are <B ID = boldCreated>created equal</B>"</P>
```

They'll help us test some features of textRanges. Specifically, we're going to track

- htmlText—the text and HTML in a textRange

- text—the plain text in a textRange

- parentElement—the HTML element that contains a textRange

- bookmark—a unique identifier for a position in an element

Starting the Script

Now we'll add some script. Create a SCRIPT element whose Language attribute is "VBScript". Some global variables will get things moving:

```
dim glblRange
dim glblMark
dim glblParentElement
dim glblResetFlag
```

The first refers to the textRange that we'll set and reset, the second to a bookmark that we'll set and move to, the third to the HTML element which contains the textRange, and the last to a variable whose value will change when we click the Reset button. We make these variables global so that we can update their values in the text area after we manipulate them in subroutines throughout the script.

Next, we initialize some values when the browser window opens:

```
sub window_onload
    set glblRange = document.body.createTextRange()
    textAreaRangeTracker.Value = ""
    glblResetFlag = 1
    updateRangeTracker
end sub
```

The first line creates a textRange on the whole BODY of the document. The second blanks out the text area. The third line assigns a value to the reset flag because we want to know when we've set (or reset) the textRange to cover the entire BODY. Why? When we get into the script, we'll add functionality that highlights the textRange as we set it. Highlighting surrounds the textRange in a color (it's set to red on my computer). Rather than bathe everything in a color when the textRange covers the whole BODY, we set a flag to tell us when to avoid highlighting. The fourth line calls a function that updates the text area.

Adding Functionality

The next subroutine adds functionality to the buttons, and takes advantage of the event model. Rather than write a separate event-handler for each button, we'll just write a function that captures a click event at the document level, examines the event's source element, and reacts appropriately for each source element. Then it updates the text area:

```
sub document_onclick

    Select Case window.event.srcElement.id
```

Skill 11

```
            Case "buttonReset"
                    call glblRange.expand("textedit")
                    textAreaRangeTracker.Value = ""
                    glblResetFlag = 1

            Case "buttonMove"
                    call glblRange.move("word",1)

            Case "buttonBookmark"

                    glblMark = glblRange.getbookmark

            Case "buttonMoveToBookmark"
                    if glblMark <> empty then
                            call glblRange.moveToBookmark(glblMark)
                      end if

        Case else
                exit sub
    End Select

        updateRangeTracker

    end sub
```

Let's examine each Case in the Select Case structure. The first one,

```
            Case "buttonReset"
                    call glblRange.expand("textedit")
                    textAreaRangeTracker.Value = ""
                    glblResetFlag = 1
```

goes into action when the Reset button is the source element of the click event. The first line calls the textRange expand method. As its name implies, this method expands a textRange. Its argument, a string, indicates the amount of expansion. When the argument is "textedit", the expanded range includes the entire BODY. The next line blanks out the text area and the last one updates the reset flag.

The second case,

```
            Case "buttonMove"
                    call glblRange.move("word",1)
```

invokes the textRange move method. This method collapses the textRange and moves the empty range by the amount indicated in the arguments. Our arguments tell it to move the range one word to the right. If we want it to move two words, we make the second argument 2, and so forth. If we want it to move to the left, we make the second argument negative. We can also move the range by sentences or characters rather than by words.

The third case

```
Case "buttonBookmark"
      glblMark = glblRange.getbookmark
```

uses the textRange bookmark method to mark a range that we can return to via the code in the fourth case:

```
Case "buttonMoveToBookmark"
      if glblMark <> empty then
            call glblRange.moveToBookmark(glblMark)
      else
            exit sub
      end if
```

The if statement prevents an error from occurring if we try to invoke this method without a bookmark set. The else prevents highlighting the entire page if you click this button when you open the page, or if you click it after clicking Reset.

 NOTE   What gets "set" when you set a bookmark? The getbookmark method generates an *opaque string* that uniquely identifies the bookmark. An opaque string is one you can't examine or modify. When the Microsofters say "opaque," they're not kidding. As you'll see when you start experimenting with this page, a bookmark string can look like this: □□B□□□□□□□□□□□□□□□□?!svp!-phb!gbuifst!csoJ□□□□□□□□□□□□□□□?!tsfiubg!scspvhiu!gpÏ

Case else exits the subroutine if a click does not occur on a button.

Mousing through the Text

Now we'll code a subroutine that moves the textRange around as we move the mouse through the opening sentence of the *Gettysburg Address*. We'll write an event-handler for onmousemove for the P element that holds that sentence:

```
sub pGettysburg_onmousemove
     call glblRange.moveToPoint(window.event.x, window.event.y)
     updateRangeTracker
end sub
```

Skill 11

This subroutine invokes the `textRange moveToPoint` method, which collapses the `textRange` and moves it to the point specified by the coordinates in its arguments. The `onmousemove` event continually updates `window.event.x` and `window.event.y` to give the mouse cursor's current position.

The next line updates the text area.

Tracking the Property Values

The `updateRangeTracker` subroutine, referred to in each of the other subroutines, takes care of the text area after performing three other tasks:

```
sub updateRangeTracker
    call glblRange.expand("word")

    if glblResetFlag = 0 then
        glblRange.select
    end if

    set glblParentElement = glblRange.parentElement()

    textAreaRangeTracker.Value = "htmlText: " & glblRange.htmlText &
    ➡chr(13) _
    & "text: " & glblRange.text & chr(13) _
    & "parent element: " & glblParentElement.id & chr(13) _
    & "bookmark: " & glblMark

    glblResetFlag = 0

end sub
```

The first task is to expand the `textRange` to include a word. When you move a `textRange`, you collapse it and relocate it to a point within the document. The `expand` method arbitrarily includes one following word. (As an exercise, you might try to create a way to empower the user to set the amount of expansion.)

The next task visualizes the `textRange` for you. If the reset flag is 0 (meaning that the Reset button has not been clicked), the subroutine calls the text area `select` method. This method applies highlighting to the `textRange`. If the reset flag is 1, the entire BODY is the `textRange`, and highlighting is not applied. In that case, highlighting would obscure the text area's contents.

The third task calls the `parentElement` method to get the HTML element that contains the `textRange`.

Next, the subroutine updates the text area as you've seen in previous Skills, and sets the reset flag to 0.

The Whole File

Here's Moving through Text.htm.

 Moving through Text.htm

```
<HTML>
<HEAD>
<SCRIPT Language = "VBScript">

dim glblRange
dim glblMark
dim glblParentElement
dim glblResetFlag

sub window_onload
    set glblRange = document.body.createTextRange()
    textAreaRangeTracker.Value = ""
    glblResetFlag = 1
    updateRangeTracker
end sub

sub document_onclick

    Select Case window.event.srcElement.id

        Case "buttonReset"
            call glblRange.expand("textedit")
            textAreaRangeTracker.Value = ""
            glblResetFlag = 1

        Case "buttonMove"
            call glblRange.move("word",1)

        Case "buttonBookmark"
            glblMark = glblRange.getbookmark

        Case "buttonMoveToBookmark"
            if glblMark <> empty then
                    call glblRange.moveToBookmark(glblMark)
            else
                    exit sub
            end if

        Case else
            exit sub
    End Select

    updateRangeTracker
```

Skill 11

```
            end sub

            sub pGettysburg_onmousemove
                call glblRange.moveToPoint(window.event.x, window.event.y)
                updateRangeTracker
            end sub

            sub updateRangeTracker
                call glblRange.expand("word")

                if glblResetFlag = 0 then
                        glblRange.select
                end if

                set glblParentElement = glblRange.parentElement()

                textAreaRangeTracker.Value = "htmlText: " & glblRange.htmlText &
                ➥chr(13) _
                & "text: " & glblRange.text & chr(13) _
                & "parent element: " & glblParentElement.id & chr(13) _
                & "bookmark: " & glblMark

                glblResetFlag = 0

            end sub

            </SCRIPT>
            <TITLE>Moving Through Text</TITLE>
            </HEAD>
            <BODY ID = bodyDocument>
            <H1 style = "text-align:center">Moving Through Text</H1>
            <HR>
            <CENTER>
            <BUTTON ID = buttonReset Title = "Click to reset the
            textRange">Reset</BUTTON>
            <BUTTON ID = buttonMove Title = "Click to move the textRange
            forward">Forward</BUTTON>
            <BUTTON ID = buttonBookmark Title = "Click to set a
            bookmark">Bookmark</BUTTON>
            <BUTTON ID = buttonMoveToBookmark Title = "Click to move to a
            bookmark">Move to Bookmark</BUTTON>
            </CENTER>
            <BR>
            <P ID = pGettysburg>Four score and <B ID = boldPhrase>seven years</B>
            ago, our fathers brought forth,
            <I ID = italicPhrase>upon this continent,</I> a new nation,
            <SPAN ID = spanLiberty>conceived in liberty,</SPAN> and dedicated
            to the proposition that "all men are <B ID = boldCreated>created
            equal</B>"</P> </P>

            <CENTER>
```

```
<TEXTAREA ID = textareaRangeTracker Rows = 10 Cols = 60>
</TEXTAREA>

</BODY>
</HTML>
```

This page, like others in this Skill, is designed as a test bed for you to discover important aspects of `textRanges` and pick up some insights. When you open it in IE, note what happens to the parent element as you move through the *Gettysburg Address* sentence, either by clicking the Move button or moving the mouse. You'll find that a `textRange` which seems, by virtue of its `htmlText` property, to be in one parent element is really in another. For example, in this phrase

```
<B ID = boldPhrase>seven years</B>
```

you would expect that both `seven` and `years` have `boldPhrase` as their parent element. When you move the `textRange` to `years`, however, and expand it to include the word, you'll find that the parent element is `pGettysburg`, the encompassing paragraph. Figure 11.4 shows this situation.

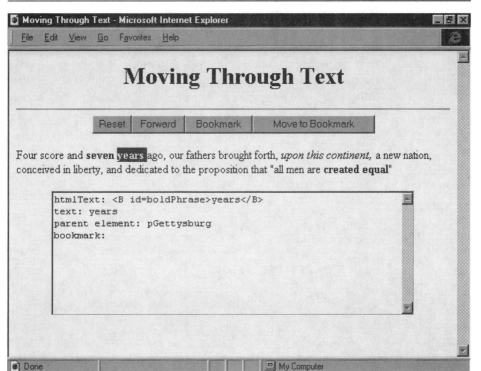

FIGURE 11.4: Moving through text.htm with the textRange on years

On the other hand, in

```
<B ID = boldCreated>created equal</B>
```

both `created` and `equal` have `boldCreated` as their parent element. The difference is that in the first case (the word "years" in the phrase "seven years") a blank space follows the second word. In the second, a punctuation mark (the close quote) follows the second word. Experiment with the document. In your text editor, replace the close quote with a letter or a word (with no space between `equal` and your substitution). What happens to the parent element of `equal`?

Note the opaque string when you set a bookmark. When you reset the `textRange`, it doesn't go away.

Searching for Text

I mentioned earlier that `textRanges` are helpful because they enable you to perform useful tasks like finding and replacing text. In this exercise, you'll learn how to implement a search capability, and in the next, you'll learn about replacement. In both exercises, we use modal dialog boxes.

We'll create the uncluttered page, `Find Text.htm`, shown in Figure 11.5. Pressing the Find... button will bring up a modal dialog box for entering text (see Figure 11.6). Clicking OK on the dialog box will close that window. In the event of a match, the matched text will appear highlighted in the main window. Otherwise, a message box will appear. It will display the searched-for text string and inform the user that no match was found.

The HTML for laying out the page is straightforward:

```
<HTML>
<HEAD>
<TITLE>Finding Text</TITLE>
</HEAD>
<BODY ID = bodyDocument>
<H1 style = "text-align:center">Finding Text</H1>
<HR>
<CENTER>
<BUTTON ID = buttonSearch Title = "Click to search for a text
string">Find...</BUTTON>
</CENTER>
<BR>
```

```
Four score and seven years ago, our fathers brought forth,
upon this continent, a new nation, conceived in liberty, and dedicated
to the proposition that "all men are created equal"
</BODY>
</HTML>
```

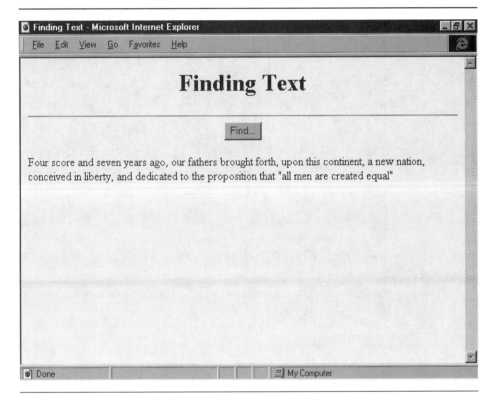

FIGURE 11.5: Find Text.htm, a page with a text search capability

Next, we have to script a `button-click` event to do three things for us:

- Open the modal dialog box.
- Take the text string that the dialog box returns and search for it in the document.
- React appropriately if no match is found.

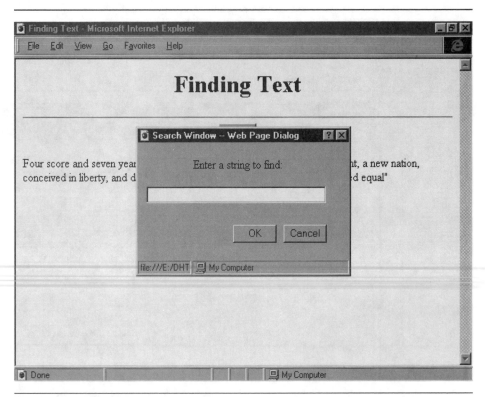

FIGURE 11.6: The modal dialog box for entering the searched-for text

Recall from Skill 10 that opening a modal dialog box is the job of the
`window.openModalDialog` method. The method takes three arguments. The
first is the name of the HTML file to open, the second is an optional argument
for sending a value to the dialog box, and the third specifies the appearance of
the dialog box. We won't use the second argument in this exercise, but we'll
have more to say about it later in this Skill.

We'll start by declaring three variables that we're going to need in this subroutine:

```
dim strDialogValue
dim range
dim match
```

We use this code to open the dialog box:

```
strDialogValue = window.showModalDialog("Search
Window.htm",null,"dialogWidth:300px;dialogHeight:200px")
```

The variable `strDialogValue` will hold the text string entered into the modal dialog box. If the return value is an empty string, we'll want to exit the subroutine:

```
if strDialogValue = "" then
            exit sub
      end if
```

If `strDialogValue` is not an empty string, we'll create a `textRange` that encompasses the BODY of the document, and then use the textRange's `findText` method to look for a match:

```
set range = document.body.createTextRange()
match = range.findText(strDialogValue)
```

If a match is found, we'll want to highlight the match. If not, we'll want to open a message box that tells the user no match was found:

```
if match <> false then
            range.select()
      else
            MsgBox "Couldn't find " & strDialogValue,,"No Match"
      end if
```

Note the searched-for text in the message box to add to the informativeness of the message.

Here's the `Find Text.htm` file:

Find Text.htm

```
<HTML>
<HEAD>
<SCRIPT Language = "VBScript">

sub buttonSearch_onclick()

dim strDialogValue
dim range
dim match

      strDialogValue = window.showModalDialog("Search
Window.htm",null,"dialogWidth:300px;dialogHeight:200px")
```

Skill 11

```
        if strDialogValue = "" then
                exit sub
        end if

        set range = document.body.createTextRange()
        match = range.findText(strDialogValue)

        if match <> false then
                range.select()
        else
                MsgBox "Couldn't find " & strDialogValue,,"No Match"
        end if

end sub

</SCRIPT>
<TITLE>Finding Text</TITLE>
</HEAD>
<BODY ID = bodyDocument>
<H1 style = "text-align:center">Finding Text</H1>
<HR>
<CENTER>
<BUTTON ID = buttonSearch Title = "Click to search for a text
string">Find...</BUTTON>
</CENTER>
<BR>
Four score and seven years ago, our fathers brought forth,
upon this continent, a new nation, conceived in liberty, and dedicated
to the proposition that "all men are created equal"

</BODY>
</HTML>
```

Before we can use it, of course, we have to code Search Window.htm:

C Search Window.htm

```
<HTML>
<HEAD>
<SCRIPT Language = "JScript">


function doOK() {
    if (textSearch.value == "") {
            alert("Enter a string or click Cancel");
            return
    }
    window.returnValue = textSearch.value;
```

```
        window.close();

    }

    function doCancel() {
        window.returnValue = "";
        window.close();
    }
</SCRIPT>
<TITLE>Search Window</TITLE>
</HEAD>
<BODY style = "background-color:silver">
<BR>
<P style = "text-align:center">Enter a string to find:</P>
<CENTER>
<INPUT ID = textSearch Type = text Style = "width:90%">
</CENTER>
<Button style = "Position:absolute;top:70%;left:48%;width:60"
onclick = "doOK()">OK</Button>
<Button style = "Position:absolute;top:70%;left:73%;width:60"
onclick = "doCancel()">Cancel</Button>
</BODY>
</HTML>
```

If you compare this file with the file for the modal dialog box in Skill 10, you'll see it's almost the same, but with a few changes to reflect the current context. In the function doOK, for example, we added an if statement to cover the case of the user clicking OK without entering anything. In Skill 10, we handled that possibility in the code for the main window.

When you have the two documents coded, open them in IE and experiment with the textRange's findText capability. You'll find that this is a quick and easy way to add a useful feature to your Web pages.

Replacing Text

Text replacement, another useful textRange–related task, enables users to change the content on your Web page. We'll work on a page which superficially resembles the page in the previous exercise. Save Find Text.htm as Replace Text.htm. In the new page, change the heading and the title to Replacing Text.

Put the *Gettysburg Address*'s opening sentence into a P element, and assign pGettysburg as the P element's ID.

In this exercise, we use the textRange's createRange method in conjunction with the document's selection property. Highlighting an item in the on-screen sentence assigns a value to document.selection, which is an object as well as a property of the document. The createRange method is especially designed for creating a textRange from document.selection. The idea is to create the range and open a modal dialog box. In the modal box, the user will enter the text that replaces the selection. When the user clicks OK on the dialog box, the box closes and the text in the main window is changed.

To coordinate with the selection process, the script is an event-handler for the onmouseup event on the P element. It starts by setting a variable to the document.selection object, invoking the createRange method, and opening the dialog box:

```
set selected = document.selection
    set range = selected.createRange()
    strDialogValue = window.showModalDialog("Replace Window.htm",
    ↪range.text,"dialogWidth:300px;dialogHeight:250px")
```

Take careful note of the second argument to showModalDialog. This argument sends the selection-based textRange to the dialog box. The box will display it in a read-only text box so that the users can see the string they're replacing.

TIP   Microsoft documentation (available at http://www.microsoft.com/msdn/ sdk/inetsdk) indicates that you can use a variable in this argument. This isn't precisely true. If you set a variable equal to a string and then put that variable in this argument, you'll get an error message when you try to open the dialog window. Apparently, the dialog box has to see a string as a property of an object, as in our example. A quoted string works in that argument, too. Incidentally, the indicated URL is a starting point for finding documentation on everything in this Skill.

If the dialog box returns an empty string because the user clicked Cancel, we'll exit the subroutine. If not, we'll assign the returned string as the new value of the range's text property. Here's Replace Text.htm:

 Replace Text.htm

```
<HTML>
<HEAD>
<SCRIPT Language = "VBScript">
```

```
sub pGettysburg_onmouseup
    set selected = document.selection
    set range = selected.createRange()
    strDialogValue = window.showModalDialog("Replace
Window.htm",range.text,"dialogWidth:300px;dialogHeight:250px")

    if strDialogValue = "" then
            exit sub
    end if

    range.text = strDialogValue
end sub

</SCRIPT>
<TITLE>Replacing Text</TITLE>
</HEAD>
<BODY ID = bodyDocument>
<H1 style = "text-align:center">Replacing Text</H1>
<HR>
<P ID = pGettysburg> Four score and seven years ago, our fathers
brought forth, upon this continent, a new nation, conceived in liberty,
and dedicated to the proposition that "all men are created equal" </P>
</BODY>
</HTML>
```

Here's Replace Window.htm:

Replace Window.htm

```
<HTML>
<HEAD>
<SCRIPT Language = "VBScript">
sub window_onload
    textOriginal.Value = window.dialogArguments
    textReplace.Focus
end sub
</SCRIPT>

<SCRIPT Language = "JScript">

function doOK() {
    if (textReplace.value == "") {
            alert("Enter a string or click Cancel");
            return
    }
    window.returnValue = textReplace.value;
    window.close();
```

Skill 11

```
    }

    function doCancel() {
        window.returnValue = "";
        window.close();
    }
</SCRIPT>
<TITLE>Replace Window</TITLE>
</HEAD>
<BODY style = "background-color:silver">
<BR>
<P style = "text-align:center"> Original: </P>
<CENTER>
<INPUT ID = textOriginal Type = text Readonly Style = "width:90%;
background-color:silver">
</CENTER>
<P style = "text-align:center">Replace with:</P>
<CENTER>
<INPUT ID = textReplace Type = text Style = "width:90%">
</CENTER>
<Button style = "Position:absolute;top:85%;left:48%;width:60"
onclick = "doOK()">OK</Button>
<Button style = "Position:absolute;top:85%;left:73%;width:60"
onclick = "doCancel()">Cancel</Button>
</BODY>
</HTML>
```

It's very similar to the dialog box in the preceding exercise, except for the extra text input that holds the original string in read-only fashion. Also, the script has an additional feature. We've added some VBScript for the window's onload event. As you can see, VBScript and JScript can peacefully coexist in a document, as long as they're in separate SCRIPT elements.

The information in the second argument of window.showModalDialog gets stored in window.dialogArguments. In the onload event-handler, the line

```
textOriginal.Value = window.dialogArguments
```

puts that information into one of the text inputs. The next line

```
textReplace.Focus
```

puts the focus in the other text input, so that the user can immediately start typing when the window opens.

Figure 11.7 shows the page with some selected text, along with the dialog box. The dialog box contains the original text and the replacement text.

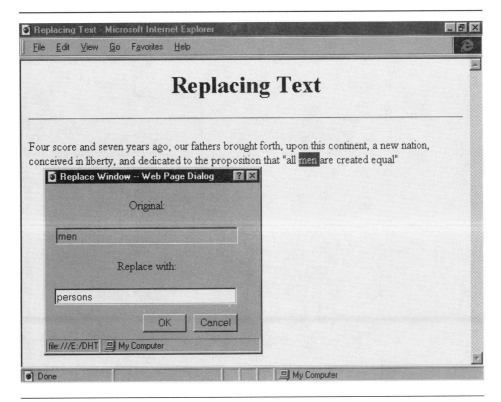

FIGURE 11.7: Replace Text.htm and Replace Window.htm, two pages designed for text replacement

With apologies to President Lincoln, Figure 11.8 shows the page after numerous replacements have updated the original message for life in the 1990s.

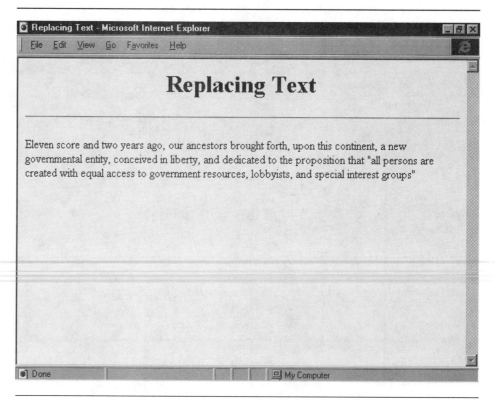

FIGURE 11.8: Replace Text.htm after numerous text replacements

Summarizing the *textRange*

The textRange has a number of useful methods. Table 11.1 summarizes them for you.

TABLE 11.1: textRange Methods

Method	What It Does
collapse	Shrinks a textRange and creates an insertion point at either the beginning or the end of the current range
compareEndPoints	Compares two textRanges
duplicate	Returns a duplicate of a textRange

TABLE 11.1 CONTINUED: textRange Methods

Method	What It Does
expand	Expands a textRange by a character, word, or sentence
findText	Searches for text in the document; sets the start and end points of the range to encompass the search string
getBookmark	Provides an opaque string that uniquely identifies a location within the document
inRange	Determines whether a specified range is within or equal to the current textRange
move	Shrinks the textRange and moves the empty textRange by a specified number of characters, words, or sentences
moveEnd	Moves the end position of the textRange and thus changes its scope
moveStart	Moves the start position of the textRange and thus changes its scope
moveToBookmark	Moves to a bookmark created via getBookmark
moveToElementText	Moves the textRange so that its start and end positions encompass the text in a specified element
moveToPoint	Collapses the textRange and moves it to a specified point
parentElement	Returns the element that completely encompasses the current textRange
pasteHTML	Pastes HTML into a specified textRange
scrollIntoView	Scrolls the textRange into view in the browser
select	Highlights the current textRange
setEndPoint	Sets the end point of one textRange based on the end point of another

Tracking Content Properties

The textRange is just one way of working with text. IE supplies another. In the IE world, most elements in an HTML document support four content properties:

- innerText—A string that specifies all the text in the element and in any enclosed elements, excluding any HTML tags. Assigning a new string to this property replaces the contents but not the end tags. Any new tags are rendered as text.

Skill 11

- outerText—Identical to innerText, but assigning a new string replaces the start and end tags as well as the text. If you assign an empty string to this property, you completely remove an element from the document.

- innerHTML—A string that specifies all the text and HTML tags in an element, excluding start and end tags. New tags inserted into this property are interpreted as tags, not as text.

- outerHTML—The same as innerHTML, but includes start and end tags.

In the next exercise, you'll build a page that will serve as a test bed for learning about these properties. You'll create the page that appears in Figure 11.9, which is based on a file called Content Properties.htm.

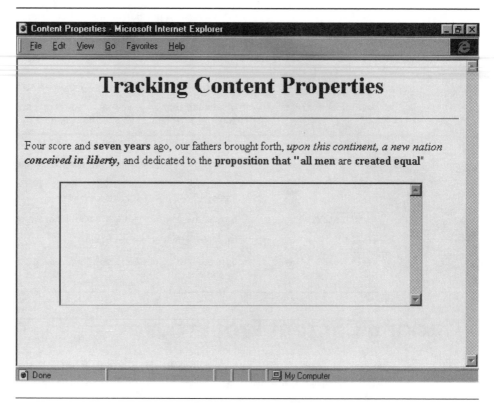

FIGURE 11.9: Content Properties.htm, a page for tracking innerText, outerText, innerHTML, and outerHTML

The HTML is similar to code you've seen before:

```
<HTML>
<HEAD>
<TITLE>Content Properties</TITLE>
</HEAD>
<BODY ID = bodyDocument>
<H1 style = "text-align:center">Tracking Content Properties</H1>
<HR>
<P ID = pGettysburg><SPAN>Four score and <A><B ID = boldPhrase>seven
years</B></A></SPAN> ago, our fathers brought forth,
<I ID = italicPhrase>upon this continent, a new nation
<B ID = boldLiberty>conceived in liberty,</B></I> and dedicated to the
<B>proposition <A>that "all men</A></B> are <B ID = boldCreated>created
equal</B>"</P>

<CENTER>
<TEXTAREA ID = textareaPropertiesTracker Rows = 10 Cols = 60>
</TEXTAREA>
</BODY>
</HTML>
```

Type the HTML for the P element just as I've presented it, and you'll see some instructive content property values in the text area.

The script consists of two VBS subroutines. One is an event-handler for **onmousemove** through the P element, and the other updates the text area with values for the four content properties:

```
<SCRIPT Language = "VBScript">

sub pGettysburg_onmousemove
    updatePropertiesTracker
end sub

sub updatePropertiesTracker

    textAreaPropertiesTracker.Value = "innerText: " &
    ➥window.event.srcElement.innerText & chr(13) _
    & "outerText: " & window.event.srcElement.outerText & chr(13) _
    & "innerHTML: " & window.event.srcElement.innerHTML & chr(13) _
    & "outerHTML: " & window.event.srcElement.outerHTML

end sub
```

Notice that we're taking advantage of the IE event model. When you move the mouse through an element, that element becomes the source element of the event, and we use the source element to update the values in the text area.

Moving the mouse through the sentence will continuously update the content properties. Take note of the values of the properties as you move the mouse. The interesting elements are the ones that contain other elements. For example, with the mouse on Four, you'll see the values in Figure 11.9:

```
innerText: Four score and seven years
outerText: Four score and seven years
innerHTML: Four score and <A><B id=boldPhrase>seven years</B></A>
outerHTML: <SPAN>Four score and <A><B id=boldPhrase>seven
years</B></A></SPAN>
```

As you can see, the innerText and outerText values look the same, and they don't include tags. The innerHTML and outerHTML include the tags, and outerHTML includes the start and end tags.

Changing Content Properties

After you've experimented with the page in the preceding section, you'll be ready to change some of the content properties. This exercise gives you a test bed for doing just that. Save the file from the previous exercise as Changing Content Properties.htm. Change the title and the heading accordingly. You're going to develop the page that appears in Figure 11.10.

Take the subroutines out of the SCRIPT element, as you'll replace them with new ones. Immediately after the HTML code for the TEXT AREA, add this code to create the SELECT element (the drop-down list) and the button at the bottom of the page:

```
<SELECT ID = selectOptions style = "position:absolute;top:340;left:350">
<OPTION Value = "InnerText">InnerText
<OPTION Value = "OuterText">OuterText
<OPTION Value = "InnerHTML">InnerHTML
<OPTION Value = "OuterHTML">OuterHTML
</SELECT>
<BUTTON ID = buttonChange style =
"position:absolute;top:340;left:450">Change...</BUTTON>
```

You'll click on the sentence to select an element, select a content property from the drop-down list, and click the Change button to open a dialog box so that you can make the change. The dialog box will present the string to be changed in a text box that you can start typing in as soon as the box opens.

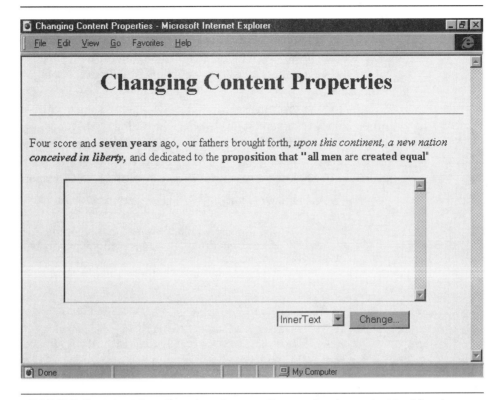

FIGURE 11.10: Changing Content Properties.htm, a test bed for changing innerText, outerText, innerHTML, and outerHTML

Now we address the script. It will consist of three subroutines. One is an event-handler for the onclick event in the P element. We use onclick rather than onmousemove so that we don't have to worry about stray mouse movements when we select an area in pGettysburg. Another subroutine is an event-handler for the onclick event for the button, and the third updates the text area.

We begin by declaring glblObjElement, a global variable that will store the element selected in pGettysburg. The first subroutine is a short one:

```
sub pGettysburg_onclick
    updatePropertiesTracker
    set glblObjElement = window.event.srcElement
end sub
```

It calls the update subroutine and sets the global variable to the source element of the click event—the element clicked within pGettysburg. Sometimes the source element will be pGettysburg. In that case, we'll have to guard against user input that changes this element. Why? Changing the name of pGettysburg would cause this event-handler to stop functioning. We'll put the safeguard into the next subroutine.

The second subroutine is considerably longer. As the event-handler for the button's onclick event, it has to open the dialog box. The dialog box it opens will contain the string to be changed, which will differ as a result of the property we select from the drop-down list. Therefore, we begin with a Select Case structure whose test expression is the value of the SELECT element:

```
Select Case selectOptions.Value
    Case "InnerText"
        strDialogValue = window.showModalDialog("Content Edit Window.htm",
        ➥glblObjElement.innerText,"dialogWidth:450px;dialogHeight:250px")
        if strDialogValue <> "" then
                glblObjElement.innerText = strDialogValue
        end if

    Case "OuterText"
        strDialogValue = window.showModalDialog("Content Edit Window.htm",
        ➥glblObjElement.outerText,"dialogWidth:450px;dialogHeight:250px")
        if strDialogValue <> "" then
                glblObjElement.outerText = strDialogValue
        end if
    Case "InnerHTML"
        strDialogValue = window.showModalDialog("Content Edit Window.htm",
        ➥glblObjElement.innerHTML,"dialogWidth:450px;dialogHeight:250px")
        if strDialogValue <> "" then
                glblObjElement.innerHTML = strDialogValue
        end if
    Case "OuterHTML"
        if glblObjElement.id = "pGettysburg" then
                MsgBox "Make another selection"
                exit sub
        end if
        strDialogValue = window.showModalDialog("Content Edit Window.htm",
        ➥glblObjElement.outerHTML,"dialogWidth:450px;dialogHeight:250px")
        if strDialogValue <> "" then
                glblObjElement.outerHTML = strDialogValue
        end if
    Case Else
        MsgBox "Should never get here"
    end select
```

In each case, we open a dialog box. One difference among the cases is the second argument, the value we send to the dialog box. (Remember the Tip in the previous section: This argument should be an object and its property.) The other difference is the content property we change when the value comes back from the dialog box (if this value isn't an empty string). You'll notice that I've widened the dialog box from the previous versions. This will accommodate longer strings.

The "OuterHTML" case's first if statement guards against changing the pGettysburg element—the possibility I mentioned earlier. If the source element of the onclick is pGettysburg, the user never gets the opportunity to change its outerHTML and thus render sub pGettysburg_onclick inoperative. Instead, a message box opens advising the user to make another selection.

One eventuality that we have to anticipate is the entry of invalid HTML code in the dialog box. For example, a P element can't contain another P element. Entering a <P> tag as the start tag for an outerHTML will generate an error message. To keep the program from crashing in this case, we add on error resume next to the start of this subroutine. We also add some code at the end that generates an informative message box if an error occurs:

```
if err.number <> 0 then
    MsgBox "Error: " & err.description & " from: " &
    ➥err.source,,"Attempt to Add Invalid HTML"
end if
```

First of all, the notation should tell you that a generated error is an object. Like any other object, it has properties, and we can examine those properties. If an error does occur, the err.number will not be 0, and the message box will display the indicated properties. (It's not the case that every error has a description.)

The third subroutine uses the source element of the pGettysburg onclick event to update the text area:

```
sub updatePropertiesTracker
    on error resume next
    textAreaPropertiesTracker.Value = "innerText: " &
    ➥window.event.srcElement.innerText & chr(13) _
    & "outerText: " & window.event.srcElement.outerText & chr(13) _
    & "innerHTML: " & window.event.srcElement.innerHTML & chr(13) _
    & "outerHTML: " & window.event.srcElement.outerHTML

end sub
```

This one begins with on error resume next so that we don't generate an error when the window opens and no source element exists.

Here's the whole Changing Content Properties.htm file:

 Changing Content Properties.htm

```vbscript
<HTML>
<HEAD>
<SCRIPT Language = "VBScript">
dim glblObjElement

sub pGettysburg_onclick
    updatePropertiesTracker
    set glblObjElement = window.event.srcElement
end sub

sub buttonChange_onclick
  on error resume next
  Select Case selectOptions.Value
   Case "InnerText"
      strDialogValue = window.showModalDialog("Content Edit Window.htm",
      ➥glblObjElement.innerText,"dialogWidth:450px;dialogHeight:250px")
      if strDialogValue <> "" then
           glblObjElement.innerText = strDialogValue
      end if

   Case "OuterText"
      strDialogValue = window.showModalDialog("Content Edit Window.htm",
      ➥glblObjElement.outerText,"dialogWidth:450px;dialogHeight:250px")
      if strDialogValue <> "" then
           glblObjElement.outerText = strDialogValue
      end if
   Case "InnerHTML"
      strDialogValue = window.showModalDialog("Content Edit Window.htm",
      ➥glblObjElement.innerHTML,"dialogWidth:450px;dialogHeight:250px")
      if strDialogValue <> "" then
           glblObjElement.innerHTML = strDialogValue
      end if
   Case "OuterHTML"
     if glblObjElement.id = "pGettysburg" then
           MsgBox "Make another selection"
           exit sub
     end if
     strDialogValue = window.showModalDialog("Content Edit Window.htm",
     ➥glblObjElement.outerHTML,"dialogWidth:450px;dialogHeight:250px")
     if strDialogValue <> "" then
           glblObjElement.outerHTML = strDialogValue
     end if
   Case Else
     MsgBox "Should never get here"
```

```
       end select

if err.number <> 0 then
     MsgBox "Error: " & err.description & " from: " &
err.source,,"Attempt to Add Invalid HTML"
end if

end sub


sub updatePropertiesTracker
     on error resume next
     textAreaPropertiesTracker.Value = "innerText: " &
    ➥window.event.srcElement.innerText & chr(13) _
     & "outerText: " & window.event.srcElement.outerText & chr(13) _
     & "innerHTML: " & window.event.srcElement.innerHTML & chr(13) _
     & "outerHTML: " & window.event.srcElement.outerHTML

end sub

</SCRIPT>
<TITLE>Changing Content Properties</TITLE>
</HEAD>
<BODY ID = bodyDocument>
<H1 style = "text-align:center">Changing Content Properties</H1>
<HR>
<P ID = pGettysburg><SPAN>Four score and <A><B ID = boldPhrase>seven
years</B></A></SPAN> ago, our fathers brought forth,
<I ID = italicPhrase>upon this continent, a new nation
<B ID = boldLiberty>conceived in liberty,</B></I> and dedicated to the
<B>proposition <A>that "all men</A></B> are <B ID = boldCreated>created
equal</B>"</P>
<CENTER>
<TEXTAREA ID = textareaPropertiesTracker Rows = 10 Cols = 60>
</TEXTAREA>
<SELECT ID = selectOptions style = "position:absolute;top:340;left:350">
<OPTION Value = "InnerText">InnerText
<OPTION Value = "OuterText">OuterText
<OPTION Value = "InnerHTML">InnerHTML
<OPTION Value = "OuterHTML">OuterHTML
</SELECT>
<BUTTON ID = buttonChange style =
"position:absolute;top:340;left:450">Change...</BUTTON>
</BODY>
</HTML>
```

Skill 11

Here's the dialog box Content Edit Window.htm.

 Content Edit Window.htm

```
<HTML>
<HEAD>
<SCRIPT Language = "VBScript">
sub window_onload
    textChange.Value = window.dialogArguments
    textChange.Focus
end sub
</SCRIPT>

<SCRIPT Language = "JScript">

function doOK() {
    if (textChange.value == "") {
            alert("Enter a string or click Cancel");
            return
        }
    window.returnValue = textChange.value;
    window.close();

}

function doCancel() {
    window.returnValue = "";
    window.close();
}
</SCRIPT>
<TITLE>Content Change Window</TITLE>
</HEAD>
<BODY style = "background-color:silver">
<BR>
<P style = "text-align:center">Edit the Content Property:</P>
<CENTER>
<INPUT ID = textChange Type = text Style = "width:95%">
</CENTER>
<Button style = "Position:absolute;top:85%;left:48%;width:60"
onclick = "doOK()">OK</Button>
<Button style = "Position:absolute;top:85%;left:73%;width:60"
onclick = "doCancel()">Cancel</Button>
</BODY>
</HTML>
```

As in the preceding exercise, in the VBS onload event-handler, the window.dialogArguments property provides the value passed from the main window. The second line in that event-handler puts the focus on the text input.

Use this window and the dialog box to change aspects of the sentence, and note the effects. After each change, you have to click the element again to see the updated values in the text area. Figure 11.11 shows the page after a change to the outerHTML of the last two words in the sentence. The change in the figure was from <B> and </B> to <I> and </I> as the start and end tags (along with a change to the ID). As the figure shows, the two words went from bold (in Figure 11.10) to italic.

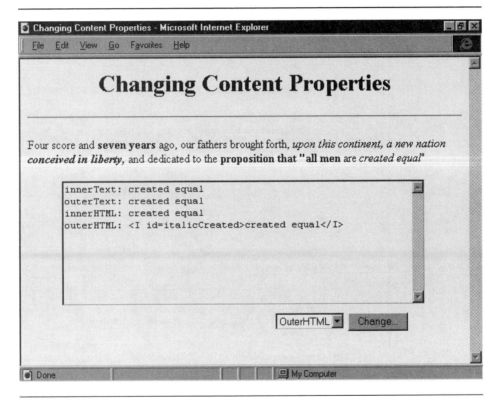

FIGURE 11.11: The appearance of Changing Content Properties.htm after changing the outerHTML of the last two words.

Inserting Content

IE provides two more methods for changing downloaded text: insertAdjacentText and insertAdjacentHTML. As their names imply, the first inserts text into an element and the second inserts HTML and text into an element. Each method takes two arguments. The first specifies where in the element to insert the string, and the second is the string to insert. For the first argument, four choices are available:

- `BeforeBegin`—Immediately before the element

- `AfterBegin`—Immediately after the start of the element and before all other content in the element

- `BeforeEnd`—Immediately before the end of the element and after all other content in the element

- `AfterEnd`—Immediately after the element

Our test bed page for working with these methods appears in Figure 11.12.

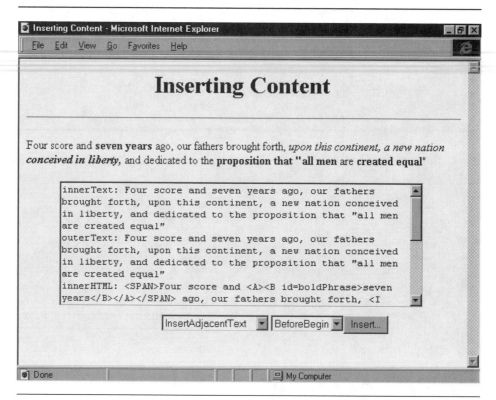

FIGURE 11.12: Inserting Content.htm, a test bed page for working with insertAdjacentText and insertAdjacentHTML

You can use the file from the preceding exercise as a template to set this one up. It's called Inserting Content.htm. The major difference in the HTML is the extra drop-down at the bottom of the page. One drop-down is for choosing the insertion method, the other is for choosing the location. That part of the HTML looks like this:

```
<SELECT ID = selectTypeOptions style =
"position:absolute;top:340;left:200">
<OPTION Value = "InsertAdjacentText">InsertAdjacentText
<OPTION Value = "InsertAdjacentHTML">InsertAdjacentHTML
</SELECT>

<SELECT ID = selectPositionOptions style =
"position:absolute;top:340;left:350">
<OPTION Value = "BeforeBegin">BeforeBegin
<OPTION Value = "AfterBegin">AfterBegin
<OPTION Value = "BeforeEnd">BeforeEnd
<OPTION Value = "AfterEnd">AfterEnd
</SELECT>

<BUTTON ID = buttonInsert style =
"position:absolute;top:340;left:450">Insert...</BUTTON>
```

The script is the same as in the previous exercise, except for the `onclick` event-handler for the button:

```
sub buttonInsert_onclick
    on error resume next
    strDialogValue = window.showModalDialog("Insert Window.htm",,
    ➥"dialogWidth:450px;dialogHeight:250px")

  Select Case selectTypeOptions.Value
   Case "InsertAdjacentText"

     if strDialogValue <> "" then
          call glblObjElement.insertAdjacentText
          ➥(selectPositionOptions.value,strDialogValue)
     end if

   Case "InsertAdjacentHTML"

     if strDialogValue <> "" then
          call glblObjElement.insertAdjacentHTML
          ➥(selectPositionOptions.value,strDialogValue)
     end if

   Case Else
     MsgBox "Should never get here"
   end select

 if err.number <> 0 then
     MsgBox "Error: " & err.description & " from: " & err.source,,
     ➥"Attempt to Add Invalid HTML"
```

```
    end if

    end sub
```

As you can see, this subroutine opens the dialog window before it gets to the `Select Case` structure. The `Select Case` determines what happens to the string when it comes back from the dialog. It bases the determination on the values selected in the drop-downs. The cases in the `Select Case` come from the drop-down that contains `insertAdjacentText` and `insertAdjacentHTML`. The location choice from the other drop-down is incorporated into the first argument of the calls to the insertion methods. Here's the whole `Inserting Content.htm` file.

Ⓒ Inserting Content.htm

```
<HTML>
<HEAD>
<SCRIPT Language = "VBScript">
dim glblObjElement

sub pGettysburg_onclick
    updatePropertiesTracker
    set glblObjElement = window.event.srcElement
end sub

sub buttonInsert_onclick
    on error resume next
    strDialogValue = window.showModalDialog("Insert Window.htm",,
    ➥"dialogWidth:450px;dialogHeight:250px")

  Select Case selectTypeOptions.Value
   Case "InsertAdjacentText"

     if strDialogValue <> "" then
            call glblObjElement.insertAdjacentText
            ➥(selectPositionOptions.value,strDialogValue)
     end if

   Case "InsertAdjacentHTML"

     if strDialogValue <> "" then
            call glblObjElement.insertAdjacentHTML
            ➥(selectPositionOptions.value,strDialogValue)
     end if

   Case Else
     MsgBox "Should never get here"
   end select

if err.number <> 0 then
```

```
      MsgBox "Error: " & err.description & " from: " & err.source,,
      ➡"Attempt to Add Invalid HTML"
end if

end sub


sub updatePropertiesTracker
    on error resume next
    textAreaPropertiesTracker.Value = "innerText: " &
    ➡window.event.srcElement.innerText & chr(13) _
    & "outerText: " & window.event.srcElement.outerText & chr(13) _
    & "innerHTML: " & window.event.srcElement.innerHTML & chr(13) _
    & "outerHTML: " & window.event.srcElement.outerHTML

end sub

</SCRIPT>
<TITLE>Inserting Content</TITLE>
</HEAD>
<BODY ID = bodyDocument>
<H1 style = "text-align:center">Inserting Content</H1>
<HR>
<P ID = pGettysburg><SPAN>Four score and <A><B ID = boldPhrase>seven
years</B></A></SPAN> ago, our fathers brought forth,
<I ID = italicPhrase>upon this continent, a new nation
<B ID = boldLiberty>conceived in liberty,</B></I> and dedicated to the
<B>proposition <A>that "all men</A></B> are <B ID = boldCreated>created
equal</B>"</P><CENTER>
<TEXTAREA ID = textareaPropertiesTracker Rows = 10 Cols = 60>
</TEXTAREA>

<SELECT ID = selectTypeOptions style =
"position:absolute;top:340;left:200">
<OPTION Value = "InsertAdjacentText">InsertAdjacentText
<OPTION Value = "InsertAdjacentHTML">InsertAdjacentHTML
</SELECT>

<SELECT ID = selectPositionOptions style =
"position:absolute;top:340;left:350">
<OPTION Value = "BeforeBegin">BeforeBegin
<OPTION Value = "AfterBegin">AfterBegin
<OPTION Value = "BeforeEnd">BeforeEnd
<OPTION Value = "AfterEnd">AfterEnd
</SELECT>

<BUTTON ID = buttonInsert style =
"position:absolute;top:340;left:450">Insert...</BUTTON>
</BODY>
</HTML>
```

Skill 11

Here's the dialog window Insert Window.htm:

 Insert Window.htm

```
<HTML>
<HEAD>

<SCRIPT Language = "VBScript">
sub window_onload
     textInsert.Focus
end sub
</SCRIPT>

<SCRIPT Language = "JScript">

function doOK() {
     if (textInsert.value == "") {
             alert("Enter a string or click Cancel");
             return
     }
     window.returnValue = textInsert.value;
     window.close();

}

function doCancel() {
     window.returnValue = "";
     window.close();
}
</SCRIPT>
<TITLE>Insert Window</TITLE>
</HEAD>
<BODY style = "background-color:silver">
<BR>
<P style = "text-align:center">Insert:</P>
<CENTER>
<INPUT ID = textInsert Type = text Style = "width:95%">
</CENTER>
<Button style = "Position:absolute;top:85%;left:48%;width:60"
onclick = "doOK()">OK</Button>
<Button style = "Position:absolute;top:85%;left:73%;width:60"
onclick = "doCancel()">Cancel</Button>
</BODY>
</HTML>
```

Since we don't pass any values to this window, we don't work with
window.dialogArguments.

Practice inserting text and HTML, and notice the effects on the page. As one of your exercises, try inserting tags with `insertAdjacentText`. You should see the tags rendered as text on the page.

Summary

As Web pages become more like standard software applications, users will expect to be able to do the same things on Web pages that they do in applications. Dragging and dropping, text insertion and deletion, and text change are all capabilities that you can add to your Web pages today. Dynamic HTML is the catalyst for making these techniques come to life on downloaded pages. Your users are no longer dependent on tedious roundtrips between their machines and servers if they want to change the positions, styles, and even the contents of your Web page elements.

By the way, if the exercises in this Skill have aroused your interest in the *Gettysburg Address*, visit `http://www.loc.gov/exhibits/G.Address/gadrft.html` to see images of Lincoln's draft. This is a wonderful Web site, particularly if you need a refresher course in the wording of the most famous speech in American history.

Have You Mastered the Essentials?

Now you can...

- ☑ Understand *textRange*s
- ☑ Build a capability for searching for text in an HTML document
- ☑ Replace text in an HTML document
- ☑ Change content properties
- ☑ Insert content
- ☑ Pass values from a document to a modal dialog box

Skill 11

PART III

Storming the Foundations

In Part I, you learned the essential skills for creating Dynamic HTML applications. In Part II, you learned how to apply them. Now that you've worked with many of the features of Dynamic HTML, it's time to examine them in a more formal way. In Part III, we'll do just that. First, we'll cover the object models at the foundation of IE and Navigator. Then we'll move on to an in-depth examination of VBScript and JavaScript. We'll finish with a look at where DHTML is headed.

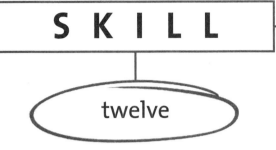

Understanding Browser Object Models

- ❑ The IE window object model

- ❑ The Navigator window object model

- ❑ The IE document object model

- ❑ The Navigator document object model

As I pointed out in Skill 1, Dynamic HTML combines HTML, scripting, and Cascading Style Sheets. The result, as you've seen in Skills up to this point, is the ability to create effects that weren't possible in traditional HTML. Elements on a page become objects that you style, position, and script.

What enables those traditional HTML elements to become objects?

Both IE and Navigator are based on *object models*, which describe the set of objects that make up the browser. The objects in the models connect the HTML elements to the workings of the browser—that is, to the browser's programs that determine the browser's look and feel, open its windows, and render the HTML code you create. An object model enables our scripts to refer to these elements and manipulate their appearances and behaviors.

This Skill will give you a firm grounding in these models. We begin by examining the window object models for IE and Navigator, and then we'll cover the document object models for the two browsers. The document objects are of major importance. They represent the HTML file that the browser renders in its window.

What does it mean to "examine an object model?" An object has properties and methods. As you've seen throughout the book, objects in Dynamic HTML are associated with events. When we examine object models, then, we'll look at their properties and methods, and the events they support. These aspects of the object models will appear in tables throughout this Skill. You'll recognize many of them, because you've already worked with them in previous Skills.

Introduction: So What's an Object Model?

The term *object model* has overtones of academic computer science and may sound a bit intimidating. Of course, you've been working with objects throughout the previous Skills. My plan was to immerse you in the objects, get you to understand their features by using them to make things happen on Web pages, and thus make it easier for you to understand object models when we examine them head-on.

When you wrote scripts, you used object models to describe and reference the elements on your Web pages or to invoke a method that works with those elements. The object model is the categorization system that enables you to do just that.

Remember our appliance example in Skill 5. I said then that if you think of your appliances as a set of objects that reside in your house, you could refer to your refrigerator as `myHouse.myRefrigerator` and to your dishwasher as `myHouse.myDishwasher`. I also said that you can go one step further and imagine your appliances as parts of a collection called `myAppliances`. When you do that, you can attach a number to each appliance based on, say, the order in which you added that appliance to your house. If you added the refrigerator first and the dishwasher second, the refrigerator is `myHouse.myAppliances(0)` and the dishwasher is `myHouse.myAppliances(1)`.

Categorization works the same way in browsers and Web pages, as you've already seen. Think of a `document` object as a container—like your house—that holds a set of elements—like your appliances. To extend the analogy, think of the `window` object as an area of land that holds your house and a number of other houses. If you happen to live in an apartment, the `window` is analogous to your apartment house and the `document` is analogous to your apartment. You might reference an element in your document, then, as `window.document.myElement`. If `myElement` is a particular kind of element, like an `IMG`, that reference is `window.document.images(0)`.

We'll take a close look at object models, but first…

A Little History

In the "good old days" of browsers, pre-1995, Netscape Navigator 1.0 was a vehicle for rendering static Web pages from servers located all over the world. People were beginning to discover the Internet and the World Wide Web, and at that stage of the game, Navigator 1.0 did its job very well.

Netscape Gets Objective

The audience became more sophisticated and Netscape got fancy. With Navigator 2.0, they introduced JavaScript and the browser world has never been the same. JavaScript 1.0 enabled you to set up interactive Web pages, work with Java applets, and more. Netscape wanted JavaScript to be object-based, and that necessitated an object model for referring to objects in a systematic way.

The object model in Navigator 2.0 was called the Navigator Object Hierarchy. The foundation of the hierarchy was the `window` object, which provided properties and methods for working with the browser window. The `window` was the parent of the `location` object, the `history` object, and the `document` object. The `location` object had methods and properties for dealing with the URL of the currently open document, the `history` object gave information about the list of recently visited URLs, and the `document` object provided the machinery for working with elements of the document.

To this hierarchy, JavaScript 1.0 added a `string` object for manipulating strings of text, a `Math` object for working with mathematical functions, and a `Date` object for handling date and time information.

When Navigator 3.0 came along, it brought with it a new implementation of JavaScript. The new JavaScript had some additional built-in objects for images, plug-ins, and applets. The version of Navigator that you use for the exercises in this book, version 4.0, works with an even newer version of JavaScript (1.2). With the current Navigator object model, you can access major page elements—forms, applets, images, plug-ins, anchors, frames, hyperlinks, and layers.

Microsoft Gets into the Game

Microsoft's IE 3.0 incorporated JavaScript and introduced VBScript. As part and parcel of this version, Microsoft delivered an object model equivalent to the model in Navigator 2.0. Thus, it lacked some of Navigator 3.0's built-in objects.

IE 4.0 goes a step beyond. As you've seen, it has extended the object model to include every element and content item on a page, not just the major ones. You can script behaviors for these elements in JavaScript and VBScript, and those scripts can hold event-handlers for every element. (Skill 6, you'll recall, showed how both Navigator and IE detect and deal with events.) IE scripts can manipulate an element's style, positioning, visibility, and even its content.

Toward a Standard Object Model?

As the Skills up to this point have indicated, IE and Navigator have some major differences. Will this situation ever change? The W3C is working on a standard object model, and Microsoft and Netscape have agreed to conform to that standard when it's finally available.

The W3C takes its time in most efforts, and this one is no exception. To see how it's going, check in periodically at `http://www.w3c.org/DOM/`. You can have a look at their Document Object Model Specification, a work in progress that's sure to pique your interest.

Common Features

Our history lesson suggests that the two browsers have common roots, and that these roots are reflected in common features of their object models.

Both the Navigator and IE models have the `window` object as their basis. Figure 12.1 illustrates the high-level object structure for both browsers.

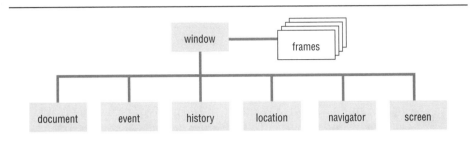

FIGURE 12.1:   The window object is a container for six other objects and an indexed set of frames.

The window object is the parent of all objects in the model, and it's a container for six other objects:

- document—represents the document in the browser window (we'll cover this one in greater detail later in this Skill)

- event—represents the state of an event, like mouse location, the element in which the event occurred, and more (see Skill 6)

- history—holds information on previously visited URLs during the current session. The information is stored in the object's History list.

- location—gives information about the URL of the currently rendered document

- navigator—represents the browser application. This object gives information about the manufacturer, version, and capabilities.

- screen—holds information about the client machine's screen and rendering capabilities

 NOTE   Why does IE have an object called navigator? IE does this to try and maintain some consistency with Netscape Navigator. Since the two have the same name and most of the same properties, accessing this object in either IE or Navigator will tell you all you have to know about the current browser.

Although the names and purposes of these objects are the same for the two browsers, the IE objects have different properties than the Navigator objects. You've already seen this in Skill 6 with respect to the event object.

Skill 12

The `window` object also holds information on frames. IE and Navigator differ on what they call the structure that holds the information. IE calls it a *collection*, and Navigator calls it an *array*. Either structure is a set of items you can index. In both browsers, the structure is called `Frames`. As its name suggests, it's an indexed set of frames defined in a FRAMESET element. Just to refresh your memory about frames, I've presented Figure 2.4 (from your work in Skill 2 on frames) here as Figure 12.2. When we get to the respective Document Object Models, you'll see many more collections in IE and arrays in Navigator.

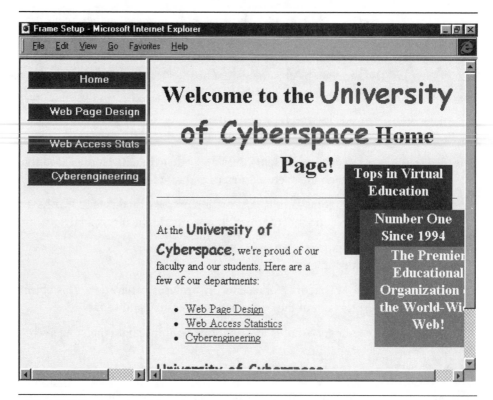

FIGURE 12.2:   The page set up by `Frames.htm` in Skill 2

THAT *FRAMES* THING: DIGRESSION 1

As long as we're talking about FRAMESETs, let's revisit some of the work we did in Skill 2. In our Frames.htm file in that Skill, the FRAMESET element specified the structure of the frames:

```
<HTML>
<HEAD>
<TITLE>Frame Setup</TITLE>
</HEAD>
<FRAMESET Cols = 28%,72%>
<FRAME Name = "leftframe"
Src = "E:\DHTML MTE\Skill 2\Navigation.htm">
<FRAME Name = "rightframe"
Src = "E:\DHTML MTE\Skill 2\UofCyb.htm">
</FRAMESET>
</HTML>
```

This set up the display in Figure 2.4, which I've presented here as Figure 12.2.

The window object model, which you're about to explore, played a major role in the rest of what we did. I'll present two more digressions at appropriate points along the way.

Now we'll take a closer look at the window object in each browser.

The IE Model

We begin our discussion of object models by examining the IE model. We'll start with the window object, examining its properties, methods, and events.

The *window* Object

The window object represents an open window in the browser. It gives you information about the state of the window. You use this object to access the document rendered in the window, the events that take place in the window, and browser features that affect the window.

The browser creates a window object when it opens an HTML document. If a document defines a set of frames, as in Skill 2, the browser creates one window object for the original document (the one that contains the FRAMESET element) and one additional window object for each frame. These additional objects are *child windows* of the original *parent* window. Actions in the parent window affect the children: If you close the parent, for example, you close the children. You can also create new windows, and hence, new window objects, via the window showModalDialog method used in Skills 10 and 11.

Properties of the IE *window* Object

The window object has a number of properties, as summarized in Table 12.1.

TABLE 12.1: Properties of the IE window Object

Property	What It Does
client	Holds information about the version and name of the browser and about whether certain features are enabled
closed	Returns whether the window is closed (true if the window is closed, false otherwise)
defaultStatus	Gives the default message displayed in the window's status bar
dialogArguments	Returns the variable or array of variables passed from a main window to a modal dialog box*
dialogHeight	Returns the height of a dialog box*
dialogLeft	Returns the left coordinate of a dialog box*
dialogTop	Returns the top coordinate of a dialog box*
dialogWidth	Returns the width of a dialog box*
document	Provides a reference to the window's document object
event	Provides a reference to the window's event object

TABLE 12.1 CONTINUED: Properties of the IE window Object

Property	What It Does
history	Gives a reference to the window's history object
length	Provides the number of elements in a collection
location	Gives the document's URL
name	Specifies the name of the window or frame
navigator	Gives a reference to the window's navigator object
offscreenBuffering	Specifies whether to use off-screen buffering for the document
opener	Provides a reference to the window that created the current window
parent	Returns the parent window. For a window created via FRAME, as in Skill 3, the parent is the window that contains the FRAMESET element
returnValue	Specifies the value returned from a modal dialog to the main window (see Skills 10 and 11)*
screen	Provides a reference to the window's screen object
self	Provides a way to refer to the current window or frame
status	Sets or returns the message in the status bar at the bottom of the window
top	Returns the top-most ancestor window object, which, by the way, is its own parent! See the upcoming sidebar for an application of this property
window	Provides a reference to the current window. It's the same as self

An asterisk (*) in this table means that the property refers only to modal windows—that is, to windows opened via the showModalDialog method. To illustrate this, try opening Replace Window.htm in Skill 11 by clicking its icon rather than by opening it as a dialog from Replace Text.htm. You'll get an error message that says the object doesn't support dialogArguments, an error message you don't get when you open this document as a dialog box from another window.

THAT *FRAMES* THING: DIGRESSION 2

Let's get back to our side discussion on frames.

When we scripted the navigation window, the one in the left frame in Figure 12.2, here's how we added functionality to the buttons:

```
<INPUT Type = button Value = "Home" Class = "UofCybButton"
onClick = "window.top.rightframe.location.href = 'UofCyb.htm'">
<P>
<INPUT Type = button Value = "Web Page Design"
Class = "UofCybButton"
onClick = "window.top.rightframe.location.href =
'WebPageDesign.htm'">
<P>
<INPUT Type = button Value = "Web Access Stats"
Class = "UofCybButton"
onClick = "window.top.rightframe.location.href =
'WebAccessStats.htm'">
<P>
<INPUT Type = button Value = "Cyberengineering"
Class = "UofCybButton"
onClick = "window.top.rightframe.location.href =
'Cybereng.htm'">
```

(This code is from `Navigation.htm` in Skill 2.)

In each event-handler, we referred to the right frame in terms of the window object. We used the window's top property, which Table 12.1 describes. We'll cover the `location.href` part in the final digression.

Methods of the IE *window* Object

Throughout this book, you've had occasion to use methods of the window object. In Skill 7, for example, you used setInterval to start a timer in conjunction with animation, and clearInterval to stop the timer.

The window object has numerous other methods, as Table 12.2 shows.

NOTE When describing a method, I use the word "specified" to indicate that something is specified in an argument or set of arguments to that method.

TABLE 12.2: Methods of the IE window Object

Method	What It Does
alert	Displays an Alert dialog box with a message and an OK button
blur	Makes on object lose focus and activates the onblur event
clearInterval	Cancels an interval started by setInterval
clearTimeout	Cancels a timeout set by setTimeout
close	Closes the current browser window
confirm	Displays a Confirm dialog box with a message, an OK button, and a Cancel button
execScript	Executes a specified script
focus	Makes a control receive the focus and executes code specified by the onfocus event
navigate	Available only to VBScript, displays a given URL
open	Opens a new window and loads the document given by a specified URL
prompt	Displays a Prompt dialog box with a message and an input field
scroll	Scrolls the window to a specified x and y offset relative to the whole document
setInterval	Repeatedly evaluates an expression after a specified number of milliseconds
setTimeout	Evaluates an expression after a specified number of milliseconds
showHelp	Displays a help file given by a specified URL
showModalDialog	Opens an HTML document as a modal dialog box

Events of the IE *window* Object

The window object supports several events. You've scripted event-handlers for one of those events, onload, in a number of Skills. Table 12.3 shows these events.

T A B L E   1 2 . 3 :   Events of the IE window Object

Event	Fires...
onbeforeunload	Just before a page unloads. This event enables you to ask the user not to leave the page. You can script an event-handler that displays a dialog box giving the user the option to stay on the page
onblur	When an object loses the focus
onerror	When loading a document or an image causes an error
onfocus	When a control gains the focus
onhelp	When the user presses F1 or clicks Help on the browser
onload	Immediately after the browser opens a specified object
onresize	When the window is resized
onscroll	When the scroll box is repositioned
onunload	Immediately before the page unloads

Those Other IE Objects

Before we move on, let's look at four of the objects that the IE window contains. We won't examine the event object because we covered it in Skill 6, and we'll cover the document object later in this Skill.

The IE *history* Object

The history object holds information about the URLs the user visited in the current session. Its one property, length, gives the number of items in the browser's history list. Its methods, shown in Table 12.4, enable you to navigate through the history list.

TABLE 12.4:   Methods of the IE history Object

Method	What It Does
Back	Loads the document of the previous URL in the history list
Forward	Loads the document of the next URL in the history list
Go	Loads the document from a specified position in the history list

The IE *location* Object

The location object provides information on the current page's URL. Its methods reload the current page or load a new page. Table 12.5 presents the location object's properties and Table 12.6 presents its methods.

TABLE 12.5:   Properties of the IE location Object

Property	What It Does
Hash	Returns the string that follows the # symbol in the HREF
Host	Provides the hostname:port of the URL
Hostname	Returns the hostname part of the URL
Href	Provides the entire URL
Pathname	Gives the file name that follows the third slash in a URL
Port	Returns the URL's port number
Protocol	Returns the initial substring that indicates the URL's access method (e.g., http)
Search	Provides any query string that follows the ? in the complete URL

TABLE 12.6:   Methods of the IE location Object

Method	What It Does
Assign	Loads another page. This is the same as changing the window.location.href property
Reload	Reloads the current page
Replace	Loads a page that replaces the current page's history entry with its URL

Skill 12

The IE *navigator* Object

The navigator object holds information about the browser's manufacturer, its version, and its capabilities. Its five properties contain the information, as shown in Table 12.7.

TABLE 12.7:   Properties of the IE navigator Object

Property	What It Does
AppCodeName	Provides the browser's code name
AppName	Provides the browser's product name
AppVersion	Gives the browser's version
CookieEnabled	Indicates whether or not client-side cookies are enabled in the browser
UserAgent	The browser name sent as part of the HTTP protocol

A couple of words about those last two properties are in order. A *cookie* is a string stored on a user's computer, and is associated with the current page. It stores information between visits to the page. The phrase *user agent* is a W3C term. It's any device that interprets HTML documents.

The IE navigator object has two methods. One, taintEnabled, concerns compatibility with Netscape Navigator and returns false. The other, javaEnabled, indicates if the browser supports execution of Java code.

The navigator object also contains two collections. One, mimeTypes, is a collection of all the different types of documents the browser supports. The other, plug-ins, is a collection of installed plug-in applications. (See Skill 8 for a discussion of plug-ins.)

The IE *screen* Object

The screen object's properties hold information about the end user's screen resolution and about the screen's ability to render documents. This information is useful if we want to set characteristics of the browser window—such as where to position it on the screen or how big to make it—or if we want to choose among several images to display in order to maximize the end user's screen characteristics. Table 12.8 shows the screen object's properties.

TABLE 12.8: Properties of the IE screen Object

Property	What It Does
colorDepth	Returns information on the maximum number of colors that the user's system supports
height	Provides the overall height of the user's screen
pixelDepth	Provides the number of bits that the system uses per pixel
updateInterval	Holds the interval between screen updates on the user's machine
width	Provides the overall width of the user's screen

Examining IE

Here's an exercise designed to give you a better understanding of the objects contained in the window object. In your text editor, create a file called Examining IE.htm and save it in Skill 12. Figure 12.3 shows what this page will look like when you're done creating it.

As you can see, we'll use a technique we've used numerous times before to investigate objects and their properties. We'll set up a text area whose value will change as a result of events, and we'll script event-handlers to give us the information we want.

The page layout is simple:

```
<HTML>
<HEAD>
<TITLE>Examining IE </TITLE>
</HEAD>
<BODY>
<H1 style = "text-align:center">Examining IE</H1>
<HR>
<BR> <BR>
<CENTER>
<TEXTAREA ID = textareaIeInfo Rows = 12 Cols = 40>
</TEXTAREA>
<BR><BR>
<FORM ID = formButtons>
<INPUT ID = buttonHistory Type = Button Value = History>
<INPUT ID = buttonLocation Type = Button Value = Location>
<INPUT ID = buttonNavigator Type = Button Value = Navigator>
<INPUT ID = buttonScreen Type = Button Value = Screen>
</FORM>
</CENTER>
</BODY>
</HTML>
```

Skill 12

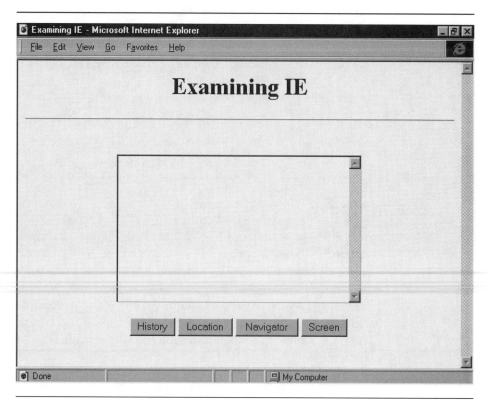

FIGURE 12.3:   Examining IE.htm, a page for looking at property values of the objects contained in the IE window object

In the HEAD, insert a SCRIPT element that looks like this:

```
<SCRIPT Language = "VBScript">

sub buttonHistory_onclick
textareaIeInfo.value = ""
textareaIeInfo.value = "history.length: " & history.length
end sub

sub buttonLocation_onclick
textareaIeInfo.value = ""
textareaIeInfo.value = "location.hash: " & location.hash & chr(13) _
          & "location.host: " & location.host & chr(13) _
          & "location.hostname: " & location.hostname & chr(13) _
          & "location.href: " & location.href & chr(13) _
```

```
            & "location.pathname: " & location.pathname & chr(13) _
            & "location.port: " & location.port & chr(13) _
            & "location.protocol: " & location.protocol & chr(13) _
            & "location.search: " & location.search
    end sub

    sub buttonNavigator_onclick
    textareaIeInfo.value = ""
    textareaIeInfo.value = "navigator.appCodeName: " &
            ➥ navigator.appCodeName & chr(13) _
            & "navigator.appName: " & navigator.appName & chr(13) _
            & "navigator.appVersion: " & navigator.appVersion & chr(13) _
            & "navigator.cookieEnabled: " & navigator.cookieEnabled &
            ➥ chr(13) _
            & "navigator.userAgent: " & navigator.userAgent
    end sub

    sub buttonScreen_onclick
    textareaIeInfo.value = ""
    textareaIeInfo.value = "screen.colorDepth: " & screen.colorDepth &
            ➥ chr(13) _
            & "screen.height: " & screen.height & chr(13) _
            & "screen.pixelDepth: " & screen.pixelDepth & chr(13) _
            & "screen.updateInterval: " & screen.updateInterval &
            ➥ chr(13) _
            & "screen.width: " & screen.width
    end sub

</SCRIPT>
```

That's the entire Examining IE.htm file. Open it in IE and find out about
your browser and your screen by clicking the buttons. Bear in mind that not all
the properties you've coded will return values. The location object, in particular, will be a little bland, as you're just opening a file and not a Web site at
an exotic URL. To get a number other than 0 into history.length, open some
other files (like the University of Cyberspace pages in Skill 3) and then go back
to Examining IE.htm.

The navigator object is perhaps the most interesting. In my system, here's the
result of clicking the Navigator button:

```
navigator.appCodeName: Mozilla
navigator.appName: Microsoft Internet Explorer
navigator.appVersion: 4.0 (compatible; MSIE 4.0; Windows 95)
navigator.cookieEnabled: True
navigator.userAgent: Mozilla/4.0 (compatible; MSIE 4.0; Windows 95)
```

As I mentioned in an earlier note, IE has a `navigator` object to maintain consistency with Netscape Navigator, which puts the same information in an object with the same name. `Mozilla` is an important word in the Netscape lexicon. It's a Netscape in-house synonym for its browser application. (It comes from Netscape's original name, Mosaic Communications.)

You'll also find that `screen.pixelDepth` doesn't return a value, and that `location.href` fills in blank spaces with %20. Between `location.href` and `location.pathName`, the slashes change direction. You'll see that these quirks don't occur when we create an equivalent page for Navigator.

THAT *FRAMES* THING: DIGRESSION 3

Let's return to our discussion on frames one last time.

In the preceding sidebar, I showed you the code that added functionality to the buttons in `Navigation.htm`, the left frame in Figure 12.2. The code used the window object model to do this.

Each frame is a window, with the properties, methods, and events of a window. As a `window` object, each frame contains all the objects that a window contains. We used one of these objects in the event-handlers.

The idea was to direct each event-handler to change `rightframe`'s `location .href` to point to a URL that would put a new page into `rightframe`. For example,

```
<INPUT Type = button Value = "Web Page Design"
Class = "UofCybButton"
onClick = "window.top.rightframe.location.href =
'WebPageDesign.htm'">
```

puts the home page of the Department of Web Page Design into `rightframe`.

continued ▶

At that point in Skill 2, I used just the file name for each source file, rather than the local file path. I wrote in a Warning that if you put a local file path into that context—i.e., as a value for location.href—you would get an error message.

If you work with Examining IE.htm, you'll see why. Clicking on the Navigator button reveals that location.href takes values that look like this:

```
file:///E:/DHTML%20MTE/Skill%2012/Examining%20IE.htm
```

In the event-handlers in Navigation.htm, fill in a value in this format for location.href, and you'll find that everything works perfectly. For example,

```
<INPUT Type = button Value = "Web Page Design"
Class = "UofCybButton"
onClick = "window.top.rightframe.location.href =
'file:///E:/DHTML MTE/Skill 2/WebPageDesign.htm'">
```

puts the Department of Web Page Design page into rightframe.

The Navigator Model

We now turn to the Navigator object model. As you'll see, the window object in Navigator has some of the same features as the window object in IE and some that are different.

Properties of the Navigator *window* Object

In Navigator 4.0, Netscape has added a number of properties to the window object from previous versions. The whole set is in Table 12.9.

T A B L E   1 2 . 9 :   Properties of the Navigator window Object

Property	What It Does
closed	Indicates whether a window is closed
defaultStatus	Gives the default message displayed in the window's status bar
innerHeight	Holds the height of the window excluding the window borders
innerWidth	Holds the width of the window excluding the window borders
locationbar	Determines if the address bar is displayed in the window
menubar	Specifies if the menubar is displayed in the browser window
name	Specifies the name of the window
opener	Provides a reference to the window that created the current window
outerHeight	Holds the height of the window, including the window borders
outerWidth	Holds the width of the window, including the window borders
pageXOffset	Gives the horizontal offset of the visible part of the page within the window
pageYOffset	Gives the vertical offset of the visible part of the page within the window
parent	Returns the parent window
personalbar	Specifies if the user's personal button bar is displayed in the browser window
scrollbars	Determines if the browser window will provide scrollbars if the browser can't render all the content
self	Provides a reference to the current window
status	Specifies the text to display in the status bar
statusbar	Determines whether to display the status bar
toolbar	Determines whether to display the toolbar
top	Provides a reference to the top-most window

Methods of the Navigator *window* Object

As is the case with IE, you've already used some of the methods of the Navigator window object. In Skill 7, you used setInterval and clearInterval to make animation work. The whole set of methods appears in Table 12.10.

TABLE 12.10:   Methods of the Navigator window Object

Method	What It Does
Alert	Displays an alert dialog box with a message and an OK button
Back	Loads the immediately preceding URL in the browser's history list
Blur	Makes the window lose the focus and activates its onBlur event
CaptureEvents	Specifies that the window should captureEvents of a particular type
ClearInterval	As in IE, this method stops a timer set via setInterval
ClearTimeout	As in IE, this method stops a timer set via setTimeout
Close	Closes the current browser window
Confirm	Displays a Confirm dialog box with a message, an OK button, and a Cancel button
DisableExternalCapture	Prevents a window that includes frames from capturing events in documents loaded from different locations
EnableExternalCapture	Enables a window that includes frames to capture events in documents loaded from different locations
Find	Returns true if a specified string is found in text rendered in the current window
Focus	Causes the window to receive the focus and to activate its onFocus event
Forward	Loads the next URL in the browser's history list
HandleEvent	Activates the event-handler of the object for the event
Home	Opens the user's Home page in the browser window
MoveBy	Moves the window horizontally and vertically
MoveTo	Moves the window to a specified position
Open	Opens a new browser window
Print	Prints the window's contents. This is equivalent to selecting File ➢ Print in the browser
ReleaseEvents	Specifies that the window should stop capturing a specified event type
ResizeBy	Resizes the window horizontally and vertically
ResizeTo	Resizes the window to a specified size
RouteEvent	Sends a captured event through the event hierarchy

Skill 12

TABLE 12.10 CONTINUED: Methods of the Navigator window Object

Method	What It Does
ScrollBy	Scrolls the document horizontally and vertically within the window by a specified number of pixels
ScrollTo	Scrolls the document within the window so that a specified point is in the top left corner
SetInterval	As in IE, this method repeatedly evaluates an expression after a specified number of milliseconds
SetTimeout	As in IE, this method evaluates an expression after a specified number of milliseconds
Stop	Stops the current download. It's equivalent to pressing the browser's Stop button

Events of the Navigator *window* Object

The Navigator window object is associated with a number of events, as shown in Table 12.11.

TABLE 12.11: Events of the Navigator window Object

Event	Fires...
OnBlur	When the window loses the focus
OnDragDrop	When the user drops a file or on object on the browser window
OnError	When loading a document generates an error
OnFocus	When the window receives the focus
OnLoad	When a document finishes loading into the browser window
OnMouseMove	During event capturing when the mouse cursor moves
OnMove	When the window is moved
OnResize	When the window is resized
OnUnload	Just before the currently rendered document unloads

Those Other Navigator Objects

Before we move on, let's look at four of the objects that the Navigator `window` object contains. As was the case for IE, we won't examine the `event` object because we discussed it in Skill 6, and we'll leave the `document` object for later in this Skill.

The Navigator *history* Object

The history object holds information about the URLs that the user has visited in the current session. Table 12.12 shows its properties and 12.13 shows its methods.

TABLE 12.12: Properties of the Navigator `history` Object

Property	What It Does
Current	Provides the current item in the browser's history list
Length	Gives the number of items in the history list
Next	Gives a reference to the next item in the history list
Previous	Gives a reference to the previous item in the history list

TABLE 12.13 Methods of the Navigator `history` object

Method	What It Does
back	Loads the document of the previous URL in the history list
forward	Loads the document of the next URL in the history list
go	Loads the document from a specified URL in the history list

The Navigator *location* Object

This object provides information on the URL of the currently rendered page. Its methods `reload` the current page or `replace` it in the browser's history list. Table 12.14 presents the `location` object's properties.

Skill 12

TABLE 12.14: Properties of the Navigator location Object

Property	What It Does
Hash	Returns the string that follows the # symbol in the HREF
Hostname	Returns the hostname part of the URL
Href	Provides the destination URL
Pathname	Gives the file name that follows the third slash in a URL
Port	Returns the URL's port number
Protocol	Returns the initial substring that indicates the URL's access method (e.g., http)
Search	Provides any query string that follows the ? in the complete URL

The Navigator *navigator* Object

The navigator object holds information about the browser's manufacturer, its version, and its capabilities. Its six properties appear in Table 12.15.

TABLE 12.15: Properties of the Navigator navigator Object

Property	What It Does
AppCodeName	Provides the browser's code name
AppName	Provides the browser's product name
AppVersion	Gives the browser's version
Language	Provides the language for which the browser was compiled (en indicates English).
Platform	Provides the name of the operating system for which the browser was compiled
UserAgent	The browser name sent as part of the HTTP protocol

As in IE, Navigator's navigator object contains two arrays. They're the same as the IE navigator object's collections: mimeTypes is an array of all the different types of documents the browser supports and plugins is an array of installed plug-in applications.

The Navigator *screen* Object

As in IE, the `screen` object's properties hold information about the end user's screen resolution and about the screen's ability to render documents. Table 12.16 shows the `screen` object's properties.

TABLE 12.16: Properties of the Navigator screen Object

Property	What It Does
AvailHeight	Gives the height of the available screen space
AvailWidth	Gives the width of the available screen space
ColorDepth	Returns information on the maximum number of colors that the user's system supports
Height	Provides the overall height of the user's screen
PixelDepth	Provides the number of bits that the system uses per pixel
Width	Provides the overall width of the user's screen

Examining Navigator

Let's create a page equivalent to the one we created for examining IE. In your text editor, create a file called `Examining Navigator.htm`. Figure 12.4 shows the completed page.

As in the IE version, the HTML for the layout is straightforward, but I'll show it to you because of a difference between IE and Navigator:

```
<HTML>
<HEAD>
<TITLE>Examining Navigator</TITLE>
</HEAD>
<BODY>
<H1 style = "text-align:center">Examining Navigator</H1>
<HR>
<BR> <BR>
<CENTER>
<FORM>
<TEXTAREA Rows = 12 Cols = 40 Wrap>
</TEXTAREA>
<BR><BR>
```

Skill 12

```
<INPUT Type = Button Value = History onClick = showHistory()>
<INPUT Type = Button Value = Location onClick = showLocation()>
<INPUT Type = Button Value = Navigator onClick = showNavigator()>
<INPUT Type = Button Value = Screen onClick = showScreen()>
</FORM>
</CENTER>
</BODY>
</HTML>
```

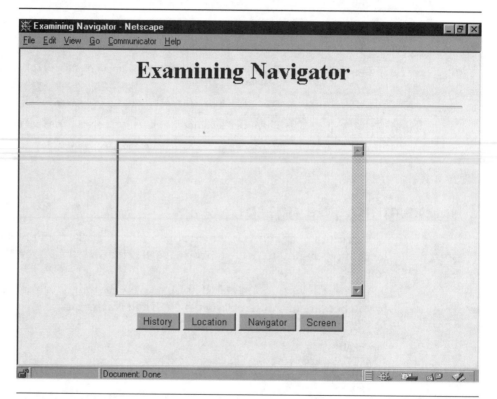

FIGURE 12.4:   Examining Navigator.htm, a page for looking at property values of the objects contained in the Navigator window object

Notice that in the IE version, we didn't put the TEXTAREA in the FORM. Here we do. In HTML 4.0, TEXTAREAs and BUTTONs can exist outside of FORMs, but apparently Navigator doesn't support this yet (at least my release doesn't; perhaps yours does). Thus, if you open Examining IE.htm in Navigator, you'll see the buttons, but you won't see the text area. (On the other hand, if you open Examining Navigator.htm in IE, everything works as it should.) Notice also that we've added Wrap to the TEXTAREA element. Wrapping is default behavior for a TEXTAREA in IE, but not in Navigator.

The next task is to write JavaScript code that adds functionality to the buttons. In each case, an onClick event will display property values for the objects. Add this SCRIPT element to the HEAD of the file:

```
<SCRIPT>
function showHistory() {
document.forms[0].elements[0].value = "";
document.forms[0].elements[0].value =
            "history.current: " + history.current + "\n"
        + "history.length: " + history.length + "\n"
        + "history.next: " + history.next + "\n"
        + "history.previous: " + history.previous;
}

function showLocation() {
document.forms[0].elements[0].value = "";
document.forms[0].elements[0].value =
            "location.hash: " + location.hash + "\n"
        + "location.hostname: " + location.hostname + "\n"
        + "location.href: " + location.href + "\n"
        + "location.pathname: " + location.pathname + "\n"
        + "location.port: " + location.port + "\n"
        + "location.protocol: " + location.protocol + "\n"
        + "location.search: " + location.search;
}

function showNavigator() {
document.forms[0].elements[0].value = "";
document.forms[0].elements[0].value =
            "navigator.appCodeName: " + navigator.appCodeName + "\n"
        + "navigator.appName: " + navigator.appName + "\n"
        + "navigator.appVersion: " + navigator.appVersion + "\n"
        + "navigator.language: " + navigator.language + "\n"
        + "navigator.platform: " + navigator.platform + "\n"
        + "navigator.userAgent: " + navigator.userAgent;
}

function showScreen() {
document.forms[0].elements[0].value = "";
document.forms[0].elements[0].value =
            "screen.availHeight: " + screen.availHeight + "\n"
        + "screen.availWidth: " + screen.availWidth + "\n"
```

```
            + "screen.colorDepth: " + screen.colorDepth + "\n"
            + "screen.height: " + screen.height + "\n"
            + "screen.pixelDepth: " + screen.pixelDepth + "\n"
            + "screen.width: " + screen.width;
    }

    </SCRIPT>
```

We'll have more to say about the document.forms[0].elements[0] format later in this Skill.

The script and the HTML make up the complete Examining Navigator.htm file. Open it in Navigator and start finding out about the property values. You'll see some differences from the IE version. For one thing, the navigator object's property values are

```
navigator.appCodeName: Mozilla
navigator.appName: Netscape
navigator.appVersion: 4.0 [en] (Win95; U)
navigator.language: en
navigator.platform: Win32
navigator.userAgent: Mozilla/4.0 [en] (Win95; U)
```

The appCodeName is still Mozilla, as you would expect, and the appName is Netscape. Also, the location property values look cleaner than in the IE version. Finally, in the values for the properties of the screen object, a value for pixelDepth shows up in my system (it didn't for IE), and the values for height and availableHeight are the same, as are the values for width and availableWidth.

 WARNING While working with this page, I stumbled on some weird behavior. In order to add to the history list and change some of the properties of the history object, I opened this page, then opened First Dynamic Nav.htm from Skill 1 in the same browser window, and then moved back to this page. When I clicked the Location button and then the History button, I got a message that the program had performed an illegal operation and would be shut down.

Introducing the *document* Object

Now that you've seen the browser objects at the window level, it's time to turn our attention to the real heart of the matter—the document object. In both IE and Navigator, the document object represents the HTML page that's currently in the browser. It holds all the elements on the page. Based on the Skills you've worked through, you know this can be a considerable amount, in terms of both number and type. For this reason, the document object can hold a variety of collections (in IE) or arrays (in Navigator) that represent all the different types of elements. When you write scripts that change properties, positions, or styles of elements, you're dealing with objects contained in collections or arrays of the document object.

We'll begin with a look at the IE document object model, and conclude by examining the Navigator object model.

The IE Document Object Model

First we'll examine the collections of the IE Document Object Model. Then we'll look at the document object's properties, methods, and events.

Collections of the IE *document* Object

The collections in the IE document object are an efficient way of organizing all the material on the page. Figure 12.5 shows these collections, and Table 12.17 lists and describes them. As you can see, the names are very descriptive.

TABLE 12.17: Collections of the IE document Object

Collection	Collects All the Document's...
All	Tags and elements
Anchors	Anchor (A) elements
Applets	APPLET objects
Embeds	EMBED elements
Frames	FRAMEs defined in a FRAMESET element
Forms	FORM elements
Images	IMG elements
Links	Links and image-map <AREA> blocks
Scripts	SCRIPT elements
Stylesheets	STYLE elements

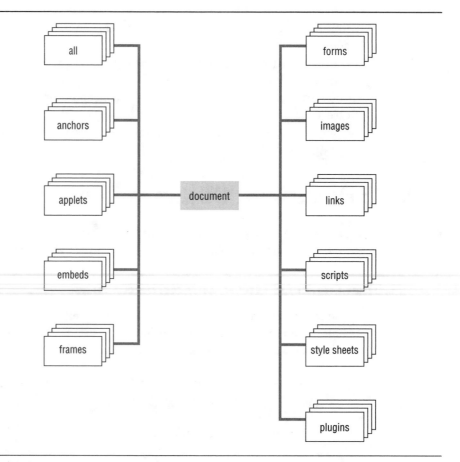

FIGURE 12.5: The IE document object organizes its information into a set of collections.

The document object works with two other collections: filters is a collection of filters for an element (see Skill 5) and plugins is an alias for the embeds collection.

Working with Collections

How do you work with a collection? One way is to refer to an element by its indexed position within the collection. If, for example, we have a page with several images on it, the first one in the document is document.images(0), the second is document.images(1), and so forth. If you've assigned IDs to those images, such as imgFirst and imgSecond, you can also reference them as document.image("imgFirst") and document.image("imgSecond").

The *forms* Collection

Within the Document Object Model, the forms collection is special. Since the FORM is a container for other elements (like TEXT, INPUT, and SELECT controls), the forms collection has its own collection of elements. We have to be aware of this whenever we refer to a control element that resides in a FORM. If we have two FORMs in our document, the VBScript notation for the second element in the first FORM is document.forms(0).elements(1) and for the third element in the second FORM it's document.forms(1).elements(2). The JScript notations are document.forms[0].elements[1] and document.forms[1].elements[2].

Properties of the IE *document* Object

The document object has properties that provide a wealth of information about the document, as Table 12.18 shows.

TABLE 12.18: Properties of the IE document Object

Property	What It Does
activeElement	Returns the element that has the focus
alinkColor	Sets the color for the active link
bgColor	Provides the page's background color
body	Provides a reference to the BODY element
cookie	Returns the value of a cookie stored by the browser
domain	Gives the document's security domain
fgColor	Provides the color of the document's foreground text
lastModified	Gives the date the document was last modified
linkColor	Sets the color for unvisited links on the page
location	Provides a URL that references the document's location
parentWindow	Returns the parent window containing the document
readyState	Returns the state of a downloading object. Can be complete (when the object is completely loaded), interactive (when the object is not completely downloaded, but can be interacted with), loading (while the object is loading), or uninitialized (when the object is not created, usually during the download)
referrer	Provides the URL of the page that referenced the currently loaded page

TABLE 12.18 CONTINUED: Properties of the IE document Object

Property	What It Does
selection	Provides a reference to the document's selection object (See Skill 11)
title	Gives the document's title as defined in the TITLE element
URL	Gives the page's Uniform Resource Locator address
vlinkColor	Provides the color for the visited links on the page

Methods of the IE *document* Object

The methods of the document object allow you to manipulate the page, manipulate elements on the page, and find out information about commands. Table 12.19 summarizes these methods.

TABLE 12.19: Methods of the IE document object

Method	What It Does
clear	Clears the contents of a selection
close	Closes an output stream
createElement	Creates an instance of an element of a specified tag. This method only works for IMG and OPTION elements.
elementFromPoint	Returns the element for a specified x and y coordinate
execCommand	Executes a specified command over a given selection
open	Opens a new window and loads a document at a given URL
queryCommandEnabled	Returns whether a specified command is available
queryCommandIndeterm	Returns whether a specified command is in the indeterminate state
queryCommandState	Returns the current state of a specified command
queryCommandSupported	Returns whether a specified command is supported or not
queryCommandText	Returns a specified string (the short name of the command or the status bar message) if the command is supported
queryCommandValue	Returns a string representing the value of a specified command if the command is supported
write	Writes HTML and text to a document in the specified window
writeln	Same as write, and adds a carriage return

Events of the IE *document* Object

The document object supports a number of events, many of which you have already scripted in previous Skills. Table 12.20 shows these events.

TABLE 12.20:   Events of the IE document Object

Event	Fires...
onclick	When the user presses and releases the left mouse button
ondblclick	When the user presses and releases the left mouse button twice over an object
ondragstart	When the user first starts to drag a selection or a selected element
onerror	When an error occurs during the loading of an image or an object
onhelp	When the user presses F1 or clicks Help in the browser
onkeydown	When the user presses a key
onkeypress	When the user presses a key
onkeyup	When the user releases a key
onload	Immediately after the browser loads a specified object
onmousedown	When the user presses a button on the mouse
onmousemove	When the user moves the mouse
onmouseout	When the user moves the mouse-cursor out of an element
onmouseover	When the user moves the mouse into an element
onmouseup	When the user releases a mouse button
onreadystatechange	When the ready state for the document has changed
onselectstart	At the beginning of a user-intiated selection

The Navigator Document Object Model

As is the case with the other browser objects, the document objects differ between IE and Navigator, although they're both designed for the same purpose—to represent all the elements on a page. You'll see some commonalities along with the differences, however.

Skill 12

Arrays of the Navigator *document* Object

The Navigator document object uses arrays to organize its information.
Figure 12.6 shows these arrays, and Table 12.21 lists and describes them.

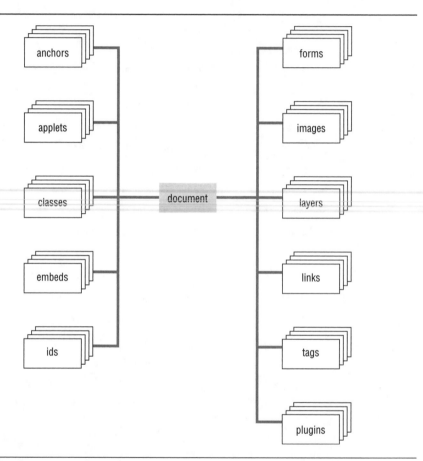

FIGURE 12.6: The Navigator document object organizes its information into arrays.

TABLE 12.21: Arrays of the Navigator document Object

Array	Is an Array of All the Document's...
anchors	Anchor (A) elements
applets	APPLET objects
classes	Style classes
embeds	EMBED elements and plug-ins
forms	FORM elements
ids	Individual element styles
images	IMG elements
layers	LAYER elements
links	Links and image-map <AREA> blocks
tags	Elements

As in IE, the Navigator document object has an array called plugins, an alias for the embeds array.

Working with Arrays

You work with arrays in Navigator the same way you work with collections in IE. You've already worked with Navigator document arrays in several Skills. In Skill 7, for example, you moved LAYER elements across a page in a demonstration of animation. This is the function that accomplished the movement:

```
function fingerMovement() {
    document.layers["layerFinger1"].offset(2,0);
    document.layers["layerFinger2"].offset(2,0);
    document.layers["layerFinger3"].offset(2,0);
    glblCounter = glblCounter + 1;
    if (glblCounter == 240) {
        glblCounter = 0;
        clearInterval(glblTimer);
        glblBackTimer = setInterval("backMovement()",100);
    }

}
```

You referred to each layer by name within the document.layers notation. You could have also used each one's index number like this:

```
document.layers[0].offset(2,0);
document.layers[1].offset(2,0);
document.layers[2].offset(2,0);
```

On the other hand, when you scripted some behaviors for LAYER elements in Skill 1, you were able to refer to each layer without having to use the layers array:

```
<FORM>
<INPUT Type = button Value = "Outward"
      onclick = "layerBox1.offset(-20,-20);
                  layerBox2.offset(20,-20);
                  layerBox3.offset(-20,20);
                  layerBox4.offset(20,20);">

<INPUT Type = button Value = "Inward"
      onclick = "layerBox1.moveTo(150,180);
                  layerBox2.moveTo(270,180);
                  layerBox3.moveTo(150,240);
                  layerBox4.moveTo(270,240);">

</FORM>
```

Why couldn't you refer to the layers that way in your script in Skill 7? In the code in Skill 1, the JavaScript for the onclick events is in the same namespace (i.e., in the same part of the document) as the indicated LAYER elements. In Skill 7, the code is in a different namespace—it's in a SCRIPT element.

An experiment will show you what I mean. Open your Skill 1 folder and make a copy of First Dynamic Nav.htm. Find the INPUT element whose Type is button and whose Value is "Inward". Move the code in the onclick event into a separate function inside a SCRIPT element:

```
function goInward() {
                  layerBox1.moveTo(150,180);
                  layerBox2.moveTo(270,180);
                  layerBox3.moveTo(150,240);
                  layerBox4.moveTo(270,240);
}
```

Now, change the code in the INPUT element to

```
onclick = goInward()
```

Open the page in Navigator, and you'll get the error message `layerBox1 is not defined` when you click the Inward button. Clicking the Outward button, however, does not give you this message. In fact, the Outward button works perfectly, and it refers to the same LAYERs as the Inward button.

Change the `goInward` function to

```
function goInward() {
            document.layers["layerBox1"].moveTo(150,180);
            document.layers["layerBox2"].moveTo(270,180);
            document.layers["layerBox3"].moveTo(150,240);
            document.layers["layerBox4"].moveTo(270,240);
}
```

and everything will work fine. Changing the function to

```
function goInward() {
            document.layers[4].moveTo(150,180);
            document.layers[5].moveTo(270,180);
            document.layers[6].moveTo(150,240);
            document.layers[7].moveTo(270,240);
}
```

will also work. The index numbers come from the positions of the `layers` in the file. These `layers` are the fifth through the eighth in the document.

The *forms* Array

As in IE, the `forms` array in the Document Object Model is special. A FORM is a container for other elements, and thus has its own array of `elements`. When we refer to a control within a FORM, we have to be aware of this. Repeating the example I used in the IE Document Object Model, if we have two FORMs in our document, the second element in the first form is `document.forms[0].elements[1]` and the third element in the second form is `document.forms[0].elements[2]`.

Properties of the Navigator *document* Object

Properties of the Navigator `document` object are similar to the properties of the IE `document` object. Table 12.22 presents these properties.

Skill 12

TABLE 12.22: Properties of the Navigator document Object

Property	What It Does
alinkColor	Sets the color for the active link
bgColor	Provides the page's background color
cookie	Returns the value of a cookie stored by the browser
domain	Gives the document's security domain
fgColor	Provides the color of the document's foreground text
lastModified	Gives the date the document was last modified
linkColor	Sets the color for unvisited links on the page
location	Provides a URL that references the document's location
referrer	Provides the URL of the page that referenced the currently loaded page
title	Gives the document's title as defined in the TITLE element
URL	Gives the page's Uniform Resource Locator address
vlinkColor	Provides the color for the visited links on the page

Methods of the Navigator *document* Object

The Navigator document object's methods enable you to manipulate the document and to work with Navigator's event capturing model. Table 12.23 presents the methods.

TABLE 12.23: Methods of the Navigator document Object

Method	What It Does
captureEvents	Indicates that the document should capture events of a specified type
close	Closes an output stream and updates the display
eval	Evaluates an object and returns a representation of its value
getSelection	Returns a string that contains the text of the current selection in the document
handleEvent	Activates the event handler of the object for a specified event

TABLE 12.23 CONTINUED: Methods of the Navigator document Object

Method	What It Does
open	Opens a new window and loads a document at a given URL
releaseEvents	Indicates that the document should stop capturing events of a specified type
routeEvent	Passes a captured event up through the event hierarchy
toString	Returns a string that contains an object's value
valueOf	Returns the primitive value of an object or the name of the object
write	Writes HTML and text to a document in the specified window
writeln	Same as write, and adds a carriage return

Events of the Navigator *document* Object

The events of the document object are either mouse-related or keyboard-related, as Table 12.24 shows.

TABLE 12.24:   Events of the Navigator document Object

Event	Fires When the User...
onClick	Presses and releases the left mouse button
onDblClick	Presses and releases the left mouse button twice over an object
onKeyDown	Presses a key
onKeyPress	Presses a key
onKeyUp	Releases a key
onMouseDown	Presses a button on the mouse
onMouseMove	Moves the mouse
onmouseUp	Releases a mouse button

Skill 12

Summary

Object models represent the objects that are at the foundation of Dynamic HTML in both Navigator and IE. Each browser's object model is a categorization scheme for referencing elements in an HTML document. Netscape was the first to introduce an object model into the browser world, adding one to Navigator 2.0. Microsoft soon followed suit, and now has an object model that includes every element on a Web page. Netscape's latest model encompasses only the major elements. Although the two browsers have different models (particularly with the way they deal with events, as discussed in Skill 6), the models share a fair amount of similarities.

Have You Mastered the Essentials?

Now you can...

- ☑ Understand the IE Window Object Model
- ☑ Understand the Navigator Window Object Model
- ☑ Work with the IE Document Object Model
- ☑ Work with the Navigator Document Object Model
- ☑ Be aware of the similarities and differences between the two browsers' models

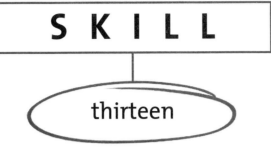

Working with VBScript

❑ Variables

❑ Arrays

❑ VBScript subtypes

❑ Operators

❑ Program flow

❑ Procedures

❑ Built-in functions

Throughout the Skills in this book, you've completed exercises in Visual Basic, Scripting Edition—better known as VBScript (or VBS). As a scripting language, VBScript is designed to work in the context of an HTML document.

As its name implies, VBScript is a subset of Microsoft's Visual Basic, a language that continues to grow in richness with each successive version. In IE 3.0, Microsoft introduced VBScript as an alternative to JavaScript. The Visual Basic syntax makes VBScript easy to learn and use, particularly if you have some Visual Basic in your background. At present, only IE supports VBScript. This situation may change, however, as future versions of Navigator may contain VBScript interpretation capabilities.

In this Skill, you'll learn and review important features of the VBScript language.

Variables

A variable is a placeholder for a value. As the word "variable" implies, this value can change. And one thing that a computer program often does is change the values in variables.

Although VBS is pretty flexible about variables—more so than most programming languages—here are some rules you must follow when you name them:

- The name must start with an alphabetic character. The rest of the name can contain any alphanumeric character, including the underscore (_).

- A period can't be part of a variable's name.

- A variable's name can't be longer than 255 characters. (You'll probably never have to worry about this one.)

- You can't have two local variables with the same name within the same subroutine, or two identically named global variables in the same HTML document.

With respect to variables, and everything else, VBScript is not case-sensitive. This is an important difference between VBScript and JavaScript. You might find that you make errors when you switch from VBScript to JavaScript because you're accustomed to VBS's case insensitivity.

Creating Variables

Use this statement to create a variable:

```
dim VariableName
```

The dim statement *declares* a variable. It tells the VBS interpreter to allocate space in your computer's memory to store that variable. You can use the dim statement to declare more than one variable at a time:

```
dim VariableName1, VariableName2, VariableName3
```

This way of creating variables is called *explicit*. Use the dim statement inside a subroutine or a function and you explicitly create a local variable. Use the dim statement outside a subroutine or a function, but inside a SCRIPT element, and you explicitly create a global variable.

VBS also has an *implicit* method for creating variables. In this method, you don't use dim to declare a variable before you use it for the first time in your script—you just go ahead and use the variable. The VBS interpreter is smart enough to know that you've created a variable.

You can force explicit declaration within a script. To do that, use the statement

```
Option Explicit
```

and be sure to position it before any functions or subroutines. If you use Option Explicit, you have to use a dim statement to declare every variable.

Why would you want to make explicit declaration compulsory, when it's so easy to just create a variable as you need it? Suppose explicit declaration isn't compulsory. If you misspell an implicitly created variable name, the interpreter thinks you want to declare a new variable (whose name is the misspelled name), and your script continues merrily on with unpredictable results. Under the compulsory method, this can't happen—VBS would give you an error message.

Creating Arrays

Sometimes you want to be able to refer to a collection of items that are similar in some way, and you'd like to be able to refer to them as "the first one," "the second one," and so forth, without having to give them unique names. The *array* is the structure that accomplishes this.

Simple Arrays

Suppose you have an array called SportNames that holds the names of sports in this order: "Baseball," "Basketball," "Bowling," "Football," "Hockey," "Soccer," and "Track." To help you understand the idea of an array, I've put this array into Table 13.1. As you can see, the index corresponds to the row, and we begin numbering indexes from 0 rather than from 1. This is called *zero-based indexing*.

TABLE 13.1: The SportNames Array

Index	Sport
0	"Baseball"
1	"Basketball"
2	"Bowling"
3	"Football"
4	"Hockey"
5	"Soccer"
6	"Track"

We can use this array to refer to "Baseball" as SportNames(0) and to "Football" as SportNames(3). In VBS, we would create this array with the statement

```
dim SportNames(6)
```

In the context of a Web page, we could put values into the array as part of a window onload event with these statements:

```
SportNames(0) = "Baseball"
SportNames(1) = "Basketball"
SportNames(2) = "Bowling"
SportNames(3) = "Football"
SportNames(4) = "Hockey"
SportNames(5) = "Soccer"
SportNames(6) = "Track"
```

Complex Arrays

Suppose we want to add a column to the table—a column that denotes whether the sport is in the Olympics. Table 13.2 shows the layout.

TABLE 13.2: Expanding the SportNames Table

Index	Sport	Olympic Sport?
0	"Baseball"	Yes
1	"Basketball"	Yes
2	"Bowling"	No
3	"Football"	No
4	"Hockey"	Yes
5	"Soccer"	Yes
6	"Track"	Yes

We can represent this kind of table in a *multidimensional* array.

We would declare a multidimensional array in a dim statement by stating the number of rows minus one, as before, and the number of columns minus one (the number of columns is two; the column that holds the index doesn't count):

```
dim Sportnames(6,1)
```

Now we would refer to "Football" as SportNames(3,0). The information in the next column in this row— SportNames(3,1)— tells us whether "Football" is an Olympic sport.

NOTE   We used multidimensional arrays in Skill 9 when we created the peg solitaire game: glblBoardArray and glblDivArray each had seven rows and seven columns.

Dynamic Arrays

VBS allows you to create an array even if you don't know how many items you're going to store in it when you get started. When you do this, you're creating a *dynamic array*. (That word "dynamic" shows up a lot, doesn't it?) Events that take place in your script can then set the size.

Here's how you create a dynamic array:

```
dim SportNames()
```

Suppose a user let you know, via a dialog or other selection mechanism, that he or she wanted to enter the names of ten sports into the array. You would use the VBS redim statement to set the number of items:

```
redim SportNames(9)
```

Beware that when you use redim, it erases the existing contents of an array unless you include the VBScript keyword preserve in the statement:

```
redim preserve SportNames(9)
```

With multidimensional arrays, the preserve keyword comes with a couple of caveats: You can resize only the last dimension and still preserve the array's contents, and you can't change the number of dimensions in the array.

Subtypes

Different kinds of values can live in variables, and VBS is flexible in this regard. Its variable type, *variant*, can hold any kind of data. Since the variant is VBS' only data type, the different "kinds" of data are *subtypes*.

The upside of the flexibility that the variant provides is that you don't have to prepare a variable in advance to hold a particular subtype. On the other hand, you often have to check or convert the subtype in a variable to insure that your script runs properly: End users are capable of all kinds of input errors, and some of these errors may result in the wrong kind of data in a variable.

Fortunately, VBS has a number of functions that help you check the type of data in a variable. One, VarType, takes the variable's name as its argument and returns a number that indicates the subtype of data currently stored in that variable. For example,

```
VarType(IntegerVariable)
```

returns 2.

Table 13.3 shows variant subtypes, describes each subtype, and presents the numerical value that VarType returns for each subtype.

NOTE   When its argument is an array, VarType always adds 8192 to another of its possible values to indicate the type of array. An array which holds integers, then, would return 8192 + 2, or 8194.

TABLE 13.3: VBS Subtypes and the Value That VarType Returns for Each

Subtype	What It Is	VarType Returns:
Array	A collection of items named by a single variable and referred to by a numerical index	8192
Boolean	Either True (–1) or False (0)	11
Byte	An integer between 0 and 255	17
Currency	–922,337,203,685,477.5808 to 922,337,203,685,477.5807	6
Date/Time	A date/time value. Permissible dates start at January 1, 100 and end at December 31, 9999.	7
Double	A double precision floating-point number	5
Empty	Indicates an uninitialized variable or a string of zero length	0
Integer	An integer between –32768 and 32767	2
Long Integer	An integer between –2,147,483,648 and 2,147,483,647	3
Null	Indicates that a variable has been assigned a Null value (the variable contains no valid data)	1
Object	An instance of an object (like an ActiveX control)	9
Single	A single precision floating-point number	4
String	A string enclosed in quotes (e.g. "I'm a string")	8

Skill 13

VBS has similar functions that test for other subtypes. Table 13.4 lists these functions.

TABLE 13.4:   VBS Functions That Test for Subtypes

Function	Returns True If Its Argument...
IsNumeric	Is a numerical value
IsDate	Is a valid date (2/31/97, for example, is not a valid date)
IsEmpty	Has never been assigned a value
IsNull	Has been assigned Null as its value. Assigning Null gets rid of the variable's contents without getting rid of the variable.
IsObject	Is an object
IsArray	Is an array

Assigning Values to Variables

We've done this so often it should be second nature by now. To assign a value to a variable, use an equal sign:

```
VariableName = Value
```

In VBS, we can update the value of a variable by adding a number:

```
VariableName = VariableName + 30
```

We can also update a variable by adding the value of another variable:

```
VariableName1 = VariableName1 + VariableName2
```

VBS has a special case regarding assignment. When the value you're assigning to a variable is an object, as in Skill 6, VBS requires that your assignment statement look like this:

```
set VariableName = objectName
```

Operators

VBS has a variety of *operators*—symbols that perform *operations* on other symbols. The plus sign (+) is an operator that adds two numbers together. As you've already seen, the ampersand sign (&) is an operator that concatenates two strings together.

VBS has three kinds of operators—comparison, logical, and arithmetic. The comparison operators appear in Table 13.5, the logical operators in Table 13.6, and the arithmetic operators in Table 13.7.

TABLE 13.5: The VBS Comparison Operators

Operator	Name
=	Equality
<>	Inequality
<	Less than
>	Greater than
<=	Less than or equal to
=>	Greater than or equal to
Is	Equivalence (two variables refer to the same object)

TABLE 13.6: VBS Logical Operators

Operator	Name
Not	Negation
And	Conjunction
Or	Disjunction
XOr	Exclusion
Eqv	Equivalence
Imp	Implication

TABLE 13.7: VBS Arithmetic Operators

Operator	Name
^	Exponentiation
–	Negation
*	Multiplication
/	Division
\	Integer Division
Mod	Modulus
+	Addition
–	Subtraction
&	String Concatenation

Of the operators in Table 13.7, Mod might be the least familiar, although we used it in Skill 9 to help us with the peg solitaire game. This one handles *Modulus Arithmetic*, a term which might be even less familiar to you. All this operator does is divide one integer by another and return the remainder. If the numbers aren't integers, it rounds them before dividing. So

```
Answer = 59 Mod 7.8
```

assigns 3 as the value for the variable Answer.

The Integer Division operator is the opposite. Denoted by \, this operator returns the integer part of a division rather than the remainder.

The concatenation operator, &, is one that we've used throughout the book. We used it to build strings that we put into text areas, as in Skill 9 when we examined dragging and dropping:

```
frmText.textAreaEventInfo.Value = "Source Element: " &
➥ window.event.srcelement.id & chr(13) _
    & "OffsetLeft: " & glblSelectedObject.offsetLeft & chr(13) _
    & "OffsetTop: " & glblSelectedObject.offsetTop & chr(13) _
    & "OffsetX: " & window.event.offsetx & chr(13) _
    & "OffsetY: " & window.event.offsety & chr(13) _
    & "screenX: " & window.event.screenx & chr(13) _
    & "screenY: " & window.event.screeny & chr(13) _
    & "X: " & window.event.x & chr(13) _
    & "Y: " & window.event.y & chr(13) _
    & "distanceX :" & distanceX & chr(13) _
    & "distanceY :" & distanceY & chr(13) _
    & "glblCurrentX: " & glblCurrentX & chr(13) _
    & "glblCurrentY: " & glblCurrentY

end sub
```

Program Flow

One of the hallmarks of any programming language is the ability to choose an alternative when a program comes to a decision point. VBS gives you several ways to do this, as you've already seen. Each method is called a *control structure*.

Select Case

The Select Case statement, which you worked with in Skill 10, enables your program to perform a test, and then based on the result, pick one of several possible paths, called *cases*. Within each path, you can have a number of lines of code. When the program finishes going through the code for that path, your program exits the Select Case. Imagine a variable called TestVariable with the possible values of 1, 2, 3, or 4. The Select Case would look like this:

```
Select Case TestVariable
    Case 1
        Statement 1
        Statement 2
        Statement 3
    Case 2
        Statement 1
        Statement 2
    Case 3
        Statement 1
        Statement 2
        Statement 3
        Statement 4
    Case 4
        Statement 1
    Case Else
        Statement 1
        Statement 2
End Select
```

Note the final case, Case Else, which executes if TestVariable doesn't contain 1, 2, 3, or 4.

While the indents aren't necessary, they make the code easy to read. The End Select *is* necessary.

The Select Case is particularly useful when used in conjunction with the IE event model. In Skill 11, for example, we developed this event-handler for a page with four buttons:

```
sub document_onclick

    Select Case window.event.srcElement.id

        Case "buttonReset"
            call glblRange.expand("textedit")
            textAreaRangeTracker.Value = ""
            glblResetFlag = 1

        Case "buttonMove"
            call glblRange.move("word",1)

        Case "buttonBookmark"

            glblMark = glblRange.getbookmark
```

```
        Case "buttonMoveToBookmark"
                if glblMark <> empty then
                        call glblRange.moveToBookmark(glblMark)
                end if

        Case else
                exit sub
    End Select

        .
        .
        .

    end sub
```

The event-handler is at the document level, and the test expression is the id of the source element in the document from which the onclick event bubbles up. The Cases specify different actions for each source element. In this way, the Select Case enables us to write just one event-handler for the document, rather than a separate event-handler for each button.

If...Then

When your program has to make a decision that doesn't have so many alternatives, If...Then is often appropriate. The format for If...Then is

```
If condition = True Then
    Statement 1
    Statement 2
    Statement 3
        .
        .
        .
End If
```

As in the Select Case, the indents make the code easier to read, and the End If is necessary. It's also important to position Then at the end of the line that starts with If.

Another way to write the first line is

```
If condition Then
```

VBS knows enough to check if the condition is True.

You can also have an If...Then start off with the condition being False:

```
If condition = False Then
    Statement 1
    Statement 2
    Statement 3
        .
        .
        .
End If
```

The alternative way to write the first line is

```
If Not condition Then
```

If...Then...Else

The If...Then structure is simple and straightforward, but it leaves a bit to be desired. It tells the program what to do if a condition is True, but what if the condition is False? As we've seen, you could write a whole additional If...Then starting with the condition being False, but it seems inefficient to have to set up everything all over again.

Here's where If...Then...Else comes in handy. Its format is

```
If condition Then
    Statement 1
    Statement 2
    Statement 3
Else
    Statement 4
    Statement 5
    Statement 6
    Statement 7
End If
```

Making Code Repeat

Another mainstay of programming languages is their ability to make portions of code execute repeatedly.

VBS has two ways of doing this:

- Do...Loop

- For...Next

Do...Loop

To repeat code, you can put it between a Do statement and a Loop statement:

```
Do
    Statement 1
    Statement 2
    Statement 3
Loop
```

The Do statement puts things into motion. The Loop statement sends the flow back to Do and everything begins again. But something's missing—how does this structure know when to stop?

Four alternatives are available: Two involve putting a condition on the line with the Do statement and two involve putting a condition on the line with the Loop statement. Let's start with the Do statement.

A Do While...Loop keeps repeating while a condition is True. Here's an example:

```
y = 14
Do While y < 30
    y = y + 2
Loop
```

A Do Until...Loop executes until a condition is True:

```
y = 14
Do Until y = 30
    y = y + 2
Loop
```

Now let's look at the Loop statement. You can put either While or Until on the same line as Loop. The Do...Loop While looks like this:

```
y = 14
Do
    y = y + 2
Loop While y < 30
```

The Do...Loop Until is

```
y = 14
Do
    y = y + 2
Loop Until y = 30
```

You put `While` or `Until` on the line with `Loop` if you want to be sure that the code executes at least once. You put `While` or `Until` on the line with `Do` if you want to be sure that the code never gets to run if the condition is `True`.

For...Next

With the `For...Next` structure, you explicitly set the lower bound and the upper bound of a variable that counts the number of times the code repeats. When the counter gets to the upper bound, the code stops repeating:

```
For y = 1 to 30
    Statement 1
    Statement 2
    Statement 3
Next
```

In these lines of code, the counter increases by one each time the loop completes. You can change that by using the `Step` statement. In the following example, the counter variable increases by 2 each time the loop completes:

```
For y = 1 to 30 Step 2
    Statement 1
    Statement 2
    Statement 3
Next
```

You can even make the counter go backward:

```
For y = 30 to 1 Step -3
    Statement 1
    Statement 2
    Statement 3
Next
```

A *For...Next* for Arrays and Collections

VBScript has a special type of `For...Next` loop for dealing with the elements in arrays and collections: `For Each...Next`. It looks like this:

```
For Each Index in ArrayName
    Statement 1
    Statement 2
    Statement 3
Next
```

You'll work with this one in Skill 15.

Procedures

Procedures in VBS are either subroutines or functions. The VBS syntax for procedures specifies that a line of code cannot continue into the next physical line in the text editor unless you provide a continuation character. In VBScript, the continuation character is an underscore preceded by a space. (As you've seen, JavaScript code can span more than one line without a continuation character.)

In addition to subroutines and functions that you design and build, VBS has a number of important functions built right into the language, which we examine in this section.

Subroutines

You've been writing subroutines throughout all the Skills. They all followed this format:

```
Sub Name(0 or more arguments)
    ...Code statements...
End Sub
```

In an event-handler, the Name is the ID of an element within the HTML document, followed by an underscore, followed by the name of an event. In VBScript, once you assign an ID to an element, you can use it throughout the script.

A subroutine may have zero or more arguments inside parentheses that immediately follow its name. Each subroutine is a piece of code that you can call from anywhere in the script. If the subroutine has no arguments, VBScript lets you omit the parentheses.

VBScript gives you two ways to call a subroutine within your script. One way is to include the parentheses around the arguments. If you use this method, you have to precede the subroutine name with Call. You can also omit the parentheses. If you do, you don't include Call in the calling statement. These two statements are equivalent:

```
Call Msgbox("This is a message",, "This is a title")

Msgbox "This is a message",, "This is a title"
```

Functions

Unlike a subroutine, a function returns a value. Its format is

```
Function Name(0 or more arguments)
        Name = Code statements
End Sub
```

The important point here is that you must set a value for the name of the function before the function finishes.

Here's an example. This function converts inches to centimeters:

```
Function In_to_Cm(Inches)
     In_to_Cm = 2.54 * Inches
End Function
```

This definition tells you that `In_to_Cm` does its computation on a numerical value for the argument `Inches`. Then, it stores the result of that computation in the name `In_to_Cm`. This enables you to call `In_to_Cm` in a script.

Within a script, you'd call `In_to_Cm` like this:

```
sngLengthConvert = In_to_Cm(75)
```

When the function finishes its work, `190.5` is the value of `sngLengthConvert`.

Consider the variable name `sngLengthConvert`. I've used two helpful techniques in naming this variable. The first is to use both uppercase and lowercase letters to make the name readable. The second is to put a three-letter lowercase prefix at the beginning. This prefix tells you the subtype of the variable. (This one stands for *single-precision floating point*.) While it's true that the variant type allows all kinds of variables, you usually know how you'll use a variable in your script. To construct a prefix, use the first three consonants of the variable's subtype. (If the subtype begins with a vowel, like `integer`, use that vowel as the first letter in the prefix.). If the variable will take more than one subtype as the script runs, the single letter v—for Variant—is a helpful prefix.

Built-in Functions

VBS has more than 80 built-in functions. You can use them as building-blocks in your scripts. We won't describe or even list them all here, but we'll tell you about a few of the ones you might find most useful.

String Functions

VBS gives you a complete set of functions for working with strings. You can use them to take apart string input from a user, to reformat a string, and to manipulate output that you want a user to see. Table 13.8 gives you the string manipulation functions.

TABLE 13.8: VBS String Manipulation Functions

Function	What It Does
Trim("String")	Removes all leading and trailing blank spaces from "String"
LTrim("String")	Removes all leading (left-most) blank spaces
RTrim("String")	Removes all trailing (right-most) blank spaces
Len("String")	Returns the number of characters in "String"
Left("String", x)	Returns the left-most x characters
Right("String", x)	Returns the right-most x characters
Mid("String", StartPosition, Length)	Returns Length characters, beginning with StartPosition
UCase("String")	Makes all the characters UPPERCASE
LCase("String")	Makes all the characters lowercase
InStr("String", Target)	Checks to see if Target is in "String". If it is, this function returns Target's position. If not, it returns 0.
String(Number,Character)	Returns a repeating string of Character of the length specified by Number
StrReverse(StringExpression)	Returns the characters in StringExpression in reverse order
StrComp(StringExpression1, StringExpression2)	Returns the result of a comparison between the two arguments. An optional third argument specifies the nature of the comparison.

In Skill 1, we used InStr and Left in the definition of our MoveElementBy subroutine.

Another important related function is Chr(), which we've been using as Chr(13) to generate a newline character. The argument for this function is a character code. That code assigns a unique number to every lowercase letter, uppercase letter, number, symbol, and for most keys on your keyboard. The Chr function returns the character associated with the code value in its argument.

VBScript also provides a function for going in the reverse direction: Asc() takes a character as its argument and returns the corresponding character code.

Message Boxes

Still another important string-related function is MsgBox, which we've used frequently throughout the book. We've used it as a subroutine because we haven't asked it to return a value.

As you know by now, a Message Box presents a message and waits for a user response. Here is a Message Box with three arguments:

```
MsgBox(prompt, buttons, title)
```

You can create some elaborate Message Boxes because

- prompt is the string expression that appears in the Message Box
- buttons is a numeric expression that specifies the number and type of buttons in the display, the type of icons in the Message Box, which button is the default button, and the *modality* of the Message Box. ("Modality" indicates the extent of operations that are suspended until the user responds to the Message Box.)
- title is the string expression that appears in the Message Box's title bar

The buttons argument has a number of possibilities. Table 13.9 shows what you can do.

TABLE 13.9: Message Box Button Settings

Value	What It Does
0	Displays OK button only
1	Displays OK and Cancel
2	Displays Abort, Retry, and Ignore
3	Displays Yes, No, and Cancel
4	Displays Yes and No buttons
5	Displays Retry and Cancel
16	Displays Critical Message icon
32	Displays Warning Query icon
48	Displays Warning Message icon
64	Displays Information Message icon
256	Makes second button the default
512	Makes third button the default
768	Makes fourth button the default
4096	Makes the modality system-wide; suspends all applications until the user responds to the Message Box

You can use combinations of these values. For example, if you set `MsgBox`'s second argument to 2 + 64 (don't add them together), you'll display a Message Box that has three buttons (`Abort`, `Retry`, and `Ignore`) and an information symbol.

The `MsgBox` function truly acts like a function when you ask it to return a value, and you do that when you're interested in which Message Box button a user clicked. Here's how you might code this:

```
intReturnCode = MsgBox("A three-button Message Box", 2)
```

Since many button displays are possible, many responses are possible. Table 13.10 shows the Message Box response settings.

TABLE 13.10: Message Box Response Settings

Value	Indicates That the User Pressed...
1	OK
2	Cancel
3	Abort
4	Retry
5	Ignore
6	Yes
7	No

Math Functions

Sometimes it's helpful to perform calculations on user input, or to get date and time information. VBS helps you with a rich set of built-in mathematical functions, as shown in Table 13.11.

TABLE 13.11: VBS Built-in Math Functions

Function	Returns...
Abs(number)	The absolute value of number
Atn(number)	The angle, in radians, whose Tangent is number
Cos(number)	The cosine of an angle of number radians
Date	The current system date

TABLE 13.11 CONTINUED: VBS Built-in Math Functions

Function	Returns...
Exp(number)	*E* (the base of natural logarithms) raised to the power indicated by number
Fix(number)	The integer part of number, and eliminates the fractional part. If number is negative, Fix returns the first integer greater than or equal to number.
Hex(number)	A string that represents the hexadecimal equivalent of number. If number isn't a whole number, it's rounded off before Hex evaluates it.
Int(number)	The integer part of number and eliminates the fractional part. If number is negative, Int returns the first integer less than or equal to number.
Log(number)	The natural logarithm of number
Now	The user's system's date and time settings
Oct(number)	A string that represents the octal value of number. If number isn't a whole number, it's rounded off before Oct evaluates it.
Rnd(number)	A random number between 0 and 1. number is optional. If it's less than 0, Rnd uses the same *seed* (the number that starts the randomization process) each successive time you run it. If number is greater than 0 (or not supplied), Rnd uses the next random number as its seed. If number is 0, the seed is the most recently generated random number.
Sgn(number)	1 if number is greater than 0; returns 0 if number is equal to 0; returns –1 if number is less than 0.
Sin(number)	The sine of an angle of number radians
Sqr(number)	The square root of number. number must be greater than or equal to zero.
Tan(number)	The tangent of an angle of number radians
Time	A variant (whose subtype is date) that shows the current system time

If you don't have a specific use for any of these math functions at the moment, it might be difficult to see how and why you would use them. Just be aware of them. As you become more experienced with Web page design, you'll undoubtedly discover uses for some of these functions.

Conversion Functions

VBScript provides a set of functions for converting expressions or variables to specified subtypes. Table 13.12 presents these functions.

TABLE 13.12: VBS Built-in Conversion Functions

Function	Returns an Expression That Has Been Converted to a Variant of Subtype...
CBool(*expression*)	Boolean
CByte(*expression*)	Byte
CCur(*expression*)	Currency
CDate(*expression*)	Date
CDbl(*expression*)	Double
CInt(*expression*)	Integer
CLng(*expression*)	Long

In Skill 1, we used CInt along with two other built-in functions (InStr and Left) when we converted a string value from a style specification into a number. We then used that number as an argument for our MoveElementBy subroutine.

Summary

VBS is a very rich scripting language. It provides a wealth of control structures, operators, built-in functions, and flexibility. You can use these features to build useful procedures. If you have some Visual Basic in your background, it's an easy language to learn. If not, you'll still find the syntax easy to pick up and become productive with.

 NOTE   For a tutorial and documentation on VBScript, visit http://www.microsoft.com/vbscript.

Have You Mastered the Essentials?

Now you can...

- ☑ Understand the ideas behind VBScript variables and subtypes
- ☑ Work with arrays, including multidimensional arrays and dynamic arrays
- ☑ Use VBScript structures that control program flow and iteration
- ☑ Understand how to create functions and be aware of VBScript's built-in functions for string-manipulation, math, and subtype conversion

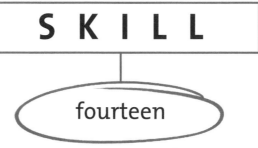

14

Working with JavaScript

❏ Variables

❏ Arrays

❏ Operators

❏ Program flow

❏ Functions

❏ Built-in functions

JavaScript started as "LiveScript," a scripting language that Netscape developed. Independently, Sun Microsystems had developed Java, formerly "Oak," as a language to control consumer electronic devices. Because of its power and efficiency, Java found a home on the Internet as a language for small programs called "applets."

Along the way, Netscape and Sun joined forces and turned LiveScript, later named "LiveWire," into a subset of Java. Ultimately, Netscape changed the name to JavaScript and the rest is history. JavaScript resembles Java syntactically, but as a scripting language, it's interpreted, as is VBS, rather than compiled, as is Java.

In its effort to gain a firm foothold on the Web, Microsoft developed its own flavor of JavaScript, and called it JScript. Microsoft's implementation has a few enhancements designed to take advantage of IE.

JavaScript Syntax

As you've certainly noticed in the Skills thus far, JavaScript syntax differs from VBScript syntax. In JavaScript, a line ends with a semicolon. Thus, JavaScript has no need for a continuation character: Until it encounters a semicolon, the JavaScript interpreter considers everything to be part of one line.

Here's another difference. A procedure in VBScript is either a function, if it returns a value, or a subroutine, if it doesn't. In JavaScript, every procedure is a function, whether it returns a value or not. In a JavaScript function, curly brackets surround the code. The left curly bracket follows the function's argument list, and the right curly bracket is the last character in the function. You've seen functions before, but for completeness, here's what the format looks like:

```
function functionName(argument1, argument2) {
    statement 1;
    statement 2;
          .
          .
          .
    statement n;
}
```

One other difference is crucial. If you're used to programming in VBScript, you've probably adopted a loose outlook about uppercase and lowercase letters.

VBScript is *case-insensitive*, meaning that "a" and "A" are equivalent. JavaScript, however, is *case-sensitive*, so that "a" and "A" are most decidedly not the same.

Comments in VBScript begin with an apostrophe. In JavaScript, you indicate a one-line comment by two slashes: //. JavaScript ignores anything on the same line that follows the two slashes. You can have a comment that spans more than one line. A multiline comment begins with /* and ends with */.

Variables

Throughout our discussion, we've used variables in our JavaScript functions. In this section, we'll cover them in more detail.

Here are some rules to follow when you name variables in JavaScript:

- The name must start with an alphabetic character (a-z or A-Z) or an underscore (_).

- The rest of the name can contain any letter, any digit, or an underscore.

- A variable's name can't contain a space.

- Avoid JavaScript *reserved words* as the names of variables.

A Word about Reserved Words

A reserved word is a word set aside for a particular purpose. Some reserved words are terms in JavaScript, others are terms in Java. Here they are:

abstract	else	if	new	static	try
boolean	extends	implements	null	super	typeof
break	false	import	package	switch	var
byte	final	in	private	synchronized	void
case	finally	instanceof	protected	this	while
catch	float	int	public	throw	with
char	for	interface	reset	throws	
do	function	long	return	transient	
double	goto	native	short	true	

The names of built-in functions and objects are also reserved.

Creating Variables

JavaScript programmers typically use variables without declaring them, although strictly speaking this isn't good programming practice. If you want to declare a variable explicitly, use `var`. This reserved word is the equivalent of the VBS `dim` statement. As in VBS, explicit declaration helps avoid conflicts in variable creation.

You used `var` in, among other places, Skill 7, when you declared variables in a script for animation:

```
var glblTimer;
var glblAnimationStartedFlag = 0;
```

As you can see, two uses of `var` are possible. One declares the variable, the other declares the variable and sets an initial value.

Notice also the `glbl` prefix. I use it to indicate that a variable's scope is global. Functions throughout a `SCRIPT` element can refer to a global variable. To make a variable global, you declare it prior to any function. A local variable, on the other hand, is created inside the body of a function, and only that function can refer to it.

To shorten the number of lines in your script, JavaScript allows you to declare more than one variable with a single `var` statement:

```
var x, y, z;
```

Variable Types

Because JavaScript is a *loosely typed* language, you don't have to specify the type of data a JavaScript variable will hold when you declare it.

JavaScript has three types of variables:

- Numeric variables—contain numbers (e.g., `var numberOfWords = 78`)

- String variables—contain text between quotation marks (e.g., `var myName = "Joseph"`)

- Boolean variables—contain logical statements (e.g., `true` or `false`)

JavaScript treats the reserved word `null` as an "empty" variable.

When you put some data into a variable, in effect you define it to be a numeric, a string, or a boolean.

In a script, you can put different types of data into a variable at different times, thus changing that variable's sub-type. You have to be careful when you do this, however, because you can get unexpected results. Here's an example:

```
var numFirst = 17;
var numSecond = 76;
var numSum;
numSum = numFirst + numSecond;
```

These lines of code result in 93 as the value for numSum. If you keep the value of numSecond as is, and change the type of numFirst to a string, however,

```
varNumFirst = "17";
```

then

```
numSum = numFirst + numSecond;
```

gives the string "1776" as the value for numSum. Why? That last expression for numSum now sees the string "17" as the value for numFirst and automatically turns numSecond into the string "76". In that context, the +, which added the two numbers together in the first numSum expression, becomes the concatenation operator you used in previous Skills.

NOTE   typeof() is a useful function built into JavaScript. It returns a string indicating its argument's type.

A Word about Numbers

You'll recall that VBScript has types of numerical variables. JavaScript, on the other hand, has one—the numeric. This type holds both integers and floating point numbers. The numbers can be in scientific notation, like 8.765e15 or 6.54e-19. Numbers can also be octal (base 8) or hexadecimal (base 16). If the JavaScript interpreter encounters a number with a leading 0, it interprets it as a base 8 number. If the interpreter encounters a number with a leading 0 followed by an x, it interprets it as a hexadecimal.

A Word about Strings

Inside a string, you can place special characters that tell the JavaScript interpreter to perform specific actions or to interpret a character in a special way. For example, when you added a long string to a text area in Skill 6, you did it like this:

```
function info(event){
textArea = document.forms[0].elements["textareaEventInfo"];
textArea.value = "target: " + event.target.name + "\n"
    + "which: " + event.which + "\n"
    + "modifiers: " + event.modifiers + "\n"
    + "type: " + event.type + "\n"
    + "screenX: " + event.screenX + "\n"
    + "screenY: " + event.screenY + "\n"
    + "pageX: " + event.pageX + "\n"
    + "pageY: " + event.pageY;
}
```

The special character here is "\n", which tells the interpreter to move to the next line in the text area before displaying the next part of the string.

The backslash is the signal for the advent of a special character. Sometimes the backslash indicates that a punctuation mark used for one purpose should be interpreted another way. For example, if you want to include a double-quote as part of a string (and not as the beginning or end of a string), precede it with a backslash. Table 14.1 shows the JavaScript special characters.

T A B L E   1 4 . 1 :   JavaScript Special Characters

Symbol	What it is
\\	Backslash
\'	Single quote
\"	Double quote
\b	Backspace
\f	Form feed
\n	New line
\r	Carriage return
\t	Tab

Creating Objects

JavaScript enables you to create new objects. You use the reserved word new to do this. The format is

```
var variableName = new ClassName;
```

This tells the JavaScript interpreter that you're creating a new instance of ClassName and you're calling it variableName. In JavaScript, strings, numbers, and arrays are objects. When you create a new instance of one of these types, as in

```
var stringName = new String("DHTML Master the Essentials");
```

it's the same as

```
var stringName = "DHTML Master the Essentials";
```

Sometimes you have no choice but to use new, as in the next section.

Creating Arrays

As I mentioned in Skill 13, sometimes you want to refer to a set of items that are similar in some way, and you'd like to be able to refer to them as "the first one," "the second one," and so forth, without giving each one a unique name. In these cases, the *array* is the appropriate structure to use.

Simple Arrays

Let's use the array from Skill 13 and show how JavaScript handles it. The array, called SportNames, holds the names of sports in this order: "Baseball," "Basketball," "Bowling," "Football," "Hockey," "Soccer," and "Track." I've put this array into Table 14.2. As you can see, the index corresponds to the row, and we begin numbering indices from 0 rather than from 1 (this, you'll remember, is called *zero-based indexing*).

TABLE 14.2: The SportNames Array

Index	Sport
0	"Baseball"
1	"Basketball"
2	"Bowling"
3	"Football"
4	"Hockey"
5	"Soccer"
6	"Track"

 NOTE In JavaScript 1.0, position 0 holds the length of the array, and the first item goes into position 1. In JavaScript 1.1 (and later) and in JScript, you put the first item in position 0.

With this array, we refer to "Baseball" as sportNames[0] and to "Football" as SportNames[3]. (Note the use of square brackets, rather than parentheses, as in VBScript.)

In JavaScript (beginning with version 1.1), an array is an object. Every array is an instance of the Array class. As you saw in the preceding section, you use the reserved word new to create a new instance of a class. Thus, we would create the SportNames array object with the statement

```
var sportNames = new Array(7);
```

 NOTE It's customary in JavaScript to begin object names with lowercase letters.

This code would create the array and insert the items:

```
var sportNames = new Array(7);
sportNames[0] = "Baseball"
sportNames[1] = "Basketball"
sportNames[2] = "Bowling"
sportNames[3] = "Football"
sportNames[4] = "Hockey"
sportNames[5] = "Soccer"
sportNames[6] = "Track"
```

JavaScript's built-in `Array` object gives you another way to initialize an array:

```
var sportNames = new Array("Baseball", "Basketball", "Bowling",
"Football", "Hockey", "Soccer", "Track");
```

It also gives you another way to refer to an array-item. These two expressions

```
sportNames[3]
sportNames["Football"]
```

are equivalent. With a string index, as in the second expression, the array-item becomes a property of the `SportNames` object. So the statement

```
sportNames.Football
```

is equivalent to the other two. This statement, however,

```
sportNames.3
```

generates an error.

Complex Arrays

To carry our example forward, suppose we add a column to the table—a column, as in Skill 13, that denotes whether or not the sport is in the Olympics. Table 14.3 shows the layout.

TABLE 14.3:   Expanding the SportNames Table

Index	Sport	Olympic Sport?
0	"Baseball"	Yes
1	"Basketball"	Yes
2	"Bowling"	No
3	"Football"	No
4	"Hockey"	Yes
5	"Soccer"	Yes
6	"Track"	Yes

We can represent this kind of table in a *multidimensional* array.

Skill 14

A JavaScript multidimensional array is an array of arrays. To make a two-dimensional array out of Table 14.3, we can consider each row as an array, and then combine those arrays into another array:

```
var baseball = new Array("Baseball", "Yes");
var basketball = new Array("Basketball", "Yes");
var bowling = new Array("Bowling", "No");
var football = new Array("Football", "No");
var hockey = new Array("Hockey", "Yes");
var soccer = new Array("Soccer", "Yes");
var track = new Array("Track", "Yes");
var sportNames = new Array(baseball, basketball, bowling, basketball,
bowling, football, hockey, soccer, track);
```

In this array, you'd refer to "Bowling" as sportNames[2][0]. Note the syntax of the two sets of brackets. The statement sportNames[2,0] generates an error.

Array Methods

The Array object provides three methods:

- join(separator)—returns a string that holds all the array-items, with the value of separator as the separator between consecutive elements

- reverse()—reverses the order of the array-items

- sort()—sorts the array-items

JavaScript Operators

JavaScript contains a full set of operators for comparisons, for logical operations, and for arithmetic. Table 14.4 shows the comparison operators.

TABLE 14.4: The JavaScript Comparison Operators

Operator	Name
==	Equality
!=	Inequality
<	Less Than
>	Greater Than
<=	Less Than Or Equal To
=>	Greater Than Or Equal To

Notice that the Equality comparison operator (==) is different from the symbol (=) that assigns a value to a variable. Table 14.5 presents the JavaScript logical operators, and Table 14.6 presents the arithmetic operators.

T A B L E   1 4 . 5 :   JavaScript Logical Operators

Operator	What It Means
!	NOT
&&	AND
||	OR

T A B L E   1 4 . 7 :   JavaScript Arithmetic Operators

Operator	Name
+	Addition
–	Subtraction
*	Multiplication
/	Division
%	Modulus
++	Increment
–	Decrement
–	Negation

Each of the last three operators is a *unary* operator, an operator that works on one entity. The expression `variableName++` is equivalent to

```
variableName = variableName + 1;
```

and `variableName--` is equivalent to

```
variableName = variableName - 1;
```

NOTE   JavaScript also has a set of bitwise logical operators. You'll probably have little use for them, so I won't cover them in this Skill.

Assignment Operators

The equal sign (=) is the JavaScript assignment operator. You can combine this operator with arithmetic and logic operators, as Table 14.8 shows.

TABLE 14.8: Combining the Assignment Operator with Arithmetic and Logic Operators

Combination	What It Means
x += y	x = x + y
x -= y	x = x - y
x *= y	x = x * y
x /= y	x = x / y
x %= y	x = x % y
x |= y	x = x | y
x &= y	x = x & y

Program Flow

JavaScript gives you a number of ways to choose an alternative when your script encounters a choice point.

switch

JavaScript's `switch` is analogous to the VBS `Select Case` statement. It enables your program to perform a test, and then based on the result, pick one of several possible paths, called *cases*. Within each path, you can have a number of lines of code. When the program finishes going through the code for that path, your program exits the `switch` if it encounters a `break` statement.

Imagine an expression called `testExpression` with the possible values of `"baseball"`, `"football"`, `"basketball"`, or `"hockey"`. The `switch` would look like this:

```
switch(testExpression) {
    case "baseball" :
            statement 1;
            statement 2;
```

```
               statement 3;
               break;
     case "football" :
               statement 4;
               statement 5;
               break;
     case "basketball" :
               statement 6
               statement 7
               statement 8
               statement 9
               break;
     case "hockey" :
               statement 10;
               break;
     default :
               statement 11;
               break;
     }
```

Note the final case, `default`, which executes if `textExpression` isn't one of the indicated values.

What happens if you don't include `break`? All the statements that follow the matching `case` will execute, even though they're within different cases.

You'll work through an exercise with `switch` later in this Skill.

if

JavaScript's `if` statement is straightforward:

```
if (conditional expression) {
     statement 1;
     statement 2;
}
```

If the conditional expression evaluates to true, `statement 1` and `statement 2` execute. If not, they don't.

else

`else` extends the `if` statement. It specifies code to execute if the conditional expression evaluates to false:

```
if (conditional expression) {
     statement 1;
     statement 2;
```

```
    }
    else {
        statement 3;
        statement 4;
    }
```

Another Kind of *if*

Sometimes a program has to set the value of a variable as the result of evaluating a conditional expression. Here's a shorthand way to do this:

```
variableName = (conditional expression) ? firstValue : secondValue
```

If the conditional expression evaluates to `true`, `firstValue` is set as the value of `variableName`. If the conditional expression evaluates to `false`, `secondValue` is set as the value of `variableName`.

Making Code Repeat

Like VBScript, JavaScript provides a set of options for making code repeat.

for

The `for` loop is a fundamental way to make code repeat. Here's the format:

```
for (starting expression; conditional expression; update expression) {
    code that runs if the conditional expression evaluates to true
}
```

Here, for example, is a `for` example:

```
<HTML>
<HEAD>
<SCRIPT>

function forExample() {
    for (i = 0; i < 10; i++) {
            document.forms[0].elements[0].value =
            document.forms[0].elements[0].value + "\n" +
                "the value of i is: " + i;
    }
}
</SCRIPT>
<TITLE> </TITLE>
</HEAD>
<BODY onload = forExample()>
```

```
<FORM>
<TEXTAREA Rows = 15 Cols = 30>
</TEXTAREA>
</FORM>
</BODY>
</HTML>
```

If you open this file (`forExample.htm`) in Navigator or in IE, you'll see

```
the value of i is: 0
the value of i is: 1
the value of i is: 2
the value of i is: 3
the value of i is: 4
the value of i is: 5
the value of i is: 6
the value of i is: 7
the value of i is: 8
the value of i is: 9
```

in the TEXTAREA. As you can see, the `for` loop stops executing when i gets to 10 because the conditional expression i < 10 is no longer true.

> **NOTE** If the expression `document.forms[0].elements[0].value` looks strange to you, go back and reread Skill 12.

while

The `while` loop is another frequently used way of repeating code. The general format is:

```
while (conditional expression) {
    code that executes while the conditional expression is true
}
```

To produce the same output as in the `for` example, the SCRIPT should look like this if you're using `while`:

```
<SCRIPT>
var i = 0;
function whileExample() {
    while (i < 10) {
            document.forms[0].elements[0].value =
            document.forms[0].elements[0].value + "\n" +
                "the value of i is: " + i;
```

```
                i++;
        }
    }
</SCRIPT>
```

and change the <BODY> tag to

```
<BODY onload = whileExample()>
```

do while

The do while loop, new in JavaScript 1.2, guarantees that code will execute at least once. In this loop, the conditional expression appears after the code to be executed:

```
do {
        code to execute
}
while (conditional expression)
```

The code in do executes, and control then moves to while. If the conditional expression evaluates to true, control moves back to do. The process continues until the conditional expression evaluates to false.

To use this type of loop to produce the output in the for example, the SCRIPT is

```
<SCRIPT>
var i = 0;
function dowhileExample() {
    do {
            document.forms[0].elements[0].value =
            document.forms[0].elements[0].value + "\n" +
                "the value of i is: " + i;
            i++;
    }
    while (i < 10)
}
```

Change the <BODY> tag to

```
<BODY onload = dowhileExample()>
```

A Special *for* Loop

JavaScript provides for...in, a for loop that enables you to examine the properties of an object or the elements of an array. The format is

```
for property in object {
        code to execute
}
```

To show you how this loop works, here's an exercise that combines some of the knowledge you acquired in this Skill and Skill 12. You're going to create a page that IE and Navigator can both open. The particular browser that opens it will determine the page heading. The script will use the for...in loop to access the properties of the browser's window object and the document.write method will display those properties and any defined values.

In your text editor, create a page called forinExample.htm. In the HEAD element, create a SCRIPT, and in the SCRIPT element type

```
function forinExample() {

}
```

The first part of the function is a switch statement. The test expression for the switch is the window.navigator.appName property you learned about in Skill 12. This property holds a string that indicates which browser opened the page. The case statements use the document.write method to put an appropriate header on the Web page:

```
switch (window.navigator.appName) {
        case "Microsoft Internet Explorer" :
                document.write("<CENTER><H1>IE Window Object
                ➡ Properties</H1><HR></CENTER><BR>");
                break;
        case "Netscape" :
                document.write("<CENTER><H1>Navigator Window Object
                ➡ Properties</H1><HR></CENTER><BR>");
                break;
        default :
                break;
}
```

Next, we set up the for...in loop that accesses the window object's properties and displays them on the page:

```
var property;

for (property in window) {
        document.write("The " + property + " of window is: " +
        ➡ window[property] + "<BR>")
}

}
```

The expression window[property] takes advantage of the JavaScript equivalence between object.property and the array reference object["property"]that I mentioned earlier in the section on arrays. Notice that we use the concatenation operator along with the HTML <BR> tag. This is like concatenating "\n" at the end of a string—it will cause the next result to appear on the next line in the display.

Add the appropriate HTML:

```
<TITLE>Accessing the Window Object</TITLE>
</HEAD>
<BODY onload = forinExample()>
</BODY>
</HTML>
```

In the <BODY> tag, the inline call to forinExample() starts things off when the page loads.

Figure 14.1 shows this page in IE and Figure 14.2 shows the page in Navigator.

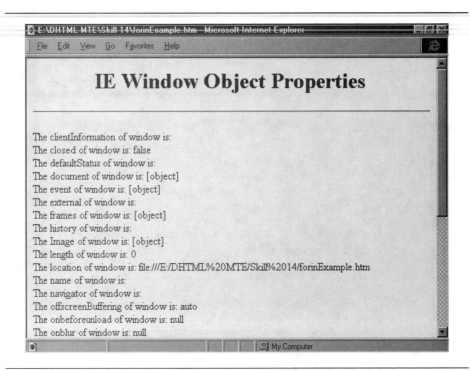

FIGURE 14.1:   forinExample.htm in IE shows the properties of the IE window object.

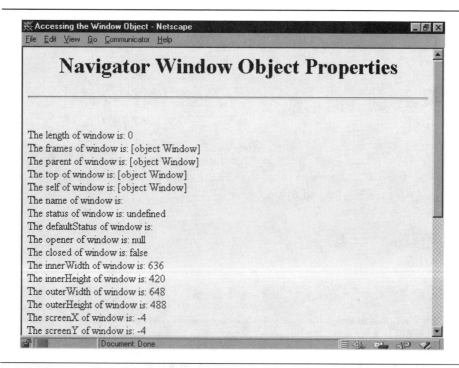

FIGURE 14.2: forinExample.htm in Navigator shows the properties of the
Navigator window object.

Note the different headings in the pages. Also, consistent with what we said in
Skill 12, you'll see how the properties of the window object differ between the
two browsers. Not all the properties will have values, but it's still an instructive
exercise.

break and continue

JavaScript provides mechanisms for getting out of a loop and for advancing to
the next iteration of a loop. The break statement, which you saw in the section on
switch, immediately moves control outside of a loop. continue moves to the
next iteration.

A quick modification to forExample.htm provides an example of continue:

```
function forExample() {
    for (i = 0; i < 10; i++) {
        if (i % 2 == 0) {continue}
        document.forms[0].elements[0].value =
        document.forms[0].elements[0].value + "\n" +
            "the value of i is: " + i;
    }
}
```

The if statement tests the remainder of dividing i by 2. If the remainder is 0, continue advances to the next iteration of the for loop. The net effect is to display only odd values of i.

Built-in Objects

In JavaScript, String, Date, and Math are objects built into the language. Each of these objects provides useful methods.

 NOTE All JavaScript objects have three methods: eval, which evaluates a string of JavaScript code; toString, which converts an object to a string; and valueOf, which converts an object to a primitive value.

The *String* Object

The String object provides a full set of methods for manipulating strings, as shown in Table 14.9.

TABLE 14.9: Methods of the String Object

Method	What It Does
anchor(name)	Turns the string into an HTML anchor tag, using name as the anchor's name
big()	Changes the string's text to a big font
blink()	Changes the string's text to a blinking font
bold()	Changes the string's text to a bold font

TABLE 14.9 CONTINUED: Methods of the String Object

Method	What It Does
charAt(index)	Finds the character in the string at the (zero-based) index position
fixed()	Changes the string's text to a fixed-pitch font
fontcolor(color)	Changes the string's text to a specified color
fontsize()	Changes the string's text to a specified size
indexOf(character,from)	Searches the string for the first occurrence of character, returning its position in the string. You can optionally start the search at from.
italics()	Changes the string's text to italics
lastIndexOf(character,from)	Searches backward through the string to find the last occurrence of character
link(href)	Turns the string into an HTML link tag, with href as the anchor name
small()	Changes the string's text to a small font
split(sep)	Returns an array created by splitting the string into separate sections at each occurrence of the string sep
strike()	Changes the string's text to a strikethrough font
sub()	Changes the string's text to a subscript font
substring(start,finish)	Returns a substring of the string beginning at start and ending at finish
sup()	Changes the string's text to a superscript font
toLowerCase()	Changes the string's text to lowercase
toUpperCase()	Changes the string's text to uppercase

How do you use these methods? Here's an exercise to show you. You're going to create a JavaScript function that incorporates some of these methods and uses the document.write() method to display the results on a Web page.

In your text editor, create a SCRIPT element that initializes a new string:

```
var s = new String("DHTML Master the Essentials");
```

Next, start a function called stringThings that takes an argument called stringName. This argument will hold a string:

```
function stringThings(stringName) {
```

Eventually, we'll call stringThings with s as the argument.

Have the first line of the function use document.write() to display the string:

```
document.write(stringName + "<BR>");
```

Now we'll add three lines. The first italicizes the string,

```
document.write(stringName.italics() + "<BR>");
```

the second makes it bold,

```
document.write(stringName.bold() + "<BR>");
```

and the third shows how you can put methods together to produce a composite result:

```
document.write(stringName.bold().italics().fontsize(25) + "<BR>");
```

That last line makes the string bold and italic, and gives it a fontsize of 25 pixels.

Now let's turn the string into an array. This line breaks up the string wherever a space occurs, and displays the resulting segments as the items in an array:

```
document.write(stringName.split(" ") + "<BR>");
```

This line forms the array and sorts the array-items:

```
document.write(stringName.split(" ").sort() + "<BR>");
```

This line forms the array and reverses the order of the array-items:

```
document.write(stringName.split(" ").reverse() + "<BR>");
```

Finally, add a line that returns and displays a substring. This expression will give you a surprising result, as you'll see in a moment:

```
document.write(stringName.substring(1,4) + "<BR>");
```

Finish off the function and the SCRIPT element:

```
}
</SCRIPT>
```

Add this HTML:

```
<TITLE>String Things</TITLE>
</HEAD>
<BODY onload = stringThings(s)>
</BODY>
</HTML>
```

The in-line function call in `<BODY>` activates `stringThings()` when the page opens. It calls the function with `s` as the argument, and `s` is the newly created string `"DHTML Master the Essentials"`.

Here's the whole `stringThings.htm` file:

stringThings.htm

```
<HTML>
<HEAD>
<SCRIPT>

var s = new String("DHTML Master the Essentials");

function stringThings(stringName) {
     document.write(stringName + "<BR>");
     document.write(stringName.italics() + "<BR>");
     document.write(stringName.bold() + "<BR>");
     document.write(stringName.bold().italics().fontsize(25) + "<BR>");
     document.write(stringName.split(" ") + "<BR>");
     document.write(stringName.split(" ").sort() + "<BR>");
     document.write(stringName.split(" ").reverse() + "<BR>");
     document.write(stringName.substring(1,4) + "<BR>");
}
</SCRIPT>
<TITLE>String Things</TITLE>
</HEAD>
<BODY onload = stringThings(s)>
</BODY>
</HTML>
```

Figure 14.3 shows the page in IE. (It looks the same in Navigator.)

Note the lines that display arrays. In each array, the items appear in a comma-delimited list.

The last line shows that surprising result I mentioned. With the arguments to `substring` set at 1 and 4, you would expect the function to return HTML. Instead, it returns HTM.

NOTE   To see a quirky little difference between IE and Navigator, go into the `stringThings.htm` file and delete + `"<BR>"` from the final `document.write()`. Reopen the page in IE and you'll see all the `document.write()` results displayed. Reopen the page in Navigator, and you'll see that the final `document.write()` doesn't appear.

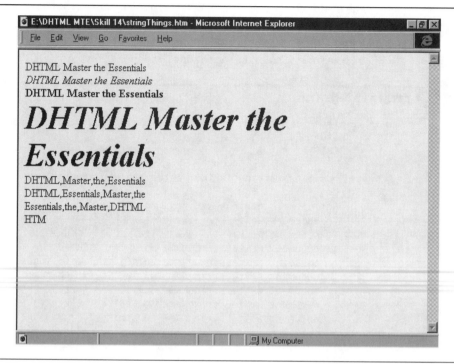

FIGURE 14.3:   `stringThings.htm` in IE shows the results of applying `String` methods.

The *Math* Object

The JavaScript `Math` object has methods that you can use to build calculations into your scripts. Table 14.10 shows these methods.

TABLE 14.10:   Methods of the Math Object

Method	Returns...
`abs()`	A number's absolute value
`acos()`	A number's arc cosine in radians
`asin()`	A number's arc sine in radians
`atan()`	A number's arc tangent in radians
`ceil()`	An integer equal to or immediately above a number

TABLE 14.10 CONTINUED: Methods of the Math Object

Method	Returns...
cos()	A number's cosine
exp()	*e* to a specified power
floor()	An integer equal to or immediately below a number
log()	A number's natural logarithm
max()	The larger of two numbers
min()	The lesser of two numbers
pow()	The value of a base to a specified power
random()	A pseudo-random number between 0 and 51
round()	A number rounded to the nearest integer
sin()	A number's sine
sqrt()	A number's square root
tan()	A number's tangent

Here are some examples that show how to use these methods:

```
var x, y, z;
y = Math.sqrt(x);
z = Math.pow(x,y);
x = Math.random();
```

The Math object has some useful properties—constants that can come in handy. Table 14.11 presents these properties.

TABLE 14.11:   Properties of the Math Object

Property	Meaning	Approximate Value
E	Base of natural logarithms	2.718
LN2	Natural logarithm of 2	0.693
LN10	Natural logarithm of 10	2.302
LOG2E	Logarithm of e to base 2	1.442
LOG10E	Logarithm of 10 to base 2	0.434
PI	Ratio of circumference of a circle to its diameter	3.1416
SQRT1_2	Square root of .5	0.707
SQRT2	Square root of 2	1.414

Skill 14

The *Date* Object

The JavaScript Date object gives you the capabilites for working with times and dates. Table 14.12 shows its methods.

TABLE 14.12: Methods of the Date Object

Method	What It Does
getDate()	Returns the day of the month in the Date object
getDay()	Returns the day of the week
getHours()	Returns the hours
getMinutes()	Returns the minutes
getMonth()	Returns the month
getSeconds()	Returns the seconds
getTime()	Returns complete time
getTimeZoneOffset()	Returns the number of hours difference between Greenwich Mean Time and the time zone in the computer running the script
getYear()	Returns the year
parse()	Returns the number of milliseconds between the date and January 1, 1970 00:00:00
setDate()	Sets the Date object's day of the month
setHours()	Sets the hours
setMinutes()	Sets the minutes
setMonth()	Sets the month
setSeconds()	Sets the seconds
setTime()	Sets the complete time
setYear()	Sets the year
toGMTString()	Changes the Date object's date into a string in Greenwich Mean Time
toLocalString()	Changes the Date object's date into a string
UTC()	Returns a date in terms of the number of milliseconds since January 1, 1970 00:00:00

Alerting, Confirming, and Prompting

We end our discussion of JavaScript with a look at three boxes that JavaScript provides for communicating with the user. These boxes are analogous to VBScript's MsgBox.

The first, alert, presents a message and a button, as shown in Figure 14.4.

FIGURE 14.4:   The JavaScript alert box presents a message and a button.

The second, confirm, presents a message and two buttons, as shown in Figure 14.5.

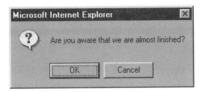

FIGURE 14.5:   The confirm box presents a message and two buttons.

Finally, as shown in Figure 14.6, the prompt box presents a message, a text box for user entry, two buttons, and a wide area.

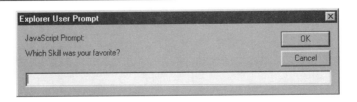

FIGURE 14.6:   The prompt box presents a message, a text area for user data entry, and two buttons.

Summary

JavaScript is a very rich scripting language. It provides a wealth of control structures, operators, built-in functions, objects, and flexibility. Some say that if you learn JavaScript, you'll have a leg up if you then try to learn Java. I'm not sure this is true, but one thing's certain: Mastering JavaScript will give you control over objects that bring a Web page to life.

 NOTE   For more information on the Netscape version of JavaScript, visit `http://developer.netscape.com/library/documentation/communicator/jsguide4/index.htm` and `http://developer.netscape.com/library/documentation/communicator/jsref/index.htm`. For more information on the Microsoft version, visit `http://www.microsoft.com/jscript/us/jslang/jstoc.htm` and `http://www.microsoft.com/jscript/us/jstutor/jstutor.htm`.

Have You Mastered the Essentials?

Now you can...

☑ Understand the ideas behind JavaScript variables

☑ Work with arrays, including multidimensional arrays

☑ Use JavaScript structures that control program flow and iteration

☑ Be aware of JavaScript built-in functions for string-manipulation and math

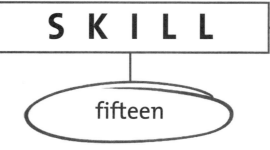

15

Summing Up, Dynamically

- ❑ Activating the Windows desktop

- ❑ Developing Active Desktop items

- ❑ Understanding potential applications

Now that you've mastered the essentials, it's time to take stock, think about the road you've traveled, and speculate on what lies ahead. You began by looking at the fundamental skills involved in Dynamic HTML—HTML, CSS, and scripting. Along the way, you also learned about object orientation. Then you learned dynamic application techniques, including animation, drag-and-drop, pages that work with data, and changing content via text ranges. Finally, you examined the foundations of DHTML—window and document object models, and scripting languages.

As you worked through the previous Skills, you probably came to an important realization about Navigator and IE: They're not just browsers anymore.

Beyond Browsing

It's appropriate to think of Navigator and IE as general application platforms. This becomes increasingly the case as Web pages become less static. You write programs in scripting languages (rather than just create nice-looking pages in HTML), test them in the IE or Navigator environment, refine them, and ultimately parade them in front of an ever-expanding audience of Web surfers.

To further expand the role of the browser, all kinds of applications are making use of browser capabilities to provide online documentation to users. IBM's VisualAge for Java, for example, is a development environment whose documents are HTML files that you can only read if you have IE or Navigator installed on your machine. Microsoft's Internet Software Developer's Kit documentation is also a set of HTML files.

Will incompatibilities between Navigator and IE ever be resolved? Netscape and Microsoft have agreed to adopt the standard that W3C produces for a Document Object Model, and that should iron out the major differences.

In the meantime, as a developer, how do you cope with the differences? Is it possible to develop Web pages that open cleanly in both browsers? In Skill 14, you saw an exercise that does just that. You created a page that uses the `window.appName` property to determine the browser in which it has opened. It opens with one heading if you open it with Navigator, another with IE.

That page, however, was a simple one. It just invoked the `document.write` method repeatedly to display properties of the particular browser's `window` object. For complex pages with dynamic effects, finding a common denominator can be an awful lot of work. Moreover, to get to common ground you'll have to forego using important capabilities of either browser. It's probably easier to generate separate versions and open the appropriate one depending on the value of `window.appName`. In the case of a corporate intranet, of course, an organization can standardize on one browser and take advantage of all the bells and whistles that browser provides.

Each browser has become a part of a larger picture. Navigator is part of Netscape's Communicator suite, which also includes

- Composer—a tool for Web page creation

- Netcaster—a component that brings information to you via "push" technology

- Messenger—an e-mail package

- Collabra—a component for dealing with discussion groups

- Conference—a component that sends and receives voice data and other types of data in real time over the Internet or over an intranet.

And IE? IE may become an essential part of the Windows operating system. Microsoft's goal is to put the Web on your computer—to make the Web-surfing experience seem like any other computer-based task you carry out, and to integrate Web-resident information with your computer-resident information. To reach this goal, the Redmond software giant is striving to integrate IE with Windows 98. The idea is to put IE icons on the task bar, and favorite Web sites into the Start menu. You'll use the browser to navigate through directories and folders, and you'll activate with a single click. If you're using Windows 95, you can preview all this by including shell integration when you install IE.

With shell integration, your screen will look something like Figure 15.1.

Activating the Desktop

The integration of IE into the operating system presents another new capability. Dubbed the Active Desktop, the shell-integrated desktop can hold Web pages. These pages, in effect, connect you to the entire World Wide Web analogous to the way regular icons connect you to applications on your hard drive.

Skill 15

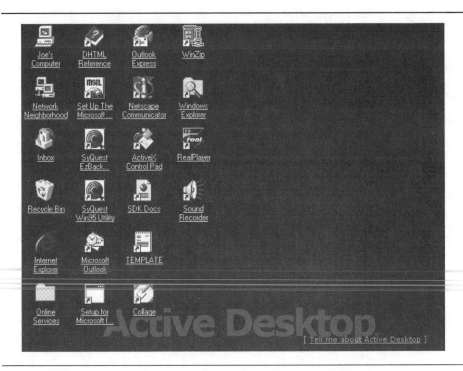

FIGURE 15.1:   The appearance of Windows integrated with IE

How do you install a Web page onto your desktop? For the remainder of this Skill, I'll assume you're working in Windows 95 with shell integration or in Windows 98. Right-click anywhere in the desktop and a pop-up menu appears. From the menu, select Active Desktop ➤ Customize My Desktop…. The Display Properties dialog box, shown in Figure 15.2, appears.

On this dialog box's Web tab, shown in Figure 15.2, click New…. The New Active Desktop Item dialog box appears. If it looks like Figure 15.3, and asks if you want to close Display Properties, click No. The New Active Desktop Item dialog box that looks like Figure 15.4 will appear.

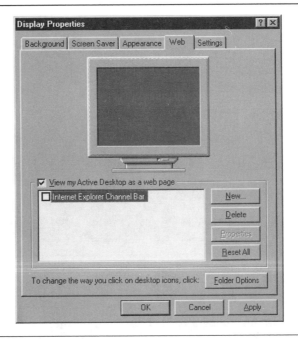

FIGURE 15.2:   The Active Desktop Display Properties dialog box

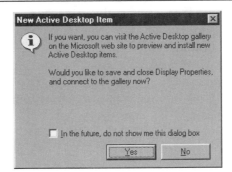

FIGURE 15.3:   The New Active Desktop Item dialog box that asks if you want to close Display Properties

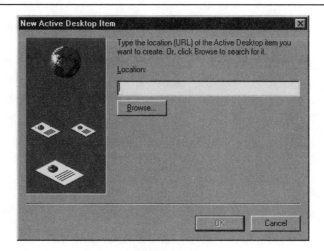

FIGURE 15.4:   The New Active Desktop Item dialog box that enables you to add a Web page to your desktop

In this dialog box, click Browse.... You're going to add the home page of the University of Cyberspace to your desktop. In the Browse dialog box, navigate to your DHTML MTE folder and then open Skill 2. Select UofCyb.htm and click Open. This puts the file path to UofCyb.htm in the Browse dialog box's Location box. Click OK, and you'll see that path next to a selected check box in the Display Properties dialog box. Click OK to close the Display Properties dialog box, and the UofCyb home page is now part of your desktop. Use your mouse to adjust size and location, and you can make this page and the desktop look like Figure 15.5.

Click one of the hyperlinks to a Department page, and the screen looks something like Figure 15.6. Notice that the newly opened page seems to float above the layer that holds the shortcut icons.

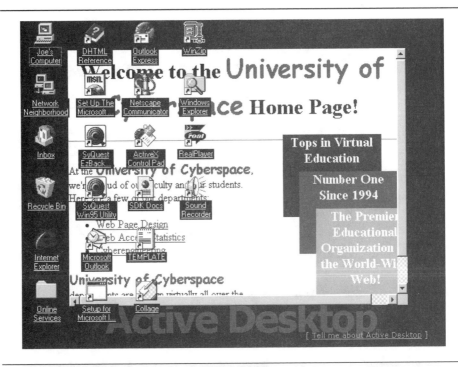

FIGURE 15.5:   The Active Desktop with the University of Cyberspace home page in the background

The Active Desktop presents new opportunities for information delivery. We can periodically change the content of the pages linked to the Active Desktop item. For example, clicking one of the department links on the University of Cyberspace home page could open a page that presents department news or current course offerings.

In fact, information delivery can take on still another dimension. You can schedule the Active Desktop item for periodic updates, so that the item's content changes on the user's machine. Thus, an Active Desktop item can display a news ticker that presents new headlines every day, a sports information service that gives scores every hour, or a cartoon that changes every week.

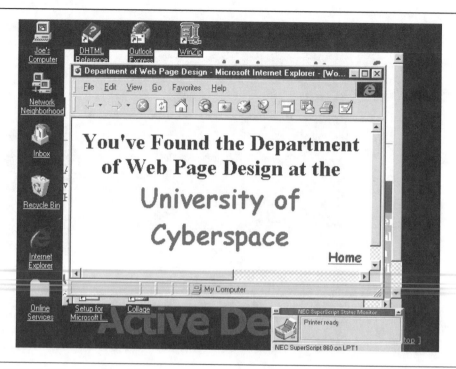

FIGURE 15.6: The appearance of the Active Desktop after clicking on a hyperlink from the background page

Drilling Down

A transparent layer holds the shortcut icons. The Active Desktop item—the Web page—sits one layer below them. The layout of the Active Desktop is the responsibility of `Desktop.htt`, a file that lives in C:\Windows\Application Data\Microsoft\Internet Explorer. Navigate through this path, right-click on this file's icon, and select Open With… from the pop-up menu. In the Open With dialog box, select Notepad and click OK. When Notepad opens, you'll see a file that looks like this:

```
<!-- The following file is an HTML Wallpaper for use with Microsoft -->
<!-- Internet Explorer 4.0. -->

<html>
<head><BASE HREF="C:\WINDOWS\Web\Wallpaper\wallpapr.htm">
```

```
</head>
<body scroll=no style="background: black; margin: 0; font: 8pt Verdana">

<table border=0 height=100% width=100% cellpadding=0 cellspacing=0 style="font:
8pt Verdana">
<tr valign=bottom>
    <td align=right>
        <span style="
                position:              relative;
                    left:                  -75pt;
                letter-spacing: -4px;
                font:                  41pt verdana;
                font-weight:    bold;
                color:                 #424242"
        >Active Desktop<span style="
                font:                  4pt Verdana;
                letter-spacing:        0;
                color:                 #424242"
        >TM</span>
        </span>
    <br>
        <span style="
                position:       relative;
                    top:            -10pt;
                    left:           -20pt;
                font:           8pt verdana;
                color:          #FF9C31;"
        >[ <a   href="res://ie4tour.dll/adinfo.htm"
                style="
                color:          #FF9C31;
                text-decoration: underline"
    >Tell me about Active Desktop</a> ]</span>
        <br>
</td></tr></table>

<IFRAME id=1 MARGINWIDTH=0 MARGINHEIGHT=0 name="DeskMovrW" src="file:
///E:/DHTML%20MTE/Skill%202/UofCyb.htm"
                resizeable="XY"
                subscribed_url="E:\DHTML MTE\Skill 2\UofCyb.htm"
                frameborder=0 style="BACKGROUND: transparent; position:absolute;
                LEFT:448; TOP:224; WIDTH:128; HEIGHT:128; Z-INDEX:1002">
</IFRAME>


<OBJECT
        classid="clsid:72267F6A-A6F9-11D0-BC94-00C04FB67863"
        id=ActiveDesktopMover
```

```
        STYLE="position:absolute; container:positioned; LEFT: 0;TOP: 0; WIDTH: 0;
        HEIGHT: 0;zIndex: 5">
<param name="Interval" value=500>
<param name="SizerID" value="ActiveDesktopMover">
<param name="Enabled" value="True">
<param name="TargetName" value="DeskMovr">
<param name="WindowOnly" value="False">
</OBJECT>

<OBJECT
        classid="clsid:72267F6A-A6F9-11D0-BC94-00C04FB67863"
        id=ActiveDesktopMoverW
     STYLE="position:absolute; container:positioned; LEFT: 0;TOP: 0; WIDTH: 0;
        HEIGHT: 0;zIndex 19">
<param name="Interval" value=500>
<param name="SizerID" value="ActiveDesktopMoverW">
<param name="Enabled" value="True">
<param name="TargetName" value="DeskMovrW">
<param name="WindowOnly" value="True">
</OBJECT>

</body></html>
```

As you've probably guessed, the part of the code that refers to the University of Cyberspace home page is

```
<IFRAME id=1 MARGINWIDTH=0 MARGINHEIGHT=0 name="DeskMovrW" src= "file:
///E:/DHTML%20MTE/Skill%202/UofCyb.htm"
              resizeable="XY"
              subscribed_url="E:\DHTML MTE\Skill 2\UofCyb.htm"
              frameborder=0 style="BACKGROUND: transparent; position:absolute;
              LEFT:448; TOP:224; WIDTH:128; HEIGHT:128; Z-INDEX:1002">
</IFRAME>
```

The start and end tags tell you that the page sits inside an IFRAME element. We haven't worked with this element before. It's called a *floating frame*, and as its name implies, it's similar to a FRAME. Like a FRAME, it's a separate window within a window. Unlike a FRAME, it can sit inside the middle of the window and have text and other elements flow around it. The subscribed_url attribute's value gives the file path to the page. Since this is a URL, you can see the potential: The page you select for an Active Desktop item can reside on a remote server that you access via the Web, or on a local area network in your organization, as well as in your local hard drive.

You can make other changes to your Active Desktop, and those changes will appear in `Desktop.htt`. For example, you might select the Windows `triangles.bmp` file as the wallpaper for your desktop. If you do (and I hope you don't), `Desktop.htt` will change the beginning of the file to

```
<!----
***** This file is automatically generated by Microsoft Internet Explorer 4.0
(deskhtml.dll) *****
-------->
<HTML>
<BODY background="file:///C:/WINDOWS/Triangles.bmp" style="border:none;"
bgcolor=#008080 topmargin=0 leftmargin=0 rightmargin=0 bottommargin=0>
```

While you have this file open in Notepad, don't bother editing it. Your manual edits will vanish, as `Desktop.htt` only changes in response to selections you make in the Display Properties dialog box.

Dynamically Activating the Desktop

Most of the time, you'd want an Active Desktop item to be somewhat smaller than the Web page you added, and yet still attract attention and be informative. Dynamic HTML supplies the techniques to meet these goals. In this section, we'll use some of the experience you gained in Skill 7 to create a simple ticker that scrolls news items from the University of Cyberspace upward through an Active Desktop item. The scrolling will begin when the mouse cursor enters the Active Desktop item. Each news item will sit in a DIV, and we'll script timed changes in each DIV's location. We'll also take the opportunity to pick up some programming techniques we haven't worked with before.

Creating the HTML Document

Create a file called `Active Desktop Item.htm` and save it in Skill 15. Start with two STYLE rules in the HEAD:

```
<STYLE Type = "text/css">
.UofCyb {font-weight:bold;font-family:cursive}
DIV {position:absolute}
</STYLE>
```

The first STYLE rule will apply the bold cursive font we've been using on the phrase "University of Cyberspace." The second sets up absolute positioning for each news-item DIV.

Next, in the BODY, add style information for the U of Cyb colors, and add a heading in a SPAN element. We use a SPAN rather than a DIV in order to differentiate the heading from the news items:

```
<BODY Style = "background-color:#FFFFCC;color:green">
<SPAN Style = "background-color:green;color:#FFFFCC;width:100%">
<H3>News from The <A Class = "UofCyb">University of Cyberspace</A></H3>
</SPAN>
```

Now add the news items:

```
<DIV>
Web Page Design: 3 new faculty
</DIV>
<DIV>
Web Access Statistics: $100M grant
</DIV>
<DIV>
Cyberengineering develops new server
</DIV>
<DIV>
New Department: Virtual Sports
</DIV>
</BODY>
</HTML>
```

Notice that we haven't assigned an ID to any of the DIVs. How will we script their behaviors? We'll apply some of those new programming techniques I mentioned earlier.

This method of setting up the DIVs will be useful when it's time to add new items or update old ones. All you have to do is surround each item with <DIV> and </DIV> tags.

Writing the Script

The SCRIPT is the next item on the agenda. You'll write it in VBScript, so in the HEAD, add

```
<SCRIPT Language = "VBScript">
```

Declare two familiar-looking variables related to event timing and initialize the second one:

```
dim glblTimer
dim glblMovementStartedFlag
glblMovementStartedFlag = 0
```

Recall from Skill 7 that the `glblMovementStartedFlag` protects you from restarting the animation timer if the animation has already started.

Now let's look at one of those new techniques I promised you. Instead of assigning an ID to each DIV, we're going to refer to each one as an item in a collection. Although the IE Document Object Model doesn't have a collection of DIVs, we can create one. First, we declare it

```
dim divsCollection
```

Then we use the document `tags` method to filter the `document.all` collection and create a collection that consists only of the DIVs in the document:

```
set divsCollection = document.all.tags("DIV")
```

You're ready to start scripting the subroutines. The first one is an event-handler for the window `onload` event. It will call a subroutine called `resetDivs` to set the locations of the DIVs on the page:

```
sub window_onload
     resetDivs
end sub
```

Next, script the event-handlers for `onmouseover` (which starts the scrolling movement of the DIVs) and `onmouseout` (which stops the movement):

```
sub document_onmouseover
    if glblMovementStartedFlag = 0 Then
           glblTimer = window.setInterval("divMovement", 200)
           glblMovementStartedFlag = 1
    end if
end sub

sub document_onmouseout
    window.clearInterval(glblTimer)
    glblMovementStartedFlag = 0
    resetDivs
end sub
```

As in Skill 7, we time the movement with `setInterval`. This method calls another subroutine, `divMovement`, to accomplish the movement. It fires `divMovement` every 200 milliseconds. We stop the movement with the `clearInterval` method and call `resetDivs` when the movement stops.

Now you have to write `divMovement` and `resetDivs`. Start `divMovement` by checking on the location of the last DIV. If it's beyond a certain point, you'll reset the DIVs and start the upward scrolling again:

```
sub divMovement

    if divsCollection(divsCollection.length - 1).style.pixelTop < -50 then
            resetDivs
end if
```

As you can see, this subroutine uses the `divsCollection` you created. Its `length` property gives the number of DIVs in the collection, and you have to subtract 1 from `length` to get the subscript of the last DIV in the collection. (The value of 50 is arbitrary. You might want to experiment with it a bit.)

Next, we have to move each DIV. To do this, we use the new VBScript `for each...next` structure that's specially designed for looping through the objects in a collection:

```
for each divItem in divsCollection
        divItem.style.pixelTop = divItem.style.pixelTop - 5
    next

end sub
```

Like 50 in the preceding `if` statement, the value of 5 is arbitrary. Experiment with it if you like.

The subroutine that sets the location of each DIV also uses `for each...next`:

```
sub resetDivs

    i = 0
    for each divItem in divsCollection
            divItem.style.pixelTop = 100 + (25 * i)
            divItem.style.pixelLeft = 10
            divItem.style.zIndex = -1
            i = i + 1
    next

end sub
```

Setting the `zIndex` to −1 ensures that the news items will appear to pass under the heading as they move up the screen. (That 25 is another arbitrary value you might want to change.)

The Whole File

Here's the entire Active Desktop Item.htm file:

Active Desktop Item.htm

```
<HTML>
<HEAD>
<STYLE Type = "text/css">
.UofCyb {font-weight:bold;font-family:cursive}
DIV {position:absolute}
</STYLE>
<SCRIPT Language = "VBScript">

dim glblTimer
dim glblMovementStartedFlag
glblMovementStartedFlag = 0

dim divsCollection
set divsCollection = document.all.tags("DIV")

sub window_onload
    resetDivs
end sub

sub document_onmouseover
    if glblMovementStartedFlag = 0 Then
            glblTimer = window.setInterval("divMovement", 200)
            glblMovementStartedFlag = 1
    end if
end sub

sub document_onmouseout
    window.clearInterval(glblTimer)
    glblMovementStartedFlag = 0
    resetDivs
end sub


sub divMovement

    if divsCollection(divsCollection.length - 1).style.pixelTop < -50 then
            resetDivs
    end if

    for each divItem in divsCollection
            divItem.style.pixelTop = divItem.style.pixelTop - 5
    next
```

```
end sub

sub resetDivs

    i = 0
    for each divItem in divsCollection
            divItem.style.pixelTop = 100 + (25 * i)
            divItem.style.pixelLeft = 10
            divItem.style.zIndex = -1
            i = i + 1
    next

end sub
</SCRIPT>
<TITLE> </TITLE>
</HEAD>
<BODY Style = "background-color:#FFFFCC;color:green">
<SPAN Style = "background-color:green;color:#FFFFCC;width:100%">
<H3>News from The <A Class = "UofCyb">University of Cyberspace</A></H3>
</SPAN>
<DIV>
Web Page Design: 3 new faculty
</DIV>
<DIV>
Web Access Statistics: $100M grant
</DIV>
<DIV>
Cyberengineering develops new server
</DIV>
<DIV>
New Department: Virtual Sports
</DIV>
</BODY>
</HTML>
```

Use the Display Properties dialog box to add this file as an Active Desktop item. After you do, with perhaps some resizing and relocation, your screen will look something like Figure 15.7.

You can probably think of a number of ways of altering and improving the page you just created. For example, it would be a good exercise to use filters to create a slide show of news items rather than a scrolling list.

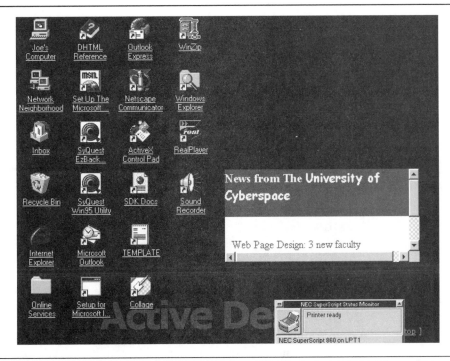

FIGURE 15.7:   The appearance of your screen after you add `Active Desktop Item.htm` as an Active Desktop item

Channeling Content

In the microworld of your own computer, updating the Active Desktop item you built is simply a matter of going into its HTML file, changing some code, and reinstalling it on your desktop.

I mentioned earlier, however, that a user can install a remotely based Active Desktop item on his or her machine. The content provider responsible for that can change the item's content, and the changes will show up on the user's desktop. That's why the `Desktop.htt` file refers to the Active Desktop item's URL as a `subscribed_URL`. When you put the item on your desktop, you are, in effect, setting up a subscription that enables you to receive scheduled changes to the content.

The beauty of it all is that these changes get "pushed" to you automatically. IE provides this service for all subscriptions. The content provider sets up what Microsoft calls an *Active Channel* to send these changes.

An Active Channel is a Web site designed to send content to IE. The mechanism that handles the sending is a file written in *Channel Definition Format* (CDF). A CDF file lists the resources available in the Active Channel and provides a schedule for updating the channel on the user's machine. If you have shell integration installed in Windows 95, you've most likely seen a *channel bar*, which provides a set of channels to which you can subscribe.

 NOTE   The details of creating a CDF File and building an Active Channel are beyond the scope of our discussion on DHTML. If you want to find out more about them, check out `http://www.microsoft.com/msdn/sdk/inetsdk/help/delivery/delivery.htm#set_content`.

Applications

As you completed the exercises in this book, potential applications from your own field of interest probably occurred to you. With its rich object and event models, both versions of Dynamic HTML tend to fire those kinds of thoughts.

Opportunities for DHTML development abound in business, education, and entertainment. In the business world, eye-catching dynamic Web pages can serve as persuasive advertisements for organizations. Animations, if done correctly, can help an organization get its message to its market. In the context of an intranet, customizing information and data for different groups is a DHTML technique that holds great promise.

In the educational realm, Web pages built in Dynamic HTML can be the basis for environments that promote active learning. Dynamic techniques present the possibility of Web-based interactive simulations that could engage students in learning by discovery. Games like the peg solitaire game we built could serve as mind-exercising diversions. It's also possible to develop games that require the user to play against the computer.

Animation, multimedia, and other dynamic techniques provide the basis for applications that entertain as well as educate. For example, you can use Dynamic HTML to create arcade-style games like Asteroids. The Microsoft site provides a version of Asteroids at `http://www.microsoft.com/ie/ie40/demos/asteroids.htm`.

Summary

Dynamic HTML represents an exciting new addition to the world of Web design. Its techniques provide the potential for remarkable new applications in business, education, and entertainment. Closer to home, the Windows Active Desktop presents additional opportunities for DHTML development and for channeling information to users all over the world.

How will DHTML fuel your dynamic vision?

Have You Mastered the Essentials?

Now you can...

☑ **Understand the Active Desktop**

☑ **Install an HTML document as a background on your desktop**

☑ **Create Active Desktop items**

☑ **Work with the *tags* method to create new collections of objects**

☑ **Use the *for each...next* structure to examine and process the items in a collection**

☑ **Understand some potential applications of Dynamic HTML**

GLOSSARY

G

Glossary

a

active channel

A Web site designed for scheduled transmissions of content to IE via a Channel Definition Format file. See also *Channel Definition Format (CDF)*.

ActiveX

A Microsoft technology for inserting software components into Web pages and other applications.

array

A set of similar items, each of which can be referred to via a numerical index.

c

cascade

A combination of Web page style specifications.

case-insensitive

As in VBScript, when uppercase letters are equivalent to their lowercase counterparts. See also *case-sensitive*.

case-sensitive

As in JavaScript, when uppercase letters are not equivalent to their lowercase counterparts. See also *case-insensitive*.

channel bar

Like a toolbar, provides a set of channels to which a user has subscribed.

Channel Definition Format (CDF)

A format for creating a file listing the resources available in an active channel, and for providing a schedule for updating the channel on the user's machine. See also *active channel*.

child

An object that inherits properties and methods from another object. See also *object* and *parent*.

class

A category that serves as a blueprint for creating objects. See also *object*.

collection

Microsoft's term for an array of Web page elements. See also *array*.

comma-delimited

A file whose adjacent values are separated by commas. See also *row delimiter*.

container

An object (like an HTML document) that holds other objects (like HTML elements). See also *object*.

contextual selector

A Cascading Style Sheet feature that enables you to specify the style of an element according to the context in which it appears.

control

A User Interface component, such as a command button, list box, or a text area.

cookie

A string value contained in a text file and stored on a user's computer. Associated with the current page, it stores information between visits to the page.

CSS

Acronym for Cascading Style Sheet, a structure for specifying the styles of HTML elements. See also *CSS1*.

CSS1

Acronym for Cascading Style Sheet Level 1 specification, a World Wide Web Consortium document that specifies the format and makeup of style sheets for HTML files. See also *CSS*.

d

declaration

In a style sheet, the specification of style information to apply to an element. Part of a style sheet rule, the declaration appears inside curly brackets. See also *style sheet* and *rule*.

deprecated

A term applied to an HTML element that may become obsolete in future versions of HTML and that offers fewer capabilities than a newer feature of the language.

dialog box

Often modal, a window that displays information to a user or gathers information from a user.

dynamic content

Web page content that changes in response to user input or code running on the client computer.

dynamic effects

Web page effects that depend on user actions or scripts executing on the client computer.

e

element

An item in an HTML document, it often consists of a start-tag, content, and an end-tag. Some elements have no end-tag, and some have no content.

encapsulation

An object-oriented term indicating that an object hides the workings of its methods from the outside world.

event

An occurrence, like a click, a double-click, or a mouse movement. An event is usually, but not always, initiated by user interaction with a Web page.

event bubbling

Microsoft's model for processing events. In this model, the object associated with an event (i.e. the source element) receives the event first. Then, the event passes up to the source element's parent, then to the parent's parent, and so forth. See also *source element* and *parent*.

event capturing

Netscape's model for processing events. In this model, the window object, which represents the browser, is the first to see the event. The document object, which represents the Web page, sees it next, and so forth. The event's target element is the last to have an opportunity to process the event before it falls off the bottom of the hierarchy and gets handled by a default event-handler. See also *event-handler*.

event-handler

A scripted procedure activated by an event. See also *event*.

explicit variable creation

Creating a variable by declaring it before you use it. See also *implicit variable creation*.

f

field

A column in a table of data.

filter

A Microsoft extension to CSS, a filter is a device for altering an element's appearance.

filtering

In the context of data manipulation, filtering is a process for specifying a subset of records.

form controls

Intrinsic HTML controls that reside between the <FORM> and </FORM> tags.

frame

An independent fully functional window that's a subdivision of the main browser window.

function

In VBScript, a procedure that returns a value; in JavaScript, any procedure, regardless of whether it returns a value.

g

GIF (Graphic Interchange Format)

An image format created by CompuServe. Each pixel in a GIF image can store up to 8 bits, so that a GIF image can have up to 256 colors. See also *JPEG*.

global variable

A variable declared outside any procedure, its scope extends over an entire script. See also *script*.

h

helper applications

Software applications that extend a browser's capabilities but are external to the browser. When you activate a helper, the helper's window opens and proceeds with the task at hand.

HTML

Hypertext Markup Language, the language for creating Web pages.

i

implicit variable creation

Creating a variable by using it in an expression without first declaring it. See also *explicit variable creation*.

inheritance

An object-oriented term indicating that an object takes on the properties and methods of its parent. See also *parent* and *child*.

inline style sheet

Consists of CSS specifications that reside inside an HTML element's start tag.

j

JavaScript Style Sheets (acronyms: JASS, JSS, JSSS)

A type of style sheet that you write in object-oriented syntax. (JASS won't work on Internet Explorer.) See also *object orientation* and *style sheet*.

JPEG

An image format named for its creators, Joint Photographer's Expert Group. Designed for transmitting complex images such as photographs, JPEG stores 24 bits in each pixel. As a result, an image in this format can have more than 16 million colors. See also *GIF (Graphic Interchange Format)*.

l

local variable

A variable declared inside a specific procedure, its scope is limited to the procedure in which it is declared.

lossiness

The information that an image format such as JPEG loses. It's usually imperceptible to the human eye. Lossiness is adjustable: If you decrease the degree of compression, you increase the image quality and lower the lossiness. You're also likely to increase download time. See also *JPEG*.

m

method

A procedure that acts upon or affects an object.

modal

A term describing an element that maintains the focus until the user initiates a specified event.

o

object

An instance of a class.

object orientation

A software development methodology based on objects that perform procedures and on procedures that operate on objects, rather than on sequences of programming steps.

opaque string

A string that you can't examine or modify.

p

padding

In the CSS format model, the empty space surrounding content on all sides.

parent

An object from which another object inherits properties and methods. See also *child*.

plug-in

A software package that extends a browser's capabilities.

polymorphism

An object-oriented term that indicates a particular method can be carried out in different ways by different objects. See also *method* and *object*.

presentation

The look of a Web page (its fonts, color, and background, for example), rather than its structure.

r

recordset

An object the IE Tabular Data Control provides for representing columns and rows of data. Its methods enable navigation through the data. See also *Tabular Data Control (TDC)*.

reserved word

A word set aside for a particular purpose by a programming language.

row delimiter

A character that marks the end of a row in a data file. See also *comma-delimited*.

rule

In a style sheet, a selector-declaration pair. The selector denotes the element to be styled; the declaration specifies the styling to apply to that element. See also *selector* and *declaration*.

S

script

Written in a scripting language such as VBScript or JavaScript, code that specifies how Web page elements work together. See also *scripting language*.

scripting language

A computer language designed to work inside a specific environment like an HTML document. See also *script*.

seed

A number that starts a randomization function.

selector

The part of a CSS rule that determines the HTML element that gets styled according to the specifications in the declaration. See also *rule* and *declaration*.

sort

To arrange a set of items, such as data-entries, in a fashion that you specify (e.g. in alphabetical order).

source element

In the event bubbling model, the Web page element in which an event, like a mouse-click, takes place.

style

A specification for presenting an aspect (such as position or color) of a Web page element.

style class

In a CSS, a way of increasing the granularity of styling. You can use a style class to set a selector so that all elements in a specified class get styled the same way. See also *selector*.

style sheet

A set of specifications for the appearance of elements on a Web page.

subclass

An object-oriented term for a subdivision of a class. See also *class*.

subroutine

A VBScript procedure that does not return a value.

t

Tabular Data Control (TDC)

A control, which comes with Internet Explorer, that enables you to work with data in ways that formerly required round-trips between your machine and a server.

tag

In HTML, the angle-bracketed term that marks the beginning or end of a document's elements.

u

unary operator

In a scripting language, an operator that works on one item. See also *scripting language*.

user agent

A W3C (World Wide Web Consortium) term for any device (e.g. a browser) that interprets HTML documents.

w

World Wide Web Consortium (W3C)

An international industry consortium founded in 1994 to develop common protocols fo the evolution of the World Wide Web.

Index

Note to the Reader: Throughout this index **boldfaced** page numbers indicate primary discussions of a topic. *Italicized* page numbers indicate illustrations.

a

C

e

f

g

h

i

m

n

O

P

q

r

S

t

U

X

y

Z

EVERYTHING YOU NEED TO KNOW ABOUT
good & bad
WEB DESIGN.

Web Pages That Suck
Learn Good Design by Looking at Bad Design
VINCENT FLANDERS, MICHAEL WILLIS

Based on the wildly popular, award-winning site, www.webpagesthatsuck.com, here's the first book to deliver practical advice from two bold and wacky experts who critique and fix real sites.

ISBN: 0-7821-2187-X • 304 pp • 8" x 10" • $39.00 • March

Effective Web Design
Master the Essentials
ANN NAVARRO, TABINDA KHAN

"I am constantly being asked to recommend a beginning web design book and haven't been able to, until now. This book delivers on its promise—with it you'll quickly gain the essential knowledge you need for effective web design."
—Eliza Sherman, President, Cybergrrl, Inc. (www.cybergrrl.com)

ISBN: 0-7821-2278-7 • 400 pp • 7 1/2" x 9" • $34.99 • February

Web By Design
The Complete Guide
MOLLY HOLZSCHLAG

The ONLY complete guide to ALL FIVE key aspects of web design: graphics; HTML design and layout techniques; typography; color, shape and space; multimedia and programming.

ISBN: 0-7821-2201-9 • 1,008 pp • 7 1/2" x 9" • $49.99 • March

Visit www.sybex.com for details on all titles from Sybex.

SYBE